miraculous air

the university of utah press salt lake city

journey of a thousand miles
through baja california,
the other mexico

miraculous air

c. m. mayo

© 2002 by C. M. Mayo
Interior photographs © C. M. Mayo
"Altar to Doña Amelia Wilkes, San José del Cabo"; "Alice and Oscar at the Cueva Pintada, Sierra de San Francisco"; "Bahia Concepción, Sea of Cortés"; "Gray whale, Laguna San Ignacio"; "Bimbo Has a Snack, Tijuana".
All rights reserved

Printed on acid-free paper

07 06 05 04 03 02
5 4 3 2 1

Library of Congress Cataloging-in-Publication Data
Mayo, C. M.
Miraculous air : journey of a thousand miles through Baja California, the other Mexico / C. M. Mayo
    p. cm.
Includes bibliographical references and index.
ISBN 0-87480-740-9 (acid-free paper)
1. Baja California (Mexico : Peninsula)—Description and travel.
2. Mayo, C. M.—Journeys—Mexico—Baja California (Peninsula)
I. Title.
F1246 .M39 2002
917.2'204836—dc21

                    2002007147

To protect their privacy, the names of the maid in Cabo San Lucas and the social worker and his clients in San Quintín have been changed, as have both the names and some of the identifying characteristics of the members of the Laguna San Ignacio whale-watching tour.

Slightly different versions of the chapters "Bay of Angels" and "In the Land of the Clouds" were previously published in the *Southwest Review;* "El Halloween and the *Día de Muertos"* in the *North American Review;* "Lay Thine Hand upon Him" in the *Massachusetts Review;* "A Touch of Evil" in *Fourth Genre;* a brief excerpt from the chapter "The Most Beautiful Dream" in the on-line journal *Brevity;* and "The Visitors" as a bilingual chapbook, *The Visitors/Los Visitantes* (Tameme, 2002).

Para Agustín
como siempre

And for Alice

The very air here is miraculous

—JOHN STEINBECK, *The Log from the Sea of Cortez*

Contents

I

the south

so close to the united states

Poor Mexico! So far from God and
so close to the United States.

—PORFIRIO DÍAZ

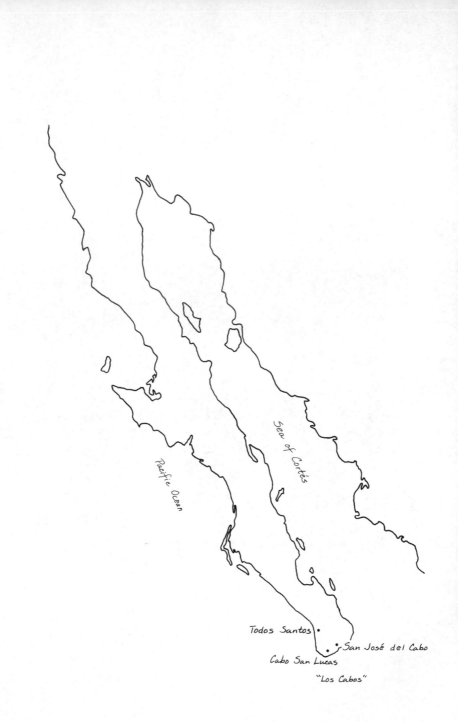

Todos Santos

San José del Cabo

Cabo San Lucas

"Los Cabos"

Sea of Cortés

Pacific Ocean

El Halloween and the Día de Muertos

Los Cabos

Yet meet we shall, and part, and meet again
Where dead men meet, on lips of living men.
—SAMUEL BUTLER, "Not on Sad Stygian Shore"

Wings

THE FIRST AIRPLANE arrived at San José del Cabo in 1931. The people couldn't believe it, that this thing could stay up above the earth, swoop over them without falling. The pilot's surname was Flores, but no one remembers his first name.

It is the town historian, Don Fernando Cota, who is telling me this story. It is late October, more than sixty years later. Most of the people who were there that day are dead.

They stood watching, Don Fernando tells me, on the stoops of their houses, at the edge of their citrus orchards, in their fishing boats: a machine with wings, its body glinting in the sun, engine droning across the pale desert sky. It had come from the other side of the Sea of Cortés; this must be so.

The dogs began to bark, mules and burros neighed and whinnied and stamped their hooves. Someone rang the bells of the church, and someone else ran to ring the bells at Municipal Hall. Everyone gathered on the beach.

It was not possible! This Flores, he started to climb and climb— Don Fernando raises his hand—and then *paf!* he would stall and dive. He did the loopy loopies! The people stood there on the beach,

3

and they clutched at their hearts because they thought he was going to die. Some of the old ladies fainted, right there on the sand.

The whole town, Don Fernando smiles, we were so grateful. We made Flores a party in Municipal Hall, a great ball, with dancing.

I am unlatching the wrought-iron gate of Don Fernando's house, leaving. He stands in the shade of leafy green plants on his patio and waves good-bye, having told me this last story. One of his caged parrots, plump and yellow, whistles like a bored child. Outside it is hot; there is no shade. A bus barrels by, a Coca Cola truck.

Half an hour later, in downtown Cabo San Lucas, by the boat ramp behind the Plaza Bonita shopping mall, I find Manuel Vega selling toy helicopters, frail contraptions made of plastic and rubber bands. He spots a group of tourists walking by, and he winds up a helicopter and throws it into the air.

"For you kids!" he calls out in English as the toy whirs over the tourists' heads. "It come back!" And indeed, like a boomerang, it does. "Twenty pesos, three dollars!"

The tourists, two blonde women in tank tops, smile and duck. Then they continue walking out toward the marina. A sidewalk runs all the way around the water, lined with vendors of painted pottery from Oaxaca, silver-plated earrings and bracelets from Taxco, iron-wood carvings of dolphins and turtles from Sonora, rugs and baskets and stacks of straw hats. One boy offers to let the tourists photograph his horned iguana for two dollars. Another boy squats behind an upended cardboard box that says, I PAINT YOUR NAME ON A GRAIN OF RICE. "Hello amigas!" they call out to the two blondes. "Cheap!"

Along the sidewalk where the vendors ply their wares are restaurants like El Shrimp Bucket, Cheezburger-Cheezburger, and the Baja Cantina, where the patrons sip strawberry daiquiris and watch hockey games on a TV mounted over the bar. "Cabo's best box lunch," advertises one restaurant; "Finest imported Black Forest ham," says another; "Swedish Massage." The marina is filled with yachts, bright, clean white vessels: the *Audacious* from Carlsbad, California; the *Treasure Chest* from Dover, Delaware; the *Natalie B.* from Coronado, California; the *Viqueen* from Portland, Oregon. Their masts make a forest of silver against the sky.

Here, back at the boat ramp behind the Plaza Bonita mall, Manuel throws his toy helicopter over the tourists' heads, again and again. A group of men in baseball caps passes by, a girl in patent-leather strap sandals, a man with a dragon tattoo. They walk slowly, squinting in the harsh light. "For you kids!" Manuel calls.

He is older than the other street vendors, who are mostly teenage boys from Guerrero and Oaxaca, coastal states on the mainland side of the Sea of Cortés. He has been selling these same toy helicopters here for fifteen years. His uncle makes them in a workshop in Mexico City. ("Helicóptero de la Vega," says the thin cardboard package they come in, "a toy for children from 6 to 60.") Manuel works in Cabo San Lucas six months of the year; the other six months he spends in Mexico City selling to tourists in the Zona Rosa and the Christmas crowds in the Alameda.

"That is *ex* cellent!" A man in mirrored sunglasses stops and watches Manuel leap to catch the returning helicopter. He laughs, lustily. "Awesome!" He buys one, paying with three crisp dollar bills.

"They like the fact that they are made in Mexico," Manuel confides to me as he pockets the money. He winds up another toy, holds it cupped in his hand. Business is good in Cabo, he tells me. Especially now, at the end of October. He lets it sail.

Around the corner from the marina, a swarm of black paper bats are taped to the street-side walls of Planet Hollywood. Cardboard tombstones and pumpkin-headed scarecrows are propped below on the broiling-hot sidewalk. Soon it will be Halloween, and there will be a costume contest.

One in a chain of franchise restaurants from San Diego to New York City, Planet Hollywood has been open for less than a year, but it has already become the dominant feature of downtown Cabo San Lucas. At night its revolving red neon sign can be seen for miles. Tourists bunch up along the sidewalk in front, examining the plaster tiles at the entrance, casts of the handprints and shoe prints of celebrities: Sylvester Stallone, Bruce Willis, Whoopi Goldberg, Keanu Reeves, Jean Claude Van Damme. ("Look!" a little boy elbows his dad. "Steven Segal!")

On one side of the building, a cobalt-blue tiled dome shades a mural depicting Planet Hollywood's celebrity shareholders: actress Demi Moore and that unholy trinity of action-picture stars, Arnold Schwarzenegger, Sylvester Stallone, and Bruce Willis. Beside them are representatives of local fauna and flora—a breaching humpback whale, seals, cardón cactus—and the curious arch of rock at Land's End.

There are no windows in this establishment, and the door to its air-conditioned interior, where a margarita costs more than what many Mexicans earn in a day, can be reached only after climbing a series of steps. Glass cabinets at street level display souvenir T-shirts and baseball caps inscribed with the words *Planet Hollywood Cabo San Lucas.* These may be purchased inside.

Cool, moist air hums from the air conditioners as one ascends thickly carpeted stairs. In the sanctum sanctorum: loud rock music, dim lights, zebra skin–patterned fabric. At strategic points through-out the bar, the dining room, and the hallways are glass-encased items of clothing neatly labeled in English: the boxing shoes worn by Sylvester Stallone in *Rocky II;* the bathing suit worn by Geena Davis in *Thelma and Louise;* Charlie Sheen's tie from *Wall Street;* the jacket worn by Stallone's sidekick in *Judge Dredd.*

Sylvester Stallone. The rumor in Cabo San Lucas, avidly spread by bartenders, hotel clerks, touts, and taxi drivers, is that he owns a house here in the Pedregal, the gated neighborhood that straddles the boulder-strewn mountain above town.

Later, Cecilia Avalos tells me, "It's not true," and she laughs. Cecilia is an old friend from Mexico City, married to Jacinto Avalos, an architect noted for, among other projects, several spectacular houses he has built in the Pedregal. Cecilia ought to know: Sylvester Stallone does not have a house here.

We are eating lunch at Mocambo, a Veracruz-style restaurant: seafood cocktails and fish, metal tables cluttered with bottles of hot sauce. Here is where the downtown begins to turn, no longer Planet Hollywood, Dairy Queen, KFC; the Cabo of *For Sale, Long Distance to the U.S. and Canada,* $EXCHANGE, but not yet the dirt-road Cabo of *se vende, farmacia, zapatería.* About half the patrons in Mocambo are tourists, half are local Mexicans. Cecilia recognizes a Mexican real estate agent whose office is across the street. The menus are bilingual, as are the waiters, reciting the day's specials in the rapid-fire clip of Mazatlán. We order tall soda glasses of shrimp in spicy tomato juice, chopped onion, cilantro, and lime.

Cecilia has spent the morning trying to find *calaveras*—the traditional sugar skulls for the *Día de Muertos,* the Day of the Dead—for her children. Her oldest boy is in boarding school in northern California, and he had wanted to make a *Día de Muertos* altar to show his classmates. She would have sent him some *calaveras* with his father, who will be flying to San Francisco on business. "But there is nothing of that here," Cecilia tells me. No *pan de muerto,* the sugar-dusted loaves of bread for the dead, either. "*Todo aquí es* Halloween," she says, shaking her head. Everything here is Halloween.

After lunch I'm back at this borrowed beach house, such a pretty little house, pastel-washed, with a swimming pool. I switch on the stereo, and the voice of Linda Ronstadt glides out to the patio. I try, but I cannot imagine Sylvester Stallone lounging here, say, on the white plastic chaise by the pool, or flexing his biceps in the shade of the palapa. Sylvester Stallone does not seem real to me, a being made of flesh and bone. Nor does Linda Ronstadt, although her voice, heartbroken now, singing of love lost, swoops as real as any bird.

I make my way down the flagstone path to the water, past the wall grown over now with matts and trailing vines of bougainvillea, sumptuous tresses of canary yellow, plum-purple, and crimson. Ten years ago, this was raw land on the edge of a hardscrabble cattle ranch named after the river Tule, a wide bed of dry sand except during the *chubasco,* or hurricane season. Behind the house and across the highway, the apron of land that spreads down from the Sierra de la Laguna is a sun-parched tan, fuzzed with cardón cacti and tangles of thorny bushes and mesquite. Below, the water is a blue so dazzling it hurts the eyes. At night the sky is awash with stars. Here at the end of the Baja California peninsula, the waters of the Sea of Cortés and the Pacific Ocean mingle. There is no land between this shore and the Antarctic.

The sand is clean and soft between my toes. The sun is hot, but the water that curls around my ankles is cool; it is nearly November.

A pair of pelicans skims by, fast and still, their wing tips centimeters above the water.

what came from the sky

"1907, 1918, oh, much suffering; another one in 1927, many animals and fruit trees lost." The town historian counted the years of the great *chubascos* on one hand. We were sitting in his living room in San José del Cabo—I was on the sofa, Don Fernando settled like a Buddha in his rocking chair. The room was small and dark despite the sun outside, crowded with family photographs, decorative dishes, mementos, and plaques commemorating his work as the town historian, as municipal deputy, as delegate for the constitutional convention of the state of Baja California Sur. Solovino, a long-backed mutt with the coat of a golden retriever, wandered restlessly between the front door and the hallway, his toenails clicking against the tiles. I'd been told that Don Fernando's nickname was El Gato, the cat, but he looked mild and kind, the retired schoolteacher that he was. If anything, with his drooping eyelids, balding pate, and tufts of hair carefully combed back above his temples, he reminded me of Mao Tse-tung.

"And then"—Don Fernando placed his hands on his knees— "there was the *chubasco* of 1939. I was nineteen years old, already a teacher in High School Number 3. Some people rode in on horseback from Cabo San Lucas—it was impossible to cross El Tule in an automobile—and they told me when they passed by the school: Cabo San Lucas is gone! So we went there on horses. We sent some mules across El Tule first because they are more surefooted, and if they can cross, the horses follow. We rode and walked through the night, and we arrived at sunup. From the sea to the foothills of the sierra"—Don Fernando swept his arm across the space between us— "there was nothing but broken pieces of cardón cactus. There were no references, everything had disappeared!"

And the people?

"Not many died, only five, because the *chubasco* came down in the daytime. Had it been at night, that would have been different. But they lost everything, their clothes, their dishes, their beds. Forty families! The governor, Lieutenant Colonel Rafael M. Pedrajo"—Don Fernando paused to spell out the name—"he delivered the material for forty houses! I don't know how he did it. The floors and walls were of wood, the roofs of corrugated iron. For forty families! Incredible, such a work. They should put his name on a street, or a monument, something."

I knew about the *chubascos*, the tropical hurricanes that hit the peninsula in late summer. A bad one hit the cape in 1993. The highway from San José to Cabo San Lucas, only recently inaugurated by President Salinas, was washed out at several points, and thousands of cardón cacti were swept down from the sierra, clogging the road and the beaches. The ocean churned up a brown froth that lasted for days. In September 1995 more than a hundred shrimpers died when they were caught out in the Sea of Cortés. More recently, in a mild *chubasco*, a tourist from Nebraska and two of his children were swept out and drowned as they walked on the beach by their hotel.

For a moment I was speechless, contemplating the furor of that *chubasco* of 1939—and the poverty and isolation that made the delivery of boards and corrugated iron for forty shacks like the miracle of manna.

Wrote John Steinbeck, "It is a miserable little flea-bitten place, poor and smelly." He visited Cabo San Lucas with the marine biologist Ed Ricketts in 1940, the year after the great *chubasco*. They were making a collecting expedition on the *Western Flyer*, a sardine boat out of Monterey, California, and they would sail, after their stop in Cabo, deep into the Sea of Cortés.

Cabo San Lucas was smelly then because of the fish cannery, the ruins of which can still be seen at the end of the pier just past the marina. Offal was tossed onto the beach for the pigs and vultures. Steinbeck noted the skinny dogs ("without racial pride"), the road into town ("two wheel-ruts in the dust"), and a "mournful" cantina where "morose young men hung about," hopelessness in their eyes.

But San José del Cabo was always different. It was a town when Cabo San Lucas was but a territory through which Pericú Indians wandered, foraging for cactus fruits. Later, Cabo became known for the whaling supply station and cattle ranch run by an English sailor named Ritchie, then for the fish-canning factory and ramshackle settlement of forty families. And San José del Cabo is still a town when Cabo San Lucas is, well, something else.

Cabo San Lucas wears a smiling, sometimes leering face that bellows, always in English. "Good morning, amigos!" the touts call out. "Something fun to do! How-are-you-today! HELLO!" Moto-tours to the old lighthouse, fishing tours, glass-bottom boat tours, tours to see the seals and the pelicans and the arch, scuba-diving tours, snorkeling tours, sunset tours, cocktails included. "YES!" The humor is hearty and forced. The Tai Won On bar does not serve Thai food; Señor Sushi serves everything but. Rules are posted: "No talking to servers, No talking to invisible people, No Jimmy Buffet music." Advice is offered: "In case of emergency: 1. Panic; 2. Pay bill; 3. Jump out window; 4. Run like hell." "Avoid embarrassment," says the sign in El Squid Roe's T-shirt shop. "Don't wear these clothes on nude beaches." At the Giggling Marlin: "If the food, drinks and service are not up to your standards, then lower your standards."

Tourists jostle down the Avenida Lázaro Cárdenas and the Boulevard Marina past T-shirt shops and jewelry vendors, the racks of postcards of bum shots and obese women ("I had a whale of a time in Cabo San Lucas"), past Pizza Hut, Dairy Queen, the Hard Rock Café, and Planet Hollywood. At the grocery store the freezer section stocks Sara Lee cakes, chicken nuggets, and White Castle microwavable hamburgers; the magazine rack carries *Vanity Fair, People,* and the *Los Angeles Times.* In the parking lot: a boy with long blond hair, shades, and a perfect gingerbread tan strolls by with a surfboard under his arm. At the intersection, hands on her hips, is a woman in black silk pants and a T-shirt that says CHANEL.

San José del Cabo, a half-hour drive around the curve of the cape, feels slower and sleepier. The tourists look older. There is a church built on the site of a Jesuit mission, and the Plaza Mijares, with its quaint little wrought-iron bandstand and benches, is heavily shaded with palms and jacaranda trees. The shops—jewelry, furniture, *zapatería, tintorería*—close for siesta.

But San José too wears a mask: postcard-pretty town, have your enchiladas and margaritas, take your photos, buy your souvenir straw hat. A nice place to retire, play golf, go fishin'. FONATUR, the development arm of the Mexican Ministry of Tourism, has been seeing to that for more than twenty years.

Not that the welcome was wholehearted.

In San José's main plaza there would be a contest for the best altar, announced *El Diario Peninsular:* "To rescue the Mexican tradition of the *Día de Muertos,* as well as to counteract foreign influences."

"Hopefully," sniffed the *Tribunal de los Cabos,* "this will leave in the trunk of forgotten things the ritual of the Americans: Halloween."

Meanwhile, in Don Fernando's house, Solovino had stopped his pacing. He sat, jaw dropped and tongue flapping loose, alert to a small figure at the front gate. *Boof,* he gave a halfhearted warning.

Don Fernando's grandson wanted to come in, to pass through the living room to the kitchen. But he was afraid of the dog.

"Solovino won't do anything," Don Fernando chided. He waved the child in. "Don't be afraid."

The boy skirted the dog warily. They were about the same size.

"*¡Andale!*" Don Fernando swatted Solovino on the haunch. "Go on! Bite him!"

Solovino wagged his tail and cocked his head, confused. Don Fernando broke out laughing.

"*¿Ves?*" he said kindly. "You see? He won't do anything."

A Real One, with Linen and Flowers

"I DON T HAVE anything against the Americans," Alfonso Fisher said. "But it's changed." He sighed and crossed his arms over his chest. He'd lived in Cabo San Lucas since 1947, he said, except when he went away to school, first in Guadalajara, then Mexico City. Although middle-aged, Alfonso was dressed like a teenager in shorts, flip-flops, and a loose avocado-green T-shirt. I had to strain to follow what he was saying; the rhythms of his Spanish were not what I was used to.

We were sitting in his restaurant in the Plaza Bonita mall, only a few steps from Planet Hollywood and the boat ramp where Manuel

Vega sold his toy helicopters. The customers had not yet arrived; it was midmorning. A cleaning lady mopped the floor with languorous sploshes of sudsy water. Alfonso's was a small but upscale restaurant, with marble-top tables, good linen, an antique piano. A stone fountain burbled softly; overhead, a ceiling fan turned, as slow as the second hand on a clock.

"My father was chief engineer of the fish cannery. You can see the ruins from here." Alfonso gestured toward the window and wrinkled his nose. "It smelled really bad."

The cannery closed in the early 1970s, to the relief of the handful of tourists who flew down for the sportfishing. In 1973, the Trans-peninsular Highway was inaugurated, linking the cape with the rest of the peninsula for the first time. Two years later, Alfonso and his mother opened El Arco, Cabo's first trailer park.

"It was small," Alfonso said. "Thirty spaces. It had water, light, good services. The people who stayed there were very interesting. Good people, the people who go to the trailer parks. And so many! The children of King Humberto of Italy came in a gigantic motor home. Peter Fonda stayed with us. All kinds of people. Some of them came every Christmas, they'd bring their piñatas and all that. Very few were Mexicans; most were Americans. A few Italians. They could buy what they needed at a general store in Cabo run by a Chinese named Chong. There wasn't a supermarket." Alfonso sighed again. "Now I feel like a stranger here. When I was a kid, we were a little town of three hundred people."

I had thought Alfonso might be part American himself, despite his accent; his surname was Fisher. When, I wanted to know, did the Fishers arrive in Baja California?

"1827." He chuckled at my surprise. "William Fisher was a sailor. There are lots of Fishers in Baja California, we're a big family. You'll find many names like that here: Collins, Green, Kennedy, Ritchie."

When did he begin to feel like a stranger?

"The last ten years." But things began to change before that, he explained. The Hotel Palmilla was built in 1955, then the Hacienda in the late 1960s, and the Hotel Cabo San Lucas in the 1970s. After that came the deluge of the Finnisterra, Twin Dolphins, Solmar,

Howard Johnson's, El Presidente, Melia, Plaza las Glorias, Marriot, Westin Regina ... Not that Alfonso hadn't been able to take advantage of business opportunities. He ran El Arco trailer park, he opened Alfonso's, which was the first restaurant in Cabo San Lucas—"a real one, with linen and flowers"—and in 1980, he and his mother built the Marina del Sol condominiums.

"You know what they say?" He grinned like a magician about to pull something out of a hat. "The world is a supermarket! And Hong Kong is the cash register." He laid both hands Xat on the table. "So I'm moving there. I'm going to open a Mexican restaurant in front of the Jockey Club, very elegant. I already have my apartment in Hong Kong, on the thirty-eighth Xoor."

I was so startled, the only thing that occurred to me to ask was whether his apartment had a view.

"Yes." He twisted his neck to one side and screwed up his eyes like Quasimodo. "If I go like this."

It Will Be a Marvel

IT WAS THE day before Halloween, and my mother was arriving from San Francisco. Late in the afternoon, I went to pick her up at the airport. The airport! I couldn't help thinking of the pilot Flores and his flight, so daring and flamboyant. ("No one remembers his first name," Don Fernando had said. "He did the loopy loopies!") Suddenly Los Cabos International Airport with its staid, boxlike terminal and its asphalt parking lot seemed monstrous in its modernity.

As I pulled in I watched my mother's plane—a Southwest Airlines 737—descend, its rumble like thunder.

I wanted X-ray vision, to see through the flesh of the present into the past. Don Fernando and Alfonso Fisher had helped me do that; now I wanted to examine a few bones on my own. As I explained to my mother, on the beach just east of the Cabo San Lucas marina was a slight sandy rise topped by the Hotel Melia. According to a nineteenth-century map, this would have been the site of the house of Thomas "Captain" Ritchie, an English cabin boy who jumped ship in the early 1800s and became, in the words of journalist J. Ross Browne, "one of the institutions of the country."

"Smuggling, stockraising, fishing, farming, and trading have been among his varied occupations," wrote Browne in an account of his travels through Baja California for *Harper's New Monthly Magazine.* "He now has a family of half-breeds around him, none of whom speak his native language. He has made and lost a dozen fortunes, chiefly by selling and drinking whiskey." Ritchie's hospitality was legendary. Browne tells us that his house was

> the home of adventurers from all parts of the world. Admirals, commodores, captains and mates inhabit it; pirates and freeboot-ers take refuge in it; miners, traders, and cattledrovers make it their home. In short, the latch-string is never drawn in. All who have money pay if they choose; those who have none he feeds and makes drunk from sheer love of fellowship and natural gen-erosity of heart.

One of that multitude was the Hungarian-born János Xántus, a naturalist stationed at Cabo San Lucas to observe the tides for the U.S. Coastal Survey and collect specimens for the Smithsonian Institution. Xántus's letters to his patron were peppered with refer-ences to Ritchie: "I send all my boxes ... which are at present pele mele piled up on the floor in Mr Ritchies house."

Browne sketched Ritchie's house as he found it in 1866, a two-storied wooden structure with a pitched roof and five large windows facing the water. This is not the house of a dupe, a drunken bump-kin; Captain Ritchie was a mogul of his time and place. He enjoyed a virtual monopoly on supplying the whalers who put in for water and fresh beef; he kept a herd of mules that he employed packing passengers and freight to the inland mines at El Triunfo and San Antonio; he ran a hotel (albeit of a casual sort); he was a moneylend-er. Ritchie may have been bullied by the Mexicans—at one point, Browne tells us, they confiscated his property and imprisoned him in Mazatlán, until an English man-of-war that happened to be in port threatened to bombard the city on his behalf. And if Ritchie was an alcoholic, he was robust. "The various injuries inflicted upon him would have destroyed any other man on earth," claimed Browne. "It will be a marvel if he ever dies."

And so, I invited my mother for a drink at the Hotel Melia, to toast Captain Ritchie, I told her. We sat in the bar by the beach, alone but for a waiter who stood off to the side staring at the water. An American yelled from the balcony outside his room, perhaps six or seven stories up; another answered, bellowing like a sick cow. They were laughing; they were drunk. The sun had fallen behind the arch at Land's End, and the lights of the hotels strung along the beach began to twinkle. Anchored off the arch was a cruise ship draped with lights as if there were a carnival aboard. The air was warm and smelled of the sea.

Afterward, we walked back through the lobby bar. A trio of American women sat dipping their straws in big tropical drinks, watching the RuPaul show on an oversize TV screen. RuPaul wore a tight, lipstick-red dress and a waxy-looking yellow wig, which contrasted sharply with his black skin. He was interviewing an extravagantly beehived member of the B-52s and an actor who was a dead ringer for film director John *(Pink Flamingo)* Waters.

"Who is that woman?" my mother said, pointing to RuPaul.

"He's a transvestite," I said.

"No," my mother said, incredulous.

Pelicans and Turkey Buzzards

AS FOR THE NATURALIST János Xántus, his camp would have lain in the lee of the massive outcropping that ends in the arch and the tall islands of rock called Los Frailes (the Friars), somewhere on the neck of sand between the ruins of the fish cannery and the Hotel Solmar. The fish cannery overlooks the placid blue of the harbor; the Solmar, only a short walk up a hill of dunes, faces the Pacific. The Solmar's is a featureless beach: swath of sand, swath of pale, hot sky. The surf pounds in, hurling up riffs of spray.

Xántus spent two years here measuring the tides and catching, killing, and preserving whatever he could: pelicans, crabs, rattlesnakes, wasp nests, scorpions, starfish, wildflowers, even (I gulp to think of it) a coyote. When he arrived at Cabo San Lucas in 1859, virtually nothing was known of the peninsula's natural history. By the time he sailed back to San Francisco in 1861, Ann Zwinger notes he had discovered and shipped to Spencer Fullerton Baird at the Smithsonian Institution nearly three hundred species new to science. Almost forty of these—among them a hummingbird, a screech owl, a gecko, and a tiny red-tailed triggerfish—bear his name.

It was a painstaking task, but Xántus worked quickly, and boxes of specimens piled up in his tent and "pele mele" at Captain Ritchie's house. Whenever a whaler dropped in for provisions—"I pray all the time for one," he wrote Baird, "like the frogs for rain"—he would send his boxes on. "[W]e must take our chances," he wrote, early in his stay, "and you shall not be surprised if you receive from me letters via the Japanese seas, or Feejee islands or by some New Bedford whaler! I wonder whether you received a dispatch from me . . . via Sandwich islands by a friendly Yankee whaler?"

His nearest neighbor was Captain Ritchie. Xántus relied on Ritchie, as his letters show, for storage, water, occasional shelter, mail deliveries, and loans of cash. Ritchie also gave him advice: about the waterbirds, gone, he said, to Socorro Island to breed; about the "quite different" birds to the north near Todos Santos; about the dangers of a rabid skunk.

The work of setting up camp and the tide gauge, and collecting and preparing specimens, absorbed Xántus for more than a year. His letters reveal glimpses of his life: a pointer dog named Jack he'd trained to dig for crabs; a visit from the governor who brought him "two beautiful magpies . . . alive in a cage . . . very funny pets"; "an old indian woman & her boy, who cook for me"; and "many presents, consisting of objects of natural history, mostly from ladies." He went hunting deer and dined "on a couple of roasted quails in a deep canyon near a spring"; another time, he was out with Jack when they came upon a mountain lion gnawing the carcass of a doe. A "very fine specimen," he boasted of the cat to Baird. "I took great pains with her, prepared very carefully, & dried well." And would Baird please "by first opportunity" send the mountain lion to the Hungarian National Museum, "also her skull, which you will find in a box."

But Xántus's ebullience began to fade. "I do not know how the world stands," he complained to Baird. "I wonder whether Empr Napoleon rules yet Europe, or somebody else?" Soon Xántus was in flat-out despair: "near my camp is at present a perfect desolation, I killed everything." His letters became fewer, brief. In his last field-book entry, he wrote:

> I am quite sick indeed of this place, every day seems a long year, and every one with the same monotonous desolation around me, not affording the least pleasure, variety, or enjoyment of any kind.
> . . . I am now of Gods grace nearly two years perched on this sandbeach, a laughing stock probably of the Pelicans & Turkey buzzards, the only signs of life around me.

Xántus's camp would have been closer to the ruins of the fish-canning factory; but the Solmar Hotel would be close enough for my purposes. I drove up the path that wound through the dunes and parked in a lot walled by a mountain of granite. The hotel rose up out of the sand, bone-white and angular. I walked through the lobby to the Pacific Ocean. The wind billowed my shirt and whipped my hair against my face. Even with sunglasses on I had to squint and shade my eyes.

The beach was deserted. The guests gathered around the swimming pool, only partially sheltered by the mass of rock at Land's End. Most of them lay on plastic chaise longues reading paperbacks: Tom Clancy, John Grisham, *The Bridges of Madison County*.

How galled Xántus would have been. To think: people would actually *pay* to come here!

I took refuge in the palapa bar and ordered coffee. Another toast, of sorts: Xántus's was a tremendous contribution to science. Not only was the sheer number of specimens he sent to the Smithsonian Institution impressive, but the condition they arrived in was almost uniformly excellent—remarkable given that the specimens ranged from birds and mammals to fish, plants, and insects, and even more remarkable given the primitive conditions in which he had to work. "The wind blows to hard all the time," he wrote Baird, "and upsets every now & then my tent, as there is nothing but quick sand to fasten the pegs in. Besides it is so small & so we have to sleep on top of the boxes." The boxes—made of wood, a scarce commodity on this remote desert cape—he nailed together himself.

According to Steinbeck, Xántus left another legacy. The manager of the fish cannery had pointed to three little Indian children and said they were Xántus's great-grandchildren. "In the town there is a large family of Xantuses," he added, "and a few miles back in the hills you'll find a whole tribe of them." Perhaps Xántus had fancied one of the "ladies" who brought him presents (a branch of milkwort? a cactus wren's egg?), a simple girl with rough Spanish and calloused hands—someone he could abandon when he returned to Europe. I had looked for that "large family" in the encyclopedic *Guía Familiar de Baja California*. I found Ritchie and Fisher, but no Xántus. It was as though his name had been covered over by the sands themselves.

The music from the bar's loudspeakers sounded like Julio Iglesias à la mexicana, marimba, and violins, something close to Muzak. It was louder or softer depending on the breeze from the ocean; in either case it was awful. Little brown birds twittered around my table; one alighted on the chair next to mine. I would have tossed it a crumb, but all I had was my empty cup of coffee.

As I stood up to leave, a gust blew through the bar, wafting away my cocktail napkin. I watched for a moment as it cartwheeled past the waiter who ran to retrieve it, like a small white animal, fleet and frisky.

Everybody Wears One

AND SO WHERE fisherfolk and farmers once gaped at their first airplane sprawls an international airport; on the site of Captain Ritchie's house, a TV screen shows RuPaul holding forth in his waxy yellow wig; and on the shifting sands where János Xántus pitched his humble tent in the roar of the wind, bleats of Muzak soothe vacationing office workers. The past lies behind the present, as strange and necessary as bones are to flesh. But to reverse the analogy, the present laid over the past, they sometimes seem foreign to one another, yet fitting as a fright mask to a face.

In the more recent past came the surfers, spearheading the first great wave of Americans to venture down the peninsula after the Transpeninsular Highway opened in 1973. As I write, hundreds are waiting for their "surf fax." It's a service—it costs some two dollars a minute—provided by a company that maintains buoys all across the Pacific. The buoys register swells from a storm, say, in New Zealand, and these predict the quality of surfing conditions in Baja California. When they're good, three or four hundred surfers from southern California alone will fly down to Cabo for the weekend. The planes will all be full, the car-rental agencies sold out.

"Live to Surf, Surf to Live," as surf star Mike Doyle inscribed his autobiography to me.

Mike was making a living as a painter now, he told me when I met with him under the big top–size palapa of a seafood restaurant. He was a rangy, square-shouldered guy in shades and a sea blue–and-white Hawaiian shirt. His heyday as a surf star was back in the 1960s. His life since then had been peripatetic: Honolulu, Aspen, Jackson Hole, Idaho, Oregon. He'd sold granola, purple surfboard wax, suntan oil, beachwear, real estate. He'd invented the single ski, precursor to the wildly popular snowboard; he'd taken up sailboarding. He'd married twice, divorced twice, dated New Age minister Terry Cole-Whitakker, remarried. It wasn't until he was in his late forties that he began to recognize the patterns in his life. "Things didn't just fall apart," he wrote. "I tore them down on purpose to get what I really wanted, which was freedom and the sense of adventure that comes from starting all over again."

That bohemian impulse had drawn Mike to surfing back when he was a teenager, inspired by the likes of Tubesteak, a surfer who lived in a shack at Malibu, surviving on a diet of roasted hot dogs financed by collecting Coke bottles. It also drew Mike to Baja California. He'd ventured south of the border before on "surfaris" with his buddies from Los Angeles, but he didn't get down to Cabo until 1974, the year after the Transpeninsular opened. "They kept saying there was no surf here," Mike told me indignantly. "But it was great!" Cabo was a village of four hundred people then, and the road to San José was unpaved. The only place to stay was Alfonso Fisher's trailer park. Mike bought a plot of land on the hill overlooking the half-moon of beach called Zippers—world famous now for its outstanding surfing—and began to construct his house. Not long after, when a legion of Americans followed Mike's lead, the area was dubbed Gringo Hill.

Mike moved down full-time in the mid-1980s. He sold real estate for a few years, but no longer. "The thrill," he told me, "is doing what you want to do. I'm really creating something. Being a salesman is not as exciting, not like putting color on a canvas." He was surprisingly soft-spoken. If I'd closed my eyes and just listened to his voice, I could have pictured someone in his early twenties.

Did he still surf?

"Surfing is *first!*" He'd looked at me as if I were insane.

Later, Mike met my mother and me at the gate of his house on Gringo Hill. The view from the patio was dark, but we could hear the rush and pull of the breakers against the beach below. His studio was a large white room lit with flood lamps placed on the floor. His canvases were big, loud, and colorful. Beach scenes predominated: a cluster of candy-colored skiffs under a lavender sky; a rim of surf, coconut palms bent in the breeze. The largest painting was of twin purple and lime-green trees rendered in strokes as broad and crude as a housepainter's. My mother admired *Squid Woman,* a red-and-yellow figure with flowing hair.

Today was a good day, Mike said. After surfing Zippers, he'd finished a six-paneled canvas of orange and fuchsia, yellow and lime-green masks, all wild and scribbly. Its title, scrawled across the bottom: *The King in Me.*

I liked the energy and playfulness of his work, and I appreciated the courage of his lifestyle. Painting was not a steady salary. "But you overcome that," Mike had told me. "You feel free again. What's the worst that could happen? I could go out surfing. I need to eat? I'll get my bag of brown rice."

But there was a pragmatic side to Mike, too. He traveled the circuit of surf trade shows, selling his book and a longboard called the Mike Doyle Waterman Special. He'd recently been commissioned to do the poster art for a surfing contest to benefit Scripps research on cancer. He himself—"surfing legend Mike Doyle," as last year's brochure touted—would participate.

Mike brought out one last painting, of a bare-chested man with a chalk-white face. The eyes were shaded with purple and turquoise, and delicate lines of scarlet scrolled around each cheek, like the war paint of the Maoris. The expression was at once watchful and amused. A self-portrait. Its title: *Everybody Wears One.*

He was going to a costume party tonight, Mike said, as he began stacking the canvases against the wall. "As van Gogh—you know, tape over one ear and add ketchup."

El Halloween

THE NIGHT WAS still young, and my mother was curious to see the new Planet Hollywood. Besides, the Halloween-costume contest might be fun to watch. We went in, up the sweep of carpeted stairs and past Charlie Sheen's tie, Geena Davis's bathing suit, Sylvester Stallone's shoes. The restaurant was dim, zebra-skinned, loud. It was also empty.

"Nah," my mom said, and we left.

We walked along the main avenue, by the restaurants and bars decked out for Halloween with black and orange streamers, fake cobwebs, paper cutout pumpkins and ghosts and skulls. The Bee Gees' "Stayin' Alive" blasted out the door of the Rio Grill. At the entrance, a peroxide blonde dressed as a dominatrix passed out candy to a group of Mexican children accompanied by their mother. The baby—wide-eyed in his stroller—was outfitted as a devil, with sequins pasted on his little red felt horns. *"El Halloween! El Halloween!"* the children cried, holding out plastic grocery bags.

The avenue was filling with children, and all along it the employees of restaurants, bars, real estate offices, and T-shirt shops were handing out candy. Several older American couples were also handing out sweets, fistfuls of little twist-wrapped licorices, strawberry chews, and Chiclets. Most of the children wore homemade witch or vampire costumes, their faces smeared with white and black greasepaint. A few sported fangs, and one tiny witch, perhaps four years old, carried an enormous plastic bone that she held like a baton. Some of the smaller children were mummies, wrapped with gauze or Ace bandages.

My mother and I decided that we too would hand out treats, and we stepped into the grocery store for a kilo bag of candies. Immediately on returning to the sidewalk we were surrounded by a crowd of children—some witches and vampires, but many without a costume—pushing their bags at us, crying, *"El Halloween! El Halloween!"* and then, a few sweets dropped in, not a *gracias,* but a chorus of "Thank you! Thank you!"

As we worked our way down the avenue we met several small groups with their parents. From their accents I guessed the parents were the white-collar workers of Cabo, shop clerks and restaurant managers recently arrived from mainland cities such as Guadalajara, Obregón, or Guanajuato. For a couple of blocks this was an agreeable intercultural kind of thing—we, delighted by the children and their costumes, they delighted with the candy, the parents beamingly polite, thanking us always in English.

And then, near the Giggling Marlin, we ran into that same crowd of unescorted children. They pressed up against my mother, crying, *"Dame el Halloween!"* Give me my Halloween!

"But you've already had your candy," my mother said, holding the bag closed against her chest.

"El Halloween!" they cried. *"El Halloween!"* A little ghoul with greasepaint circles around his eyes and a penciled scar that looked more like a centipede tugged at her blouse, his face an agony of hurt. I believe he'd already gotten candy from my mother twice.

I had to laugh. I was glad not to be home in Mexico City, where my doorbell would be ringing at all odd hours for days. I usually drew the line at two visits for candy, and steeled myself against the begging and whining on the third. How I missed the orderliness of a suburban American Halloween, all the children in costume, accompanied by parents, saying "Trick-or-Treat!" between the hours of seven and ten P.M. on the thirty-first of October. (Anyone having the cheek to ring the bell twice at least goes to the trouble of changing masks.)

Feeling somewhat put-upon, we moved off the street to the patio bar at the corner of Plaza Bonita, a good vantage point for watching the Americans who were beginning to file out of their hotels and houses to explore the costume parties along the avenue. There was a Batman, a woman in a Dodgers baseball uniform, a pirate with a stuffed fake-fur parrot Velcroed to his shoulder. A clique of girls in fright wigs and black leather miniskirts rated whistles from the waiters. One of the waiters crouched behind a potted bougainvillea and yelped like a coyote.

It was nearly nine o'clock when we headed back out to the avenue. The air was cooler and the bass bleat from the restaurants and bars-cum-discos louder, muddled. Most of the children were gone, or flagging. I spotted the devil asleep in his stroller. One little mummy, his unraveled bandages revealing an expanse of diaper, held his father's hand as he slowly scaled the steps of Pizza Hut.

Like an Island You Can Drive To

"LOS CABOS is an island," my friend the architect Jacinto Avalos told me. "It's isolated from Mexico and from the United States, but it's sufficiently close to the U.S. and sufficiently far from Mexico, so that as a Mexican you feel strange, as if you're not in your own country."

When Jacinto and Cecilia arrived from Mexico City—he was to open his own architectural office in the Pedregal—their youngest son was five years old. When the little boy asked the price of a T-shirt, the saleswoman answered him in English (probably because he was blond): "Seven dollars." The menus in many of the restaurants were printed in English; the bathrooms said "Men," not *"Hombres,"*

"Ladies," instead of *"Damas."* He was confused and he asked his parents, are we in the United States?

%

"YOU KNOW WHAT they say?" In the cool of his living room, the town historian, Don Fernando Cota, rocked forward in his chair and crossed one leg over the other. "It would be very easy to break off Baja California, and all the world's ships could push it out to sea, and not a thing would change. Someone told that to the governor of the Territory of Baja California Sur, an old Revolutionary general named Francisco J. Múgica, when he first arrived from Mexico City. The general started to laugh. He said, 'You're right!' He understood that the peninsula was completely cut off from the rest of the country. And that's when he got the idea to build the Transpeninsular Highway, in 1941. So he brought over an engineer who made all the necessary studies, and he sent them to Mexico City. But they ignored the reports, as well done and detailed as they were. What they did was begin a ferry service from Mazatlán to La Paz, and later, four other ferries.

"When Luis Echeverría arrived on his presidential campaign, he said he would build the highway. He said he would not set foot again in Baja California until it was constructed. We all figured it was the usual demagoguery. *¡Pero híjole!* But goodness! *Punto y seguido,* Right away, they built the highway. It was inaugurated on December 1, 1973. President Echeverría himself came to the ceremony at the twenty-eighth parallel, the border between the state of Baja California and what was then the territory of Baja California Sur.

"I myself inaugurated the stretch between San José and La Paz. This was in 1970, the 150th anniversary of Mexico's independence from Spain. A representative of the president came, and I told him that the government had not yet done anything as important for Baja California as what the Jesuit missionaries did. He didn't like that, not one bit."

%

THE HIGHWAY changed everything. Wrote Mike Doyle, Los Cabos is "like an island you can drive to." The year after the highway opened, he was surfing Zippers. Thousands of Americans followed— surfers, kayakers, snorkelers, sportfishermen, golfers, businessmen, artists, retirees, in cars and trucks and motorbikes and caravans of great lumbering Winnebagos. This was precisely why the Mexican government did not build it earlier. They waited until ferry services from the mainland and a series of wells drilled deep into under- ground aquifers had helped populate the peninsula with a small but critical mass of Mexicans. And with good reason: they had nearly lost Baja California to the Americans, and more than once.

"Here Is a Place for Someone Like Me"

BUT THE IMMIGRATION from mainland Mexico was not without its costs. "The local people, they are lost in the crowd," Father Luis Alvarado told me when I met with him at his parish office in Cabo San Lucas. "Their hometown has changed. They've sold their land, they're moving out towards the edge of town—into better houses, to be sure, but they are no longer living where they used to. A new community is being formed, and this is very difficult."

Father Alvarado spoke with a strong, clear voice. A handsome man in his early forties, he was a native of Jalisco and a graduate of semi- naries in Guadalajara and Puebla. He was new to Cabo himself, although he'd arrived in Baja California nearly fifteen years earlier, to serve the fishing communities on Natividad and Margarita Islands, and then for six years, the inland cape town of Santiago. Cecilia Avalos, who'd arranged the interview, told me Father Alvarado paint- ed, wrote poetry, and could play several musical instruments. Outside, traffic clattered past on an unpaved road, churning up clouds of dust.

"Let me give you an example," he continued. "When a local per- son dies, *everyone* goes to the church. But if a person from elsewhere dies, maybe three or four people show up. Usually, the body is sent home 'a mi tierra,' as they say, to Guerrero, Puebla, Oaxaca, Nayarit, Sinaloa. They come for land and for work. Their roots are not here."

The next day was All Saints' Day. "At the graveyard," Father Alvarado said, "almost none of the new people will show up. The community had a tradition of going to mass and taking flowers to the graves, but that's being broken now." (And—he didn't mention this—a new tradition, of *Día de Muertos* altars and altar contests, was being imported from the mainland.)

The tourist industry had brought money and jobs, but also social problems. "There have been murders," he said, "people beaten up, very aggressive behavior. Before one never saw such things. Decent, hardworking people come to Cabo, but also criminals who are hiding their identities. We're seeing drug trafficking, young people smoking marijuana, alcoholism. Also, a lot of homosexuals come here, and they hire male prostitutes, even little boys, and take them out on their boats. You get the impression the tourists are kings. Some of them come here to get drunk. When the town wants to have its dance, the hotels complain because the tourists want to sleep. Well, they have the money."

Didn't this breed resentment?

"Not yet. People want jobs and tourism benefits the worker. The new people don't consider Cabo their home. It's something for tourists, something apart. The community hasn't yet been created."

The challenge, for Father Alvarado, was to help build that community, "a Cabo San Lucas that is for everyone." But it was, he said again, very difficult. "Some of the new people don't come to church because they are afraid, they think we won't get along. On the other hand, it's like an explosion, there are so many people. We don't have enough priests, we don't have enough buildings. People willing to volunteer, they're hard to find. Everything is makeshift."

Father Alvarado was one of three priests in the Cabo San Lucas parish. Among them they divided the work of eleven masses each Sunday, plus weekday masses, Wednesday visits to four chapels in the sierra, training lay preachers, confessions, counseling, baptisms, first communions, marriages, and funerals—not to mention the mountains of attending paperwork. "Just this year we gave catechism and first communion to 1,311 children in Cabo. Next year we expect to have 2,000."

And now there was the problem of the poor who'd arrived with the economic crisis that followed the collapse of the peso in late 1994. (Near the Plaza Bonita mall I had spotted beggars in Indian garb—probably Mixtecs from Oaxaca on the mainland.) Father Alvarado had organized a group of concerned parishioners, and led their first meeting the night before. They'd collected the foodstuffs stacked in the hallway: bags of flour, canned soup, and jugs of orange juice.

"You have many challenges," I said. I was beginning to feel embarrassed at having taken so much of his time.

"But many satisfactions," he answered, clasping his hands together. "We do it with love. We must construct with love."

LUPE, WHO COOKED and cleaned at the beach house where I was staying, was one of the many workers who had come to Cabo from Acapulco. She was short and copper-skinned and moon-faced, her hair parted down the middle and pulled back tightly with a rubber band. She wore oversize T-shirts, shapeless skirts, and plastic sandals, comfortable clothes for moving around in hot weather.

Lupe had been in Cabo for less than a year. Shortly after her arrival, she joined the *paracaidistas,* or "parachutists," the hundreds of squatters who invaded ranch land behind the old workers' barrio. When the police came to evict them, Lupe ran away and hid in an arroyo while they tore down her tar-paper shack and burned everything in it.

This happens all over Mexico. In Mexico City, I used to work as an economist. One Sunday afternoon several years ago, when I was doing research on microenterprise lending in a working-class barrio, I watched from the upstairs window of a candy factory as parachutists took over the empty lot next door. Some two dozen men, women, and children appeared as if out of nowhere. Lengths of white string were knotted around nails and pulled from one end of the lot to the other to mark the parcels, then sheets of corrugated iron and tar paper were carried in, the men like ants beneath their loads, and deposited in the squares. The people moved silently and fast. In time—if they weren't evicted—they would have power, water, telephone lines. Perhaps a school or a clinic. They would vote—usually for the PRI (the then ruling Party of the Institutional Revolution), but increasingly for an opposition party—as a bloc.

Like the other evicted parachutists, Lupe was offered a lot in Lomas del Sol, the newest workers' barrio in Cabo, a long bus ride down a dusty dirt road. Already Lomas del Sol (which means Hills of the Sun) had bus and sewage services, water, and light.

But it's in an arroyo, as Cecilia Avalos told me, dangerous in the *chubasco* season, and it borders the garbage dump. The people who live there suffer respiratory infections, diarrhea, and skin diseases.

When we were first introduced, Lupe was washing tomatoes in the sink. She had barely said *mucho gusto,* pleased to meet you, when she told me, her hands still under the running water, that her baby had been born dead. Now I was back from downtown, and again Lupe was at the sink, slicing celery. I said hello, and then I asked her to be sure to soak it in Microdyne. As if in answer, she told me her brother had died.

"He drank too much and wrecked his liver." This happened two weeks ago; she'd just returned from Acapulco, where she'd gone for the funeral.

"I'm so sorry," I said.

"He was young," she said. "He left a wife and a three-month-old baby."

Quickly, she patted her hands dry and then passed me three brown buns shaped like ghosts, their eyes made of raisins. *Pan de muerto,* a gift for me of bread for the dead. I was touched. Also surprised: Cecilia had told me she couldn't find *pan de muerto* here in Cabo. This bread was not made in a bakery, Lupe explained, but in a house in Lomas del Sol. She was selling it door-to-door.

"That must be a good business," I said.

"Not really." Lupe shrugged. "They sell for only a peso and a half." A handful of pennies.

The cost of living is high in Los Cabos, but here maids like Lupe can earn double, triple, even quadruple what they could earn in their hometowns and villages. Some of them have glamorous lives, of a sort. One left the beach house where I was staying to go work for a family that was moving to Madrid. Another had worked for the billionaire Jimmy Goldsmith at his mansion in Careyes, Jalisco. She later left the beach house because she was convinced that the gatekeeper, jealous that his wife did not have the job of cooking and cleaning, had paid a witch to cast a spell on her.

Once, when I was using the telephone at Jacinto Avalos's architectural office, three women came in and asked how they might find work as maids in the Pedregal. They bunched together, shyly. Their eyes were shining; this was what they had come to Cabo for. They were copper-skinned and moon-faced, like Lupe. Probably from Acapulco.

٭

AS FOR JACINTO AVALOS, when I asked him why he had chosen to come here, he said, "Cabo is a zone that is still defining itself. I thought: here is a place for someone like me."

It was late in the afternoon, and Jacinto, Cecilia, and I were sitting in their living room under the gaze of an antique painting of the Virgin of Guadalupe. There was a sculpture by Zúñiga on the coffee table, and a child-faced merman in bronze by Sergio Bustamante next to the swimming pool. Jacinto had designed and built the light-filled house himself. Perched up high in the Pedregal, one of its most remarkable features was that from the living room, the swimming pool appeared to blend into the Pacific Ocean.

Unlike the majority of Cabo's immigrants, Jacinto had had attractive opportunities at home. He'd studied architecture at the Iberoamericana, Mexico City's prestigious Jesuit university, and he held a master's degree in urban design from Oxford. But after working in Mexico City for several years, he began to feel frustrated.

"There I was with all these incredible museums, restaurants, cinemas. Mexico City has a very active cultural life, but I couldn't take advantage of it. You never have time, you're always tired, or you go to the Gauguin or Chagall exposition and find so many people that you can't enjoy it." (I smirked with recognition: I'd spent my recent weekends at home in Mexico City watching Blockbuster videos— *Die Hard II,* etc.—wedged onto the sofa between my snoring dogs.) "Therefore, what was the point of putting up with the pollution, the traffic, and the crime, if I couldn't take advantage of the cultural life? It occurred to me that if I moved to Cabo I'd still get the same culture, because I could go do those things on visits to Mexico City."

But the most important consideration for Jacinto and Cecilia was their three children.

"There were two problems with raising children in Mexico City," Jacinto explained. "First, for a variety of reasons, including physical security, they lived in a ghetto without any contact with other sectors of the population. It bothered me that other people within my own ghetto had developed attitudes that were negative, even unchristian, towards other people from other sectors. Second, in Mexico City you get the idea that you as an individual don't have an impact, that everything—the garbage collection, the road repair, water, and electricity—functions like magic. I wanted my children to see that they could contribute to and enrich their community. For the Mexico they are going to live in, I felt it was very important that they learn to live with people of different social and economic classes, and that they feel they can be—that they are, already—important in the development of their community. In Cabo, I have time to be with my family. We eat together every day, and often we have time together in the afternoons. We spend the weekends on the beach. In Mexico City I couldn't enjoy my family. I'd have to leave for work early, I never had lunch at home, I'd get home late. And although we miss our extended family in Mexico, the distance allows a more autonomous family life. Also, I like to be in contact with nature. Every morning I see the ocean"—he gestured toward the open patio, flooded now with golden light. "I see the sierra, and rocks, and plants. That's so much better than buildings, cars, and sidewalks."

It sounded idyllic. I turned to Cecilia, who'd been nodding with agreement at everything he said. "The first moment I arrived in Cabo," she said, "I was happy."

But hadn't moving here had its drawbacks?

She didn't hesitate to answer. "You always feel nostalgia. You don't want to go back to Mexico City, but you long for your country, for your people."

"It's hard to make friends," Jacinto said. "In Mexico City you can have a group of friends who all live in the same neighborhood, go to the same schools, dress the same, look at the world in the same way. But think how many millions of people you need to filter out those five or six best friends who are just like you. Here there are very few people with whom we share common interests, activities, and values. On the other hand, you can at least find something to bring you together."

"I've made two good friends here," Cecilia said. "I mean, people who think the way I do."

They'd left Mexico City eight years earlier. Cabo was still defining itself, but Jacinto had already designed and built an important part of its emerging profile—the remodeled wing of Cabo's church, a number of restaurants, many of its most beautiful homes.

Jacinto looked wistful. He said, "I miss giving classes at the university."

Couldn't he teach architecture and urban design here?

"Where?" He gave a bitter laugh. "To whom?"

That was when I noticed there was something peculiar about their dog, a miniature schnauzer named Biscuit, who was napping under the coffee table. Biscuit looked healthy—plump, his chest rising and falling evenly—but he seemed (that was it) a different shape, smaller than when I'd last seen him. His hind legs looked like a pug's now, and his chin, where there'd been a silken boxlike little beard, was shaved to a stubble.

"I took Biscuit to be groomed, and they sent him back to me like this." Cecilia rolled her eyes. "It's like that old saying: you leave Mexico City, and everything is Cuautitlán."

Which was why they'd had to send their two older children to boarding schools in northern California.

"We expected their education in adolescence to be a problem," Jacinto said. "It *is* a problem. But we're trying to improve." The youngest was still at home, attending one of the local private schools.

Jacinto and Cecilia had helped push for more qualified teachers, higher teacher salaries, better textbooks, computers, and sports; recently, Jacinto had joined the board. This was in addition to their work with Amigos de los Niños, a group that aids Cabo's abused and abandoned children, and PRONATURA, which promotes environmental protection.

The separation from two of their three children was difficult; they were counting the days until Thanksgiving weekend. Nevertheless, sending the older girl and boy abroad ensured a quality education for them, and future admission to top universities—probably in Mexico City.

When I left, the sky was a medley of mango and raspberry. Standing at the gate to the street, I could see the sweep of ragged shore far below, silver in the fading light. Biscuit trotted out along the edge of the pavement, his cobby little body silhouetted against the horizon.

Cecilia and I stood watching for a moment as the colors deepened over the shimmering water. Breeze from the ocean brushed against our bare arms.

Dreamy Gardens

But there was another side to the picture-postcard Cabo San Lucas: the workers' barrio. The day after Halloween I drove down the dirt road to Lomas del Sol, plowing up the dust behind me. The surrounding land was undeveloped, a wilderness of cacti and plastic detritus, rusted cans and Coke bottles. A farm truck overtook me, spitting back billows of grit. Workers were packed tight onto its deck, only the dark bouncing crowns of their heads visible above the wooden slats. It was late afternoon, and the sky was streaked with cottony pink clouds. Their barrio was a grid of wide unpaved avenues lined with cinder-block houses, most of them unpainted, their corner studs protruding like brown flowerless stems. Here and there, mongrels nipped at their tails or scratched at their chins with a hind leg. A girl with fluttering pink ribbons in her pigtails pedaled across an intersection; a man stood behind a fence, picking at his stomach. It could have been a slum anywhere in Mexico, I thought: the outskirts of Acapulco, Ciudad Juárez, Mexico City. Always there are the unpaved roads, the dogs, the half-finished gray cinder blocks.

But Lomas del Sol, I began to notice, had more than the usual number of businesses: here was a furniture store, there an ice cream shop, a beauty parlor. I stopped at the Mini-Super Joss (cement floor washed turquoise, a boy plugging coins into a video game) and bought a cold Coke. Across the street was a *papelería*—a stationery store—with a banner hung over its entrance that said HALLOWEEN. The shops were mixed in among the houses, many of which had satellite dishes, some as large and fine as Jacuzzis, anchored to a roof or plunked at an odd angle in a side yard. More stores, five or six of them, sold *materiales de construcción:* cement, wood planks, plumbing fixtures, paint. And everywhere bright notes, like harbingers, of color: a spray of bougainvillea, coffee cans planted with geraniums, the raw green of a sun-glistened banana tree. And then it was dark. On the road back, I passed a woman walking toward Cabo with a tray of candies on her head, then a mariachi carrying a violin. The headlights of my car picked out the silver buttons on his trousers.

❧

WROTE ONE ARTHUR NORTH, an early traveler to San José del Cabo, "It certainly is a dreamy garden." It always seems like magic to me, the way things grow—the moment they're watered—in the sun of Baja California. As late as the 1980s, for instance, much of the land between San José del Cabo and Cabo San Lucas was an unrelieved desert shore of thorn and scrub. Today, there are rolling green carpets of golf courses and landscaped drives. The garden of this beach house is a thriving profusion of velvety hibiscus, birds-of-paradise, pillowy tufts of daisies, tangerines, limes, and pomegranates, as fat as baseballs. Thick tangles of bougainvillea have matted over the trellises; great bushes of it burst from terra-cotta tubs. Tendrils shoot out overnight, festooned with blossoms. In the slightest breeze, the blossoms blow onto the swimming pool and drift, like the loose beads of a necklace.

In the mornings, when I walk along the beach, the rollers crashing loudly, I pass a grove of transplanted coconut palms shielding a compound of fantastic palace-size palapas. Farther on, after a nude brown arroyo, is the house of a European prince, with its orchard of fruit trees. His lawn spills toward the sea down a hill, a carpet of emerald. The sprinkler system twirls out sprays of water, *phut-phut.*

They are an extravagant lot, these neighbors. Next door is a real estate magnate, the owner of vast tracts of suburban Los Angeles. One owns a hotel in Europe. Another is a rock star. I hear rumors: that one of them flew in Elton John to play the piano at his birthday party, that another bought a Hummer and hired a helicopter to spot him in the Baja 1000 off-road race.

The gardener tells me the hotel owner likes to shoot ravens with his hunting rifle. One expired a little ways away, and fell into the pomegranate tree outside my bedroom.

The Día de Muertos

AND SO HALLOWEEN had passed, and the first day of November, All Saints'. On the second, I drove my mother back to the airport. The airport was filled with franchises: Domino's Pizza, Carnation Ice Cream, Mrs. Field's Cookies. Long lines snaked to the counters of Continental, Mexicana, Alaska Airlines. The bar was packed with Americans, all watching football on TV.

"Touchdown!" they shouted, raising their fists.

Today was the *Día de Muertos,* that tradition—the local pundits claimed—so in need of rescue from "foreign influences." A blend of European folk practice and pre-Hispanic ritual adapted to the Catholic All Souls', it is celebrated in mainland Mexico as a happy day. Families visit the graves of relatives, sweeping and then decorating them with flowers, candles, and offerings of food—tamales, chocolate, beans, and tortillas. In some parts of Mexico an altar with the offering is assembled inside the house, and may include photographs, favorite toys, musical instruments, and even clothing. Until recent years this celebration was an intimate one, the dead honored by those who knew and loved them. Now tourists, both Mexican and foreign, crowd into the mainland Indian towns of Mixquic and

Pátzcuaro, jumbling through the narrow rows between the pretty graves, cameras clicking away. "Mexico has sold its cult of death," writes Mexican critic Carlos Monsiváis, "and the tourists smile, anthropologically satiated." Even the urban middle and upper classes—in generations past, at a careful remove from any taint of the indigenous—revel in their *mexicanidad,* assembling altars to no one in particular, loudly colorful constructions for the lobbies of museums, offices, shops and hotels, schools and universities, and town plazas . . .

On my way back from the airport I stopped in San José's. A hot afternoon. Trees thick with birds. An old man sat nodding on the steps of the church, which was a pretty little building, buff-yellow and cream with twin bell towers flanking its entrance. In front of the ice cream stand, a tourist in a golf hat and cork-soled sandals fanned himself with a folded brochure. At the far side of the plaza, I found one *Día de Muertos* altar, half assembled in the shade of a lush, feathery palm.

Like all the many others I had seen, it looked impersonally attractive. A riot of color and pottery (from Puebla and Michoacán), it beckoned the camera, its chief purpose to win a competition.

I almost didn't notice that the little paper cutout skull taped above a bowl of apples and bananas read:

AMELIA WILKES

Water, Then Fire

At the mention of the name Amelia Wilkes, the town historian, Don Fernando, rocked back in his chair. *"Ah, la profesora,"* the schoolteacher. He'd been stroking Solovino behind the ears; now he laid both hands Buddha-like across his belly and closed his eyes for a moment before he began.

"Amelia Wilkes—Wilkes is a name like Ritchie or Fisher, from a sailor—was born in Cabo San Lucas in 1907 and died in 1989 at the age of eighty-two. She was a teacher and a community leader. She served as president of the electricity supply, she directed the water commission. This was around 1930, a long time before the *chubasco*. When they named Amelia Wilkes subdelegate for the territory, she became the first female authority in Baja California Sur. She was *un personaje,* a real character, very respected. They dedicated the plaza of Cabo San Lucas to her in 1976.

"I'll tell you a story that shows you what kind of person she was. She used to collect money from the townspeople in order to buy heating oil for the generator that produced the town's electricity. She would buy the oil and keep it in barrels in her house. Her house was made of wood. This was after the *chubasco;* it was one of those from the governor. She was also the director of the school, so she had all the savings of the students in her house, along with the barrels of heating oil. One night her sister knocked over a kerosene lamp, and the house caught fire. As fast as they could, so the house wouldn't explode, Amelia and her sister began rolling out the barrels of oil. And then she ran back into the house—the flames were every-where!—and grabbed the children's savings. That was what she res-cued, nothing of her own. She lost everything."

Just as in the *chubasco* of 1939.

When John Steinbeck and Ed Ricketts went ashore at Cabo San Lucas in 1940, Amelia Wilkes would have just moved into that wood house given to her by the governor. Like János Xántus, that unhap-py Hungarian, Steinbeck and Ricketts had come to collect speci-mens; in their case, marine animals. To put it less nicely, they were there to kill things, and seal them in little bottles of formaldehyde and take them home. Ricketts, the author of a standard reference work on Pacific tide pools, owned a laboratory on Monterey's Cannery Row. Steinbeck had just published *The Grapes of Wrath,* which, on his return from Baja California, would be awarded the Pulitzer Prize.

Perhaps from her window, *la profesora* saw the Americans in their yachting caps and sweaters swagger through her "sad little town"; perhaps she even saw them push through the doors to the "mourn-ful" cantina. I like to think that Amelia was inside, one elbow on the bar—why not? The novelist's wife, Carol, was there, although she isn't once mentioned in his *Sea of Cortez.*

It is painful to read the scene in the cantina. The Americans are ignored; they order a round of beer for the Mexicans; still they are ignored. They buy straw hats; they are ignored. For their beneficence with the beer and the straw hats, indeed, for their very presence in Cabo San Lucas—which Steinbeck likens in importance to the great *chubasco* itself—the Americans compare themselves to God, no less, and to the Mexicans' "golden angel."

O irony! Slung as thick as wet sand.

Even the pirates didn't think much of Cabo San Lucas. It did have interesting rock formations at Land's End, "like the Needles at the Isle of Wight," noted the English pirate Woodes Rogers. The people—Pericú Indians then—were poor and primitive. Their women, especially, wrote Rogers's second-in-command, Edward Cooke, "are very disagreeable to look to, of a middle Stature, let their Children suck 'till very big, and when traveling, carry them on their backs; they sit and lie in the Sand, like Swine."

The reason the English came was to capture the annual Manila Galleon, which they did on two occasions, bloody battles of cannon and musket fire and hand-to-hand combat. The Spanish survivors were left to fend for themselves on the beach.

·✤·

DON FERNANDO had gone to the back of his house for something to show me. When he returned, he handed me a letter. Deeply creased where it had been folded and refolded many times, it was dated 1968.

It began: "*Querido Fernandito,*" Dear little Fernando. Amelia Wilkes sent her congratulations for his appointment as delegate—one of the most important political positions in the territory. (Only a few years later, in 1974, Fernando Cota was named one of seven *constituyentes,* members of the first constitutional assembly for the state of Baja California Sur.) She had allowed herself to use the diminutive because Don Fernando had once been her pupil.

"I'll tell you something else," Don Fernando said. "There were many times when there weren't enough men at the dances, so she would play that role. She used to dance *el jarabe tapatío.* She would put on trousers, a mustache, a big *sombrero charro*"—that broad-brimmed Mexican hat. Don Fernando planted his hands on his knees and chuckled.

"I even have a photo of her dressed like a man with Mercedes, another teacher, as a *china poblana*"—flouncy skirts and petticoats all in red and green, a loose white cotton blouse low on the shoulders. Don Fernando slapped the arm of his rocking chair. "Ready to go out dancing!"

He Lives

AS I WALKED out to the gate of Don Fernando's house, Solovino dashed down the length of the front fence, barking at a pair of tourists, his tail wagging like a whip. Solovino: *el que solo vino,* he who just showed up. He'd been abandoned as a newborn puppy, Don Fernando had told me, and they'd found him naked, too weak to cry, on the sidewalk.

"We didn't think he'd live," Don Fernando said. *"Pero miralo,"* But look at him.

The parrots rustled in their cages.

And then, as we stood there, Don Fernando told me that last story, the story of the first airplane to arrive in San José del Cabo in 1931.

Later, as I sat in the Plaza Mijares eating an ice cream cone, I thought of the pilot Flores and what he would have seen from the sky. He would have been flying low, in an open cockpit. He would have worn a leather skullcap and goggles, a red silk scarf, say, snapping behind his shoulder. I imagined that he'd taken off from the mainland. Soon he would have lost sight of shore; for a time, there was only the pale dome of sky that blended into the sea, a rippling navy blue flecked with sparkles of swells catching the sun. The engine droned. Below (Flores looked down), the shadow of his plane passed over the water like a crucifix.

Baja California, when it first appeared on the horizon, was a shimmering sliver wedged between the sky and sea. Gradually it loomed larger, yielding shape and color: the peaks and pleats of its mountains, rosy-gray and brown; the curve of the cape jutting into the sea like a tongue. And beyond the jagged line of sierra, a hint of light: another sea.

🔖

> Know ye that on the right hand side of the Indies there is an island called California, very close to the Earthly Paradise, and inhabited by black women without a single man among them, for they live almost in the manner of Amazons. They are robust in body with stout, passionate hearts and great strength. The island itself is the most rugged with craggy rocks in the world. Their weapons are all of gold as well as the trappings of wild beasts which they ride after taming, for there is no other metal on the whole island.

So begins the famous passage of Garci-Ordóñez de Montalvo's *Exploits of the Very Powerful Knight Esplandián, Son of the Great King Amadís of Gaul,* a chivalric romance published in Spain in the year 1510. Words like honey to Hernán Cortés and the conquistadors who were gullible enough, in that dawning of the age of literacy, to swallow what Montalvo claimed: that the manuscript "on parchment so ancient," penned in Greek by the great master Elisbad, had been found beneath a stone tomb in a hermitage near Constantinople, thence brought by a Hungarian merchant to Spain, where it fell into the hands of himself, a mere and humble translator. Like its predecessor, the phenomenally popular *Amadís of Gaul, Exploits of Esplandián* purported to be an ancient history. "Amadises," these novels based on the legends of chivalric romance came to be called, and, by those in the know, "lying histories."[1]

But Montalvo did not invent the Amazons. Greek tradition held that the women warriors—so fierce they cut off one breast to better position their bows—lived in Anatolia. Medieval European travelers, among them Marco Polo, reported sightings in Asia and Africa. Columbus claimed to have spied Amazons hiding in caves on the coast of a Caribbean island. The name California also had its antecedents: the rebellious land of "Califerne" appears in the *Chanson de Roland,* a troubadour's ballad first committed to paper in the eleventh century; "calif" is a variation of "caliph," a successor to Mohammed as head of Islam. Hence Montalvo's Calafia, queen of the Amazons, she of the island of California and its man-eating griffins, ally of the Turks. (Queen Calafia is vanquished, of course, by Esplandián's masculine charms, and the world made safe for Christendom.)

Less than a decade after *Exploits of Esplandián* came off the presses at Seville, Cortés landed at Veracruz. He had been directed by the governor of Cuba to investigate, among other exotica including dog-faced men, "where and in what direction are the Amazons." What Cortés found after an inland march was the Aztec empire and its pyramid-studded metropolis of Tenochtitlán, which he and his band of five hundred men and sixteen horses subdued in an epic of violence and intrigue as fantastic as the Amadises themselves.

Yes: there were Amazons to the north, reported the Indians of Ceguatán. Therefore, ran the logic of the conquistadors, there must be an island called California. Cortés would go there himself.

❧

AS FLORES BEGAN to descend, he could make out the detail of the town—the boats on the beach, small as pellets; a clutch of thatched roofs, huddles of green, streets like scratches in the hide of the earth. And then (he banked around for landing) the bell towers of the church, a mule in a corral, staggering with fright, and everywhere—running now toward the salt marsh—the people, as tiny as dolls, their faces turned up in wonder.

Only four years earlier, in 1927, Charles Lindbergh had flown solo across the Atlantic, from New York City to Paris, an ordeal of thirty-three and one-half hours that made him a world celebrity. Later that same year, at the invitation of U.S. Ambassador Morrow, Lindbergh flew nonstop for twenty-seven hours from Washington, D.C., to Mexico City. When the *Spirit of St. Louis* touched down on Balbuena Field, the throng of 150,000 that had been waiting for hours went wild, shouting and cheering *"¡Bravo!"* the men tossing their hats in the air. President Calles gave him a full *abrazo*—that highest of Mexican honors—a handshake followed by two hearty back slaps. As Lindbergh made his way off the field with President Calles and Ambassador Morrow and family, the ecstatic crowd rushed from the grandstands, trying to touch him, tearing at his clothes. Once in the open touring car, the Morrows' youngest daughter was nearly smothered under the wreaths and bouquets piled on by still screaming fans. The embassy gave a reception for a thousand guests; there were dinners with President Calles; the mayor presented him with the keys to the city; the Chamber of Deputies awarded him a gold medal for his "noble feat and glorious mission." For weeks, the Mexican press was abuzz with Lindbergh's supposed romance with Ambassador Morrow's daughter Elisabeth (in fact, he would marry her sister Anne). He was young and handsome and daring, "Lucky Lindy," a man who it seemed might live forever, like a god, or a saint.

Flores knew what to expect.

❧

IT IS, we know now, a peninsula. And we don't call it California, but Baja California. Baja, which means "lower": unfortunate adjective.

At the end of the eighteenth century, the missionaries moved north into the more fertile and populous land of Alta, or Upper, California. The United States took that territory in 1848, and with it the name California. The memory of that rankles in Mexico, like so much else. Halloween, for instance.

"*¿Qué significa el* Halloween?" What does it mean? a Mexican teenager asked me with a defensive cock of the chin, a sneer. He'd sauntered up to where I was sitting on the steps of Planet Hollywood. In the melting light we were surrounded by the decorations, the bats and pumpkins, the plaster tiles with their shadow-filled handprints and shoe prints of American movie stars. I answered his question. He'd had no idea that Halloween meant All Hallow Even, the eve of All Saints' Day, *Todos Santos.*

"*¿De veras?*" Really?

I nodded. His expression relaxed; the foreign was familiar, after all.

He was from Mazatlán, he said; he'd been here two weeks. He lived with his sister in Lomas del Sol. He had on jeans, new white running shoes, and a T-shirt that said simply: CABO.

"You know what?" he said, pointing with his chin toward the rocky mountain of the Pedregal. "Sylvester Stallone has a house here."

❧

IT OCCURRED to me later that, awful as it seemed, there was an appropriateness to Planet Hollywood. I was thinking of the plaster handprints and shoe prints that seemed to say, "He lives," inviting mere mortals to compare theirs for size; I was thinking of the items of clothing in glass cases, enshrined like relics; and in particular, I was thinking of that trinity of shareholders in the mural by the entrance—Arnold Schwarzenegger, Bruce Willis, and Sylvester Stallone—when I realized: They are our Amadises. They may be cops and soldiers now, instead of knights; they may battle mafiosi and narcotraffickers and aliens from outer space, in addition to postmodern varieties of "Turks" (Arab terrorists, mainly). But the damsels remain fair and faithful, the heroes blessed with skill and valor and luck beyond belief, the locales exotic, weapons lethal, endings triumphant. In short, that trinity of action-film stars, they are heroes incarnate, not just of some rock-'em-sock-'em American-manufactured trash, but of stories as old as the troubadours'.

Esplandián may not have his house here, but: we can go to his restaurant.

The Visitors

Todos Santos

The Visitors

IN THE GALERÍA DE TODOS SANTOS there was a painting by an American named Derek Buckner. I'd found it propped against the wall in the back room, the paint still fresh. It was a curious tableau: a man in a turquoise skirt and a brick-red fez; another man, also in a fez, his smile a slash of white between a mustache and a goatee, arms spread wide as if to say *Voilà;* a woman with smooth red hair pinned into a topknot, her rose-colored dress catching the light of morning sun, the dappled shade of trees; another woman, wielding her tambourine like a weapon, chastising a dog. These exotic characters stood around a table, the dog with its paws on the edge of the tablecloth. Plunk in its center, like a soup tureen, sat a flying saucer.

The painting was titled *The Visitors.* There was a woman who wanted to buy it, but the Galería de Todos Santos was asking two thousand dollars. It was worth it, she acknowledged. But she was remodeling her kitchen, and she had to buy a stove.

"Who needs a stove?" the gallery owner said. His name was Michael Cope, as in "I can't," he liked to say. He was blond and apple-cheeked, Danny Kaye as Hans Christian Andersen. He was from L.A., a refugee of corporate life, a painter himself. He placed his arms akimbo.

43

"We don't need food," Michael said. "We need art!"

What had brought the first big-spending visitors to Todos Santos, however, was in fact the food—specifically, lunch at the Café Santa Fé, an Italian restaurant on the plaza. Todos Santos was only an hour north of Cabo San Lucas on the highway, a narrow, shoulderless pavement threading through a wilderness of cardón and cholla cacti, the sea on one side, the sierra on the other. Cattle browsed around the tangles of cholla cacti at the edge. Sometimes they wandered into the road and stood there chewing their cuds. Every ten miles or so was a clump of palms: a fishing village of cinder blocks and thatch-roofed adobes, a roadside stand offering Tecate beer and cold Cokes.

Todos Santos seemed like just another of those villages, although larger, with a gas station. It also had a stoplight and a grocery store. A few Americans lived here, some in an RV park, others—many of them artists—in the old downtown, which was no more than a plaza with a whitewashed theater and the requisite church, around which clustered a few blocks of nineteenth- and early-twentieth-century brick town houses and shops. Some were newly renovated, painted bright fruity colors, but many remained empty, their rotted wooden doors padlocked, roofs caved in.

Todos Santos had once boasted a prosperous bourgeoisie whose fortunes were built on sugar. With water from a spring, they grew the cane, milled it for its juice, then boiled it down to a syrup in great cauldrons with orange peel and spices, which was then poured into molds to make the hard cones of *panocha*. But in 1950, the spring slowed to a trickle and the mills closed, one by one. The few families that remained in Todos Santos lived by hunting turtles and sharks. The spring revived in the early 1980s, but now the water was used to irrigate tomatoes, papayas, mangoes. The ruins of the sugar mills, their rusted machinery and brick smokestacks, dotted the tiny town of four thousand people. Most of the streets were dirt.

The air in the Café Santa Fé was cool; the tables were of pink marble. *Nuevo* flamenco played on the stereo, intricate and delicate as fluttering gauze. I sat out back under the pergola in the garden. I spread the napkin—a great flannel-soft square—across my lap and ordered lunch: rosemary focaccia, lobster ravioli with basil, roasted new potatoes, and mesquite-grilled dorado drizzled with balsamic vinegar and olive oil.

The restaurant was full: Americans up from Cabo for the day, most of them. The women were in espadrilles and linen; the men sported Rolexes and baseball caps embroidered with the names of golf resorts.

The owners of the Café Santa Fé, Paula and Ezio Colombo, had just returned from Paris. "We took in a fashion show," Paula said when she stopped by my table. "Oh! And a film opening, and the Francis Bacon show." She'd been a fashion model once herself, an African American cover girl for *Essence* and *Seventeen*. That was more than twenty years ago, but Paula still seemed girlish, fine-boned and bubbly. Ezio, a thick-waisted fellow in the background, striding like a worthy burgher between his bar and his kitchen, was a painter from Milan.

As I was leaving I saw the gallery owner, Michael Cope. He was having lunch with two of his artists: Robert Whiting, who also owned the new Todos Santos Inn, and Gloria Marie V., a petite woman with long, straight chocolate-brown hair. She wore a straw boater with silk flowers bunched at the brim. Birds were singing; something rustled in the thick matt of bougainvillea over the pergola. Their table was a still life: goblets of chilled white wine glistening with condensation; a vase with a sprig of desert wildflowers bright as raspberries.

If I were a painter, I thought, I would have liked to paint that.

Charles Stewart's Cat

TODOS SANTOS, I'd been told, was like Cabo used to be. An American invasion was under way here too, although on a smaller scale and with a different sensibility. It was the sensibility here that interested me. I wanted to meet Derek Buckner, and ask him about that flying saucer on a table. I wanted to talk to Michael Cope and his artists and ask them why and how they had come here. And the local Mexicans, what were they like? What did they think about the Americans? I would experience, if only for a few days, Baja California's artist community by the sea.

First on my list when I checked into Robert Whiting's Todos Santos Inn was the painter Charles Stewart, whom I'd read about in a recent *Los Angeles Times* article, "Baja Bohemia." The first American artist in Todos Santos, Stewart arrived in 1985. I'd seen his house, an ancient sagging structure that seemed to be mostly porch—a corrugated iron roof cantilevered out over a jumble of potted plants, broken-down furniture, garden hose, and caged birds. A stone's throw from the Café Santa Fé, his house was also a gallery open to the public.

But only when Charles Stewart was in town, Robert said. Robert had a voice that was as mild and smooth as Yankee cheddar. He was perhaps in his midthirties, with a pallid unlined face and ice-blue eyes. Despite the heat, I could easily imagine him in a suit and tie.

We were standing in the foyer of his inn, which had been a house back in the heyday of the sugar business, single story, the rooms opening onto a flagstone terrace and a garden. Robert had bought it as a ruin and restored it carefully, supervising every detail. As we spoke, a Siamese cat wandered in from the street and began to rub against my legs.

"Well," Robert said with a lopsided smile. "You can say you've met Charles Stewart's cat."

He showed me to my room, one of the two he'd finished. He'd opened his bed-and-breakfast only a few months before. My room had handmade tiles on the floor and a high ceiling with wooden beams. A mosquito net as gauzy as a bride's veil canopied the bed; an antique English print hung over the desk. I switched on the light.

It was quiet. A dog barked. I listened for the sound of the sea, but not even that: the beach was down the hill on the other side of the highway. There was no traffic.

I had supper by myself at the Caffé Todos Santos around the corner. The café, in another nineteenth-century building, high-ceilinged and plain, had a few small tables with hand-painted wooden chairs: yellow with red chiles; turquoise with birds; white and black like a cow. Other than a madonna-faced Mexican teenager filing her nails at the cash register, the place was empty. A bulletin board was thick with flyers, all in English: surfboard for sale, house for sale, Spanish lessons, AA meetings, English spoken. On a side table lay a stack of well-thumbed *Fortune*s. One had Lee Iacocca on the cover: "How I Flunked Retirement."

I sat in a chair painted with the moon and stars, and I had a mango smoothie and a chocolate muffin.

Some Artists of Oz; or, Something Feels Right Here

"ARTISTS ARE moving in," trumpeted the May 1993 *Travel and Leisure* about Todos Santos, which it dubbed the "new Mexican Oz in the making."

Derek Buckner, for example. "He came here and saw the light," Michael Cope told me. "It's like Los Angeles used to be, like Morocco, Egypt, this incredible light in the morning. Derek paints on-site. When he saw the light here, there was nowhere else he wanted to go." I was in the back room of the Galería de Todos Santos again, my eye on Derek's *The Visitors*. I was impressed with its technique and composition, and enchanted by its humor, the men in skirts and fezes, the dog, the flying saucer on the table.

The light: that was why Michael Cope had come here too. He'd been with Revlon in Los Angeles for seventeen years. He'd always painted, but it wasn't until after his first child was born that he came down to Todos Santos to paint. He and his wife, Pat, bought property and stayed. That was three years ago. Their gallery had been open for a year and a half. They rented the space, a corner of the Todos Santos Inn building, from Robert Whiting. Light filtered in through the slats of the wooden door from Robert's flagstone terrace. "I was really lucky meeting Robert," Michael said. "He was the one who said, you know what? Try it."

The Galería de Todos Santos was one of three galleries in town, but the first and only gallery—so far—dedicated to fine art.

"The reputation and stature of an arts community depend on fine arts, rather than crafts," Michael said. "Who's to say whether something is fine art or craft? It's difficult sometimes. I get artists coming in all the time—Americans, they knock on my door twenty times a day. When I choose what to take for the gallery, I try to be across the board, surreal, impressionist, collages. It's not like the States, where you can focus on one artist.

"Also, I try to keep an equal balance between Mexican and American artists. I never forget for one minute that I am an American in Mexico. I'm a guest here, it's at their discretion. I put the responsibility on myself to represent good Mexican art. And the Mexicans fill a void for expression that Americans just don't have. The Mexicans are influenced by Tamayo, Orozco, they're not afraid to make political statements. They're very serious about their art."

Who were the Mexican artists in the Galería de Todos Santos? Well, there was Carlos Uroz, a photographer who lived in Loreto. Antonio Viveros, who lived in San José del Cabo. Paulino Pérez and Gabo, who lived in La Paz. The majority had been trained in Guadalajara or Mexico City. None had a home or studio in Todos Santos.

"There's not much fine art in Baja," Michael admitted. "It's mostly pottery and weaving."

But the Mexicans who came into the gallery looked at each painting, in detail. "Mexican families come in from La Paz, and they look. I don't make a sale, but it's great. The kids from across the street have come in. They're a bit intimidated, though." Some of the Americans and Canadians, however, could be annoying. "They go, 'Jesus Christ! What the hell piece of crap is that? Who'd pay five hundred dollars for that?' And the artist is standing there! You know, he's had to bring in all his art materials, canvas, everything, which is expensive. And art is his life—it's what he does for a living." Michael rolled his eyes. "Some people don't have any sense of gallery etiquette."

Nevertheless, business was brisk. Movie and music producers from L.A. bought paintings, as did businessmen from Mexico City and Cuernavaca, and Americans with houses in Todos Santos and Cabo. Most of the gallery's clients stopped by before or after lunch at Paula and Ezio Colombo's Café Santa Fé.

And the American artist community?

"I've seen people stand in the middle of the street and say, 'Where is it?'" Michael chuckled. "They come up from Cabo for the day, and all they see are a few old buildings and dirt streets. Years ago the

Mexican government started calling this an artist community. It was an area that was beautiful, by the sea. It would be nice. Now the newspapers are saying that Todos Santos is going to be the new Taos, New Mexico, the new Carmel. There are a lot of artists here— painters, writers, musicians. But you're not going to find them in a store on the corner. And anyway, you want fine art, not poster shops.

"An artist community is a way of life, a place where people live and produce. If you want to find the artist community you have to go to the Caffé Todos Santos, to the Café Santa Fé. You have to meet the people."

≈

SO I MET Paula Colombo for an early lunch at the Café Santa Fé.

"We've had some wonderful publicity," she said when I asked her about the artist community. "*Travel and Leisure* and the *L.A. Times* had the biggest effect. But after the *L.A. Times* article, people came here in droves expecting to find shops and galleries, this *artist community.* Then they go, That's it?! Where's the shopping?"

She giggled. A bowl of tossed greens and a platter of breaded and fried calamari rings had arrived at our table. Paula squeezed a lime over the calamari. There was a simple elegance in her gesture, like her appearance: she wore linen trousers and a loose white blouse, and her hair was pulled back into a neat braid. "But quite frankly," she said, "Todos Santos has become the hip thing with music and movie people. Chris Isaak came here with his mom. The producer of U2 stayed for three months in a portable studio."

I was more interested in the artists who lived here. Paula and her husband, Ezio, were among the first. Ezio was a painter; Paula—her career as a model long past ("When African power came," she once told me indignantly, "I wasn't black enough")—was an interior and furniture designer.

How had she come to Todos Santos?

"I was living in Malibu, doing houses, these shacks that cost five million dollars, when I came to Baja for the first time. That's when I realized: here I could have Malibu, but without the garbage."

Paula met Ezio in San José del Cabo, where he was building the oven for Da Giorgio's, an Italian restaurant on the highway to Cabo San Lucas. Ezio had moved to the United States from Italy in the early 1970s. When the Transpeninsular Highway opened, he drove down the peninsula. Then he went back to the States, sold everything he owned, and bought a one-way ticket to Cabo.

Paula returned on another vacation in 1988. "I'd just finished a big fourteen-month interior job for a famous writer-director. I was desperate to get away, so I came to Cabo. And there was Ezio, everywhere I went. One night I went to Da Giorgio's for dinner. Ezio got this feeling, and he drove over there at night from San José. Nobody does that here; nobody drives at night. So we had dinner. I saw him everywhere, at Squid Roe, at this fashion show on the beach. I was about to leave when he invited me to Todos Santos. So I went. He showed me this building. I said, I'm going to buy it. He said, no ... I said: I saw it in my dreams. I know I am going to buy this building. So Ezio introduced me to the owner. I bought this building. It was owned by the Santana family; they were big in the sugar business. They were the town before the water ran out.

"I went home and I sold my house in two days. It was like it all came together. The roses in my garden were in bloom, beautiful big roses—and then after I sold my house, they never bloomed again and the market froze. It was really meant to be.

"We were both artists, Ezio and I. He was considering this place for his studio and a house. He had the reputation of being a wonderful cook and party giver. People kept coming to our house for dinner. So we thought, why not do a restaurant? Our talents just really complemented each other."

Paula and Ezio worked every day for a year and a half to restore the building. On the plaza next to the church, the Café Santa Fé was the handsomest of the historic buildings in Todos Santos. It was tall and box-shaped, cream with salmon-colored trim around the entrance and windows. The main seating area was an airy, high-ceilinged room that opened onto the sunny garden with its vine-covered pergola. Around the pink marble-top tables were ladder-back chairs handmade of *palo de arco,* a native bush with slender but strong stems. Paula designed the chairs herself.

The Café Santa Fé opened in December 1990. At the time, Todos Santos was a village of farmers and fishermen, most of whom had never seen a restaurant with waiters and linen. The main community of Americans and Canadians were retirees who lived behind the gas station in El Molino Trailer Park. "People were really discouraging," Paula said. "They thought I was out of my mind, they thought I would wreck things by paying my workers too much. But I knew I would not be relying on local patrons."

We'd finished our lunch. The restaurant had filled, and it was time for Paula to make the rounds of the tables, greeting her customers.

❧

TODOS SANTOS, said *Travel and Leisure,* "is crying for a swank little inn in the spirit of the Santa Fe."

When Robert Whiting read those words they changed his life.

We were sitting on the flagstone terrace of his Todos Santos Inn, at one of the tables where he served breakfast. An antique wooden angel hung on the brick wall. There was shade here, the smell of foliage. I sipped a cup of fresh-brewed coffee as I listened to his story.

Some years earlier, when he was night manager at the Four Seasons in Boston, Robert decided he would open his own hotel, a classic New England inn. He took a job at Fidelity, the Boston-based investment firm. His idea was to make big money quick to buy a hotel. But when he looked into the New England real estate market, he found the prices too high and the hotel business saturated. So he began considering more exotic places, like Belize and the Caribbean.

"I always looked for places that hadn't been discovered but had the potential I couldn't find in New England," Robert said. "When I read that *Travel and Leisure* article, I thought: this is my opportunity! Like a low fruit hanging there . . ."

He was days from leaving for Costa Rica. Instead, he booked a flight and flew to Cabo.

"I'd never been to Mexico. I never had the desire to come to Mexico. I expected to see kids bathing in sewage. It was the idea a lot of Americans have, you know, that you're going to find either that or Cancún. In Cabo I got on the bus. It broke down in the middle of the desert. Everybody had to get off and it was roasting hot. I didn't speak any Spanish. Finally, the driver fixed the bus and we arrived in Todos Santos. I didn't know the layout of the town, so I got off too early. I actually fell into a ditch. I had to straggle all the way up here with all my luggage.

"My first impression was my god, *Travel and Leisure* was a little exaggerated! Paula and Ezio were away, so the Café Santa Fé was closed. But Todos Santos was a friendly little place. People like Jane Perkins, the owner of El Tecolote bookstore, were very welcoming. The Caffé Todos Santos had just opened. There was a handful of people starting things here.

"I saw this building with a FOR SALE BY OWNER sign. I knocked on the door, and this big, obnoxious Papa Hemingway–type said, 'Come on in! I can't sell the goddammed place, can't get rid of the fucker!' He was a retired California highway patrolman, and every other word he said was *Fuck*. Fuck this, fuck that. He was almost bald and he looked like Mr. Clean, so the kids in town called him Maestro Limpio. The house was a ruin, and he was living in a trailer on one side of the garden. His asking price wasn't cheap. But I thought: This is it. If I can't make this work . . .

"I'd gravitated so much towards the corporate life, I felt trapped. I'd bought a house in the suburbs but I never enjoyed it; I was working all day. My house was twenty-three miles south of Boston in a really nice town, but the traffic was bumper-to-bumper. My average commute was an hour and a half each way, and in the winter it was just horrendous, two and a half, even three hours. Working at Fidelity was always meant to be a means to an end, working hard and saving pennies. But that last winter I was chronically depressed. It was like that Talking Heads song, you know, This is not my house, my god, what have I done? I'd always wanted a life that was interesting and exciting."

It took six months of negotiations before Robert and the patrolman agreed on a price. Finally, one night in the dead of winter the patrolman called and said: "I think we got a deal." Robert put his own house on the market, and it sold on the first day, a thousand dollars above the asking price.

"I thought: something feels right here. . . . But I didn't tell anyone at Fidelity. I needed to keep working for another six months to save money to fix up the place. One month before I left I made my announcement in a meeting. There was just this silence. The treasurer said, 'Robert, you sure know how to ruin a meeting, don't you?' I thought people would feel betrayed, threatened. But mostly they were like, 'Yeah! Go do it!' A number of people said, 'Oh, my wife and I always thought we'd do something like that.' You know, people in their midfifties. You know they never will.

"I bought a pickup truck and loaded it up with my Georgian partner's desk and other antiques, nothing practical. I should have brought down plumbing fixtures, things like that. I was kind of naive. My truck looked like an upscale *Grapes of Wrath*. It took me nine days to get here. It was a horrific trip. I didn't speak Spanish, and my friends were all like, Oh, my God, aren't you scared of *bandidos*? I was scared of driving across Texas! I had no idea what to expect. I crossed the border at Tijuana. I had no idea what would happen in customs. The guy took one look at my truck, all that old furniture piled into it, and he said, Get outta here! He waved me through without even looking. And then driving down the Baja peninsula, I misjudged the distances altogether. I had this big, overloaded camper shell, I could barely keep it on the road, which has no shoulder! Of course I ended up driving at night. Going around all those mountain curves, I could smell my brakes burning. Good thing it was dark and I couldn't see how steep the drops were."

But Robert made it to Todos Santos. He'd opened his office and two rooms for business a few months earlier; soon he would construct nine more rooms.

And best of all, Robert had begun to paint again, after a hiatus of a decade. The first painting he'd done here hung over his desk in the office. We walked over so he could show it to me. It was of Compton Wynyates, a manor house in England, from a photograph he'd taken when he was in school there. The painting had a brooding and dreamlike feeling, like a stage set for a Gothic mystery: darkened windows, ominous rain clouds. The details were so careful, down to each brick and leaf on the trees, that it looked as if it had been painted on a larger canvas and then shrunk.

"I'm an Anglophile," Robert said. "Why I'm in Mexico, I don't know."

We went back to the terrace and sat down again. An Irish setter wandered in and accepted a pat on the head before wandering back out.

"It's funny," Robert said after a while. "I figured I'd be one of the crowd that read the *Travel and Leisure* article and said, *Ah ha!* I'll go to Todos Santos and open my 'swank little inn in the spirit of the Santa Fe.' It turned out I was the only one."

Smelling the Dirt; or, Paradise with an Italian Restaurant

MICHAEL COPE, Paula and Ezio Colombo, Robert Whiting: all were artists, but all owned businesses that catered to an upscale tourist, the sort of person who might stand in the middle of the street and say, Where is it?

Now: I wanted to meet Derek Buckner. And Bob Luckey, a surfer who wrote three-line poems. But neither was in town.

The next morning I woke to a rooster's crowing. Soon after the sun came up, I heard the *scrick-scrick* of someone sweeping the street outside my room. I pulled on my boots, which were thickly powdered with fine yellow-brown dust. There wasn't any point in cleaning them.

The street was filled with teenagers walking from their dormitory—the *albergue* run by the state of Baja California Sur—to the school. I hadn't realized that when Michael Cope mentioned "the kids across the street," he meant the several dozen students in the *albergue*. They were ranch kids, from towns and settlements up in the sierra and along the coast, places too small to support their own school. The boys wore khaki pants and white shirts, the girls A-line dresses in pink or burgundy with knee socks. Most of them carried smart-looking backpacks.

"They could get a hundred thousand dollars for that place, easy," one American had told me about the *albergue,* a nineteenth-century stuccoed brick building. "They should sell it and build a better one away from the center." The center was what *Travel and Leisure* dubbed the "gringo gentrification zone" with its shops lining Calle Juárez; the Café Santa Fé on the plaza and the cluster of businesses behind it: Robert's inn, Michael's gallery, the Caffé Todos Santos, El Perico Azul with its colorful (Made in Indonesia) sundresses.

Mexican-owned shops and houses were scattered around the center and the outskirts. Behind the Café Santa Fé I found the Siempre Vive, a brick-front grocery with a "Raleigh cigarettes" sign and an ice locker parked on the sidewalk. There were dust-covered tins of juice, Campbell's soup, and Carnation condensed milk; in the back, the refrigerator door was broken, and the jugs of milk inside felt warm to the touch. Flies buzzed over bins of avocados and lumpy-looking papayas speckled with mold. At the register I said, *Buenos días,* Good morning, and the cashier looked right through me.

"Twenty pesos," she said in English.

I left the bottled water I'd bought in my room at Robert's inn. From there I walked down the dirt road that meandered toward the beach. I passed a large brick building (once part of a sugar operation), a couple of thatched adobes, and then suddenly, I was in the country. Date palms and cocopalms towered above, silvery in the sunlight. I swatted away flies from my face and tried to ignore the stink of horse droppings. And then there was rolling grassland, where a handful of Americans were constructing modest, thatched-roofed beach houses, some with trailers parked outside. An old Mexican in a cowboy hat was sweeping his yard with a broom made of twigs. He smiled a broad, toothless smile and waved.

After a while, I came to two white horses standing by the ruin of a sugar mill.

❧

LATER THAT MORNING, I met Nanette Hayles. I'd seen some of her work in the Galería de Todos Santos: a mosaic portrait of Frida Kahlo made of tiny hand-ripped squares of magazine paper.

"Art is connected with the spiritual," she said when we met on the terrace at Robert's inn. Nanette had a wild mane of black hair and big hoop earrings. "Here you're more in touch with your quiet side, you're closer to nature. In the city, you have to look for a park, smog blocks the sky. Here you see birds, you smell the dirt, the horses. It's slower paced here. Out of peace the creativity can flow."

And the artist community, had that helped?

"Michael has been really supportive. I feel very close with the artists connected with the gallery, Michael, Gloria, Derek. We're very supportive of one another, very constructive. It's almost storybook. All of us are struggling, but once in a while we'll go to the Café Santa Fé, drink scotch and smoke a cigar, pretend we're Hemingway and Picasso." She laughed a zithery laugh, threw her hair over one shoulder.

But the artist community, Nanette stressed, was not the town. "Mexicans make the town, they are why I'm here. Todos Santos has a soul, it's not like Cabo. There is a large group of Americans who love Mexico, but they don't like Mexicans. Cabo, for example, attracts a party animal. They don't like it here, they see Todos Santos as a dirt town, and they just keep moving. Other people stop, they really feel what this place is about. I've traveled all over the world, and I feel that God gave this place a big kiss. People who really like Todos Santos are people with good hearts. They're usually artists, or people in touch with the artist part of themselves."

"Softer things result from that," said Jane Perkins, when I asked her about the influence of the artist community. Her bookshop, El Teco-lote, carried mostly English-language books: used paperbacks, travel guides, books on Baja California, Chicano literature. El Tecolote was in a white adobe building that also housed the Message Center, a beauty parlor, a gallery, and a patio restaurant. Across the street were the town's two main real estate offices, their windows plastered with advertisements: *excellent view lots / watch the whales from your hill top terrace / trailer with satellite dish, washing machine, freezer, TV, BBQ, USD 28,500.*

"It's a state of mind," Jane said. "You can throw up your hands and do nothing, or you can make a friendly atmosphere towards artistic endeavors. If people come because they like the artistic aspect of the community, then that's good, we can delay high-rises like they have in Cabo."

Next door, however, Jennifer Deaville scoffed. "Artist community? *Ha!* If there's an art thing here, Michael did it with his gallery. Before that, no. Charles Stewart was here, a few other people. That was it."

A Canadian from Nova Scotia, Jennifer owned the Message Center. At first I'd misread the sign next to El Tecolote books as the Massage Center, imagining something new agey, aromatherapy acupressure perhaps. But no, it was the Message Center, which offered long-distance phone service, fax, and message taking. Few people in Todos Santos had a telephone, and service in any case was unreliable. The phone at Robert's Todos Santos Inn, for example, hadn't worked in more than a week.

Jennifer pursed her lips. She said, "Todos Santos is just a traditional little fishing and farming village."

She wasn't the only one to stiffen at the idea of an "artist community." Paula's friend Euva Anderson cringed. She said, "I find the idea embarrassing! I feel there are still places we can cherish without turning them into something else. Todos Santos is a real town, close to nature. People are harvesting chiles and onions, you still walk in the dirt."

Euva was a painter who owned a twenty-acre horse farm on the beach. A tiny, nut-brown woman, she wore a sleeveless sundress she'd designed herself, with big pockets and big buttons. It was late afternoon when we talked over tall glasses of iced mint tea at the Café Santa Fé.

But things were changing, I said. Look at Cabo.

"Cabo! With the golf courses and the fishing, it's become a Disneyland! Even a granny can come up with a five hundred–pound marlin. People go there, they build a wall around their air-conditioned house, and they could be back home! It's the epitome of my worst nightmare."

Euva first came to Cabo from San Francisco in 1967 on a yacht with friends. Some of them were making a film on whales, others were enamored with Steinbeck's *Sea of Cortez,* some were surfers. "I had no idea where we were." Euva giggled. "It was like landing on the moon!" She and her husband came back ten years later and bought a house near San José del Cabo. "You felt like an explorer then. There was nothing to buy. If you wanted milk, you had to go to the ranches and ask them to milk a cow. My husband is a surfer. For a wild adventure we would drive the dirt road into Todos Santos and follow the goat paths to the beach. Once we found an idyllic surfing spot with these huge, huge waves, twelve feet high! That was Punta Lobos—now everyone comes. And we discovered La Pastora. We used to camp in this coconut grove, never imagining that we would live here."

Their house near San José was now in the middle of a posh golfing community. They'd put it up for sale; Euva planned to dedicate herself to her horse farm.

"What I would like to do here in Todos Santos is be a preserver. We were attracted to the pristine ambiance, and I don't want to forget that. I think Todos Santos can escape the fate of Cabo, the big-money development. I want to encourage the people of Todos Santos to preserve the land, the sea, their culture."

Euva was born in Brazil to a Mexican mother and a Swedish-Peruvian-Guatemalan father, an engineer who built roads. "I've lived on every continent, so I have an outsider's perspective. I'm a Libra to begin with, so I can see many sides of a question. I can see it as a Mexican, as a Latin American, an Indian, a European, an American. As a Mexican I can appreciate that many of the local people feel resentful of foreigners. But their plight is brought on by trying to profit from the land. They just barely eke out a living. To sell their land for, say, twenty thousand dollars is very tempting. But I've seen the result of their selling the land. The land is what gave them peace. I always tell people, value your land. Once you sell it, what do you have? Where will you go?"

This from a woman who'd purchased twenty acres on the beach! But I kept in mind what she'd just told me, that her identity was fluid and complex.

"Many things are sad to see," she continued. "Television arrived ten years ago. The kids are seeing Nike, Adidas, all these foreign products, that's become their goal. Now there's all this paper and plastic. Some people say, I can't stand the people here, how can they litter? But I understand. Before, all their garbage was organic. You'd throw out a corn cob and the cows would eat it. It takes time to educate people; you have to work on the children. Every single person can add, make a difference, so that we can survive the colonization."

And how did she make a difference?

"I'm not so good on organization, I'm better one-to-one, just in my own little network. Through the horses, I'm trying to encourage a way of life, to be an example. I used to complain about the trash out on the beach. I would say, somebody should do something. But now I realize that somebody is me! I have to put in energy and love. So I ride my horses and pick up trash. I make it a zen practice, part of my daily ritual. And I am sort of the humane society. Whatever little dog comes to my house, I give it food, have it spayed. Instead of complaining, let's help.

"I feel that Todos Santos has a really strong and beautiful energy People think, oh, it's an *artist community*! But there's a lot of dirt! I look like a little filth monger at the end of the day. I sometimes say to Paula, did you think you'd ever end up in a dusty little village? And she says, no, but I'm in Paris and all I can think about is going home!"

Euva sipped the last of her tea.

"I thank my lucky stars. I live in paradise, with a good Italian restaurant.

Nos Están Invadiendo

"Nos están invadiendo," They are invading us, the girl tending the Sueños Tropicales fruit-and-vegetable stand told me. *"¿Pero qué podemos hacer?"* What can we do? She had a big toothy smile. She shrugged. *"Nada,"* Nothing. *"Sólo mirar,"* Just watch. She pointed to one eye.

Sueños Tropicales sat on the highway just a skip south of Todos Santos, in the village of Pescadero. I'd stopped by before. Sueños Tropicales sold the reddest, sweetest strawberries I'd ever eaten in my life. Braids of garlic hung from the thatch-roofed ceiling; tiny gold-en teardrop tomatoes, glossy cucumbers, pearl-white onions, and bags of dried papaya were neatly piled in baskets; jars of homemade fruit jam were stacked behind the scales. Sunlight seeped in through the walls of *palo de arco.*

"They are taking over Todos Santos," the girl said in Spanish, "and they are beginning here in Pescadero, too." She pointed toward the beach. "The entire beach is for sale. We Mexicans are being pushed to the outskirts. We are selling the country. We sell our land because we need money. Here in Mexico we are poor. But we sell the land very cheap. And then what will we do with the little that we get for it?

"*Ay,*" she said, crossing her arms over her chest. "Some of the Americans are really rude. One came in here and shouted at me, and I answered her, Don't you shout at me like that, and especially not here. You are a visitor. This is Mexico." She shook her finger, and then she smiled a big smile, as if this were all a silly joke.

"On the other hand, some are decent people. The owners of this fruit stand, for example. They're Americans and they are really nice. We Mexicans are lazy, that's the problem. No one here would open a fruit stand like this."

She sighed. She frowned.

"In five years everything will be different, nothing but Americans here. We will all go to Cabo San Lucas to work. That place is totally invaded. Nothing but people from the Republic—Oaxaca and Sinaloa."

🌹

"CABO IS the shining example of what we don't want," Robert Whiting had told me. That seemed to be one thing Americans and Mexicans in Todos Santos agreed on. In the center of Todos Santos again, in another art gallery, Ricardo Torres told me he knew about Cabo: he'd worked there in construction and sportfishing before returning home to work in Todos Santos.

"The Americans who come to Todos Santos are different," Ricardo said. "They come for the culture, they're interested in Mexico.

The Americans who live here are careful, they don't want problems. Yes, some people complain about them. They say, how come they get all the business? I get mad about that because that's how I make my living. I think it's good that we get more investment, the restaurants and galleries provide jobs. What I'm worried about is that if Todos Santos changes, people from the rest of the Republic will come, like in Cabo San Lucas."

Juan Manuel Nuñcz was visiting, taking a break from his job at the jewelry shop next door. He added, "In Cabo, there are many people from outside. Very ambitious people. In Cabo, if somebody talks to you it's because he wants a tip. They give you a service, they put a price on it. They pull out a chair for you to sit down, and they say, *Three dollars!*"

"The people here," Ricardo insisted, "are from *here.*"

◆

AND YET—first grip of a first tentacle—workers from the mainland had already arrived in Todos Santos. They hadn't come to wait tables or clean hotel rooms; they'd come to pick tomatoes for Agrícola Bátiz, a grower from Sinaloa.

Two and a half years earlier, the local *ejido*, or agricultural cooperative, had sold Agrícola Bátiz a vast tract of land east of town for what one resident described as "a few pickup trucks and nothing." The *ejidatarios* had expected the tomato business to provide jobs and benefit the town. Instead, Agrícola Bátiz brought in workers from Oaxaca, one of the poorest states in the Republic, and housed them in shacks near the tomato fields.

"We'd never seen true poverty before," one woman told me, "not here in Baja California." Some of the Oaxacans stole fruit from the gardens. Agrícola Bátiz made an arrangement with the town. Since then, the workers stayed in their dormitories. "Sometimes," another Todos Santos resident said, "the *oaxaqueños* come into town on Sunday, to buy food at the Siempre Vive. But we don't want them here."

Oaxacan workers were not the only problem the Sinaloan tomato grower brought to Todos Santos. Somehow, despite the fact that Todos Santos had been declared a restricted water zone, Agrícola Bátiz obtained permits from Mexico City to exploit the local aquifer. Within two years, the flow of water had decreased by more than 50 percent. According to the Todos Santos water authority, it took twelve to sixteen hours to irrigate fields that once took only eight hours. For many, the town's collapse after overplanting sugarcane in the 1940s was a fresh and painful memory. For those too young to have lived through it, the ruins of the sugar mills were plain to see.

After a citizens' committee confronted Agrícola Bátiz, a technician from Israel was brought in to help economize its water use. Then, heavy rains during the *chubasco* season replenished the aquifer.

During my visit, Agrícola Bátiz was building an office on Calle Juárez.

꙳

AND THERE'D been yet another disturbing arrival, this one from Colombia.

As first reported by the *Los Angeles Times,* near midnight on Saturday, November 4, 1995, local fishermen saw the lights of a large jet move inland from the Pacific and land on a dry lake bed just north of town. On landing the jet smashed its nose gear. A convoy of four-wheel-drive vehicles pulled up; twenty men wearing federal police uniforms jumped out and began unloading the cargo. None of the fishermen dared alert the authorities—until at sunrise they saw flames. When the state police commander and his deputies showed up, they caught the twenty men in federal police uniforms destroying the disabled plane, a converted Caravelle passenger jet the size of a Boeing 727. The "federal police" insisted that "the situation was under control." And so, as Baja California Sur's chief federal prosecutor put it to the *New York Times,* "The state police commander opted to withdraw."

An investigation determined that the men had worked for several hours with cranes and tractors. They ripped out the jet's black box

and avionics equipment, sawed off its wings, and attempted to dyna-
mite it. That failed, so they set it on fire. Then they drove a bulldoz-
er over the remains, partially burying them with sand. Nevertheless,
investigators retrieved the jet's serial numbers from the turbines and
traced it to the Cali cartel in Colombia. Its cargo of cocaine, U.S.
officials estimated, may have been as large as fifteen tons, with a street
value of at least two hundred million dollars.

At first, Mexican and U.S. officials assumed the shipment belonged
to the Tijuana cartel, the "family" that controlled the drug trade
along Baja California's 150-mile border with the United States. But
in fact, the Todos Santos cocaine belonged to the Juárez cartel, based
in Ciudad Juárez on the border with Texas. The Juárez cartel was at
that time headed by Amado Carrillo, otherwise known as "Lord of
the Skies" for his brazen use of jets to fly in massive shipments of
cocaine from South America. Once on Mexican soil, the cargo was
unloaded to be shipped north in smaller parcels: in cars, on small
planes, and in trucks sometimes, concealed among loads of agricultural produce.

The drug-smuggling business is like a half-filled balloon: you push
down there, it pops up over here. In the early 1980s, the U.S. Drug
Enforcement Agency's interdiction campaign closed off the Colombian cocaine smugglers' Caribbean and coastal-Florida routes into
the United States. So the Colombians simply shifted west, making
alliances with Mexican drug traffickers, specialists until then in marijuana and heroin. South Americans continue to grow and process
coca leaves into cocaine; Mexico, with its two thousand–mile border
on the world's biggest drug market, has become the major transshipment point.

The drug business is also like a cancer, metastasizing to every level
of government. Officials are lured with money on the one hand, and
on the other are intimidated with ruthless, often grotesque violence.
Many are murdered. The 1994 assassination of PRI presidential candidate Luis Donaldo Colosio in Tijuana, for example, was widely
believed to have been ordered by *narcopolíticos,* allies of the drug
traffickers within the ruling party itself.

Shortly after the Todos Santos scandal, Baja California Sur's entire federal police force was transferred to Mexico City. The army set up roadblocks along the highway to search for weapons and drugs. By now I'd been through the one near Todos Santos several times. The soldiers were dark-skinned boys from poor states on the mainland. They wore combat boots with white laces, and they clutched their rifles tightly, close to their chests. Usually they waved me through. Once in a while, they would flip open the glove compartment, maybe glance beneath the front seat. If I'd draped it with a blanket, I could have smuggled through a hippopotamus.

The Colombian jet may explain a curious incident in Graham Mackintosh's *Into a Desert Place*. While camping in the mountains east of Todos Santos, he saw what he believed was a UFO: four lights in formation flashing through the trees in a night that was "absolutely still and quiet." Mackintosh was in Baja California in the mid-1980s, precisely when Mexican drug traffickers began using clandestine landing strips for the transshipment of Colombian cocaine. On the other hand, maybe Mackintosh did see a UFO. I'd heard of sightings in the mountains of Sonora, just across the Sea of Cortés. And there'd been a rash of sightings, many of them videotaped, around the mountain near my house in Mexico City. But these—what the Mexicans called *OVNIs*—zigzagged wildly at fantastic speed, unlike any aircraft.

Derek Buckner's painting with the flying saucer was on my mind.

Pueblo chico, Infierno Grande

THAT AFTERNOON there were some new paintings on display at the Galería de Todos Santos: Michael Cope had unfurled his newest canvas on the floor, a series of life-size nudes kneeling over machetes and yellow banana leaves. On the wall was his painting of his three-year-old son playing with a hawk's feather on the beach. Derek's *The Visitors* hung next to it.

Derek would be back, Michael said, in a couple of days.

So I ambled down Calle Juárez and across the highway, to Esperanza—Hope—the new barrio of cinder-block houses. Dirt roads, satellite dishes, mutts: it could have been one of more prosperous workers' barrios in Cabo San Lucas. At the foot of the hill by the beach someone was burning trash.

Tucked between that hill and the gas station—incredibly, without a view of the sea—I found El Molino Trailer Park. Residents had built shaggy palapas to shade their trailers and the concrete strips alongside them that served as patios. These were large trailers, luxury Winnebagos many of them, with license plates from Oregon, Alberta, Manitoba. In the shaded patios were tables and chairs and potted plants: bougainvillea, hibiscus. Several had well-stocked bars, their cocktail glasses neatly lined up. Next to one trailer a fluffy gray kitten slept in a padded basket. The trailer park's swimming pool was built around the ruins of a sugar mill *(un molino)*—rusted machinery and a brick smokestack.

On my way out, a woman asked me if I knew how to hook up a generator. She had neatly bobbed white hair and wore white shorts and white sandals. Her skin looked a dangerous pink.

"I can't figure these out," she said, showing me the manufacturer's instructions. She'd said "out" like "oot."

I hadn't a clue.

The light was soft, almost lemony in the late afternoon. I kept walking, south toward Punta Lobos. A sandy track led to the beach from the highway. Soon I was walking through a field of tall dry grass littered with plastic bags, soup cans, and diapers. A flock of vultures roosted on the tops of cardón cacti; behind them soared the peaks of the Sierra de la Laguna, distant blue.

The beach at Punta Lobos was empty but for an abandoned turtle-processing plant. *Arriba y Adelante México* was stenciled over its entrance: Upward and Onward Mexico, the slogan of Luis Echeverría, the president who built the Transpeninsular Highway in the early 1970s. Its walls, some of them still covered with easy-to-hose-down white tile, were scribbled with graffiti.

Turtle meat, I'd been told, is a tender spongy white, almost like a fatty veal sausage. It was famous as a local delicacy. Turtle fishing is illegal now; the Carey and Olive Ridley turtles once processed here by the thousands are endangered species.

I'd been trespassing. A sign said:

❧

"IT'S NOT EASY to live here," Robert Whiting said when I met with him again for tea on the terrace of his Todos Santos Inn. "To go to a decent supermarket I have to drive an hour to La Paz. And when the Café Santa Fé is closed . . ." He grabbed the edge of the table and sucked in his breath.

I braced myself for the start of the usual expatriate's litany of gripes. But Robert wasn't telling me about Mexico so much as he was about life in a small town.

"My mom lived in a little town in Maine. She hated it, just hated it! Everybody knows what you had for dinner, you have your roof fixed and everybody knows what you paid. But your good neighbors look out for you too."

Although Robert's inn had only two rooms, it represented an important investment for Todos Santos. He'd employed as many as sixteen people putting down the tile floors. "The town knew about me, of course, and people started to gossip. They said my father owns all these hotels in Florida." He laughed. "Where did *that* come from?"

Almost everyone in Todos Santos had a nickname that was used behind their backs, especially by the kids in the *albergue*. Maestro Limpio (Mr. Clean), who'd sold Robert his property, was one example. Robert still sometimes gave his address to delivery people as *la casa del* Maestro Limpio.

"Well, hey, that beats *Cara de Rata,*" another American told me later. *Cara de rata* means "rat face," which was the nickname of a retiree in El Molino Trailer Park. Someone else was called El Pozo, the Deep Hole, because you wanted to walk around him.

Pueblo chico, infierno grande, goes the saying. Small town, big hell. Robert knew his nickname. It was El Padrecito, the Little Priest.

❧

WHEN EVENING CAME, it was comfortably warm, and so I felt like walking again—a luxury I wouldn't dare in Mexico City. Up the street from the Café Santa Fé, I came to the Salón Recreativo "Filis," the local pool hall. All four of its doors along the Calle Centenario were flung open, the fluorescent light flooding onto the sidewalk and the dirt street. I caught sight of the corners of two billiard tables and a foosball game. A bristly-faced man in a baseball cap leaned against the back wall, strumming a guitar. He sang in a quavering voice, *la bella, corazón, hasta no verte . . .* I couldn't make out the words over the clicks and clanks of the games. I sat outside on the curb and listened. One of the men began to whistle along off-key.

When they stopped, a dog barked.

Around the corner, next to El Tecolote bookstore and the Message Center, I wandered into the patio restaurant. Robert was there, and Michael and Pat Cope and their three-year-old son, and the painter Gloria Marie V. and her boyfriend, a writer named Michael Mercer. They'd pushed together several of the tiny tables, and their faces were lit with the flickering golden light of candles. They'd almost finished with their chicken mole. Empty wineglasses littered the tables. Robert pulled a chair out for me, and I sat with them for a while. They seemed so happy. Overhead the sky was spangled with stars.

In Which I Meet Don Quixote

SO THERE WAS the Salón Recreativo "Filis," and then there was the patio restaurant, et al. Fifty pesos—less than ten dollars—was a day's wage for many Mexicans here, while the Galería de Todos Santos was asking two thousand dollars for Derek Buckner's *The Visitors.* It might have seemed there was an incipient apartheid in Todos Santos, the Americans in their "gentrification zone" and trailer park, the Mexicans increasingly nudged toward the outskirts. Yet there were intersections, expressions of goodwill: Nanette and Paula, for example, ran the local Rotary chapter with Juana Salgado, owner of the Siempre Vive grocery. A number of American businesspeople, a realtor and a restaurant owner among them, were married to Mexicans. And Michael, Nanette, Paula, and Robert all urged me to talk with Professor Néstor Agúndez, director of the Todos Santos *casa de cultura.*

The *casa de cultura,* or House of Culture, is a government-sponsored institution common in towns and cities throughout Mexico. But this one was no longer a mere *casa de cultura,* Professor Agúndez explained when I met with him in his office. Now, having moved into the old teachers college on Calle Juárez, it was the Centro Cultural Siglo XXI, the Twenty-First Century Cultural Center. In its foyer were important 1930s-era murals—Rivera-like groupings of workers in overalls, tractors and wheelbarrows, schoolchildren and athletes. One mural featured a red banner bearing a hammer and sickle, another a cameo of Revolutionary hero Emiliano Zapata and the slogan *"La tierra es de quien la trabaja,"* The land belongs to those who work it. Inside, laid out around a central patio and a basketball court, were a library, a small museum of Mexican handicrafts and regional history, an art gallery, and an auditorium with stacking chairs and a baby grand piano.

Professor Agúndez had founded the *casa de cultura* in 1978, when he was director of the student *albergue,* which he had also founded. He had retired as a schoolteacher in 1993. Since then he had been working without pay.

"Lo hago con mucho amor," I do it with a lot of love, he said. Sometimes he spent his own money for repairs and special projects. "I believe in saving. I worked for fifty years to educate the children and save my pennies. But to work is not the same as to serve. To serve is to love."

He had a gaunt, gray face and neatly combed-back hair. His eyes looked smallish behind his glasses, and some of his lower front teeth were missing, which caused him to lisp when he spoke. But his diction was formal, his bearing distinguished. "My greatest concern," Professor Agúndez said, "is to bring culture to the children and young people of the region, both current and future generations."

He'd had little help aside from a few donations—the piano, from an American who died; some paintings from Ezio Colombo and Michael Cope; sundry arrowheads and old photographs for the museum. For nearly twenty years, his little *casa de cultura* had struggled by in a cramped building some blocks away. Several years earlier he'd been granted the abandoned teachers college on Calle Juárez, but it was in such disrepair—the roof had collapsed—and funds were so scarce that the new Centro Cultural Siglo XXI had not been able to open until only three weeks earlier. Nor did Professor Agúndez have enough people to help him. Above all, he needed someone who spoke English, because he could not. "*El debido y justo apoyo,*" The deserved and just help, he said sternly, the government does not provide.

I couldn't help noticing the portrait of Don Quixote on the wall behind his battered metal desk. Directly below that was a framed color photograph of Luis Donaldo Colosio and his wife, Diana Laura. It was a candid shot: Diana Laura's face aglow with sunlight, the two of them smiling at each other as if they were sharing a private joke.

"*Si, yo soy un Quixote,*" Professor Agúndez said when he saw me looking at the portraits. Yes, I am a Quixote. On top of his filing cabinet was a little statue, another Quixote, weary, sitting slumped on his horse.

"One time I dreamt that I wrote to your President Clinton. I asked him to connect me with several people of goodwill. And you know what? He sent me five truckloads of furniture, televisions, all kinds of useful things. He also presented me with a check. And you know what else? In my dream, President Clinton spoke perfect Spanish."

Professor Agúndez may have tilted at windmills, but here, after all, was his Centro Cultural Siglo XXI. I'd seen the fat guest book in the foyer by the murals. I ventured that many people had visited.

"*Es muy visitado,*" It is frequently visited, he nodded, "by people from all over the world." He stepped outside his office and brought in the guest book. "Look," he commanded, turning the book toward me, "Japanese!" He ran his finger down the page. "Spain!" He turned the pages slowly, examining each entry, gleaning the exotic from the long lists of overwhelmingly Mexican and American signatures. "Cuba!" he said happily, and then a page or so later: "New Zealand, how about that?"

Suddenly he looked up as if he'd remembered something. "You know who's been here? Donna Summer!"

He went back to the guest book. "Ah! Holland."

I'd been told that Professor Agúndez wrote poetry, so I asked him about that. He took in a breath and sat up tall. A most exciting thing had happened. He'd found a directory with the names and addresses of poets in Spain and Central and South Americas. "I started to write to them. Many of them answered me, they sent me books. From Brazil I received a certificate naming me protector and promoter of popular poetry, a very elegant certificate in Portuguese."

But then with the economic crisis, he couldn't afford to buy stamps. "I lost contact," he said, and his eyes seemed to fade behind his glasses.

The economic crisis, Colosio's assassination, they were inextricably linked in my mind. When Colosio was killed, it was like the beginning of a nightmare. Within the year, his wife, Diana Laura—the pretty blonde in the photograph on the wall—died of cancer, orphaning their two children. Then came the devaluation and the crisis and the scandals about ex-president Salinas, *thud* after sickening *thud,* like a bowling ball down the stairs.

Why did he have Colosio's photograph on his wall?

The professor's eyes flashed fiercely, his chin jutted forward. "To talk about them, I must stand at attention." He pushed back his chair and stood up and saluted. Ramrod straight. Then he sat down again at his desk.

"Luis Donaldo Colosio was going to be president of Mexico. He was going to be our president, president of the poor, president of hope." Professor Agúndez sighed deeply. "I had so much hope, so much trust. I knew his parents."

Colosio's parents lived in Sonora. How had he known them?

"The story begins this way. When Luis Donaldo Colosio was named presidential candidate what was the first thing he did? He went to pay his respects at the grave of President Adolfo López Mateos.[1] I admired López Mateos because he was a pacifist, but also because he came to La Paz. Todos Santos sent a troupe to La Paz, to show him the sugarcane cutters' dances. He reformed the school system, he built the airstrip. He came here to Todos Santos for the inauguration. López Mateos . . ." His voice trailed off for a moment as he savored the memory.

"So when Colosio went to visit the grave of López Mateos, I was very moved. I saw Colosio's address in a magazine: Corregidora 26, Mexico City. I wrote to him, and I told him why I admired López Mateos so much, because he was a pacifist, he helped the schools, and because he was the only president who visited my town. I said: You must be the second."

But then, on March 23, 1994, three months into the campaign, Colosio was assassinated. Professor Agúndez found out when he came home and turned on his television. I'd seen the same images on my own TV in Mexico City: Colosio's body on a stretcher, his head a mess of blood; a doctor in a white coat explaining why he couldn't be saved; the supposed assassin, Mario Aburto, looking wild-eyed, bloodied from a savage beating from the crowd. Colosio had been wading through a throng in a Tijuana slum when he was shot in the abdomen and the back of the head at close range.

An experienced career politician, Luis Donaldo Colosio was handsome as a cinema star, only forty-three years old. He'd been sure to win; the candidates from the two main opposition parties were relatively weak, and his party, the Partido Revolucionario Institucional (PRI), had won every presidential election since 1929. Mexico wasn't like Central and South Americas; no presidential candidate had been assassinated since General Alvaro Obregón in 1928. With the news that Colosio had been killed, all over Mexico traffic stopped, people walked out of theaters and restaurants. Television cameras panned the crowd that had gathered outside Los Pinos, the Mexican White House, in vigil.

"There was no one in my house. I ran out into the street, but there was no one!" Professor Agúndez went back into his house where the TV was still on: the body on the stretcher, the crowds in vigil, the droning words that said nothing. He walked up and down, he drank several glasses of cold water, trying to control himself. "Oh, I had so much hope for Mexico! I cried, I sincerely cried."

Two days later, a letter arrived. Colosio had accepted his invitation to visit Todos Santos.

I hadn't cried when Colosio was killed. But now, as I pictured the old schoolteacher opening his letter, I began to cry.

"I wrote to his parents in Sonora. They sent me this photograph of Luis Donaldo and Diana Laura." He pushed back his chair and gazed at the picture.

Later, he said, Colosio's parents came to Todos Santos for a mass in his honor.

I blew my nose.

Professor Agúndez slammed his hand on the desk. "We lost a great hope! And we don't know why. Who killed him? I think it was Salinas. But why?"

❧

Nos engañaron, They deceived us. Every Mexican I knew felt that way about the government. So did many Americans—investment bankers, businessmen, economists, politicians who had laid their reputations on the line to pass NAFTA, and who'd posed with a beaming President Salinas, that "leading economic reformer."

Colosio was killed by a lone gunman, said investigators. Then they revealed an elaborate, intricately choreographed plot involving his Tijuana bodyguards. Then they backtracked: no, it was a lone gunman after all. For some reason, photographs of the assassin at the scene in Tijuana did not resemble the man in custody in Mexico City. "Aburto Is Not Aburto!" screamed the newspaper headlines.

Then: more assassinations, arrests, suitcases crammed with cash, buried bodies, detectives gunned down, union monies diverted to the Zapatistas, an investigating official a suicide with two bullet holes through the heart (yes, deadpanned a government doctor, it was possible to shoot oneself in the heart twice)—in short, a Gordian knot of plot twists, like a crummy novel that no longer made sense.

Perhaps it never would. "We tell lies," wrote Octavio Paz in *The Labyrinth of Solitude,* "for the mere pleasure of it . . ." Especially at parties. They begin as a kernel of anecdote, then in the retelling shoot out tendrils of the fantastic: a crocodile that wandered into a hotel room in Cancún, told again includes a flamingo that flapped through the window; or, say, a U.S. Customs officer poured out a bottle, two bottles, and then, in the third retelling, raved like a *loco* as he upended a whole case of Dom Perignon, bottle by hundred-dollar bottle, splash over someone's shoes. The point is not truth but style. In another context, self-preservation. Mexico is not a literal culture: yes may mean no, no may mean maybe. One learns to listen between the words, watch the eyes, ponder motives. One ventures questions only timidly, like Alice before the Cheshire cat.

Even the Zapatista rebels in Chiapas hid behind black knit ski masks and told lies. Subcomandante Marcos was not named Marcos but Rafael Guillén. He was not a subcommander, but the leader of an uprising that was led not by indigenous Mayans but by Mexico City radicals, who were not social democrats but hard-line Marxist-Leninists.

Or were they?

"The people of Chiapas accuse him of being Indian," Subcomandante Marcos wrote of himself in an letter to the Mexico City newspapers. "Guilty. Traitor Indians accuse him of being mestizo. Guilty. Male chauvinists accuse him of being feminist. Guilty. Feminists accuse him of being a male chauvinist. Guilty. Communists accuse him of being an anarchist. Guilty. Anarchists accuse him of being orthodox. Guilty . . ."

"Curiouser and curiouser!" said Alice.

But I'd begun to suspect Mexico was a place where nothing was as it seemed, years earlier. I was teaching economics in Mexico City when I started to write stories—the urge was sudden and compelling—because somehow, I sensed that through fiction I could capture my intuition of reality in a way I could not with "facts" and "objective," reasoned analysis. It was a sort of intussusception: enveloped in irony, I sought truth through fiction, wordless knowledge through words. Soon I was no longer working as an economist; I'd become a writer. A teller of tales. Which was not so great a change. Economists use facts and logic, but also metaphor to tell stories. The sun is an orange, writes the novelist; the interbank credit market is represented by supply and demand, says the economist. As Donald McCloskey points out, "No one has so far seen a literal demand curve floating in the sky above Manhattan."

"Once upon a time, there was an economy . . ."

Always, I had the conviction that the stories I told were mine: I sought them out, or as with my fiction, I made them up. But now, as I followed Professor Agúndez through the dusty rooms and corridors of his museum, past arrowheads and Indian skulls, yellowed photographs of the sugar mills and spindle-legged burros laden with *panocha*, I had come to understand that the stories I would tell about this wondrous length of land were unlike anything I might have imagined.

Propped on a shelf next to a Brownie camera and a rusted clothes iron was a daguerreotype portrait of a young, pale-faced priest, his eyes so deeply shadowed they appeared rimmed with kohl. He was looking up, but there was nothing innocent or spiritual in his expression. On an index card tucked into the lower corner of its frame, Professor Agúndez had typed:

EL PADRE GABRIEL GONZALEZ

. . .

DESTACADO DEFENSOR DE LAS CAUSAS BUENAS
QUE BENEfiCIARON AL PUEBLO

Father Gabriel González
outstanding defender of the good causes
that benefited the town.

Like Blighting Wind

"COOL, CUNNING & INTELLIGENT," wrote U.S. lieutenant Henry Halleck of Father Gabriel González, the Spanish-born president of Baja California's last Dominican missions. And, he added, "destitute alike of principle and honor."

Father González sired eleven children. He lived with his family south of Todos Santos on his ranch, the most prosperous on the peninsula's Pacific coast, producing sugar, tobacco, rum, and corn, and boasting a great herd of cattle, horses, and mules. His ranch was on mission land, though the Indians—the mission system's raison d'être—were nearly extinct. Following independence from Spain in 1821, the Mexican Congress voted to secularize the California missions. As a result, the assets and land of the Franciscans' Alta (Upper) California missions were sequestered—but not those of Baja California's Dominican missions because when the secularization decree was pronounced, Father González organized a revolution against the governor. When the next governor attempted to enforce secularization, Father González had him arrested by the garrison at La Paz. The governor escaped and sent troops to Todos Santos, but Father González fled to Mexico City where within a few months he had the ear of President Santa Anna, no less, and the mission lands were restored.

By 1843 Father González was firmly entrenched as Baja California's caudillo, or strongman. It was, as Mexican historian Enrique Krauze titled his book, the *Siglo de caudillos,* the century of *caudillos,* and from 1833 until 1855, none was stronger, or stranger, than Antonio López de Santa Anna. President of Mexico on eleven different occasions, first liberal, then conservative, always mercurial, always ruthless, Santa Anna drained the treasury and lost—or sold—large chunks of national territory even as his own landholdings accumulated to hundreds of thousands of acres. Why would President Santa Anna deign to receive a priest from a province so poor and remote? What prompted him to reverse the secularization decree for Baja California? A whim, perhaps.

He had many. In 1842, the year he received Father González, Santa Anna ordered a state funeral for his leg. Blown off at the knee by a French cannonball during the "Pastry War" of 1838 and buried at his hacienda, Manga de Clavo, the leg was disinterred and brought to Mexico City, where the army and the presidential guard—twelve hundred "Lancers of the Supreme Power"—carried it in solemn procession through the streets to a specially built shrine. The ceremony was attended by Congress, the diplomatic corps, and the entire cabinet. "The name of Santa Anna," declared one of the many ora-tors, "will endure until the sun no longer shines and the stars and planets return to chaos."

Five years later, Mexico was still under Santa Anna's rule when in the summer of 1847, 115 New York Volunteers ran the Stars and Stripes up the flagpole in La Paz. Over the previous year the cities of northern Mexico had fallen to the U.S. forces like dominoes: Chihuahua, then Monterrey, then San Luis Potosí. In March, General Winfield Scott's ten thousand–man Army of the Occupation had bombarded Veracruz with mortars, and now it was marching on Mexico City where it would be met with a ferocious if inept resistance, the crowds throwing stones and shouting, "Death to the Yankees!"

On this far-off and forgotten peninsula, however, many—including its governor and the Dominican father resident in La Paz—were openly enthusiastic about U.S. rule.

"A kinder hearted, more hospitable class of people never lived," reported New York Volunteer lieutenant E. Gould Buffum in his memoir. "Their thatched houses are ever open for the reception of visitors, and a glass of wine and a paper cigar are always offered to any one who chooses to enter." Officers were permitted to rent rooms in town; Buffum found one in the home of a Portuguese trader, where he lived for the next few months "in a style of Eastern luxuriance," sleeping in a hammock sheltered by "a silken canopy," gorging on turtle steaks, mussels and oysters, "ripe, fresh figs," clusters of grapes, and pitahaya, "the most delicious fruit I ever ate." Together with the other American officers, Buffum went on "little excursions on the broad and placid bay" and took Spanish lessons from "a beautiful creature." "Our military duties were so light, that they never interfered with this pleasant mode of life, particularly as our commanding officer was not very strict in his enforcement of them, and the reveillé drum seldom disturbed my morning slumbers."

In the midst of this idyll Father González arrived from Todos Santos. As president of the missions, he maintained a residence in La Paz, to which he invited the American officers, among them Lieutenant Buffum:

Soon after we entered, when he had brought out a bottle of good old wine, he very quietly took from a pocket in his cassock a pack of montè cards, and asked us if we had any objection to a quiet game. Out of courtesy we told him that we had no objection, and the padre commenced dealing and we betting.

After our amusement had been in progress about half an hour, during which time the padre had beaten us to the amount of a few dollars, the bell of the church tolled. The padre laid down his cards and said with perfect *nonchalance:* "Dispensarne [*sic*] Señores, tengo que bautizar un niño." (Excuse me, gentlemen, I have a child to baptize.) He invited us to proceed to the church with him, and when we arrived, we found a woman with a child anxiously waiting in the doorway. When, however, the padre was ready to commence operations, it was found that there was no one present to stand in the capacity of *compadre* (godfather). Gabriel invited me to perform this service. I told him I was not a Catholic. "No le hace," was his reply; and I accordingly stood at the baptismal font while the padre sprinkled the youngster and muttered over it some Latin after which, he turned to my companions and myself, and said, "Ahora, Señores, vamos a jugar otra verz [*sic*]." (Now, gentlemen, we will go and play again); and we accordingly returned to the house and resumed the game.

All the while, Father González was passing intelligence to the Mexican forces that had landed on the peninsula to the north. The following month, a contingent of mounted marines took possession of his mission headquarters in Todos Santos. Soon the priest himself appeared, friendly as ever, according to the report of Lieutenant Henry Halleck,

> assuring us that he greatly regretted the disturbance that had taken place, and would use all his influence to put a stop to it. . . . All the respectable people of the country were of the same opinion as himself respecting this matter, being fully aware that it was much better for them to quietly wait the negotiations of the U[nited] States & Mexico respecting their future destiny; that

some were in favor of remaining a Mexican colony while others prefered annexation to the U.S., but all were fully convinced that nothing they could do would have the least influence on the result of those negotiations, and now to get up a revolution in the country could only lead to disaster & ruin.

Notwithstanding, Father González had already slipped word of the Yankees' arrival to the *Guerrilla Guadalupana*. The following day, in defiance of Halleck's orders, he sold several of the marines rum. By the time they were ready to leave, some half dozen were so drunk they could barely stay on their horses. One of Father González's sons had stolen the flints from their pistols. "He at first positively denied it," Halleck reported incredulously, "but the flints were found in his pocket."

The Mexicans attacked a week later in La Paz, and then the week after that in San José del Cabo. They suffered heavy losses—including Lieutenant José Antonio Mijares, shot dead in San José del Cabo. They made a second attempt to take La Paz, but with ammunition running low, the *Guerrilla Guadalupana* was forced to retreat to the sierra. Soon thereafter, additional New York Volunteers arrived to mop up the last of the resistance in the cape region. Father González was taken prisoner in the last, brief battle of Todos Santos. (Americans: one man and one horse slightly wounded; Mexicans: eight wounded, ten killed.) Lieutenant Halleck then delivered the father—who'd gotten himself, in the words of the ship's commanding officer, "royally drunk"—to the American authorities in Mazatlán.

Father González may not have been sincere when he told Halleck "that nothing they could do would have the least influence on the result of those negotiations." But he was right. What neither knew at the time was that the Treaty of Guadalupe Hidalgo had already been signed, though not yet ratified. In the treaty Santa Anna confirmed U.S. title to Texas (annexed in 1845), and signed away the vast territories of Nuevo México and Alta California—which today constitute the states of California, Nevada, Utah, Colorado, Wyoming, and parts of Arizona and New Mexico.[2] In exchange, the United States

Army would withdraw from occupied territory—essentially, the whole of Mexico—and the U.S. government would assume claims and make cash payments equal to some eighteen million dollars.

What of Baja California? Less than two months before the treaty was signed President Polk had promised Congress that the Californias—both Alta and Baja—would "never be surrendered." That was what United States Army and Navy commanders had been told as well. When they hoisted the Stars and Stripes over San José del Cabo, Cabo San Lucas, La Paz, and Todos Santos, they never expected to have to lower it.

"Polk the Mendacious," his Whig opponents called him. What he told Congress was not what he confided to his diary, that Baja California was of only marginal consideration. The war was unpopular and expensive, and Polk was eager to conclude a treaty. The chief U.S. negotiator received top-secret instructions to "not break off the negotiation if New Mexico and Upper California can alone be acquired."

Someone—a Whig clerk in the State Department was suspected—leaked the instructions to the *Boston Post* and the *New York Herald*. The newspapers may or may not have come to the Mexicans' attention, but this much is known: Polk's secretary of state sent a second set of secret instructions to the negotiator in Mexico City with a courier—again, stating that Baja California was not a sine qua non for a treaty. When the courier arrived at Veracruz, he fell ill and died; Mexican agents rifled through his luggage, found the document, and delivered it to Santa Anna.

In the spring of 1848 the American officers in Baja California received orders to withdraw. They were aghast. Wrote one marine to the *New York Commercial Advertiser,* the news of the treaty was "like blighting wind; [the *bajacalifornios'*] hopes of a free and liberal government gone; the promises held forth to them were a delusion." Young Lieutenant Buffum was scathing: "Never in the history of wars among civilized nations was there a greater piece of injustice committed, and the United States government deserves for it the imprecations of all who have a sense of justice remaining in them."

Ever hopeful, an assembly of *bajacalifornios* led by the governor and the Dominican father in La Paz determined to secede from the Mexican Republic and request annexation to the United States. Failing that, they would request annexation to the British Empire. After a meeting with U.S. naval commanders in the vicinity, however, they accepted transportation to Alta California, and, for some individuals, cash compensation.

Shortly thereafter, in October 1848, the New York Volunteers and 350 *bajacalifornio* refugees set sail for Alta California. There, in their new lives on new territory, they would be buffeted on the sweet breezes of fortune. Gold had been discovered at Sutter's Mill.

As for Father González, he returned to Todos Santos. The missions, at last, were secularized. He retained his ranch; he'd registered title in his family's name. He died, apparently of syphilis, in 1868, twenty years after the American warships had weighed anchor.

The Artist Who'd Gone Away

I COULDN'T stop thinking about Derek Buckner's painting. It was ridiculous—the men in skirts and fezes, the dog, the flying saucer on the table—yet at the same time, strangely beautiful. There was the light, the way it played on the faces and the fabrics, and the way the figures were gesturing, wonder struck, or merely posing?

I went to the Galería de Todos Santos to see it one last time.

Derek was back, Michael said. He would meet with me at the Caffé Todos Santos around the corner.

And there he was: a twenty-five-year-old American in shorts and a T-shirt. He needed a shave, but he had a good-natured face and intelligent pale-blue eyes.

I sat in the same chair I'd sat in the first night I arrived in Todos Santos, the one painted with the moon and stars. I ordered a mango smoothie and a chocolate muffin.

He was from New York, he said, but he'd come to Todos Santos by way of Chicago, where he'd studied at the Art Institute.

"I was unhappy with the lifestyle," he said when I asked him why he left. "You're surrounded by people who are making careers *around* the arts, not as artists. It's high profile, high pressure, making connections, knowing the right people." Art school was a minefield of criticism and egos, and after graduation, pressure to keep producing.

"In Chicago I would paint and paint," Derek said. "I felt like I was punching a time clock. I felt like: you have to work, keep working."

He came down to Todos Santos with his father, the painter Walker Buckner. The first thing Derek noticed was the more relaxed pace. "In Chicago, if you want to see people you have to make an appointment. In Todo, I could spend four hours painting, then come to the café and people were here. It was spontaneous, it felt more real. There are all kinds of people. I could have neighbors, I could have animals. Go to bed early, get up early, go surfing, paint. And then, maybe talk to somebody about, say, their house. I was thinking of Corot, artists who'd gotten out of the scene and gone away. I realized, I don't have to stay in a cold studio in Chicago."

The other artists were not the attraction. "There's this idea that Todos Santos is an artist community, but it's paper thin. Charles Stewart had been keeping up the image. Then Michael came here, my dad, a few other people. There *is* a sense of colony, of gringos. Everyone shares the same immigration experience, you see everybody at the restaurants. But being an artist is a lonely lifestyle. It's not romantic, it's long hours in the studio. You create this other world of light and color. Then you have dinner."

I was intrigued by the idea of the artist who'd gone away. Many of my favorite writers were expatriates: Paul Bowles, Ruth Prawer Jhabvala, V. S. Naipaul. For painters, there was always the example of Gauguin, ordinary in France, a genius in Tahiti.

"My color palette is very different with the light," Derek said. "In Chicago, my colors were muted, darker. Here, there's all this color, a white wall has purple and yellow shadows."

But his influences remained largely the same: Caravaggio, Sorolla. "I like painting figures, people. I like to have a person there doing things. And I love big drapery things, flowing things; the light can play off them. I'm also influenced by Goya. He painted a lot of people dancing, wars, very dramatic gesturing."

Like his painting *The Visitors,* I suggested.

"I like having the big table, square in the middle," he said. "All this movement around it. Things tend to get bigger, get more mass. It's a feeling of things moving out, people getting fat."

Why the men with the fezes?

"The guy I rented a house from had a fez. I did a self-portrait in the fez. I like the affectation of some nineteenth-century paintings. I don't feel the outfits of my time and culture are very interesting. It's fun for me to escape to a timeless place."

The dog?

"I have this little Jack Russell terrier. I like drawing dogs. Dogs connect the floor to the ground."

And the flying saucer on the table?

"There's usually a bowl. I screwed it up, it looked like a convex thing, so I made it a flying saucer. I had a lot of fun with that." He laughed.

"In Chicago," he said, "you can freeze up with self-consciousness. Here I just paint a dog, a woman with a tambourine jumping around. You know, have a little fun! Don't take everything you create as this precious thing."

And there was the irony: it was a precious thing Derek had created.

Around a Table

MICHAEL COPE and Gloria Marie V. shared a studio, a corner in the garden of Robert Whiting's Todos Santos Inn, sheltered with a wall of woven straw *petate*. Michael had left for the day, but Gloria was there, perched on a stool in front of a newly stretched canvas. She looked smaller than she was in her Buddy Holly glasses a size too large. The sun had just gone down, and the crickets were chirping, a loud electric buzz. A moth ticked at the bare lightbulb overhead.

Nanette Hayles had just finished a collage, a scene of fishing boats at Punta Lobos. "Oh," Gloria said. "That's really great."

"Really good." This was Gloria's boyfriend, Michael Mercer.

The little studio was crowded; Nanette held up the canvas so I could see too.

Later, at the Café Santa Fé, Robert, Gloria, Michael Mercer, and I shared a platter of marlin sashimi and rosemary focaccia.

Gloria had started painting seriously only four years ago. She used to be a makeup artist and set designer in L.A. She liked to paint Mexican women, she said, "but not like the images we see in the North American media, you know, fat, baby in one arm, grinding corn." I'd seen one of her paintings in Michael Cope's gallery: a huge blue sky, strings hung with colorful *papeles picados,* two laughing schoolgirls.

Michael Mercer was writing a novel. He was also thinking of starting a press. "It's the foco theory," he said. "You build it, they will come."

They all agreed: there was an artist community in Todos Santos, but it was recent and very small. "Paper thin," Robert said—exactly the words Derek had used.

I had sensed a concern among many of the people I'd interviewed in Todos Santos that an "artist community" would prompt an invasion of tourists. Almost every American I'd talked to here mentioned the *Travel and Leisure* and the *L.A. Times* articles. They'd had an effect on the tiny town like a rock dropped into a teacup.

"But art is meant to be shared," Robert said. "Perhaps artist colonies are temporary by nature. Already there are people here who will tell you it's become gentrified and yuppie."

"There was some resistance to the gallery," Gloria said.

Robert nodded. "People were saying, Who are you to charge that much for your painting? I had a lot of hostile reactions to setting my price for a room at eighty-five dollars a night."

"But we've proven them wrong," Gloria said. "The paintings sell, people do stay at Robert's."

"There's a lot of money in Cabo," Robert said.

We ordered tiramisu. Nanette waved to us from across the room; she'd arrived to have a drink with Paula.

The tiramisu was velvety rich, sponge cake and whipped cream laced with liquor.

For a moment, no one spoke. Our spoons clinked deep into the bottoms of our glasses.

II

the interior

strange treasures

...and thou shalt have treasure in Heaven.

(Matt. 19:21)

† Santa María Cabujakaamung

Calamajué †

DESIERTO CENTRAL

Guerrero Negro

SIERRA DE SAN FRANCISCO

† Santa Gertrudis

† San Ignacio

Guadalupe Huasinapí †

† Santa Rosalía de Mulegé

† Loreto

† San Javier de Biaundo

LLANO MAGDALENA

† La Paz

Todos Santos †

† Santiago

† San José del Cabo

Like People You See in a Dream

The Llano de Magdalena to San Ignacio

> A dream hangs over the whole region, a brooding kind of hallucination.
> —JOHN STEINBECK, *The Log from the* Sea of Cortez

Mission: Loreto

FROM TODOS SANTOS the peninsula stretched north for hundreds of miles, terra incognita. Was it nothing more than the Giant Sandbar, as one of my childhood friends in California called it? At first I was afraid I wouldn't be able to get my mind around it, the vastness, what I'd imagined was a merciless monotony. But of course I could. Stories make a map.

Strangely enough, they begin on the other side of the world, in the year 1291, when, having sacked Jerusalem, the Turks were marching toward Nazareth. With their mangonels and giant catapults, if they could have they would have reduced the house of the Virgin Mary to a pile of ignominious rubble, but, just in the nick of time, in a ray of light from Heaven, a company of angels appeared and lifted the little red-brick house into the air, and then flew it across the sea (with a stopover in Yugoslavia) and, ever so gently, set it down on a hill near a laurel grove on the Italian coast south of Ancona.

This was a story dear to one Giovanni Salvaterra. When he was born in 1648 in Milan, the House of the Virgin—or, as he came to know it, the Santa Casa—had long been enclosed within a magnificent edifice of marble, its sumptuous sculptures and frescos and paintings by some of the greatest artists of the Renaissance: Bramante, Lotto, Sangallo, Signorelli, Sansovino. The town that had grown up around it was named Loreto, after the Latin for "laurel grove." At the age of thirty, now a Jesuit priest with his name Hispanicized to Juan María Salvatierra, he was sent to New Spain, where he carried his devotion to Our Lady of Loreto to the very farthest reaches of the northwest frontier, and then in the year 1697 across a sea to the barbarous island of California. On his arrival at that far shore, wrote a Jesuit poet, *Aligerum coetus, unoque tenore triumphis,* A chorus of angels sang in triumph.

When I first read this story of the rescue of the Virgin's house, I laughed. But it turns out that the little house enshrined in Loreto, Italy, may in fact be the house of the Virgin. The crusaders carried back all sorts of rubble and relics on their return journeys. One of the main shipping families on the Adriatic during the Crusades were the Angelis—hence, angels? In any case, here was my itinerary for the interior. For the story of the Jesuit conquest, which was made in the name of Our Lady of Loreto, is the bones of Baja California. From Todos Santos, I would drive to Father Salvatierra's first mission in Loreto, nearly three hundred miles north on the Sea of Cortés, and from there travel west into the rugged mountains to Mission San Javier de Biaundó, then along the inland coast again, north to Santa Rosalía de Mulegé, San Ignacio Kadakaamán ... I had a long list of missions, meaningless names at this point. They ended with Santa María Cabujakaamung, near the north of the immense wastes of the Central Desert, the last outpost founded in 1767, not a year before the Jesuit order was expelled from the Spanish realm.

But if the Jesuits conquered this peninsula, indigenous peoples had conquered it too, in a distant, pristine past. More recently it had been conquered by Mexicans from the mainland, all kinds of foreigners, most of them Americans—miners, ranchers, and adventurers. One of my favorites was a fellow Californian, a journalist named Arthur North who came through with a mule train in 1906. So many conquerors, so many conquests; even me, even now as I write these lines.

Onward, to Loreto.

But first I would have to cross the vast desert of the Llano de Magdalena, and then a range of mountains named for the queen of the Amazons, La Giganta.

On the Llano de Magdalena

IT WAS A FEW DAYS after Christmas when I headed north from Todos Santos through cardón forest. The cardón looked like giants, rubbery, thick cactus arms raised to the sky. The Transpeninsular Highway ran northeast toward La Paz, touched its bay on the Sea of Cortés, then angled northwest through sierra. More cholla, barrel cacti. A herd of goats nibbled at the highway's broken asphalt shoulder; a Winnebago with Vermont plates whooshed past. A van, two motorcycles, a Pemex truck, fishtailing slightly, its rear-wheel flaps flying. I began to notice the roadside shrines, spare little iron crosses, whitewashed concrete boxes, places where someone had died. At the El Cardón Microwave Tower: a panorama of the Pacific, razor-sharp blue. And then I headed down onto the vast plain called the Llano de Magdalena. This went on and on, sandy white ground covered with cacti, for two hours.

Still in the middle of it, I stopped my car and walked into the desert. I wanted to photograph the fat, twisty-limbed *torote*, or elephant tree; the Spanish moss that hung like rags from the tips of the cardón; perhaps find *chirinola* or "creeping devil," a long, red-tipped cactus that grows horizontally, like a snake. From the highway the ground appeared thickly covered with tangles of green; up close, I could see wide, parched spaces between each plant. The cacti bristled with thorns, from pea-size burrs to barbs long and sharp as hypodermic needles. The dome of the sky was leached pale with heat, the air felt dry and hot as a sauna. Shadows fell small and dark, as if they were some viscous, fast-evaporating substance oozing from the trunks of the cacti. There were a good number of cow patties and coyote scats, which surprised me, until I realized that some of them might have been lying here for years. A few more yards in, I came to a cow's femur, two ribs, a scattering of vertebrae, all of them bleached salt-white from the sun.

Once, more than four million acres of this were leased to an American syndicate.

"Quite a farm," remarked Arthur North.

Back on the Transpeninsular, an hour later: the desert was now broken, gnawed barren in places, more goats, cattle with long, sharp horns. Some were Brahmins, putty-colored hides, their rabbity ears twitching. A water tower, an orchard: bright globes of fruit in dark-green trees. More desert: cholla, cardón. A patch of green: Radishes? Tomatoes? But then, close behind an Allegro RV with Arizona plates, I had to slow down. Cinder-block houses, palm trees, then desert, then citrus. A power station. Overhead, a Cessna zoomed down just as the highway widened and became Boulevard Olachea, two lanes on each side of a median neatly planted with fan palms.

Ciudad Constitución: pickup trucks, men in cowboy hats sitting on benches, a store selling wheelbarrows. At the stoplight: a truck with a bumper sticker that read, *La ciudad limpia no es la que más se asea sino lo que menos se ensucia,* The cleanest city is not the most tidied but the least dirtied.

Ambling down the main boulevard was a woman wearing an apron and sunglasses, twirling a ruffled pink parasol.

"Fossil water" made Ciudad Constitución possible. Deep wells were sunk into the aquifers in the 1950s; soon workers began to arrive from the mainland. Hundreds of acres of sorghum and citrus orchards and vegetables now spread far into the Llano Magdalena. But water was being drawn up at a faster rate than it was replenished. It was the same story from Los Cabos to Tijuana. The problem wasn't so much lack of rainfall—although indeed, there was very little other than the occasional *chubasco*—but the narrowness of the sierra catchment, the spine of jagged mountains running the length of the eastern peninsula.

As for the Llano de Magdalena, wrote Arthur North, "Its theme is ever thirst, *thirst.*"

But in the morning, I learned about another kind of rainstorm, called a *torito,* because it comes back like a little bull. Rain came into the restaurant the other night, said my waiter, and the carpets were still soggy. He stamped his foot and made a squishing noise.

I was the only customer in the Hotel Maribel's restaurant, although there'd been several breakfasting here earlier, so I guessed from the tablecloth stained with coffee-cup rings and a smear of ketchup. The TV blasted on at full volume, a music program with Michael Jackson and Los Caifanes. My waiter pointed toward the patio. "Last summer a *torito* came in that was so strong it threw a table with its umbrella all the way onto the roof." He had a moon-shaped, guileless face. He spoke country Spanish, rough, with a strong *norteño* accent, nasal and braying.

On the TV, pop star Luis Miguel, a cherub-faced blond boy in a tuxedo, crooned into a microphone. Then the news came on: something about the Colosio investigation, and an earthquake in South America.

"There was an earthquake here a week ago," the waiter said when he brought my hot chocolate. "The lamps started swinging. It's because of the French."

And how was that?

"Every time the French explode a bomb we get an earthquake."

He drifted back toward the TV. Los Caifanes were singing now, loud, buzz-sawing rock-and-roll. Purple, green, and yellow stars floated over the stage. The lead singer snarled at the camera.

I had almost finished with my chocolate when a little boy came into the restaurant and sold me an *El Sudcaliforniano*. I like to read the local newspapers when I'm traveling, especially the small-town papers with their news of children's birthday parties, a lost pet, a bake sale for the new football club. *El Sudcaliforniano* had all that, as well as a section the likes of which I'd never seen before: "*Aeropuertos y Turismo,*" interviews and photographs taken at the La Paz Airport. "Isis Amador and her baby daughter traveled to their destination Los Mochis, Sinaloa," was one caption, and another: "Businessman Amadeo Murillo could not travel on flight 601 so he went on Aerocalifornia 801."

I leafed through the rest of the paper. It also had international news: The king of Bahrain had offered Luis Miguel a harem of nine hundred women. And, on an American Airlines flight to New York City, a Brazilian orthodontist "lost control of himself" and bit a stewardess.

I started driving north toward Loreto in the full heat of the day. The air wavered over the asphalt, making a mirage of puddles, always in the distance. The highway shot straight over the plain for a few miles; then at Ciudad Insurgentes—a bantam version of Ciudad Constitución—it cut inland and slowly up the rise of the escarpment.

Nothing to be seen but rocks, *Man erblickt nichts als Felsen,* reported the Jesuit missionary Wenceslaus Linck. Cliffs, sheer mountains, and sandy deserts, *Klippen, steile Berge, sandige Wüsten,* whose monotony is interrupted only by stony heights, *gleichsam mit Fleiss aufgethürmte Steinklippen.*

The Sierra de la Giganta was the color of almond marzipan. It dropped into the sea at Loreto.

Loreto: Like People You See in a Dream

IF, AS THE POET CLAIMED, Father Salvatierra's arrival in 1697 excited a chorus of angels, my own arrival late in the day was as unremarkable as the town of Loreto itself, a windblown little *pueblo* just a jog off the highway. I followed Calle Salvatierra past a Pemex gas station and a bus stop, the El Nido steak house (two Winnebagos parked out front), a cluster of fish-taco stands, a sign for "RV Park Villas Loreto." And then I trailed a van (California plates) with two candy-colored kayaks strapped to its roof all the way to the *malecón,* the long waterfront lined with benches and, protecting the shore, great piles of cement block riprap.

The Sea of Cortés was smooth as a mirror. Terns and pelicans wheeled above. The mountains of Isla del Carmen stretched out in the distance, an ethereal rosy-gray. There was no one on the water, only birds. Their cries filled the air, which felt light and smelled slightly metallic.

It was nearly three hundred years later.

"*Santa María, ora pro nobis,*" Holy Mary, pray for us, the Indians said to Father Salvatierra and his eight men when they landed. The Indians also said the Spanish words for *butter, dog,* and *sir.* "*Almilante!*

Almilante!" said one chief, over and over. He was buck naked, and half his body was ulcered with cancer. His name was Ibó, the Sun.

Almilante was Admiral Isidro de Atondo, who had attempted to establish a colony a few miles north. Admiral Atondo and his colonists—among them the Jesuit Father Kino—had sailed back to the mainland a dozen years before.

Ibó sat down with Father Salvatierra. Delighted, Ibó asked about Father Kino and the others.

Conchó, Red Mangrove, was what the Indians called this place. Walking along the empty beach, it was easy to lose myself in time, to imagine this scene, these voices. The water lapped softly, like whispers against the sharp, angry-sounding cries of the gulls and terns. I passed a twisted trunk of driftwood, its shadow a long slice across the sand. I settled down nearby. I drew my fingers through the grains, still warm from the day's sun.

Here the Indians had gathered to watch as Salvatierra and his men began unloading many things, leading through the surf many strange animals.

Hunter-gatherers, these people had no corn, no metal, no shelter, no animals, not even dogs. Some had tasted corn at Admiral Atondo's camp; some had seen and even touched the hard, shiny weapons, and the strange, deerlike animals that were horses and cows and goats. But never had any of them seen pigs. The women wore skirts woven with reeds that rustled when they moved, a sound like kernels being shaken in a sack. As they approached, the pigs snuffled and grunted, expecting to be fed, and the women ran away giggling, their skirts rustling louder, the pigs trotting after them. The Indians laughed, delighted with the spectacle. Some helped unload, carrying boxes and bales, corn, flour, and clothing. Out came the Jesuits' standard-issue copper cauldron, a fire was lit, and a corn gruel called *pozole* cooked up and ladled out to all who helped.

The Indians pressed close, wanting more. But Father Salvatierra and his men piled their cargo like a wall and dug a trench around it, which they lined with thorny mesquite branches. The Indians must have shouted and cursed; perhaps they began to gather up rocks? "So fierce was their angry reaction," reported Salvatierra, "that we feared they would begin their attack on us at once." And so he had the rock-launching mortar unloaded from the galliot and mounted next to the harquebuses.

The next day, with great solemnity and to a salvo of gunfire, Salvatierra and his men brought out an effigy of the Virgin of Loreto, baby Jesus in her arms. Her church was a tent on the beach. A cross had been made of *palo de arco* and surrounded with bunches of wildflowers.

This place, Salvatierra announced, was now called Loreto.

"Mary lives, Mary rules, Mary conquers," wrote Salvatierra. This, "the realm lost through Lucifer."

What did the Indians think as they stood watching on this beach? We don't know.

Salvatierra kissed the cross. The soldiers kissed the cross.

Some of the Indians kissed the cross, too.

On the mainland, almost two centuries earlier, a seer had told the Aztec emperor Moctezuma, "Be forewarned, in a very few years our cities will be laid to waste, that we and our children and our vassals will be annihilated. . . . And I tell you more: that before many days there will be signs in the skies that foretell of what I say to you." Soon a comet streaked across the night sky.

"What shall I do?" cried Moctezuma. "Where shall I hide?"

Then, in the year 1517 a Spanish ship landed in the Yucatán. Bearded men from the East, reported the Mayans, as in the legend: the feathered serpent god Quetzalcóatl had returned. One year passed before Spaniards were sighted again off the coast of Veracruz. Moctezuma's spies told of "a house on the water, from which emerge white men, white of face and hands, and with long, thick beards and robes of all colors." These must be *tueles,* gods. When Moctezuma heard the news, he covered his mouth and moaned.

These Stone Age people of California were as remote from the Aztecs and the Mayans as Laplanders from Romans, or as bushmen from the kings of Dahomey. But they would have seen that same comet. They would have told stories about it that passed from generation to generation. Surely, they too had their theories about

Admiral Atondo, and now this pale-faced and black-robed Father Salvatierra and his men.

Having wandered for years lost among the tribes to the north of New Spain, Alvar Nuñez Cabeza de Vaca affirmed that "among all these peoples, it was held for very certain that we came from the sky." In the Papua New Guinea highlands there are people still alive who remember first contact with an Australian patrol in the 1930s. A Huli man named Telenge Yenape told an ethnographer that when he first saw the white men "so pale they seemed to glow," he knew they were *dama,* ghosts or powerful spirits. As an Etoro man put it, "they were like people you see in a dream."[1]

"Castrate the sun, that is what the foreigners have come to do." So it is written in the Mayan *Chilam Balam.* "Oh! Let us be sad because they arrived!"

❧

I ARRIVED at my hotel, fifteen minutes south of Loreto in the FONATUR development at Nopoló. The government's idea, as with Los Cabos, and Cancún and Ixtapa on the mainland, was to generate dollars and jobs. But the golf course had large amoeba-shaped patches that looked as dry as straw. The road to the beach, which was paved but in need of repaving, wound through a wilderness of empty lots choked with scrubby brush. Here and there emerged a stuccoed, red-tiled house. "FOR SALE OR RENT UNFURNISHED," said one sign in English. In the lobby, I could hear the restaurant's TV blaring. It was not an encouraging sign; for something to eat I got in my car and hightailed it back to Loreto.

"*Hoy es cabrilla,*" Today it's grouper, the owner said, as I settled onto a stool at the counter of McLulu's, a fish-taco stand on Calle Salvatierra. "Tomorrow it might be snapper. Depends on what's fresh."

Lulu Armendáriz was a large woman who nearly filled the space of the shack's tiny kitchen. The walls were plywood, the floor dirt. She held up a plastic bag of fillets, tinged pink down their middles.

She pulled one out and held it to my nose. *"Es muy fresco,"* she said. Very fresh. It had cost her five pesos more per kilo than frozen.

She flopped it in a bowl of batter and then with a pop and sizzle slid it into a tub-size skillet of corn oil. One wall by the counter was covered with snapshots of Lulu with her customers, Americans in baseball caps, girls in university T-shirts, tanned and smiling.

"I'm alone here all day," she volunteered. "Ever since my husband died twelve years ago." She slipped another fillet in the pan. The cooking fish smelled of corn and flour, light and comforting.

She had five children to support, she said. Two still lived at home; three she'd managed to give university educations—a lawyer, an accountant, and a teacher, she said proudly. She eased the fish from the skillet with a spatula.

"No es para hacerme rica," she added. It's not to get rich. "But it sure beats working for someone else."

She set the plate with my fish tacos on the counter and pointed to the condiments: mashed avocado; a sauce of chopped tomato, onion, cilantro, and serrano chile; shredded cabbage; and fresh cut limes. The taco melted in my mouth, like a bite of heaven.

Before I left, I had to ask: why did she call her taco stand "McLuLu's"?

"Pues," Well, she put her hands on her hips. "An American told me there's a restaurant over there called McDonald's and they sell a lot. I want to sell a lot, too."

Americans again, whether invited or invading, we seemed impossible to avoid. We were at McLulu's, on the beach, at the gas station. The parking strip in front of the Supermercado El Pescador was crowded with vans and RVs, their plates: Oregon, California, Arizona, Alaska. Around the plaza by the mission clustered souvenir shops and street vendors, waiting for our business with ironwood carvings of whales and dolphins, Kodak film, T-shirts, earrings, and postcards.

But a short walk away, I wandered into a square that seemed to have been forgotten in time. Its little bandstand was dwarfed by date palms and eucalyptus trees that shivered and whispered in the breeze. On one side were a municipal building and a *Servicios Funerales,* on the other, a dentist's office and a couple of boarded-up houses, the planks nailed across the doors and windows cracked and faded like driftwood. At the far end was a tiny shop, Regalos Lunenoma, "Gifts since 1965."

I stepped down into a cavelike room, crowded with a jumble of merchandise, coral necklaces, fossilized shells, a turtle's carapace, Aztec-style flutes and pipes. A whale vertebra the size of an elephant's foot gathered dust on the floor. The owner, a bald man in a track suit, held a branch of black coral, fantastic twizzles as large and flat as a Chinese fan. He'd just finished dusting it off; it had a dark, licorice-like sheen.

I bought a coral necklace. He asked me where I was staying, and when I said the hotel at Nopoló, he frowned. I didn't think much of it either, I said. And why was the FONATUR development so far from Loreto?

"Humph." He crossed his arms over his chest. *"Algunos chilangos picudos,"* Some Mexico City bigwigs, "they showed up in the 1970s and said they were going to expropriate land in Loreto. The titles we had were no good, they were going to rezone. Well, I'll tell you what. My title is from 1856 and it's signed by Benito Juárez!" He laughed sardonically. "We all got together and refused to cooperate. *Habrá balazos,* A shoot-out, we threatened. So—" he pointed his thumb over his shoulder—"they had to go south."

❧

THE JESUITS had not been long ashore when Ibó warned Father Salvatierra: the Indians were planning to kill them and take the food. Salvatierra was a veteran missionary to the Tarahumara, a fierce mountain tribe in the mainland's Sierra Madre. With his rock-launching mortar and harquebuses in place, the priest took the news in stride.

The attack came from the heights, a rain of arrows and rocks and dirt clods that lasted for two hours. Finally, the Indians charged. Salvatierra stood up and warned them away, gesturing toward the harquebuses. But the Indians did not understand what harquebuses were; they loosed three arrows at him. "In this desperate strait," Salvatierra wrote, "God inspired me. . . ." He manned a harquebus, and together with his soldiers opened fire. The Indians "were struck down from every side—some were injured and others were killed outright. Disheartened and terrified at our valor, they all withdrew simultaneously at sunset."

Then: absolute silence. After about fifteen minutes, Ibó appeared in the reeds facing the trench. He walked slowly toward the priest and his soldiers. And then he entered their compound, sobbing.

❧

A BRONZE BUST of Father Salvatierra was mounted on a concrete pedestal in the plaza facing Loreto's mission church. His expression was grim, like a man watching his house burn down.

Carved into the stone above the door to the church were the words

CABEZA Y MADRE DE LAS MISIONES
DE BAJA Y ALTA CALIFORNIA

I savored that for a moment: Head and Mother of the Lower and Upper California Missions. In grade school, we'd been taught that the California missions began in San Diego. Father Junípero Serra and the Franciscan order played the heroes—or villains, depending on one's point of view. Salvatierra, Loreto, the Jesuits, none were so much as mentioned.

For years I'd had a recurring dream about finding a room in my house that I hadn't known was there. Sometimes the door was at the back of a wardrobe, other times I found it behind a cabinet. I suppose that's common, like dreams about flying. Baja California, I was beginning to realize, was like my dream about the room. Except that it was true.

The stone church looked small and plain, but inside was a luscious confection of an altar, all gold and Wedgwood blue, with an effigy of the Virgin in gold-leafed robes set back into a niche of pleated satin.

The pews each had a plaque: *En memoria de Teresa Valadez Bañuelos; Familia Benziger Davis; En memoria Ernesto Davis Drew*. Names like Davis and Drew, I'd read, were from sailors, like Fisher and Ritchie and Wilkes in Los Cabos.

The building had been heavily restored. A *chubasco* ravaged the town in 1829 (the capital was moved then to La Paz); earthquakes did further damage. By the mid-eighteenth century, the Indians had died off, and everyone who could had left for the gold rush and other mining booms. With no one to rebuild it, the church remained a ruin. When John Steinbeck came through in 1940, the only room left intact was a side chapel.

It was that simple whitewashed room that interested me, because here was the original Virgin of Loreto carried ashore by Salvatierra himself. I was so struck by Steinbeck's description of the brown-haired wooden effigy that I'd made a note of it: "[S]he has not the look of smug virginity so many have—the 'I-am-the-Mother-of-Christ' look, but rather there was a look of terror on her face, of the Virgin Mother of the world and the prayers of so very many people heavy on her."

Which was a remarkably creative thing to say, I thought, as I gazed up at the shiny, polychromed face. To me, she had a vapid expression. Her eyes were open, but she looked as though she hadn't yet woken up.

San Javier de Biaundó: A Finger toward Heaven

NEXT STOP, San Javier. Early in the morning I left Loreto, driving west into the Sierra de la Giganta on a graded dirt road, my tires spitting back gravel. Abruptly, the road began to rise, running in places along sheer canyon walls. Everywhere there were cacti, rooted even in the rock, in the thinnest pockets of soil: cardón; thorny twists of cholla; fat little barrel cacti crowned with flame-colored flowers; and tangled-looking pitahayas—the low-growing cacti famed for their delicious, seed-laden fruit. Just below the road, a vulture settled onto the top of a cardón. It turned its head, an evil-looking red, and followed the progress of my car.

Soon the towering date palms that crowded the arroyo had become tiny tufts of green far below. Occasionally, when I dared to peer down, I spied settlements tucked near a thread of water, ranchos of one or two families with their adobe buildings and corrals made of twiggy little *palo de arco* branches. Always, there were dogs and a rusty-looking truck, sometimes a few goats, or a mule tethered to a post. At one particularly stunning vista—the hazy blue of the sierra dissolving into the sea, Isla del Carmen floating on the horizon—I passed a pair of crosses, each draped with a wreath of red carnations. Two people had gone over the side. A sickening vision. I gripped the steering wheel and inched, my foot quivering on the gas pedal, ahead.

❧

SALVATIERRA's right-hand man, Francesco Pìccolo, came this way in 1699, to the heights the Cochimí called Viggé and the watered valley they called Biaundó. Father Pìccolo was a native of Sicily, tall and blond with blue eyes, and he too had established missions for the mainland Tarahumara. By comparison, the Cochimí at Viggé-Biaundó seemed docile. Pìccolo returned six months later with his soldiers and built a crude adobe structure with a thatched roof. This was San Francisco Javier de Biaundó, or simply San Javier, the second mission of the Jesuit conquest.

However, the Indians had shamans they called *guamas,* who were unhappy with the competition. One day when Father Pìccolo was out, the Indians destroyed his mission, smashed all the furniture, and split the crucifix into pieces. Then they shot arrows into a painting of the face of the Virgin because, they said, she was his friend.

But when I read this account, I couldn't help wondering, did the Indians really call the Virgin Pìccolo's "friend"? The missionaries' grasp of the Indians' languages (and their profusion of dialects) must have been tenuous. Every word had to be divined. For example, *resurrection.* "They made use of a curious measure for the purpose of finding it out," wrote the Jesuit historian Francisco Javier Clavigero:

After they had caught some flies and submerged them in cold water until they seemed quite dead, they first put them on ashes and then exposed them to the sun to resuscitate them with the heat; they were very attentive, meanwhile, in observing and writing the first words that the Indians uttered when they saw the flies revive, being persuaded that the words would mean resurrection. But they were disappointed, because the words then used by the Indians . . . were these: *ibì-muhuet-ete,* which does not express resurrection but means only "It died a little while ago," or "Just now it was dead."

Father Juan de Ugarte—Piccolo's successor at San Javier—had a particularly difficult time learning the language. Some of the Indians would tell him nonsense when he asked the meaning of a word or its pronunciation, and then when he used it during catechism or mass, they would break out laughing. And even when Father Ugarte found the right words, he was not always able to express ideas in ways they could understand. Hell, for example, seemed to the Indians a fine place, because with an everlasting fire they would never suffer cold.

❧

THE VILLAGE OF San Javier straddled the bottom of a valley eroded from lava flows many millions of years old. The mountaintops pushed up bare and rocky; below were sudden bursts of bougainvillea, date palms, orange and grapefruit trees. As I pulled into town, past a clutch of cinder-block houses with satellite dishes on their roofs, a trio of nanny goats waddled onto the road, their udders wobbling like half-filled balloons.

In lieu of a plaza, San Javier had a wide avenue flanked by thatch-roofed adobes that dead-ended at the Moorish-style church of San Francisco Javier, a perfectly proportioned jewel of Jesuit architecture. Stark and fortresslike, its stone walls and pinnacles rose sheer from the valley floor, its whitewashed cupolas shining in the sun as if they'd been dusted with snow. Built over many years by Father Miguel del Barco and his Indian neophytes, it was completed only in 1759—

long after Pìccolo's and Ugarte's tenures, and less than a decade before the expulsion.

Inside, the air was cool like a cellar. The walls were white as talc. A shaft of light, shimmering with swirling dust, fell from the central dome. An old man sat slumped at the edge of a pew, snoozing. Intermittently, his hiccuping snores echoed down the nave.

I sat down on the other side of the aisle. It felt odd to be sitting in a church; I hadn't sat through a mass since I was a child. I admired the altar, which was small but impressive, a gilded busywork of rosettes and carved cupids framing darkened oil paintings of saints and angels and a sacred heart. How different, I couldn't help thinking, from the church my dad went to in suburban California, which had the feeling of a multipurpose room with its brown plastic stacking chairs. The only decoration I could recall was a life-size effigy of Jesus on the cross, his skin a cadaverous gray, liver-colored blood dribbling down from his forehead and the nails in his hands and feet. How I pondered those mysterious gold letters at the top of his cross when I was a child, letters that read "INRI."

My mom preferred the Protestant church on the other side of the parking lot. Instead of catechism, my sister and I attended Presbyterian Sunday school. I remembered our teacher, Miss Helen, who wore her gray hair pinned into a bun. Once, to demonstrate the parting of the Red Sea, she held a Marie Callender's pie plate filled with water up to a floor fan.

I asked Billy Thompson, who was twelve, what "INRI" meant.

He said: "I'm nailed right in."

❧

FATHER UGARTE was famous for his size and strength. One day, when an Indian began laughing at him, Ugarte grabbed him by the hair, and holding him up, feet wriggling limply, he shook him several times. And once, when a brave challenged him to wrestle, the priest seized his arm and pinched until he cried. Ugarte was disdainful: "He who cannot endure such a slight pain is not capable of fighting with me."

The Apostle, Salvatierra called him, the Atlas and the Column of

California. A Honduran-born Creole aristocrat, Ugarte was a professor of philosophy at a Jesuit college in Mexico City when he joined Salvatierra in the spiritual conquest of California. In Mexico City, he collected monies; in Sinaloa, he gathered provisions, and then he sailed across the Sea of Cortés and trekked deep into the sierra here to Viggé-Biaundó—where the Indians would have killed Piccolo had they found him—and he waited, alone. When the Indians appeared, shyly, suspiciously, Ugarte offered them food and began to catechize. He rebuilt the mission, he planted corn and wheat, the first citrus trees and date palms, he pressed the first wine, he taught the Indians to weave with wool.

What we know of Father Juan de Ugarte is, of course, Jesuit hagiography. Just as—with the haunting exception of their rock art—almost all we know of the Indians is the little recorded by those same soldiers of Christ.

🦗

THE ALTAR'S CENTRAL FIGURE was San Francisco Javier, that first and greatest of the Jesuit missionaries. A doll-size effigy with ivory-colored skin and an ink-black beard, it gazed out over this poor congregation—one agnostic American, one snoring old man—as it pointed a finger toward Heaven.

A woman in a thin brown cardigan tapped me on the shoulder. She was so short, the top of her head came only to my shoulder. There was something officious in her manner, her jaw set with disapproval. ("You in the bermudas," says a sign at the entrance of many a Mexican church, "This is a house of worship.") But I wasn't wearing shorts, I hadn't been using my camera. Without a word, the woman took me by the arm and led me through a door in the side of the nave.

We were in the sacristy. On the table was a collection basket with a ten-peso bill lying as flat as a little flag. She pulled a key from her pocket and unlocked the weathered door of a wardrobe: priests' vestments were hanging there, richly embroidered silks, crimson and fern and gold.

"Originales," she said, with a smile that showed her broken teeth. The missionaries had brought them from Mexico City on mule trains to the coast, she said, and then on boats across the Sea of Cortés.

I touched the stiff fabric.

It seems incredible, I said, that the priests would come here from so far away.

She stared at me.

"Tenían la fe," she said. They had faith.

Precious as Pearls

INDEED, THEY HAD FAITH. But as the Bible says, "Faith without works is dead"—and works require cash. In the Jesuits' mainland Mexico and South American missions—as on their Sonoran cattle ranches, or the maté plantations in the Jesuit-Guaraní "Republic"— the Indians were well fed and clothed, their days a regimen of closely supervised prayer and work. Here in peninsular California, however, there was not enough water or enough arable land to support the missions. Supply lines from the mainland had proved weak and unreliable. For all their planning and preparation, the California Jesuits began running out of food. And now, in the scorching peninsular summer of 1701, their grain sacks empty, the cattle dull-eyed and bony, Fathers Salvatierra, Piccolo, and Ugarte had to turn away their neophytes to hunt and gather as they had from time immemorial.

This was bitter failure, for in the wilderness the Indians would turn to their *guamas,* those "agents of Satan," and "quacks" as the Jesuits called them. Away from their missions, the neophytes would throw off the clothes the missionaries had given them, and they would "commit unchastities," as one missionary very delicately put it, and then after a dance, they might "switch their wives and do their unchastity with them." They would wash their faces with urine, pierce their noses, and observe "all kinds of absurd and superstitious rites, which, for reasons of decency, cannot be described." It was the summer pitahaya season, and the Indians were eager to roam the highlands and gorge on the ripening cactus fruit—and whatever else they could scavenge. And that was among the worst of it, "all [the] kinds of disgusting things" they would eat, as the later missionary Johann Jakob Baegert described in a letter to his brother:

> for example, the guts of animals, still with, if you will excuse the expression, filth; two species—as far as I know—of naked cater-pillars. One of these species is quite green, the other is black, red, yellow, and other colors and three times as big as the first, also full of fat—as the Indians say—and therefore more highly valued . . .

As for cooking, wrote this same Jesuit in his *Observations in Lower California,*

> they simply burn, singe, or toast in or on a fire everything which is not eaten raw. Meat, fish, birds, snakes, field mice, and bats are simply thrown in the middle of the fire or flames or on the glow-ing embers like a piece of wood, then left there to smoke or sweat for about a quarter of an hour. Then the roast, which is charred on the outside, but raw and bloody within, is thrown on the ground or on the sand. After it is sufficiently cooled off, they shake it a little in order to remove the sand and dirt, and the ban-quet is ready.

Most revolting was the so-called second harvest, when the Indians would pick the seeds of the pitahaya from their own shit and then roast and grind them into a flour that they would lick from their fingers. But pity, more than disgust, was what the missionaries felt for the Indians—and a terrible fear for their souls, "precious as pearls," as Father Piccolo wrote, that they might be lost in eternity, never to know Paradise.

NOW WEAK WITH HUNGER, Salvatierra had to face the inevitable and summon his fellow missionaries to Loreto. Ugarte, ever the most energetic, convinced him not to abandon the missions. Pìccolo left for the mainland to seek help. For an entire year, they waited. "We were reduced to skeletons," Salvatierra lamented, "because our stomachs rebelled against the monotonous diet of lean meat." He even ate, he claimed, the very quill he used for writing.

Meanwhile, Pìccolo had made his way to Mexico City, where, to solicit the support they would need to make the mission viable, he printed the *Informe on the New Province of California*. Promising "all frankness and truth," his report described the desert peninsula as blessed with "plenty of water, which promises good harvests with very little effort"; "beautiful meadows, very pleasant valleys, many springs, creeks and rivers"; "fine pastures throughout the year," as well as an "abundance of wild grape vines," not to mention "so many pearl fisheries that they are numbered in the thousands," and the "promise of many minerals." Translated into several European languages, widely read by a public eager for news of California, the legendary land of gold and pearls, Pìccolo's *Informe* fanned rumors of hidden Jesuit treasure, rumors that would become increasingly baroque as they spread through the courts of Europe. In the short run, however, the *Informe* had its intended effect: a royal subsidy, and from several nouveau riche donors, endowments for four new missions.

Father Pìccolo then made the long trip from Mexico City back to Loreto.

So did I.

The Road to Mulegé

I WAS BACK in Loreto in February. I would leave Father Salvatierra behind; now the man to follow was Pìccolo: north toward Mulegé. This time I was with my sister, Alice, and driving a rented refrigerator-white four-wheel-drive jeep. I drove fast, hugging the Sea of Cortés.

The landscape reminded her of Alaska, Alice said. If only the cacti were pine trees, it could be the tundra: the same wide spaces between the plants, the gravelly soil, barren mountains pink in the distance, the sky hard and bright.

My sister had traveled to some of the odder pockets of the world—northern Alaska, Bhutan, Burma, the Isle of Skye. A lawyer in Palo Alto, California, on weekends she volunteered as a captain in the Civil Air Patrol. I was quite sure she'd read everything ever published by and about the Lindberghs.

"Imagine," Alice said as we drove by Bahía de la Concepción, placid as the waters of a fjord. "What if you could ice skate on that?"

We seemed to glide up the highway until, at the mouth of the Río Mulegé we came to El Sombrerito, a hat-shaped hill with a lighthouse smack on top like a knob. On the near bank of the river was the Hotel Serenidad and its dirt landing strip. A chain and padlock draped the gate to the hotel. We knew why: one of Alice's pilot friends, a lawyer who'd flown down for the fishing and the Saturday-night pig roast, told us about a dispute between the owners and the *ejido,* the local agricultural cooperative. Later, there was an article in the *Los Angeles Times.* The Hotel Serenidad was full when armed campesinos took over the building and threw everyone out. Nancy Ugalde de Johnson, who ran the hotel with her American husband, claimed title, but so did the *ejido.* This happened in July 1996. For nearly thirty years, the Johnsons' Hotel Serenidad had been one of Mulegé's major employers. These many months later, it was still closed, as we could see, the suit tied up in the courts.

But there was a handful of small planes, Mooneys and Pipers, parked to the side of the runway. A Mexican in a rugby shirt was standing at the edge, talking into what looked like a cellular telephone.

"An unofficial FBO," Alice said.

Excuse me?

"Fixed base operator," she said. She guessed he was a taxi driver, waiting to hear from planes coming in to land. Which was exactly what he was, although, he said, he used to be the cook at the Hotel Serenidad.

"For twelve years." He gave a rueful smile. Business had really fallen off in Mulegé. There wasn't any aviation fuel here anymore. But the Bush Pilots, members of a U.S.-based travel club, were in town for the weekend. Three groups of ten planes would be coming down in turn, like a caravan in the sky.

The Johnsons and their gringo guests versus the campesinos: I could picture my sister's lawyer friend, a guy in a golf shirt, huffing and red-faced in the heat, hefting his duffel bag and fishing gear out to his plane. (So much for the Saturday-night pig roast.) And the campesinos in their hand-me-down T-shirts and broken shoes, gripping their guns and sticks with sweating, nervous hands. Rafael García was the leader of the campesinos who took over the Hotel Serenidad. According to the *Los Angeles Times,* he was a toothless man who lived in a one-room plywood shack. "What would you do," he asked the reporter, "if you had a shop with large profits and you received nothing, and the store is yours because you can prove it?" I'd thought of following up on that, of looking for Rafael García and the Johnsons. This was the biggest thing to have happened in Mulegé in years. And yet, it was not very big. It was sad, that was all.

Like the Battle of Mulegé, fought right here in the lee of El Sombrerito. In September 1847, the uss *Dale* steamed up from La Paz and demanded the Mexicans' surrender. The Mexicans refused, so the Americans began to batter the town with bullets and grenades. Mexican infantry on the beach blasted back with artillery fire, shouting "*¡Viva la República Mexicana!*" At five in the afternoon, with two men wounded, the uss *Dale* withdrew. That was it.

Lush green date-palm fronds and banana trees, citrus and bougainvillea: Mulegé burst out of the desert dense and tall. The air was sweeter here, softer, smelling of earth and mint. There were songbirds, and cats, many dogs, the sounds of a town: a radio pumping *ranchera* music, trucks, boys playing baseball in the street.

A large white prison sat on a bluff overlooking the town; a stone church perched on another, across the Río Mulegé.

Water, a wide green river flowing to the sea: it was like a miracle. Here comes Father Pìccolo.

A Prison and a Church

IN THE MORNING we hiked up the bluff to Mulegé's prison, a curving sweep of ivory-colored facade so grand-looking from below that tourists were apt to confuse it for the mission church. The prison had a curious history: from 1907 until 1975 no sentries stood guard, only a soldier who blew a conch shell at sunrise to signal the prisoners that they were free to go, and again at sunset to signal that they should return. Prisoners had jobs in Mulegé, families, and friends. At night they slept in the unbarred cells that opened onto a whitewashed courtyard. It was a museum now, a poor one, with pigeons roosting in the exposed rafters. At the entrance hung a blown-up reproduction of an American sailor's painting of that sorry Battle of Mulegé. Inside: old typewriters, a broken sewing machine, Indian arrowheads, a cross fashioned out of crystallized salt. The exhibition rooms, once administrative offices, smelled of mildew.

Ah, but *there* was something of interest, in a dank space off the foyer: the desk that once belonged to Erle Stanley Gardner. Uncle Erle, his secretaries called him. Creator of the *Perry Mason* TV series, he also wrote several books about his adventures in Baja California, so crudely composed they read like transcriptions from his Dictaphone, which, to a large degree, they probably were. But what marvelous tales he tells! Before the Transpeninsular Highway was built Gardner traveled through the rocky wastes like a pasha on safari, in a fleet of four-wheel-drive jeeps, on custom-made dune buggies and all-terrain Pak-Jaks, by plane and by helicopter and by Goodyear blimp. "I have seen things no other writer has ever seen," Gardner wrote. "I have seen things perhaps no other human being has ever seen within modern times." All the while ("where I travel I keep one foot in Hollywood") Gardner was churning out *Perry Mason* scripts, his secretaries balancing notebooks on their knees as they huddled around the campfire—or as in Mulegé, as they sat at this desk.

I ran my hand over its chapped wood surface.

But if the old prison was grand and white and open, Mulegé's mission church was mean, made of stone, and closed. There was no sign to indicate when mass might be held. Two Americans with matching fanny packs were trying to peek through a gap in the door.

"Bush Pilots," Alice said.

The woman wore a baseball cap that said MOONEY. The man was in spotless white trousers with knife-edge pleats. They looked about our parents' age. We chatted. Which hotel were we staying in? The same one. Terrible, sewer pipe running through the room, she said. Shame about the Hotel Serenidad, he said. No aviation fuel, she said.

Just below the church rose a rocky promontory that faced west, toward the jagged line of the Sierra de Guadalupe. Below, wisps of cloud were reflected in the gem-clear waters of the river. A woman in bike pants and a purple windbreaker was videotaping the view, the lush clusters of date palms like a scene out of the Bible.

Piccolo named this mission after the patron saint of his native Palermo, Santa Rosalía, a Norman princess whose remains were discovered on Monte Pellegrino during the plague of 1640. The plague ended when her bones were carried through the streets. Ironically, not long after the founding of Mission Santa Rosalía in 1705 came an outbreak of smallpox, the most lethal of the epidemics that over the course of the next century would sweep up and down the peninsula and exterminate all but a few tiny remnant communities in the mountains near the present-day U.S. border. In the space of about two years, half the adult neophytes and nearly all the children in the Jesuit missions perished. Piccolo himself almost died in the epidemic that followed, probably of typhoid. At San Javier, Father Salvatierra found Father Ugarte "prostrate with a violent form of colic and high fever, with chest and stomach so swollen that he could scarcely breathe."

The missionaries recovered to spend the next years ministering to the sick and burying the dead. Every day, at every mission—the Jesuits had five now—there were last rites to be given and graves to be dug.

In the Sierra de Guadalupe: Strange Treasures

THEIR BONES have sunk in the dry soil and become the earth itself. The Indians, masters of this land for generations, left only traces—a skull here, a cache of arrowheads there. But a few of them left more than themselves, strange visions painted onto the high ceilings of caves in canyon walls. West of Mulegé, in a remote and rugged arroyo, was the cave at San Borjitas, one of Baja California's most important rock-art sites.

To go there I needed a guide. Salvador Castro, one of two in town and until recently a waiter at the Hotel Serenidad, would drive me out in his high-clearance pickup truck. *"Ojalá,"* he said, *"si nada malo pasa,"* God grant it, if nothing bad happens. Salvador had a round, boyish face and nervous eyes, shifting and blinking in the dim light of the bar at the Hotel Hacienda. *"Ojalá,"* he said for the third time, after we'd agreed on his fee.

I was therefore pleasantly surprised when Salvador showed up the next morning on the dot of seven, the church bells clanging as if to herald his entrance.

So: leaving Alice behind in Mulegé, I went west again, into the Sierra de Guadalupe.

⅗

THE ROAD WAS STONES. Salvador's pickup truck crunched along, jolting over the big ones, as I tried to keep my knee from hitting the gearshift, or my shoulder on the door. The noise was deafening: squeaky jangly, *thump thump,* and every now and then a *bang* loud as a gunshot on the truck's bottom. Cacti and scrubby brush scraped at its sides. But the landscape was stunning: reddish bluffs and cliffs, a sky of liquid blue, the early morning moon still floating above, round and thin as a wafer. We were driving through a valley thick with trees, acacia, *torote,* mesquite, *palo blanco* with its ghostly pale trunks, *dipugo* with its delicate green leaves and kiwi-colored branches. Here and there, cattle nibbled at the leaves, on the tall sepia grasses, the cholla cacti. We passed a calf whose face was Velcroed with thorny bits of cholla; its muzzle was close enough to my open window that I might have brushed them off. It gazed at me with sad brown eyes. *"Pobrecito,"* I said, Poor little thing.

"Not to worry," Salvador said. "Cattle like the cholla cactus for the watery juice. Their tongues are thick and tough." He had another personality today: confident, in control.

Every half an hour or so we came to a ranch with its *palo de arco* corral, palapas, cinder-block house with a satellite dish, barking mongrels. Sometimes, someone waved to us from the shade of a porch. Salvador would jump down and open the gates we had to drive through, homemade affairs of *palo blanco,* barbed wire, and rope. On the wind was the smell of goat dung and a distant tinkle of bells.

After about two hours we encountered our first vehicle, a battered pickup heading toward town. Salvador pulled to the right to let it pass. The driver had the milky-white freckled skin and apricot-colored hair of an Irish boy.

"Es muy güero," He's very fair, I said, as his truck plowed down the road behind us in a cloud of dust.

Salvador laughed. "In the *ranchitos,* they are *muy güeros,* very fair, lighter than Americans some of them."

He'd grown up on a ranch himself, he said. So far from town, maybe miles from the ranch out rounding up goats and cattle, you had to know how to use the trees and plants. Cholla buds you could peel and suck for their water. Cardón, there's nothing better to put on a wound to stop the bleeding. There was lomboy for pimples, cat's claw for cancer, sage—he braked the truck, leaned out the window and snapped off a handful of fragrant white flowers and leaves—put this in your shoes, he said, and they'll never smell.

We bounced along for another half hour. The valley broadened. A man was riding a mule through a field of yellow grass, trailing his lariat over his shoulder. He reined to one side and rode toward us as Salvador slowed the truck. His face, I saw as he drew near, was leathery but *güero* as a Montana rancher's. A cigarette dangled from the corner of his mouth.

"Ví a su hijo," Salvador said. I saw your son.

The man nodded, tipped his hat. And then he rode away through the grass, which undulated gently in the breeze. A hawk sailed overhead, spiraling into the depths of blue.

It was very near here that Father Pìccolo discovered the first and only good timber on the peninsula, stands of a tall white-barked poplar. A godsend for the missionaries, who were dependent for both supplies and any coastal exploration on donated ships, leaky old hulks that often wrecked, drowning men and animals, the timber was cut and hauled to the beach at Mulegé. There in the lee of El Sombrerito, an Englishman named William Stafford built a sloop, which Pìccolo blessed and christened on July 16, 1720, *El Triunfo de la Cruz,* the Triumph of the Cross. Its crew included six Europeans, among them William Stafford (Capitán Guillermo, they called him) and an Irishman named Joseph Murphy, in addition to a Peruvian and thirteen Filipinos. That cosmopolitanism was characteristic of the Jesuit enterprise in California—hardly the picture I'd been given in grade school of "the padres," Spaniards all.

The founding missionary in these parts was a German educated at the Jesuit seminary in Prague. There was almost nothing left of his Mission Guadalupe de Hausinapí. Most of the stones had been carted away long ago, the adobe walls melted into the ground.

Salvador downshifted, the gears moaning as we heaved forward, stone by stone.

At the end of the road, rust-colored cliffs rose ahead of us, green with cacti and brush and *palo de arco* clinging wherever a crevice had caught a patch of soil. Finally—it was so luxurious to stand and stretch—we got out and walked through an empty corral and then hiked along the side of a narrow canyon, the trail winding around boulders the size of trucks. All around were cholla, cardón, pitahaya, nopal, and the wild fig trees called *zalates,* their roots gripping the walls of the canyon like the tentacles of giant octopi. The air smelled of herbs; there was water below: still, jewel-like ponds flashing in the sun. Flies buzzed. A pair of doves fluttered by, cooing loudly. The canyon was alive with chirrups and singsong. When I clapped there was an echo, a hollow *ping* that ricocheted like a pinball under glass.

After about twenty minutes we'd hiked some hundred feet above the canyon bottom. At the top of the trail the wall opened, a dark, yawning mouth. On its roof and lip, up high—perhaps twenty-five feet above us—were enormous vivid-red and black figures as crude as paper cutouts. Some were impaled with arrows, some were half-black–half-red, so many of them, their arms and legs overpainted, figure upon figure, sprawled like the bits in a humongous kaleido-scope. Were these memories—or intentions? Their arms were raised as if in surrender.

I was mesmerized; I couldn't stop looking. They were like visions from a nightmare, obscene gingerbread men with weird protuber-ances on their heads, colors like blood and soot. This strange, crude caroming crowd of giants, it woke me like a slap in the face: Look.

Giants from the north made them, the Cochimí said. They them-selves, they assured their missionary, did not paint. They showed him a giant skeleton they'd unearthed, perhaps of a whale.

The cave paintings were not studied with any seriousness until the 1880s when a Dutch and later a French researcher viewed and sketched a handful of sites. In the 1960s, Erle Stanley Gardner ex-plored the sierra in a helicopter, then popularized the cave paintings with a photo-filled article in *Life*, and later in his books. Not until the 1970s were the extent and significance of the peninsula's rock art fully established. Over a period of several years, guided by local ranchers, American historian Harry Crosby and his Mexican associate the photojournalist Enrique Hambleton hiked and rode mules through-out the maze of the sierras, photographing and mapping some 180 previously undocumented sites. Both published books (most recent-ly, Crosby updated and expanded his magnificent *Cave Paintings of Baja California*). To date, more than 250 sites have been located in the central mountain ranges—the Sierras de Guadalupe, San Francisco, and San Borja—and extending up into the Central Desert around Cataviña, an area known as the Great Mural Region.

"The Painters," as Crosby calls the artists, were probably a Paleolithic people from the North. To reach the high ceilings and overhangs they would have used scaffolding made, most likely, of cardón skeletons or palm trunks lashed together with deer hide. Their paints were a slurry of water and ground volcanic rock.

Radiocarbon dating of artifacts unearthed in the caves proves they were occupied some 10,800 years ago, but when exactly the caves were painted remains a mystery. Crosby's guess is that the most recent cave paintings are well over 500 years old, and the oldest 2,000 years old or more. North of here, in a cave in the Sierra de San Francisco, Crosby found a tantalizing clue that, he argues, suggests a date for one painting: a red sun peeking over a bicolored sphere—a half moon? This is highly unusual, for almost all the art in the Great Mural Region depicts human figures and animals; moreover, it looks similar to rock art found in Arizona and New Mexico that juxtaposes a sunlike object with a crescent moon. Of the latter rock art, other researchers have made the case that this records a spectacular coincidence in the year A.D. 1054, visible only in North America, when the supernova that was the birth of the Crab Nebula appeared in the night sky off the point of a crescent moon.

I leaned back against the boulder at the entrance to photograph the figures.

Toward the back, where the cave was blackened from ancient campfires, wasps' nests were wedged into the fissures, honeycombed with holes as if they'd been poked with a stick. Some fifty carvings that looked like leaves or horseshoes, all the almost exact size of my hand, decorated one wall. Supposedly these were symbols of fertility—common, according to anthropologists, to some stage of almost every known human culture.

The floor of the cave, a soft, powdery dirt, was littered with cow patties and dimpled with the half-moons of hoof marks. From here, the light at the mouth of the cave was blindingly bright. Outside, birds twittered.

I gazed for a while longer at the sprawl of figures. One of them looked like a giant frog.

It was funny to think of cattle standing in here alone.

Rancho El Perididio: The Lost, and the Found

BACK IN THE TRUCK, Salvador had me sign the National Institute of Anthropology and History Register. An entire year's worth of visitors had not yet filled the first page. A family of Italians had been here, another group of five from Austria, a handful of Americans, two Canadians, a lone Mexican from Mexico City. Immediately I guessed why Salvador had been so nervous at our first meeting. The fee I would pay him must have been a rare chunk of income.

Sometimes people came in without guides, Salvador said when I commented on the register's few entries. But that was illegal.

Even still, other than the red-haired boy in the pickup and the ranchers, we hadn't seen anyone else all morning.

Salvador looked to be in his midthirties. His middle was growing thick from sitting in a taxi, driving his truck. He missed his old job as a waiter at the Hotel Serenidad, he said. I'd asked him about the dispute between the Johnsons and the *ejido* on our way in, and his face became shifty again, his eyes darting and blinking. He didn't want to talk about it. Whoever was right, whoever was wrong, he just wanted his job back.

Meanwhile, I was exhausted by the drive, the interminable bumping and shaking and rattling. Still more than an hour from Mulegé, we were passing yet another little ranch. A man deep in the shadows of a porch waved hello, good-bye.

What was the best business out here, I wondered, meat or hides?

"Goat cheese," Salvador said.

Chèvre, I imagined, those tart, crumbly bits on salads—would they sell me some? "Sure," he said, and he U-turned the truck and pulled into the broad, swept turnaround in front of the porch. A pack of mongrels charged the truck. The man on the porch waited, immobile as a statue until we came to a full stop. Then and only then, he placed his hands on his knees and slowly stood up. Already the dogs were spent; most of them slunk back into the shade.

They were out of cheese, the man said. Delivered their stock two days ago. He shrugged, smiled, picked at his tooth. He was young, perhaps twenty, in jeans and a baseball cap, olive skin, brown hair. Maybe at the next ranch, he said. Yes, we could see the goats if we wanted. There were about twenty of them over in the corral.

Grateful to stretch my legs, I hopped down from the cab. A honey-colored cur ran after me, making frantic little rushes at my ankles.

The goats were bleating nervously, *bh-hah, bh-hah, hihihi.* Once the goats could see me—elbows and a head over the corral—they quieted. A dozen were sitting in the dirt, another dozen were standing. They were large goats, their bellies big and round as barrels. Some were white, some black, some brown and black. A few had beards, some had short ears, others long, floppy ears. Their stink was rich and herby. Two nanny goats staggered to their feet, udders swinging, and ambled to the far wall of the corral. They didn't seem frightened, rather, primly offended by my presence. Mostly, the goats simply gazed at me with their glassy, oblong eyes and continued chewing.

I gazed back. There was something endearing in the way their little jaws worked their cuds, open and around, showing their little yellow teeth and pink tongues, *chomp, chomp.*

The next ranch, another forty bone-rattling minutes down the road, was El Perdido, the Lost. They not only had goat cheese—a cake-size kilo round in a knotted plastic grocery bag—but also had, Salvador was quick to tell me, a *perro chivero,* a goat-herding dog.

"*Pues sí,*" Señor Aguilar said proudly. "And not every goat ranch has one." He was as tall as a basketball player, with a leathery face and ill-fitting black glasses. We were standing around an open palapa furnished with a lumpy-looking mattress and a shrine (candles, plastic flowers in jelly jars) to the Virgin. The goat corral was just across the road.

"The *perros chiveros,* they nurse with the goats," Salvador said. "They don't mix with other dogs, they stay with the herd all their lives and protect them from mountain lions and coyotes."

Were they a special breed, like collies or German shepherds?

"They only have to be strong," Señor Aguilar said, pushing up his glasses. "He goes out with the goats for three, four days at a time, up in the mountains. I feed him when he gets back. Ay, he eats a lot."

His son, a wiry teenager in a baseball cap, sat on the corner of the mattress. He stuck his fingers in his mouth and whistled. A coal-black dog with the ears and pointed nose of a jackal came loping over from the corral.

"Chivero," the boy said, and the dog knelt down on its knuckles in front of us.

Its head was as smooth and soft as seal fur.

"We were on the highway one day when our truck broke down," Señor Aguilar said. "And this puppy wandered up, out there in the middle of the desert. Someone had abandoned it, reckoning it would die. But our truck broke down, right then and right there. He looked like a good dog, so when we got our truck fixed we took him with us."

The boy chucked the dog on the chin. Its eyes were bright, its paws as burly as a Rottweiler's. It trotted off, back to its charges in the corral.

"On the highway," the boy said, still in awe of Chivero's happy fate. *"En la carretera, pues."*

Santa Rosalía: En Passant

BACK IN MULEGÉ, Alice was on the patio of the Hotel Hacienda, settled on a rocking chair, an empty glass of *limonada* at her side. She'd been reading my copy of Arthur North's memoir, *Camp and Camino in Lower California*. Tomorrow we would make Mission San Ignacio Kadakaamán; en route we would stop in the French copper-mining town of Santa Rosalía, apropos of which she'd found a passage she wanted to read to me. But first, our goat cheese, more *limonadas*, tortilla points, and *pico de gallo* (chopped tomato, onion, and chile). The goat cheese crumbled nicely onto the tortilla points. It had a firmer texture than chèvre, and a saltier and milder flavor.

By the time Alice began to read to me, the swimming pool was filling with shadows and the palm tree near the entrance splayed black against the sky. I rocked back in my chair, the glass cool in my hand. Not long ago, Baja California was a great blankness, a piece of geography I could explore; now it felt less like a place on a map than a wide, swift-moving river of stories. As I half-listened to North, my fellow Californian who'd traveled through in the year of the San Francisco earthquake, I thought: and here, as I live it, is my story, quicksilver fish swimming by.

We left Mulegé in the morning. The Transpeninsular ran through stark country, bare mountains to the west, and to the east, metal-smooth sea. The mass of Isla San Marcos rested on the water like a slab of neapolitan ice cream. Nearing Santa Rosalía we passed the replacement for Mulegé's quaint prison: a modern penitentiary with rifle-toting guards and a parking lot. And then suddenly around a curve, a sprawl of cables, streetlamps, roofs scattered hurly-burly over a hill, scraggly palm trees poking out here and there like weeds. COLOSIO announced a tattered billboard overlooking the highway. A fungus-black jetty of stones enclosed the harbor. The ferry terminal, a mildewy green, squatted over a mud-colored beach. Then rusted smokestacks, warehouses, soot-blackened, broken, abandoned; a junkyard ("YONKE"), shacks, trash, drooping lines of electric wires. We'd missed the turnoff into Santa Rosalía, driven right by it.

Back and up the hill.

Santa Rosalía was made of wood, peak-roofed structures bleached and peeling, sagging with age. We tooled around its few square blocks, Calle 1, Calle 2, Calle 3, which were crammed with shops *(panadería, farmacia, zapatería)*, and cars (decrepit Datsuns, vw bugs), pickup trucks, and vans. Everything was coated with dust, even the people, almost all of them in T-shirts and tennis shoes or cowboy boots.

Santa Rosalía's lifeblood was the ferry and Transpeninsular Highway traffic, but once it was a company town, built to mine copper. From 1885 until the mines played out in the 1950s, Santa Rosalía was run by the French Compagnie du Boleo. Scattered around the town were references to this past: mining locomotives repainted and displayed like monuments, the Panadería El Boleo, the Hotel Francés. On the bluff perched the Museo Histórico-Minero, once the offices of the Compagnie, a two-story mint-green building topped with a clock tower.

For all the wooden construction (the lumber was from Washington, ballast on the return trip from Tacoma's copper refinery), Santa Rosalía was billed in my guidebook as reminiscent of the Wild West, like an Arizona mining camp. But that did not seem quite . . .

"Africa," Alice said. "French Africa. Look at the windows, look at the doors—" Of course, they were French doors, French windows.

And the peaked corrugated iron roofs, built to deflect heat and the tropical rains typical in French colonies. Many of the buildings had porches, long and generous, furnished with broken-down sofas and rocking chairs. It was easy to imagine Arthur North sitting on one, palavering with his friend the mayor, Monsieur Bouchet.

Even the church, flanked by two cylindrical topiary ficus, was built for Africa. Made of prefabricated iron panels designed by Alexandre-Gustave Eiffel, no less, it was a homely little thing, its rivets showing through the paint. Along with his tower, Eiffel displayed it at the 1889 Paris World Exhibition as the prototype for cheap, easy-assembly mission churches. Packed away in a Brussels warehouse, Eiffel's church was forgotten until 1895, when a Compagnie du Boleo official had it shipped to Santa Rosalía and reassembled.

It seemed a miracle, we agreed, that it hadn't crumpled, or been swept out in some long ago *chubasco* to the Sea of Cortés.

Arthur North, Alice sniffed, hadn't bothered to mention it.

San Ignacio Kadakaamán: Everything That Is in the Bible

WE WERE ALMOST midway up the peninsula now, moving toward its center. The Tres Virgenes volcanos loomed in the distance like an admonition. As we closed in on the nude gray cones, the Transpeninsular wound down the escarpment, inland through a vast and terrible desert tangled with bristling pitahayas and streaked with lava hardened to rock beds and rocks. Beyond and below was a dense green huddle of date groves: San Ignacio, the favored.

"Down the camino we plunged," wrote Arthur North, "following hard in the wake of our thirst-crazed burros. . . . '*Agua, agua!*' we demanded, gaspingly, with naught by way of preliminary greeting . . . "

Water: broad, deep reservoirs that mirrored the sky. Two of Father Piccolo's horses drowned when they tried to cross.

The road into town wound through a grove of date palms. The scaled trunks snaked up into parasols of green; the shadows were green. The ground was bare between the trees, the air cool and muffled like the air in a living room shuttered against summer. I thought of Morocco, a date grove near Marrakech where I'd seen two men in djellabas sitting on a carpet, taking small white containers from a hamper. Dates, perhaps? Wine and olives and figs, wedges of goat cheese dripping with whey. I'd forgotten until now what one of the ranchers said: in Baja California we have everything that is in the Bible.

The date palms were planted by the Jesuits. When the missionaries were gone and Indians scarce, the date palms grew wild. By the second half of the nineteenth century, farmers hacked back some of the dates to grow citrus, tomatoes, melons, squash. Still, San Ignacio had thousands of date palms. Dates were good business.

Later, at Guerrero Negro, I met the owner of San Ignacio's oldest date palm. It was so tall, he said, that the only one who dared climb it was the electric-line repairman. The owner's name was Leonardo Villavicencio. The Villavicencios descended from a soldier in the mission presidio at Loreto. He also owned a lot of land, Leonardo Villavicencio told me, a historic building on the plaza, and the post office (well, he said sotto voce, the building it's in). Heavyset, he had a mustache and thick fudge-colored hair slicked back over his forehead. His son had studied food processing. He had this idea: he was going to package the dates with a label, very pretty, with a picture of the mission. No one had done that before.

Instead of a stoplight where the road fed into the plaza, a policeman stood waving his arm left to right, left to right, like a windmill too low on energy to get it up and around. *Pase, pase,* he intoned as we drove by. *Pase.*

San Ignacio's plaza was canopied with trees, ancient Indian laurels with their elephantine trunks daubed white. At the far end was a stand selling *nieves,* ices with syrups—cherry, lime, pineapple. A group of boys kicked a soccer ball from one end of the plaza to the other. The traffic (a pickup, a Winnebago) circled the trees and the *nieve* stand and the boys, slowly. We made the circle and then parked in front of the church, a few feet from where the policeman stood waving, *Pase, pase.*

The church of San Ignacio was of stone with a carved and whitewashed facade as fussy as a petit four. Its altar looked like San Javier's, a baroque, gold-leafed profusion, only larger and dedicated to San Ignacio—Saint Ignatius of Loyola—whose effigy stared down sternly at the pews.

Born Iñigo López de Oñaz y Loyola, Ignacio was a Basque soldier given to gambling and womanizing, until 1521 when his leg was shattered by a cannonball. Recuperating at the castle of Loyola, he was bored. There were none of the chivalric romances—Amadises— he so loved to read, so he had to settle for the *Life of Christ* and *The Flower of Sanctity*. By the time he was able to walk out of the castle, limping badly, Ignacio had determined to change his life. He would go on to found the Company of Jesus, the pope's knights in the Holy War of the Counter Reformation.

When Father Piccolo arrived here in 1716, at this oasis the Cochimí called Kadakaamán, Creek of Reeds, the Jesuit order was one of Rome's most powerful. Thousands of Europe's and the New World's brightest young men joined its seminaries, going on to become leading teachers and intellectuals. Hundreds committed themselves to missionary work from the Philippines to Paraguay, India and China and the far frontiers of Mexico, "to help souls."

But if the Jesuits had powerful patrons, they also had growing ranks of enemies, both Protestants and fellow Catholics jealous of their wealth and influence. Only the walls of San Ignacio Kadakaamán were up when the Jesuits were expelled in 1768. A Dominican finished the work.

Over the nave soared a high whitewashed dome from which dangled a golden cherub, as pretty as the decoration for a cupcake. It held a banner that read (I could make it out if I squinted):

GLORIA IN EXCELSIS DEO

San Zacarías: Wine in the Desert

SAN IGNACIO was but the largest of several oases in the Vizcaíno Desert. At one oasis called San Zacarías, as they had since Jesuit times, a few families kept vineyards and made wine. I'd heard of Baja California's wine industry—the supermarkets and restaurants in Mexico City were stocked with bottles of Padre Kino, Calafia, L.A. Cetto, and Monte Xanic, long-standing brands based in the fertile Valle de Guadalupe up near the border. But wine in this desert? It made me think of tea in the Sahara.

In the morning, keen to try a bottle, we drove out to San Zacarías, west down the unpaved road to the Pacific. The soil was reddish out here, rubbly with rocks, and the cacti looked shriveled, grayish, and burned. In an hour and a half we passed only one pickup, whose driver waved at us as he clattered by.

The landmark at San Zacarías was a government SEDESOL rural store, a shack by the road. Its door was padlocked. On the ground sat an enormous satellite dish and a sparkling-blue solar panel recharging itself in the sun. Behind the store, we could see two cinder-block structures and then, dense like a jungle, date palms and bougainvillea.

We got out of the jeep and stretched. Across the road, waves of heat were rising off the desert floor. From behind the store and the cinder blocks, in the thicket, came a burble of running water and the cackle of insects and birdsong. Just as we were about to walk in, a banged-up butterscotch-colored pickup truck rumbled off the road and braked with a loud squeal. It was the man who ran the store.

I asked him about the wine.

"*No hay vino*," he said shaking his head. No wine, not in the store. "And where then might we buy some?"

"*No lo comercializan*," They don't sell it. "It's just for us." He laughed. For some reason, he said, lots of tourists came out here looking for wine. Especially French people. If we wanted, we could buy Cokes.

He let us into the store. It was well stocked: bags of beans and rice stacked waist-high, a shelf of Campbell's soups and tinned juices, burlap bags of potatoes, and by the cash register a basket of home-made beef tamales. The refrigerator—very cold—held a row of canned Cokes.

I paid for two.

"The wine was very sweet this year," he said, as he counted out my change.

I took this as my cue. "Is it always sweet?"

"My grandfather used to make different types of wine. Some were dry, others sweet. Well, it depends on the crop. This year's is very sweet." He went on talking about the wine, how they would crush the grapes with their hands and age the wine in oak barrels. "Now they do it in leather vats, but they still make it with their hands, so it's more expensive than elsewhere."

We weren't going to quibble.

His uncle Antonio Arce was the one who made it, he said, and he lived a kilometer down the road. Through there, he said, gesturing toward the date palms and bougainvillea.

I recognized the name Arce (pronounced *Ar-seh*). It belonged to a Jesuit-period presidio soldier. Was he named Arce, too?

"One of my grandmothers was half Arce," he said. "Everyone here is related, everyone's my cousin." His name was Reyes Murillo. We shook hands. He insisted on driving us there in his truck.

The road to Antonio Arce's house was stones, bulky and loose like the road to San Borjitas, only here the vegetation was lush, tropical. We crossed a creek, then switched back through a grove of date palms, and past several little garden plots, garlic here, melons and lettuces there, a stand of lime trees.

The road ended in a clearing where there was a stone house with a thatched roof that cantilevered out over a veranda. The veranda was strewn with old furniture, a vinyl sofa, metal chairs, and rocking chairs. On every chair, someone was sitting. A bare-chested man with a beard sprawled on the sofa. Twin girls in matching white shirts and new white sneakers stared at us from behind an unplugged refrigerator. There must have been fifteen people, plus dogs. They hadn't been watching TV or listening to music. They were just sitting. I'd forgotten; it was Sunday.

The old couple was Reyes's aunt Victoria and uncle Antonio Arce.

Bienvenidas, Welcome, they all said, and Antonio Arce pulled up chairs for us. One of his daughters brought us a tumbler and two jelly jars of wine. It was a dark sweet wine, like a madeira. Reyes gulped his down as if it were juice.

Everyone was a child or grandchild, Antonio Arce said when I asked him if everyone was family.

"They have nine children," Reyes said. "But not everyone lives here all the time," he added.

"Part of the year we live at a fish camp on the coast," the barechested man said. He wore a gold pendant in the shape of the peninsula. He seemed to have melded with the sofa, as limp as a Gumby doll.

"Here they grow grapes, citrus, mangoes, and sugar cane." Reyes seemed to be enjoying playing tour guide. "They make *piloncillo*, and my aunt Victoria makes really good mangoes in syrup."[2]

She smiled shyly, clasping her hands together in her lap.

Several more children had come in from the yard and were standing now behind the chairs, watching, listening. A Siamese cat slinked by, nuzzling my leg. We sipped our wine.

"Their house is unusual because it's built of stones," Reyes said.

"We built it in the 1930s," Antonio Arce volunteered. "But we've been here since the 1790s. We have a title signed by Benito Juárez."

We came to the object of our visit. Yes, of course, they would sell us some wine, Don Antonio said. He opened the unplugged refrigerator that stood behind us on the veranda. Inside were clothes and a jumble of things. He picked out a funnel and passed it to his daughter. In a moment, she returned from the kitchen with a milk jug topped with wine.

"Two dollars," Don Antonio said. He didn't want pesos.

When we stood to leave, everyone shook hands with us. The barechested man stayed on the sofa.

Someone said something, I couldn't hear what, and the man on the sofa chuckled. *"Mejor ser flojo que joto,"* he said. Better to be lazy than gay. And he sank down deeper.

On the ride back, Reyes said he liked to read *Proceso* (a Mexico City weekly magazine featuring political news and the arts), as well as *Reader's Digest* (published in Mexico in translation). He drove much faster than he had on the way in. He checked his watch. It was almost time for the news, he said, Televisa from Mexico City. He would power his TV with the battery in his truck.

He let us off at the SEDESOL rural store. We thanked him for his trouble. Then we exchanged addresses. When he saw my name, he said, "Ah, like the Mayo brothers' clinic."

I was sorry to tell him that we were not close kin.

"Where Are We Going?"

ON THE DRIVE back to San Ignacio we did not see a single soul. If someone had told me it hadn't rained here in ten years, I would have believed him. For as far as the eye could see: parched red soil, desiccated-looking cacti, and a huge, cruel sky. In the days before automobiles and good maps, if you missed a watering hole you could die.

A lot of forty-niners died out here, adventuresome boys who'd spent what they had to travel through Panama to La Paz, but didn't have enough to get to San Francisco. They'd figured they could walk. In 1906, the journalist Arthur North almost died crossing this desert. He was in the middle of it when his burro brushed against a cactus that tore open one of his canteens.

Indians must have died of thirst here too, although we'll never know their stories. Like the Polynesians who set out across the Pacific: some found the Marquesas, some encountered Hawaii, others Rapa Nui. But how many rafts went out filled with families, pigs, birds, dogs, only to drift, never to land? Apparently most of the Indians migrated to the New World from Siberia, however, walking across on a strip of tundra exposed when sea levels fell during the last Ice Age. Inexorably, they moved south, populating Mexico, the isthmus, and South America. By 9000 B.C. they'd reached Tierra del Fuego. To enter the Baja California peninsula was to enter a cul-de-sac, a hot, harsh land surrounded by sea. Other peoples were pressing, hungry for game, from behind. As demographer Homer Aschmann wrote, "there was no turning back." The Pericú made it across the deserts to the cape and southern islands. Behind them came the Guaycura, behind them the Cochimí.

Long before the Jesuits arrived, the peninsula's Indians had evolved a way of life that enabled them to survive. They knew about little shoots and fatty worms, how to spear fish and hunt mice, how to make medicine from herbs and cacti. In small groups they wandered, perhaps ten miles on a typical day, lying down to sleep in the open air. When they had to, they practiced abortion and infanticide. They knew when the pitahaya would be ripe; they knew where the watering holes were.

But that way of life was pathetic to a European sensibility; the missionaries were determined to destroy it.

"Only by the crazy time, by the crazy priests, was it that sadness entered us," said the Mayan Chilam Balam. "Because the very Christian arrived here with the true God; but that was the beginning of our misery."

Lamented an Aztec poem about the conquest, *Where are we going? Oh friends?*

San Ignacio Revisited: Pathways to Paradise

"COME, ALL OF YOU," Father Sebastián Sistiaga would cry as he walked among his neophytes, "come to the faith of Jesus Christ. Oh! If only I could make all of you Christians and take you to Paradise."

A professor of belles lettres at a Jesuit college in Mexico City when he became convinced that God had called him to the missions, Sistiaga did most of the work of founding San Ignacio, which was to be, for a time, the largest and most prosperous of the California missions. There were ten missions now, overseen by a new generation of Jesuits. Salvatierra had died more than a decade earlier, at the age of seventy-three. Piccolo would die in Loreto in 1729, aged seventy-five; Ugarte—"the Atlas and the Column of California"—would follow him within the year at San Javier, at the age of sixty-eight.

The Jesuit enterprise in California was now more than three decades old, a third of the way into the century that would belong to the likes of Locke, Rousseau, and that "monkey of genius," as Victor Hugo called François-Marie Arouet *dit* Voltaire. In the late 1720s, the steam pump was in use, as were the mechanical seed drill and the microscope. The Dutch, inspired by Chinese porcelain, were manufacturing delftware; in England, Jonathan Swift published *A Modest Proposal*. Vivaldi was in Venice; in Leipzig, Bach composed his *Passions*. And in the caverns of Mexico City's rococo cathedral—it is easy to imagine young Father Sistiaga among the congregation, a tangle of rosary beads as cool as pearls in his hands—the chapel master conducted his choral works, celestial clockwork made music, trumpets trilling and tumbling against a fretwork of violins, each voice as pure as oil and precise as a lathe-cut sliver of silver: *las dichas, las glorias,* the joys, the glories.

"Oh!" To float among the cottony clouds of Paradise.

But, if the fervent Sistiaga did the work, it was Father Juan Luyando who was given the credit for founding Mission San Ignacio because he paid for it with his patrimony. Indeed, on his arrival in 1728, Father Luyando found his five hundred Cochimí already instructed.

But to be instructed was not necessarily to be converted. When Luyando concluded his first sermon, "a loud noise was heard and such a commotion in the audience that the missionary feared that they wished to kill him." A famous *guama* was the instigator. After the sermon, the *guama* gathered the Indians together and argued that they had seen none of what Father Luyando told them—of God, the Trinity, Heaven and Hell and the Devil who, so the missionary claimed, "made use of the *guamas* to deceive them." But, records the Jesuit historian Clavigero,

on the contrary, that they had seen *Fehual,* who was the directing spirit of human actions, and had heard him speak on many occasions . . . as children, they had learned no other doctrine than what *Fehual* taught them. Finally, he added that *Fehual* was very angry, since the Christians had entered the country, and, for this reason, he had driven away all the deer.

Not so, said some neophytes from Mulegé. On their way to San Ignacio they had seen seven deer.

Two months after Father Luyando's arrival, a distant tribe of Indians came to San Ignacio asking for baptism. "I shall gratify you very willingly," he told them, "providing you learn the Christian doctrine first and bring me the superstitious instruments which your *guamas* make use of to keep you in error." To his amazement, they'd brought these things with them—capes of human hair, probably, deer hooves and feather fans and wooden tablets. They'd been told to do so by a child, a neophyte from one of the missions, whom they'd invited to their country to instruct them. Luyando would likely have made a bonfire, as had done the missionary at Guadalupe de Hausinapí, to which, as Clavigero tells us, "he assembled all the Indians. The latter then showed the scorn in which they held those things by the stones which the men as well as the women and children threw at them."

Eventually, Father Luyando induced that famous *guama,* the devotee of Fehual, to seek baptism. Once baptized, he was made governor of the Indians, a typical strategy the missionaries used to co-opt their rivals. Nevertheless, Clavigero relates, the *guama* was "not long in returning to his more ungovernable vices"—probably healing rituals and adultery. In doing so, he posed a threat the missionary would not countenance.

Father Luyando assembled all the Indians one day, and, in their presence, he severely reprimanded the governor for all those scandals. . . . All were silent, with the exception of a more zealous and daring neophyte named Tomás who confirmed in a loud voice what the missionary was saying; and after encouraging the others, he took hold of the Indian governor to whom the usual punishment of lashings was applied after he had been deprived of his office.

The *guama* then urged an uprising against the missionary, and when that failed, he tried to kill him. Soon however, "God freed Father Luyando from such a fierce persecutor and the latter from perdition; he was the first victim of the epidemic which followed, dying very repentant and kindly nursed and comforted by his Father in Christ."

Clavigero does not reveal the name of San Ignacio's "famous" *guama.* Nor the name of the child who went to evangelize that distant tribe. So many of the Indians in the Mexican Jesuit's chronicle are nameless, like the deaf-mute girl who, when at last Father Luyando consented to baptize her, showed her elation "with leaps and other singular demonstrations of happiness, looking up and pointing to Heaven, as if she wished to give all to understand that now she could go to Paradise."

We hear of Tomás, so loud, so eager to humiliate. What was his Indian name? What was his story? And the catechist baptized Andrés Comanají, "his exemplary integrity," his zeal, his "particular charm"? Although he was blind, he was able to design and build structures, among them Mission Santa Gertrudis, by touch. Interesting, but vague.

The Indians appear only dimly, like ghosts.

Without the immunity of Europeans, developed over millennia of exposure, Baja California's Indians began dying of influenza, measles, smallpox, typhoid. Some of the *guamas* blamed the sickness on the holy water and holy oil. Baptism caused the sickness, others said, and during San Ignacio's great plague of 1729, many Indians hid their children from the missionary.

Not so, said the more seasoned neophytes. Half of those who fell ill had been baptized and half not, and of those who died, they claimed, there were more who were unbaptized. Indeed that plague "was very advantageous," wrote the Jesuit historian Clavigero, "because it took the lives of some of the *guamas* who were most opposed to Christianity." Clavigero, writing in exile in the 1780s, didn't have any idea what was causing so many Indians to die, either.

On the mainland, European diseases had long since decimated the Aztecs, the Mayans, and dozens of other tribes from the Purépecha to the Tarahumara. By the eighteenth century the Mexican countryside, in places, had been emptied of people, and the outdoor chapels, built to accommodate the hundreds and even thousands of Indians who would congregate for mass, were no longer in use. Yet over the whole of New Spain, there were still millions of Indians, enough to provide gang labor for the haciendas and the silver mines. Baja California's Indian population, however, was too small and lived too precarious an existence to withstand the epidemics. Sherburne Cook estimated a preconquest peninsular population of 41,500. Thirty years later, in 1728—the year Mission San Ignacio was founded—there were only 30,500. Forty years after that, the Jesuits expelled, the Franciscan census counted a mere 7,149, and when they turned the missions over to the Dominicans four years later there were but 5,094. Within the space of a few generations, the Cochimí, the Guaycura, and the Pericú would be extinct.

Disease would have arrived on the peninsula without the Jesuits and their soldiers. Infested trade goods such as blankets spread measles and smallpox, and as early as the sixteenth century, pearlers and pirates may have infected the cape region's Pericú with syphilis. But the mission system, by congregating Indians in centers, narrowing their diet, and forcing them to sleep and worship in confined spaces, promoted contagion. It may also have compromised the Indians' defenses and further depressed their birth rates, as attacks on their culture wrought social instability, confusion, rage, and despair.

Of the Ibero-American frontier mission system, writes historian David Sweet, "there was nothing voluntary about it. . . . Every mission had its whipping post, its jail cell, its set of iron shackles, its stocks." Even in his sugarcoated history, Clavigero lets slip the occasional flogging or execution, a corpse strung up and left on display.

The missionaries ran schools where the children were taken from their parents to be instructed in the Christian religion, as well as reading, writing, and simple arithmetic in Spanish. Mass was obligatory. The Indians had to kneel and cross themselves and recite their *Ave Marías*, and they had to sing the *Alabado,* a hymn in praise of the sacraments, with proper solemnity as many as five times a day.

Elsewhere on the frontiers of the Spanish realm Indians labored on mission plantations and cattle ranches. In Baja California, however, the missionaries had no choice but to let some of them roam at least some of the time. Bands of hunter-gatherers called *rancherías* were obligated to appear at chapels on given days of the lunar month. Those in residence at the missions might be required to make adobe bricks, build roads, tend cattle, or plow fields. Soldiers would recapture neophytes who strayed.

And the soldiers would punish any who mocked the priests, who hunted the mission's cattle or stole its crops, or who sinned without repentance. There would be no more pagan rites and witchcraft, no stealing, no more abortions, no adultery, no masturbation, no going about without clothes. And no "second harvest" of pitahaya seeds, at least not at Father Baegert's mission. Twenty lashes for transgressors.

Yet the missions did have their attractions. There was the corn gruel ladled out from cauldrons, above all, as well as many novel and nutritious foods such as oranges and dates, goat meat, beef jerky, and wheat bread. The churches, however rustic, must have been impressive to these Stone Age people: the gong and tinkle of bells, the glow and flicker of candles, censers slowly swinging, trailing clouds of fragrant smoke. There were altars shiny with gold, effigies of white-faced Virgins and saints robed in velvet, chalices of silver, altar cloths of finest, whitest linen. The priests themselves appeared in silk vestments richly embroidered in the colors of flowers. There was singing, simple chants at first; later, Father Bischoff and Father Nascimben, a Venetian contemporary of Vivaldi, introduced choral singing at Mulegé, Guadalupe, and San Ignacio, "beautiful Lauretan litanies," according to Father Baegert.

Work was sometimes encouraged with contests, who could carry away the most rocks, for example, or clear away the most brush. One priest encouraged the children at his mission to help tread the mud for adobe bricks by slipping off his shoes and then dancing and jumping barefoot with the children in the mud.

And what a relief it must have been for many of the Indian women, especially, to at least occasionally settle in one place, without having to carry their infants as they roamed in search of food. From the priests and the wives of the soldiers they learned to weave and sew and embroider.

Power too, raw and crude, was an attraction. The tall white priest with his food, his soldiers and weapons, was powerful. His was the new order, the winning team.

And finally: what if it were true what the missionary said, that here was a chance for Paradise?

"Santa María, ora pro nobis," said the Indians. Holy Mary, pray for us.

As for the missionaries, life on the frontier was an interminable struggle. Jesuits were well-educated men, many from Europe, or from noble families, and here they could find themselves unbearably lonely. Their only company besides the Indians were the soldiers and their families, who were *gente de razón,* people of reason, but simple folk. "Louts," Father Johann Jakob Baegert called his soldiers. He spent his free time, he wrote his brother, "reading, and now and then I do some small handicraft work. As the sun at all times burns down from the ever bright sky, and everything everywhere is covered with stones or thorns, I less and less feel the desire of leaving my house or setting one foot outside the yard except to visit sick people."

Father Sistiaga, that fervent professor of belles lettres, suffered a nervous breakdown. Father Luyando too was sent back to Mexico City when his health failed after only a few years at San Ignacio and Mulegé. And Father Hellen, for fifteen years the missionary at Guadalupe de Hausinapí, retired to the seminary at Tepotzotlán near Mexico City after he developed a hernia tending his flock during an epidemic of dysentery. Of Father Hellen's neophytes, 128 died, "beside very many babies," Clavigero noted, "who were baptized by him and who fluttered away to Paradise."

To Paradise, among the stars in those devil-black nights.

5.

HALFWAY THROUGH this story—the bones as yet in partial outline and many more miles to drive before I might see the last Jesuit mission of Santa María Cabujakaamung—I returned home to Mexico City. From there I drove the hour north to Tepotzotlán, where I toured its churrigueresque chapel of San Francisco Javier, resplendent with altars and effigies, paintings, frescos, cockleshells, and cherubs. The effect was dazzling, dizzying. After a while, I hurt my neck.

The former Jesuit seminary was now a government-run museum. The corridors were long and high-ceilinged, and as I walked my footsteps echoed loudly. The rooms, once the quarters of the novices and their professors—Salvatierra, Ugarte, Hellen, the historian Clavigero, and so many, many others—smelled musty, as if the windows had been left open when it rained.

I perused the displays: a sedan chair upholstered with silk; a portrait of a viceroy; Chinese ginger jars; a chest inlaid with mother-of-pearl. In the corridor a window opened onto a patio below. There were orange trees planted all around, heavy with fruit. In the center a stone fountain dribbled softly. Between classes the novices used to gather here, boys in their soutanes, destined some of them for the missions.

I went back to the chapel of San Francisco Javier. In all the baroque splendor I'd missed the Santa Casa, a replica of the house of Our Lady of Loreto. There it was, wedged into one side of the nave, a red-brick box, plain as a toolshed. I peered through its window. Inside was a painting of angels flying the little house over the water.

The Most Beautiful Dream

In the Sierra de San Francisco

> There were giants in the earth in those days.
> —(Gen. 6:4)

> [To fly] is the most beautiful dream that
> has haunted the hearts of men.
> —LOUIS BLÉRIOT

The Most Beautiful Dream

PERHAPS THERE *are* beings in the heavens. Deep into his first flight across the Atlantic, Lindbergh began to sense the presence of "friendly, vapor-like shapes." He may have been a Lutheran, but one of the few things he'd carried with him into the cockpit was a medal of the Virgin of Loreto—whom, seven years before, the pope had declared the patroness of aviators and air travelers.

Surely Lindbergh would have been amused to know that among the magnificent Renaissance treasures in the shrine in Loreto, Italy, is a fresco that depicts—together with the Santa Casa being flown over the water by angels, a commercial pilot, an astronaut, and Laika, the Russian dog—his little tinfoil-silver *Spirit of St. Louis.*

"Lucky Lindy," they called him, a man who it seemed might live forever.

Laika, however, seems an unfortunate choice for that fresco. It has been more than forty years since she was rocketed into orbit; yet, I like to think that Laika is still up there, sweet trusting angel, watching down on us as she speeds over the continents and the oceans.

Of Baja California she would see what satellite photographs show:

a withered arm the color of sand. From such a height it looks flat, but in its heart lies the great geologic mass of the Sierra de San Francisco. To mere mortals, feet planted on the ground, the Sierra de San Francisco soars. From the depths of its rock-strewn labyrinths the sky is seen only in ribbons of blue. It is a blue you are certain you can someday, somehow fly right through. I hadn't stopped to think: of course, I already had.

The Last of the Californios

HIGH IN THE Sierra de San Francisco the missionaries grazed their cattle. For the few Cochimí they found, they built a chapel. Once the Cochimí were gone, descendants of the presidio soldiers moved in. They were still here at the end of the twentieth century, the *Last of the Californios,* as Harry Crosby titled his book about them. In the ranches of the Sierra de San Francisco, an antique culture has survived in the isolated mountain coves.

But things were changing now with radio, satellite dishes, better roads, and the attraction of schools and jobs in San Ignacio and the coastal towns. Like Rip Van Winkle, the Californios were beginning to wake up. For the people of the Sierra de San Francisco, the changes were being accelerated by the increasing number of tourists who come to see the Indian cave paintings in the Cañón de Santa Teresa, the most spectacular rock art on the North American continent. Erle Stanley Gardner and, later, Harry Crosby and Enrique Hambleton had encouraged a tiny trickle; their numbers increased somewhat after 1993, when the Sierra de San Francisco was named a UNESCO World Heritage Site. But they were still too few to have brought genuine prosperity. The road in from the highway was bad. And while there was water in the Sierra de San Francisco, there was precious little of it.

We'd bought our supply at the supermarket in San Ignacio, several gallon jugs, along with tinned juices and chocolate milk. As for food, Alice had packed a supply of MREs—meals ready to eat—which she carried in her survival kit on Civil Air Patrol flights. We would be in the Cañón de Santa Teresa for three days, and, as per the instructions we'd been given at the National Institute of History and Anthropology office in San Ignacio, we'd brought food for our guide, too. They'd radioed him that we were on our way.

Into the Sierra de San Francisco

FROM SAN IGNACIO, the Transpeninsular Highway arrowed through the Vizcaíno Desert. The Sierra de San Francisco rose bronze-gray and ragged to the east; to the far west, toward the Pacific Ocean, the scattered pointed peaks of the Santa Claras faded to a dusky lavender in the distance. The sand and the cacti were bathed in golden light when we angled off the highway onto a long, straight stretch of graded dirt road. Ahead, just above the ridge of the mountains, hung a full moon, though the sky was still blue with day.

Where the desert met the mountains, the road suddenly wound upward like a corkscrew, no railings, all rocks and rubble, wheel ruts and potholes. I shifted the jeep into four-wheel drive and we continued climbing, the water jugs and tins and duffel bags sloshing and bouncing in the backseat. Soon we were on a high mesa where everything looked green, although the green was cacti. A few feet from the road, the green opened up, a yawning chasm of canyon, its walls sheer black rock.

We'd driven a few hundred feet higher when we stopped for the view. Behind us, the plain of the Vizcaíno Desert looked like sea, the peaks of the Santa Claras like islands in the hazy blue. Ahead was the moon, bright now in the Prussian-blue sky. The air had cooled, become crisp. A small white goat leaped across the road.

More climbing, another mesa. A herd of goats swarmed down the embankment onto the road behind us, their heads bobbing like pigeons', their bells tinkling chimes. In the rearview mirror, I saw a small boy jogging behind them, flailing at them with a switch. The road went on, 180-degree turns around cliff edges, for which I braked to a rolling crawl. The canyons were so deep we couldn't see their floors. And then the road leveled into a high cove ringed with rocky peaks. More goats, two here, three there tearing at a cactus.

Around a corral came a herd flowing like a slip of black river. The goats sounded like children laughing, a pretty, silly sweet sound.

We'd arrived at Rancho San Francisco, a huddle of thatch-roofed shacks, a school, the tiny cream and coral-pink chapel, an airstrip. Fluffy snow-white chickens pecked at the hard-packed earth. A pair of dogs sniffed at the air as we drove past. We were headed to the far end of the settlement, to Enrique Arce's house.

More goats, more chickens, more dogs. A little caramel-colored dog with a sharp snout rushed at our jeep, hopping onto his hind legs the better to bark at us. Enrique Arce's thatched-roof house sat on a bare-earth yard strewn with goat droppings and junk: broken glass, bits of twine, a charred metal barrel. Parked to one side of the house was a battered camper trailer.

A light-skinned man in a cowboy hat and the homemade shoes called *teguas,* Don Enrique had a face that was weathered and kind. He invited us onto his porch, where Alice and I sat on a sofa draped with a quilt. He took a chair from a table that was pushed against the wall. There was a dirt-floored kitchen behind us. A chicken wandered in; he shooed it out.

Don Enrique was not our guide; he was the National Institute of Anthropology representative in charge of supervising visits. We had reported to him, and now we were to sign the visitors' register. Don Enrique's movements were calm, deliberate, like a man who has just eaten a good meal. He crossed his arms over his chest and waited, motionless, while we signed the book.

We could use the camper if we wanted, he said. Alice and I were grateful for that; the light was almost gone, and we would have had to put up our tent in the dark. And we could boil some water in the kitchen, if we needed to.

Don Enrique's daughter Gertrudis watched us unload our sleeping bags and duffels. His name is Cowboy, she said of the peppy little caramel-colored dog, now lifting his leg on one of the jeep's tires. She began stuffing the metal barrel with firewood.

The camper was a wreck—the floor was splintered, the sink's faucet busted, the oven door knocked askew. Every one of its windows was broken and draped with a sour-smelling sheet. But it had two mattresses where we could spread out our sleeping bags. Above mine was a campaign poster of President Ernesto Zedillo, *"Bienestar para tu familia,"* stuck onto the wall with stubs of black electrical tape.

When we came outside, the mountaintops were glowing orange and red like embers. Cowboy nosed my calves; he wanted a pat. Gertrudis was flipping tortillas on the grill.

In the kitchen, Señora Arce put a pan of water on to boil for our tea. It was cold now, and even though Alice and I had on sweatshirts, we hugged ourselves and huddled close to the little stove, a gas range hooked up to a propane tank. The lightbulb flickered a weak, bluish gray. Gertrudis had wandered in with the tortillas. She stood with us around the stove, eating salted orange slices.

Didn't we also want hot water for our supper? Señora Arce asked. She'd assumed that we'd brought dehydrated food like the other tourists.

We had MREs, Alice explained. They came with a chemical packet that needed only cold water. She tore open her brown plastic MRE kit and took out a pouch: chicken à la king. She added a few fingers of cold water to the chemical packet, slipped in the chicken à la king pouch, and presto: heat. This was quite something to see. The packet began to fizzle, giving off wisps of gassy smoke. The thing was warm in a minute or two, then hot to the touch. The smell it made was sour and chalky.

"Qué curioso," Señora Arce said with a little giggle. How curious. Gertrudis cocked her head.

It was meant for soldiers in the field, Alice said. She pulled out the rest of her MRE: another pouch with Cheez-Whiz and crackers, another with a Tootsie Roll, another with a spoon and condiments— salt and pepper, a miniature bottle of Tabasco sauce, powdered coffee, powdered creamer, sugar, a box of chewing gum, a Handywipe, and a packet of Kleenex.

Alice gave Gertrudis her Tootsie Roll. We ate quickly.

Outside the air was sharp. The moon hung low, every pock and shadow clear on its mottled face. The stars looked dense, clotted. The sky was so bright that we could see everything, the rocky peaks, the thatch on the house, a glint of glass on the dirt.

Still, we needed flashlights inside the trailer. Our lights darted over our duffels, the broken oven door, the floor, the ghostly sheets that draped the windows.

"He looks awful," Alice said. Her flashlight was trained on the campaign poster of Ernesto Zedillo.

He did. His smile amounted to baring his teeth; the rest of his face was slack with shock and grief. As I explained to Alice, the photo for this campaign poster was taken only days after Colosio's murder. I wished it weren't hanging directly over my bed.

We burrowed into our sleeping bags. I lay awake for a long time, listening to Cowboy bark. The barks seemed to hang in the air, like bubbles in the space and the silence.

Into the Cañon de Santa Teresa

THE CHICKENS woke us up. And the goats, out of their corral now, a great chorus of bleating and clanking from all directions. The radio on the porch had burst into life with scratchy voices and static. Don Enrique rapped lightly on the camper door: our guide, his nephew Oscar Arce, was waiting for us at Rancho Guadalupe, three kilometers down the road.

We packed up the jeep, augmented our food supplies with two rounds of goat cheese purchased from Señora Arce, and left. Gertrudis, heating tortillas on the grill, waved good-bye.

A short way down the road we came to Rancho Guadalupe, a tiny settlement of thatched huts. Again the goats, the chickens, the dogs. Several men were standing around, their hands in their pockets. All of them wore cowboy hats and *teguas*. A radio crackled loudly.

We parked the jeep next to a hitching post. A pair of burros and a pair of mules were tethered to it, waiting with stonelike patience. Oscar Arce introduced himself. One of the youngest of the men, Oscar had a handsome, strong-boned face that looked the more boyish for his felt-tip pen–thin mustache.

He would be walking, Oscar said. He had only the two mules— they hadn't been able to find a third—one for me and one for Alice. The burros would carry the loads.

We could take turns riding the mules, I suggested.

"*Ay no,*" he insisted as he rolled up his sleeves. "*Yo camino rápido,*" I walk fast.

The men began to load the burros with our duffel bags and supplies. First the men draped the animal's back with a heavy woolen blanket, then a packsaddle of straw-stuffed leather called an *aparejo.* The packsaddle had a strap that belted the burro's stomach; to cinch it tight, one of the men braced himself with a foot on the animal's ribs and pulled. The burro steadied itself against the tugs, hopping on its little hooves, its rusted goat bell clinking. This burro was snow-white. His name was Güero, Oscar said, Fair One. On top of the *aparejo* came our duffels, and our water and food packed into plastic milk crates. These were held in place by two men, while a third anchored them onto Güero with a rope. On top of that came a bright Popsicle-blue tarpaulin, also anchored with a rope.

The other burro, bean-brown with a white nose, was loaded up in the same way. His name was Pinto, Oscar said.

And why didn't Pinto have a bell?

Because he always stayed close to Güero, Oscar said. "*Son buenos amigos.*"

When we were all ready, the men—five of them plus Oscar—suddenly ran after the fully loaded burros, pelting them with small stones and sticks, shouting "*Bro! Brrrro!*" Off the burros trotted, Güero's bell clanking, his bright-blue load bouncing down the trail. Pinto trotted after him, the pebbles the men threw glancing off his rump. "*Brrro! Brrro!*" they shouted.

Oscar followed on foot, and then Alice and I on our mules. My mule, stout and henna-colored, was named Macho de Mata. I took the reins firmly, steering him toward the head of the trail. I was a bit rough, I thought, but I figured it was best to start out showing him who was boss. The mules moved as though through wet sand, their heads drooping. I had to dig my heels into Macho de Mata's side to keep him from stopping altogether. We hadn't been going for three minutes when suddenly he swung his head around with an indignant snort, leaped off the trail and up the hill at a full gallop back toward the ranch. I didn't even have time to yank the reins before he slipped beneath a low-hanging acacia branch that clipped me on the fore-head. My baseball cap flew off, and I doubled over the pommel, cup-ping my hand to my head in pain.

That's who was boss.

I opted to walk for a while. Oscar led Macho de Mata back down the trail by a rope, encouraging the mule with a sound that was halfway between a kiss and a cluck, *"tch tch tch."* Every few minutes Oscar would pick up a stone or a twig and throw it ahead at the bur-ros. *"Brrro!"* he would say, then turn around and give Macho de Mata's rope a tug, *"tch tch tch."*

I had to keep my eyes on my feet—the trail was littered with dung, ankle-twisting rocks, and blankets of loose gravel. Unfortunately, for the scenery was spectacular: we were on a rocky mesa edging along the rim of a vast reddish canyon dusted with green. The sky was huge.

"This is what the road to San Ignacio was like before," Oscar said. "It took us three days to get to there with our burros. We suffered a lot."

And when was the road constructed?

"A little more than ten years ago."

I'd thought it was older, because it was so bad.

President De la Madrid himself had come to its inauguration, Oscar said, a special ceremony in the Salón Social—hadn't I noticed it, there by the chapel at Rancho San Francisco? Carlos Salinas came too; this was just before he was named presidential candidate. The day after the dignitaries left, the Salón Social collapsed. Had they been in it, they might have been killed.

"De la Madrid promised to have the road paved." Oscar shrugged. *"Tch tch tch,"* he pulled Macho de Mata.

We'd begun to descend into the canyon. Its slopes were thick with cacti: cholla, pitahaya, cardón, and soon we were beginning to see more ocotillo, a thorny, bushlike plant with slender, woody branch-es. Goat bells tinkled all around us. On the other side of the canyon I could make out tiny figures, some black, some white, moving like insects among the cacti.

This canyon was called La Tinajita, Oscar said. Little Water Jug.

A low groan, horrible, like a deranged man in agony, floated up from the canyon. I imagined someone had fallen, broken a leg. Once more, the groan. Who was that?

"Goats." Oscar laughed and explained that it was the echo of their voices, warped as it carried across the canyon.

More groans, tinkles, and clanks: La Tinajita was filled with an eerie music. There were no shadows, and only a wisp of a breeze. The sky was solid blue, with nothing in it.

Lying across the trail was a goat carcass, not much more than a blackened rib cage and a few shreds of skin. Oscar picked it up and flung it away. It sailed over the side, into the unseeable depths of the gorge.

The mules moved forward slowly but surefootedly. I was riding Macho de Mata now, his high spirits subdued by the midday heat. We'd been on the trail for more than two hours, and now from the crest of a ridge we had a view of another canyon, its sides looming above, carpeted with the nubby gray-green of cacti and crowned with bare, craggy rock. A scar of dry, stony creek bed ran down from the heights to a palm-lined arroyo, far below. I might have missed the tiny ranch nestled at the bottom. It was just a few *palo de arco* buildings with thatch, a corral, and a postage stamp of an orchard.

"Rancho Salsipuede," Oscar said.

Salsipuede, I liked the way that tripped off the tongue, like a child's taunt: *sal si puede, sal si puede,* get out if you can.

"*Brrro! Brrro!*" he tossed a pebble at Pinto.

It was hard going riding the mules, because they brushed close to the cacti that lined the trail. Leather cups protruded from the stirrups, protecting our feet, and we'd all had the sense to wear long-sleeved shirts. But without gloves, my hands, which I put up to shield my face, were soon stinging with nicks and scratches. And I was saddle sore, too. In places, it was too steep to ride, so we had to get off our mules and walk, long stretches that were like descending a rubbly, dung-strewn staircase. Then we would remount the mules. I'd begun, even at this early stage, to appreciate Harry Crosby's caveat, that Baja California's rock art "gives up its secrets in grudging increments and only to those who persevere." I'd yet to see a cave painting and I was ready to lie down.

Oscar was walking fast, between us and the burros. Every quarter hour or so, he would burst into song: *"No tengo orgullo de ser del Norte!"* Or, *"Camino los valles, mi amor, mi amor!"* He would pick up a pebble and pelt Pinto. *"Brro!"* Sometimes, far ahead of us on the trail, I caught sight of Güero's bouncing bright-blue load.

It was afternoon when we descended, at last, to the bottom of the palm-lined Cañón de Santa Teresa. The palms towered above, their smooth, willowy trunks swaying in the breeze, their shaggy heads rustling like running water. The bed of the arroyo was wide and dry, nothing but giant boulders and rocks and sheaves of bone-dry palm fronds that crunched and cracked as the mules trod on them. On either side of the arroyo rose the canyon walls, tall as a block of skyscrapers, stacked layers of ocher and pink and putty-colored rock. Already the canyon was dimming gray with shadow.

We made camp on a sandy spot beneath a lone mesquite. Sheltering us were three boulders as big as huts, and behind them a stand of palms. Unsaddled, the mules and burros rolled on their backs in the dirt and on the stones like dogs, snorting and whinnying with lusty pleasure. Oscar knotted hobbles around the forelegs of the mules and Güero. Pinto, the burro without the bell, didn't need to be hobbled because he would stay close to his friend. There was no feed for them; they would have to forage. A palm tree, some seventy or eighty feet long, had fallen across the arroyo, forming a barrier as high as my waist. Güero, with his hobbles on, hopped right over it. By the time we'd set up our tents, the animals were nowhere to be seen.

Just beyond the fallen palm tree was a little spring. It burbled from beneath a tumble of boulders, trickling into a scummy green pond. A dragonfly had fallen into the water; its wings shivered weakly, making faint ripples. In the *chubasco* season, water might rage through the canyon; but for now, this pond was it. I was glad for the jugs of water we'd brought from San Ignacio.

Alice and Oscar had upended the milk crates and covered them with oilcloth for our table. Lunch was ready: MREs of hot corned beef hash, along with fruit juice and water. Alice and I sat on flat rocks, Oscar on a log of palm trunk.

The MRES were a great success with Oscar. They were practical, lightweight, well packed, waterproof, no need to light a fire, and quite good.

One time, he said, he took an American couple down here to see the cave paintings, but they didn't bring any food, just some diet pills and powdered coffee and one melon. "One melon!" he said, shaking his head. "They were crazy."

We went on talking. Our legs were sore, and it felt good to stretch them. Overhead, the palm fronds rushed in the breeze, as loud as the ocean.

Oscar asked Alice where she'd gotten the MRES. When she told him they were from her Civil Air Patrol survival kit, he was fascinated. Was she really a pilot? What kind of search-and-rescue missions did she fly?

There had been an accident near his house at Rancho Guadalupe earlier that year, he said. A woman flying with her two children from Loreto to Guerrero Negro. When she was over the Sierra de San Francisco, the wind picked up and she couldn't control her plane. She started circling and circling, wobbling in the wind, then she crashed. She broke a finger, that was all. Someone came to repair the plane so it could be flown out. The problem was, the people of Rancho Guadalupe had to build a runway for it. That was illegal— the Mexican Army didn't allow private airstrips anymore, not with all the drug running. The only authorized airport in these mountains was at Rancho San Francisco, and the soldiers would have destroyed it if Enrique Arce hadn't shown them his permit. Anyway, Oscar said, they cleared a runway at Rancho Guadalupe, the plane took off, and then they had to do all the work of covering it up again.

But one time, before the road was built, an American couple had a terrible accident. When their plane took off, it hit a rock and exploded. They escaped before it burned, but he broke his thigh bone and she broke her arm. There was no way to get them down to San Ignacio except on burro, which took three days. "They suffered a lot," Oscar said, flinching at the memory.

The canyon had cooled. In our jackets and sweaters, we were sipping steaming mugs of sugared coffee now, still talking. We were in no hurry; there wasn't time to hike to the cave paintings and back before sunset.

"One time a seaplane landed," Oscar said. "It had these huge things like boats on its wheels."

"Pontoons," Alice said.

"Oh," Oscar said. "And many, many helicopters."

Did people still talk about Erle Stanley Gardner? I asked. He was the first to fly into the Sierra de San Francisco. This was in 1962, before Oscar was born.

"Oh, yes," Oscar said. "They admired him for his helicopter very much. They'd never seen one before, they didn't know such things existed!"

In his book *Off the Beaten Track in Baja,* Gardner writes that, on his second visit to Rancho San Francisco, when the women spotted the helicopter they all ran inside to change into their best dresses. He'd brought the villagers a case of beer, flashlights with extra batteries, and old clothes. One of his party brought crayons and paper. Another took photos of the people—who'd never seen photographs of themselves—had them enlarged, and later dropped over the village by parachute.

What Oscar knew about was the toys. Gardner, he said twice, had brought toys for all the children.

When night fell the canyon was drenched with noise and moonlight. Frogs were croaking; the palm trees rushed like surf, casting shadows like wiggy, swaying heads on the walls of the canyon. We'd hiked up and down the canyon a ways, and now we were back in camp. For supper Oscar had brought a stack of homemade flour tortillas that he shared with us. We wrapped the tortillas around chunks of Señora Arce's goat cheese sprinkled with Tabasco sauce.

Oscar was good company. He told a story about his little dog, Kayla, and how she'd sniffed out a mountain lion sleeping in a cave near here.

So tiny a dog had come all the way down into this canyon? I'd seen Kayla at Rancho Guadalupe: she looked like a cross between a dachshund and a curly-haired chihuahua.

Oh, yes, Oscar said. Kayla helped him find goats.

I was getting an education here; I'd thought the small dogs were merely pets. I asked about the mules and the burros. Mules were expensive, Oscar said, about 250 dollars—for a good one. Burros, on the other hand, were cheap.

"Nobody wants them anymore," Oscar said. There were roads now, and trucks. "People are killing them for their meat. Burro sausages, they are very bad. You have to be careful, very careful about what meat you are eating. Especially in Tijuana. That is a lost city." He nodded gravely.

We knew, didn't we?

Tijuana, that was where they killed Colosio.

❧

STARS, STARS, STARS: from the bottom of the canyon we had a fat slice of sky so crowded I couldn't identify any of the constellations. The red dot of a high-flying airplane slipped slowly among them.

The Giants, They Came from the North

WHEN WE AWOKE Oscar was gone. We waited for more than an hour, sipping our coffee. It was a glorious day, sun spilling into the canyon, and we were eager to leave for the cave paintings. Finally, from far up the arroyo, we heard the tinkle of Güero's bell.

The animals had wandered all the way back to Rancho Salsipuede, Oscar said, when he arrived out of breath. He wiped his brow with his shirtsleeve.

Salsipuede! That was more than three hours round-trip.

"I walk fast," Oscar said. He conceded that he'd been up before dawn. He tethered the two burros and two mules to the acacia tree behind our tent. Macho de Mata gave me a withering look.

We left the animals at camp and began to hike down the arroyo over boulders and rocks and crunchy carpets of fallen palm leaves. Then we made our way up the side of the canyon on a trail so faint we would never have found it without Oscar. In places, we had to turn sideways to ease ourselves between the rocks and the cacti. Soon we were edging along ledges, slowly so as not to lose our footing on the loose dirt and rubble; within inches were sheer drops. Far below, the tops of the palm trees shimmered silver-green. A hawk swooped by, its screech echoing across the canyon.

"That was where Gardner's helicopter landed." Oscar pointed to a widening in the stony bottom that was bare of trees. "My uncle Tacho was their guide."

When we'd stopped to rest, Oscar asked me about Erle Stanley Gardner's education. *"¿Tiene muchos estudios?"* He wondered how he'd gotten the money to travel here in a helicopter. I told him Gardner was a lawyer, but his money—millions of dollars—had come from the *Perry Mason* TV show and his pulp novels.

Oscar nodded, frowning thoughtfully.

Halfway up the canyon wall we came to "Gardner's Cave"—or, as the ranchers had always known it, La Cueva Pintada, the Painted Cave. "This grand cave," as Harry Crosby describes it, "the most painted place in the most painted part of the entire range of the Great Murals."

Nothing, not all the reading I'd done or the photographs I'd seen, prepared me for the Cueva Pintada's stunning scale, its weirdness, its seething black-and-blood-colored mass of animals and birds and men. It wasn't a cave really, more a ledge with an overhang, like a bubble between the cakelike layers of the canyon wall. The rocky ceiling jutted out, ablaze with enormous figures, many of them ten, twenty, even thirty feet high up the ceiling and the rock face. To view them all fully would have been dangerous—too easy to slip back off the ledge. It was as if the Painters—what wizards!—had worked as they floated in the air.

As at San Borjitas, the human figures faced front, red or black, some bicolored, arms stiffly raised. But here there were also many animals—bighorn sheep, deer, rabbits—all in silhouette, fat-stomached, many of them pierced with arrows and spears. The figures overlapped, a man imposed on a deer, a red man over a black man, an arm over a hind leg, a head obscuring a head. This was ritual magic, prayers of a people without the written word.

But what people?

The giants, they came from the north, said the Cochimí.

Flechas, which means Arrows, was on the opposite side of the arroyo, at about the same height up the canyon wall. With rests, it took us nearly a half hour to climb there.

The cave was called Flechas after the two giant red men overlaid from thigh to face with black arrows. They made a foursome with another pair of figures, half-black–half-red, one in a headdress, the other without a neck, its head a triangular lump. Their arms were raised like criminals under arrest. The larger of the two bicolored figures—perhaps ten feet tall—was superimposed on a leaping, open-mouthed deer. Smaller figures were scattered among them, tiny red men floating upside down above their shoulders, painted animals underfoot—a rabbit perhaps, and antelope and deer.

Here was a story lost, like hieroglyphics undeciphered. It was intriguing but maddening, like a movie with the sound switched off, or a novel without an ending.

I was moved by the simple fact of their presence, now, after such a desert of years. And I couldn't help wondering, when the Painters brushed these colors into the rock, if they could possibly have imagined the likes of me, in my duck-billed baseball cap and waffle-stomper boots one day in the far future, coming from a great distance for no other purpose than to see them. We were so different, and yet, this delight in seeing images, and the urge to make them—like listening to and telling stories—is woven into the very fabric of what makes us human.

There were five major rock-art sites in the Cañón de Santa Teresa. But it was clear to us now that we would not have time to see them all. I'd been told at the National Institute of Anthropology and History office in San Ignacio—where we'd obtained our permits and reservations—that three nights was sufficient. They were wrong. In any case, we had food and water to last only until midday the next day; to make it back to our jeep at Rancho Guadalupe by then, we'd have to camp tonight at Rancho Salsipuede. Of the remaining three sites, we had time to see one. Oscar said Boca San Julio was the most interesting. We began the long hike.

The shade of a boulder was a good excuse to stop for lunch. Nearby, a spring burbled from the rocks, chill and fresh, into a necklace of emerald-green ponds. Water beetles skimmed their surface; pearl-size snails speckled the shallow, rocky bottoms. We drank the water we'd bought in San Ignacio, which was warm and tasted of plastic.

These MRES are good, Oscar said. He sighed.

Could Alice send him more? How much did they cost?

Another hour down the arroyo, I fell and scraped open my hand. When we'd found a sandy spot to sit down, Alice opened her backpack and unzipped her first-aid kit, an Elizabeth Arden cosmetics bag decorated with roses. Efficiently, she cleaned the wound with an antiseptic wipe, rubbing vigorously (which hurt like hell), then applied Neosporin and a gauze bandage, which she secured with tape.

"I come prepared," she said.

What else did she have in there? Oscar and I watched as she pulled out each item and laid it on the sand: an Ace bandage, Benadril, bandages for burns, a triangle of cloth to make a sling, safety pins, more tape, more antiseptic wipes, surgical sponges for soaking up blood, a signaling mirror.

"A signaling mirror!" I chuckled.

Oscar stood up and took a small, round mirror from his front pocket. "I've got one too," he said shyly, and he held it out so that it caught the sun.

Alice smirked at me. "You laugh."

In fact, we hadn't seen another soul in more than twenty-four hours.

Not until midafternoon did we finally arrive at Boca San Julio, which turned out to be a small site framed by leafy green *torote* trees. The mural of red-and-black animals was dominated by two life-size leaping deer, their front legs arching forward, heads thrown back in terror.

We know this much: the Painters were hunters. More than one researcher speculates that the paintings were made at a time when game was becoming scarce. As the first Indians swept south from the Alaskan taiga, they found a New World teeming with animals. The largest and slowest moving were the first to go: mammoths, mastodons, giant ground sloths. The bones of these extinct species litter the Americas, many of them embedded with arrowheads and charred by ancient fires. European conquest only accelerated a long-ongoing process.

A few deer still foraged in Baja California's sierras, although we'd yet to see any. The gazellelike pronghorn antelope was in imminent danger of extinction, as was the bighorn sheep. Bighorn (population unknown, but possibly fewer than three hundred on the peninsula) were still hunted, not here in the Sierra de San Francisco, but farther south, in the Sierra de la Giganta, and in the mountains north of La Paz. The government had recently auctioned off permits, which cost as much as thirty thousand dollars. I knew a Mexican who'd bought one. His house was crammed with trophies, including the head of a yawning hippopotamus. *El chiste,* The thing, he'd told me through the fug of his Cuban cigar, was to get a "Grand Slam," one head of each of the "big four" sheep: Dall, Rocky Mountain, stone, and desert bighorn.

A government biologist accompanied his expedition, identifying which animals could be shot. I'd spoken with that biologist. He informed me that the bighorn were "a resource." He admitted they had not yet identified what might be a "sustainable rate of exploitation." And yes, there was, as everyone knew, a lot of poaching.

Now there were goats. I'd asked Oscar what he'd done about the mountain lion his little dog, Kayla, had found sleeping in a cave. He'd shrugged.

"Mountain lions and goats, they don't mix."

By sunset we'd made it to Rancho Salsipuede. Quickly, we set up our tents in a sandy clearing between the mountainside and a thicket of palms, prickly-pear cacti, and scrub, just outside the gate to the orchard. By the time our tents were up, it was night.

Among the three of us, we'd finished Oscar's tortillas. Here we could buy more, he said. So we hiked down the dry, stony bed of the arroyo toward the ranch house. We didn't need flashlights; the stones, oval like dinosaur eggs, were aglow with moonlight. Across the arroyo, the palm trees cast shadows onto the canyon wall.

We rounded a corral (faint tinkle of goat bells) and came to a crude *palo de arco* fence. *"Buenas noches,"* Good evening, Oscar called out, and announced that we wanted to buy tortillas. In a moment, the owner appeared and unlatched the gate. I couldn't see his face in this dark, and he didn't give us his name. He shook our hands with a hand as hard as a hoof.

Once in the compound, we walked by a shack made of loosely spaced planks. A light was on inside, sending spears of gold onto the path. People were talking in there, a woman, a girl? A child stood in the doorway and stared at us. There was a good cinnamony smell, of wood burning in an oven.

We sat on the darkened veranda of the house on mismatched metal chairs. The radio, a white box hung on the wall, was on, crackling loudly. A dog appeared out of the darkness, pressing a wet nose against our legs. The owner whapped it on the snout with the back of his hand; it shrank back into the darkness. Oscar and the owner began to talk, but I couldn't follow what they were saying. Their Spanish, unlike the Spanish Oscar used with us, was singsongy and slurred, as if the ends of the words had melted off. They paused now and then to listen to the radio.

"¿Dónde estás?" Where are you? A man's voice asked. Static. Then a woman's voice, as pure as the notes from a flute: "Guerrero Negro, and the night is very clear and the moon is bright."

Someone began to moan in the shack by the entrance. Oscar and the owner continued talking, listening to the radio as the moaning from the shack twisted into a screech, like a monkey with its hand caught in a door. The voice was a man's; it erupted into frantic babbling and hooting. Then, a noise like gargling. We'd been waiting for about ten minutes, pretending to ignore this, when the owner's wife, a tired-looking woman in a head kerchief, brought out our tortillas. We paid and left.

Their son was born like that, Oscar said when we were back in camp. Now the son was twenty-five years old. He couldn't speak, he couldn't walk, he had constant seizures.

We were sitting around a campfire, boiling a pan of water for tea. Alice fed a dry palm leaf into the flames. We watched it curl and burn.

"They say that's what happens when people of the same blood have children," Oscar said. "But in this family, the parents are not cousins."

The isolation of this place was staggering. They had the radio, at least, to bring news and help in an emergency. But treatment for their son (was he autistic? epileptic?) would have been impossible. There was no road, no airstrip. Everything that family owned was made by hand or carried in on the back of a burro.

The children, did they go to school?

"No," Oscar said. "Their father doesn't want them to go." He poked at the fire with a twig. Oscar had attended the little school at Rancho San Francisco. "I didn't like it, though," he said. "I didn't realize how important school is until now." He told us about one of his wife's relatives, who'd gone to high school in Guerrero Negro. She was a secretary now at Exportadora de Sal, the salt company owned by the Mexican government and Mitsubishi. She would buy groceries at the employees only subsidized supermarket, then send some to her family at Rancho Guadalupe. "We are very grateful for that," Oscar said.

We made our tea. And then we ate, spooning the hot beef stew of our MREs into the tortillas. The tortillas were still warm, blistered from the griddle, and they had a nutty flavor.

"The Flying Samaritans used to come here," Oscar said. "Two American doctors named Jaime and Tomás. They used to fly into Rancho San Francisco from Mulegé. They would fix your teeth." But they'd stopped coming about five years ago, some problem with the doctors in Santa Rosalía. *"Hace mucha falta, mucha falta."* There were many, many needs. Did Alice know Jaime and Tomás?

Jim y Tom, she said.

He nodded.

No, she didn't.

Oscar poked another twig at the fire, and then tossed it in.

How do you fly a plane? he wanted to know. Alice told him it was like riding a mule, you pull the control yoke the way you pull the reins; you work the rudder pedals with your feet.

They went on talking about flying. I'd nowhere else to go, so I sat and listened. Once in a while, I got up to gather more twigs and palm leaves to add to the fire.

Oscar said he collected pictures of airplanes. Did Alice have any?

Yes, she'd bought postcards at Oshkosh. That was the world's biggest air show, hundreds of planes, World War II fighters, B-1 bombers, even a Concorde, she said, which can flash across the Atlantic Ocean in under four hours.

Oscar watched for planes. There was one that flew toward Laguna San Ignacio every week on the same day at the same time. There was also one that flew south toward Loreto twice a day.

That must be the Aerocalifornia flight from Los Angeles, I said. I wondered whether he'd seen the jet that flew the length of the peninsula from Los Cabos to San Diego. I'd taken that Aeroméxico flight many times.

"Oh, yes," he said. "It leaves a white trail."

Up Again

THE CLIMB UP from Rancho Salsipuede exhausted the mules. I could feel Macho de Mata's rib cage heaving, his heart pounding under my legs. "She feels like she's shuddering," Alice called out about her mount, Soguía, halfway up that first ridge. We began to alternate as we climbed toward the mesa, riding for a while, then dismounting the mules and walking when we anticipated a particularly steep stretch. But the trail was narrow, curving with the contours of the mountainsides, and difficult to anticipate. Several times I found myself on my gasping mule, hard by the rock wall, his hoofs treading within inches of the abyss.

Oscar hiked ahead of us, tossing pebbles and branches at Pinto. *"Brrro! Brrro!"*

The morning went by this way. The sun beat down like a hammer as we pitched and lurched in our saddles, then clambered over rocks and rubble. Sometimes, where the trail widened, we stopped and Oscar cinched tight the loosened saddles. Always there was the smell of horse and hot leather, the clop of hooves, and the clank, far ahead, of Güero's bell.

As we neared La Tinajita, we began to hear the goat bells, a tinkly clinking like a chorus of ethereal chimes. Once on the mesa over-looking the canyon, we stopped for lunch. The sky was lapis lazuli in its center, paling to an opalescent, cloud-wisped rim. To the horizon: canyons, deep, razorlike cuts and gouging scoops into the rust-red earth. The mules waited, their heads drooping low as we drank the last of our water and fruit juice with great greedy gulps.

Oscar cinched the saddles. We were about to mount the mules when we heard a buzzing. It was coming from the northwest.

"An airplane," Oscar said.

It was the plane he'd told us about, the one that always flew on the same day at the same time toward Laguna San Ignacio. It drilled through the sky, a small black cross. The canyon filled with its noise, a deep, reverberating rumble.

🎵

AT RANCHO GUADALUPE we found our once white jeep gray with a thick coating of dust. Children had drawn figure eights and smiley faces on all of its windows; there were dribbles where dogs had marked the tires. Parked next to it was a gleaming white high-clear-ance van with Oregon plates, three fiberglass kayaks strapped to its roof. The two vehicles, the only ones in the settlement, looked pre-posterous amid the goats and dogs, the thatch-roofed adobes, solar panels, and tack.

The men were polite but businesslike. They began to unload the burros and unsaddle the weary mules. Oscar's little dog, Kayla, was there, sniffing around our ankles as we piled our bags into the jeep. Finis.

"She is a pilot," Oscar announced.

· A pilot! Really! What kind of plane? Did she own her plane? Or did she rent her plane? Did she fly in California? Did she fly in Mexico?

Oscar's father shook our hands. "Bonifacio Arce," he said. We were invited in for coffee.

Their house, down a flower-lined path, was painted moss green with snow-white trim. We sat on the veranda on padded flip seats from an old movie theater. Clustered throughout the kitchen garden were plantings of calla lilies, daisies, and a sprinkling of magenta cosmos, the blossoms bobbling in the breeze. Kayla rested her paw on Alice's boot.

Did she know Jaime and Tomás? What did she think of the runway at Rancho San Francisco? In Los Angeles, was the runway paved?

As Alice answered their questions, I leaned down and scratched Kayla behind her ears. Brave little dog. The sun fell on us honeyed and warm. Kayla let her tongue loll out just a little. She closed her eyes.

Fine Kings

Beyond the Vizcaíno

Across the Vizcaíno

BACK ON THE Vizcaíno Desert, Alice and I headed northwest on the Transpeninsular to Guerrero Negro, where we planned to stay the night. Here the ground was forested with datilillo, a spiky-headed, bark-trunked yucca like a Joshua tree. They clustered in threes and fours, their hydralike heads bent low toward the ocean, like a vast field of Mohammedans bowing toward Mecca. There were cardón too, and thick tangles of cholla. The wind was blowing hard across the plain; the sky was brushed clean. The afternoon sun bleached the mountains in the distance bone and slate gray.

But the Vizcaíno was not quite the wilderness I had expected. Electric cables ran alongside the highway; we passed trucks, blasting Macs, Winnebagos, vans, a bus with its destination—CIUDAD CON-STITUCION—emblazoned across the crown of its windshield. There were even the occasional farms irrigated with "fossil water"—sudden spreads of emerald green, improbable atolls cluttered with cinder-block houses, broken-down pickups and signs advertising

"YONKE." At Vizcaíno Junction, where a dirt road forked west toward the fish camps on the jagged elbow of the Vizcaíno Peninsula, we bought Cokes and filled our gas tank at the Pemex station. And then, for a long while, we drove through a lowland denuded of everything but pickleweed.

It was incredible to think that the Jesuits set out across these merciless wastes with their soldiers, their horses, and their crowds of loyal neophytes. They wanted to save souls, and to scout watered sites for new missions. Souls they found, more of the nomadic Cochimí, but little water other than a handful of alkaline springs trickling from between the bone-dry rocks of remote canyons. The deserts—the Vizcaíno, then the Central—stretched north, vast and pitiless.

Wrote forty-niner William C. S. Smith, a greenhorn who blundered through without a map or a guide, "there was a curse resting upon this region; this perfection of eternal desolation."

But here, hurtling north to the cusp of ruin, the Jesuits' story must backtrack to the time and the place that everything started to go wrong.

The Devil on His Throne: The South, 1720–1766

THE SOUTH is that fat foot of land dangling from an ankle carved thin by the Bahía de la Paz. At its heel are waters rich with shellfish, from its arch rise high sierras good for grazing cattle, while its toes— Los Cabos and Todos Santos—dip into the Tropic of Cancer, watered (by the standards of the peninsula) and fertile. For the Jesuits, here were souls to be saved; for the king, a safe port for the Manila Galleon.

"Now we are rich," gloated Thomas Cavendish as he marveled at the great glittering heap of booty piled on the beach at Cabo San Lucas. When Cavendish seized the *Santa Ana* in 1587, and Woodes Rogers the *Encarnación* in 1709, the king lost his "fifth," and hundreds of Spanish and Creole merchants were ruined.

Cortés, Father Salvatierra, and many others had attempted to conquer the South. All had been defeated by thirst, hunger, and the fierce, roving tribes of Guaycura and Pericú—until the Jesuits' *nueva entrada en el Sur,* new incursion into the South: more glory among the heathens, the wild men in feathers. By 1733 the Devil was no longer on his throne, as one Jesuit put it. Four missions had been established in the South. And so, the following year, the Manila Galleon put in at San José del Cabo.

Relief at last, it seemed. For more than a century the Manila Galleons had heaved over the smashing open ocean or drifted in the doldrums, sails slack under a blistering tropical sun, for as many as eight months without touching land. Dozens were lost at sea; on those that reached New Spain the ranks had thinned, the victims of beriberi, scurvy, plague, and thirst wrapped in shrouds and slid into the sea. The first sight of America was usually the coast of peninsular California. And now they could drop anchor here, safe from pirates and Indians. Thus it was with enormous satisfaction that the viceroy sent orders to the Philippines that the next year's Manila Galleon should put in again at San José del Cabo.

Yet trouble was bubbling in the South. A careful reading of Jesuit journals and letters reveals, for example, an Indian flogged; an "old heathen and a great wizard" hanged from a tree; an Indian shot, his head cut off and displayed on a stake. But it was the missionaries' campaign against polygamy that most enraged the Indians in the South. Those who would not give up their women were publicly humiliated and whipped. And with this, wrote Father Sigismundo Taraval in his journal of the Rebellion of 1734–1737, "the Devil began to scatter the germs of an uprising." Within a matter of months all four missions had been sacked. At Mission Santiago the father was shot full of arrows and clubbed to death by a mob; at San José del Cabo the missionary's head was hacked off with knives and his body thrown on a bonfire. From Todos Santos, Father Taraval fled north with his soldiers and loyal neophytes; the twenty-seven neophytes who'd stayed behind were all butchered. And then, "as though instigated by the demon," the rebels torched the church, mutilated the communion tables, and snapped the cross to splinters.

Three months later the Manila Galleon sighted the cape. Land: it was an oppression lifted, like springtime after ten winters. Slowly, as the peaks of the Sierra de la Laguna emerged over the horizon, those who could gathered on deck to sing *Te Deums*. The captain dropped anchor off San José del Cabo and sent out a longboat of sailors to look for the missionary. When the thirteen walked inland, they were met by a phalanx of Pericú in war paint and slaughtered in a hail of arrows.

Four missions destroyed, two priests killed: for the Spanish authorities, this was nothing compared to an attack on the Manila Galleon. When the news reached the viceroy in Mexico City, he convened an inquiry. The Jesuits blamed the viceroy for not dispensing the funds that would have supported an adequate number of soldiers; the viceroy retaliated by dispatching the military governor of Sinaloa and Sonora. This was a bitter blow. In Sonora, the Jesuits knew the governor as a philistine who would deliver their neophytes to the miners and ranchers. For his part, the governor viewed the Jesuits as arrogant obstructionists. In California, the governor would answer to the viceroy, not the priests. In short, at the stroke of the viceroy's pen, the Jesuit theocracy, at least in the South, had ended.

In short order, rebellious Indians were chased down, their ringleaders executed or exiled or flogged. Some were repentant, but others were defiant, like the prisoner who shouted: "When are they going to kill us? What are they waiting for?" Some simply despaired, like the Guaycura whose last words were that "he had always been and was still a bad man, that he was tired of living, wished to die, and that they might as well kill him."

The soldiers raped some of the women. Epidemics of measles and smallpox and typhoid soon reduced the thousands of Indians in the South to a few hundred, and of those, many were scabbed and fevered with syphilis. Long after the governor returned to the mainland, uprisings continued like sparks from a waning fire: as far north as Mission Comondú a *guama* shot an arrow at the missionary; shortly afterward, a gang of Pericú killed a mission herdsman by smashing his head with a rock; briefly, the roads between the southern missions were cut off. A band of Guaycura roamed the sierras, harassing the missions until 1748, when the presidio captain executed the adults and dispersed their twenty children among the missions to the north.

By that time, so few Indians were left in the South that the Jesuits closed Mission La Paz and converted Mission San José del Cabo to a mere visiting chapel. Like piles of chips pushed across a gaming board, the Pericú at Todos Santos were marched to Mission Santiago, while La Paz's remaining Guaycura were relocated to Todos Santos. Children were held inside the walls so that their parents would not attempt to return to their homelands.

As the Indians were dying off in the South, miners and pearlers and cattle ranchers moved in, and with them, everything the Jesuit fathers had struggled to avoid. The first was an ex-presidio soldier named Manuel de Ocio, who began trading pearls in 1741. Within a few years, he'd purchased fourteen houses in the city of Guadalajara, married into one of its most distinguished Creole families, and begun mining silver in the sierra south of La Paz with a raggle-taggle crew of Spaniards, mestizos, and Yaqui Indians from the mainland. For the Jesuit fathers, Ocio's mining camp was a cancer, spreading drunkenness, whoring, gambling, and blasphemy like the tentacles of a metastasis, even as it sucked at the resources of the missions. At his own expense, the missionary at Santiago would ride out to minister to the miners, those "dregs of humanity" as the Jesuit historian Clavigero called them. Sometimes, miners would appear at the missions begging for food. All the while, Ocio was building a herd of mules and cattle that would eventually amount to sixteen thousand head, inexorably encroaching on the missions' grazing lands and watering holes.

The Jesuits made claims to the viceroy, Ocio counterclaims and claims. Neither party was satisfied with the rulings. In June 1766, Ocio was in a wrangle with Mission Todos Santos over grazing rights. He argued his case before the Jesuit presidio captain and lost. Not long afterward, a letter arrived in Madrid addressed to the king that charged the California Jesuits with working secret mines, enslaving the Indians, and feeding them only corn, while keeping them in ignorance of the fact that they were subjects not of the priests, but of the king. "It is difficult to imagine," concludes the historian Harry Crosby in his meticulously researched *Antigua California,* "that these charges did not originate with Manuel de Ocio."

Certainly, the allegations were read with interest in Madrid and Mexico City. Besides the Jesuits, who'd made every effort to keep out anyone but themselves, who knew the truth about California, the legendary land of gold and pearls? As Crosby points out, no central government official had ever visited the peninsula.

It was a land as remote as a fairy tale, but that was about to change.

El Arco: Fine Kings

THE SHADOWS were lengthening, the eastern sierra tinged with rose. Alice and I were still barreling north on the Transpeninsular Highway through the Vizcaíno Desert. We'd rolled our windows down to let the air blow into the jeep; the plastic grocery bags on the backseat—our leftover water and food—crinkled and flapped. We had entered a forest of datilillo and cacti, scraggly, sour pitahaya, barrel, cholla, cardón, agave. The earth here was red with iron, almost powdery and mixed with pebbles. Somewhere deep in the mountains to the east lay the ruins of Mission Santa Gertrudis, the fifteenth and third-to-last mission of the conquest, founded by Father Georg Retz in 1751. A native of Düsseldorf, Father Retz remained here in these sierras, Santa Gertrudis's only missionary, until the expulsion seventeen years later. It must have been a hard seventeen years. He had to store his wine in hollowed-out stones. To bring water to his meager gardens, he had to carve a three kilometer–long aqueduct from solid rock.

The Transpeninsular angled northwest, toward Guerrero Negro on the Pacific Coast. We had just enough time, if we were to make Guerrero Negro by nightfall, to go halfway to Mission Santa Gertrudis, to the old mining town of El Arco. We turned off the highway and aimed east, bucking over the dips and rises of a dirt road.

For a good forty minutes, we saw no one and nothing but cacti.

"Now then!" wrote the Jesuit missionary Father Baegert. "Those who have ears, listen! What is California? Nothing but innumerable stones and these you will find in all directions. It is a pile of stones full of thorns . . . or to quote the scripture, a pathless, waterless thornful rock, sticking up between two oceans."

But had not Father Piccolo's famous *Informe* mentioned "plenty of water," "beautiful meadows," and "fine pastures throughout the year"? Had he not boasted of "many pearl fisheries" and the "promise of many minerals"? And had not this ex-soldier Manuel de Ocio become a rich man harvesting pearls and mining silver?

Already, in 1759, the Jesuits had been expelled from Portugal and its dominions. They had controlled too much Indian labor, their plantations were too grand, their monies too great. They'd even had the temerity to raise an army of Guaraní and use it to fight on the side of the Spanish over the Brazilian border. The Jesuits were "traitors," declared the document of that expulsion, "rebels and enemies." The French did not want them either. In 1766, after a series of intrigues that involved credits to Jesuit-run coffee and sugar plantations on Martinique, troubles with the Jansenist Paris Parlement, the duc de Choiseul and madame de Pompadour, King Louis XV dissolved the Jesuit order on French soil. Applauding on the sidelines were the Jesuits' rivals at the Vatican, as well as Protestants and philosophes. "Now that we have broken up the Jesuits," gloated Voltaire, "it should be no great matter to be rid of the Pope as well."

Protestants and philosophes held little sway in Catholic Spain. As the English said, "a Spaniard without his Jesuit is like beef without mustard." On the other hand, as the Spanish saying went, "Hang a Jesuit and he'll make off with the rope."

That old exaggerator Father Piccolo told the truth on one count, however: there *were* many minerals in Baja California—silver in the south around El Triunfo, copper at Santa Rosalía, gold here in these mountains around El Arco. Dotted throughout the northern half of the peninsula and the islands were more silver mines, more copper and gold, salt, iron, onyx, sulphur, even guano and gypsum mines. But with the exception of Ocio's crude silver mines in the South, none were worked during the Jesuit period.

Yet who would believe that in Mexico City and Madrid? Unlike the mendicant Dominicans and Franciscans, the Jesuits were a worldly order. A priest might make a career as a missionary, or at court as a confessor to kings; he might be an astronomer, a cattle rancher or a banker. Why not a miner? No one knew the exact amount of the Jesuit order's wealth, but anyone could see their schools, their splendid seminaries, so many churches and chapels aglitter with gold. In their dedication to "helping souls" and defending papal supremacy, the Jesuits curried favor with the nobility and managed well their endowments. They managed haciendas producing hides, wool, meat, and cheese, as well as cacao, coffee, hemp, maté, and sugar plantations, many of them worked by Indians, others by branded African slaves. They even operated an international banking network, trading in foreign currency and bills of exchange. The Jesuits, as the gossips would have it, were as cunning as foxes. Sophie and Michael Coe relate in their *True History of Chocolate* that one year the Spanish flotilla arrived from the Indies with eight crates marked "Chocolate for the Very Reverend Father General of the Company of Jesus." When the strangely heavy cargo was inspected at Cádiz, it was found to be bars of solid gold, each painted with a thin crust of chocolate.

And now, in 1766, here was the ex-presidio soldier Ocio's letter about Jesuit California, its secret mines, Indian slaves fed only corn, and the arrogance of the priests, who fancied themselves kings.

"Fine kings!" answered Father Baegert, years later, from exile in the Rhenish Palatinate.

In truth, kings who, as someone said, drank with their horses, ate corn with the chickens, and slept at night with the dogs on the bare soil! Great honor indeed! Honor such as one could seek among the Indians of California or expect from them! . . . As for the Catholic King, what could the missionaries say to the natives about him? Should they preach about the number of his subjects and soldiers, his revenues, his court, palaces, summer residences, and the like? How could a priest speak of these things to a people hardly able to count to six, without knowledge of silver and gold—a people more appreciative of a knife and a pound of meat than a hundred pounds of gold; a people that believed the Jesuits, like the cowhands and soldiers, had come to California for their support, and that, aside from them, there was no one on earth except such cowhands and soldiers?

Indeed, the Jesuit missions in Baja California were pitifully poor. The peninsula's mining boom—boomlets, rather—began nearly a century after the Jesuits' expulsion, as a minor sequel to the gold rush in Upper California. Most of the miners were Americans, although many Mexicans from the mainland came to try their luck, as well as Frenchmen and Germans. The first bonanza was in copper, the richest mines around Santa Rosalía. Gold was discovered in the Calmallí gold fields—which included El Arco—in the 1880s. Hundreds descended on these remote desert placers, some as employees of an American-owned mining company, others as independent prospectors digging in the nearby ravines. Among them was a woman, "a pretty young *Americana,*" as the story was told to the journalist Arthur North,

> traveling alone, her outfit packed on a gray mule, her garb the regulation miner's red shirt, overalls, felt sombrero and heavy boots, her ready six-shooter strapped to her belt. Around her claim the mercurial Mexicans flocked at once, intent on fond demonstrations. But the fair prospector had views of her own.
>
> "I come from Tombstone," she asserted, in perfect Spanish, "Tombstone, Arizona, where three times a day the Coroner makes his regular rounds, and I have always done my modest share in furnishing him with employment. You must understand I do not want any Greasers making love to me." And with this she nodded in a most cordial manner, swinging forward the holster of her formidable revolver. "I do hope, caballeros," she concluded, smilingly, "that there will be no misunderstanding of my views."

The gold may be gone now, but the stories remain—or pieces of them, like this gem-bright cameo. One, above all, is elaborately detailed, told and retold like a ghost story at a children's summer camp, The Legend of the Jesuit Treasure: pearls, gold doubloons, silver chalices and candlesticks, mortared into the adobe walls of a lost mission . . .

The road passed a microwave tower, curved, and then took us straight into El Arco, a ramshackle settlement that sprawled over the bald pate of a hill. At the near end stood a derelict wooden church, a beige box with a steeple, one of its windows clapping in the wind. Other than that, the nineteenth-century mining town was a huddle of shacks cobbled together with tar paper, corrugated iron, cardboard, and adobe. There were no people that we could see, although a rusted pickup was parked in front of one house.

A dog wandered across the bare earth of what might once have been a plaza of sorts. The dog walked slowly, its head low and tail between its legs. The breeze ruffled its fur.

We turned around and left for Guerrero Negro.

Guerrero Negro: Arriba y Adelante México

FOG HAD ROLLED IN over Guerrero Negro, snuffing out the stars. The wind was blowing in from the ocean, clammy and chill. The Jesuits never settled here; Guerrero Negro was a new town, founded by an American salt company in the 1950s. I would be back for a longer stay later. For now, Alice and I lugged our bags into the Hotel La Pinta on the highway. We showered, ate dinner, and collapsed.

The morning dawned clear, the sky so bright it looked brittle. Directly in front of our hotel, on an island in the center of the highway, was the Twenty-eighth Parallel Monument, a 140-foot-tall steel abstract sculpture. Supposedly this was an eagle, Mexico's national emblem, but it looked more like a cross between a construction crane and some odd lengths of railroad track. It was surrounded by a city block–size ring of sandbags, chain-link fencing, and low cement walls. Inside—we saw as we drove around the island—were army offices. An osprey's nest sat undisturbed on the top of a traffic sign.

We drove around the circle once more. Unveiled on December 1, 1973, by President Echeverría as part of the ceremony to inaugurate the Transpeninsular Highway, the Twenty-eighth Parallel Monument marked the boundary between the peninsula's two states, Baja California Sur and Baja California (Norte). I remembered what Don Fernando Cota had told me back in San José del Cabo, that he'd figured Echeverría's campaign promises were the usual demagoguery. "¡Pero híjole! But goodness! *Punto y seguido,* Right away, they built the highway."

And it wasn't bad. I'd driven more than six hundred miles of it by now. True, the lanes were narrow and occasionally potholed, and unfenced cattle grazing at the shoulder posed a hazard. But any passenger sedan could have traversed it; many did, along with trucks and buses, RVs and jeeps and motorcycles and vans.

Erle Stanley Gardner's *Off the Beaten Track in Baja* has a photograph of a character who called himself Outdoor Franklin, a scarecrow-thin American in a Panama hat and World War I–issue riding boots. In the mid-1920s, as a publicity stunt for an automobile dealer, Outdoor Franklin drove from the California border down to Cataviña in the Central Desert. It must have been a herculean task. One photo from the expedition shows his team armed with crowbars, levering the battered Model T from a ditch. Another is simply titled "Marooned among Rocks." Outdoor Franklin's was the first automobile the people at Cataviña had ever seen. When "Uncle Erle" came through in the late 1940s, dirt roads had been carved out all the way to Cabo San Lucas, but most were passable only in high-clearance vehicles. The road that zigzagged along the cliff edges of Bahía Concepción had a point so narrow and a drop so steep, it was marked with a skull and crossbones. *La Punta de la Pintura de Muerte,* it was called, the Point of the Picture of Death.

With the Transpeninsular Highway, Echeverría changed everything. And so, this monument marked a boundary at the twenty-eighth parallel not only in space, but also in time: the year 1973, Before and After.

Arriba y Adelante México, Upward and Onward Mexico, was President Echeverría's slogan. He was a ruthless spender—a road here, a clinic there, schools, airports, why not some hotels? Here, have a steel factory. By the time he left office in 1976, the peso—steady for twenty-two years—had devalued by 80 percent, and Mexico owed its foreign creditors more than twenty billion dollars. The average worker's purchasing power was half what it had been before he took office, while Echeverría, a career bureaucrat who had styled himself leader of the Third World, retired to an ambassadorship in Paris.

In the Boojum Forest

NORTH OF GUERRERO NEGRO we'd passed through the checkpoint (no fruits or vegetables, no guns or drugs) and had been speeding north, over smooth asphalt. Like that intrepid Outdoor Franklin, we too were headed to Cataviña. From Cataviña, still following the story of the Jesuits, we planned to visit Santa María Cabujakaamung, the last of the Jesuit missions.

"A boojum!" Alice cried. Suddenly, we were in a forest of the things, the strangest plants we'd ever seen. They were as tall as any tree, thin as pencils, or very skinny candles, and tapered at their tips. Some of them were topped with a puff of golden flowers, like the crown of a heron. Every one was unique: some had two tips, some had three, or six; some curled and dipped, like strings of spaghetti. They made me want to laugh out loud.

"'For the Snark *was* a Boojum, you see.'"

What?

"Lewis Carroll," Alice said.

The Mexicans called these *cirios,* wax candles. But we agreed: *boojum* was better.

Wind buffeted our jeep, sudden gusts that might have swerved a smaller car. It roared by, it whispered, it whistled. Yet on the plain of the desert, nothing moved. The cardón, the cholla, the datilillo, the forest of slender boojums remained still, like a world under glass.

What beautiful country this was: the mountains in the east as stark as the tundra, the sky a flawless, silken blue. But beauty, of course, is in the eye of the beholder. As he walked through this, shoes worn to shreds, tongue swollen thick from thirst, forty-niner William C. S. Smith kept a diary. Every other entry mentions a horse that lay down to die. "Rocks, thorns," he lamented, "and this horrid cactus! The devil's own plant."

In this desert it did not rain for seven years. "This should give an idea," wrote Father Wenceslaus Linck, "how unproductive and unpleasant the region is." In this wilderness north of San Ignacio, the missions were fewer and spaced farther apart. First Mission Santa Gertrudis, in the sierra east of El Arco; then Mission San Francisco de Borja. From there, Linck made four expeditions, exploring as far north as the Colorado River country. The only site he found that was suitable for a mission was a tiny oasis the Cochimí called Velicatá, 150 brutally hard miles north. That was too far. Another mission was needed as a way station. The best candidate was a spittle of a stream named Calamajué, its water so bitter with copperas that it was undrinkable. Two priests, Juan José Díez and Victoriano Arnés, arrived at Calamajué with ten soldiers and a troop of neophytes in 1766. They sowed a small field of wheat, but it turned white from the copperas and was ruined. Then Father Díez fell ill, leaving Father Arnés alone.

On the straight black ribbon of empty highway, I'd floored the accelerator. Now the road rose gently and onto a higher plane, skirting the edge of an immense, dry lake bed—Laguna Chapala, named after the lake near Guadalajara. ("Well," reported Father Linck in the diary of his 1766 expedition, "our Lake Chapala had no water.") A fringe of pickleweed lined the roadbed. Otherwise, the landscape was nothing but brown, gray, bone-dried mud and the rock of the sierra in the east. Deep, deep in those sierras trickled the miserable, little copperas-tainted stream of Calamajué.

The road signs, we'd begun to notice, were peppered with bullet holes. Some sharpshooter had blasted an asterisk into one. We were in boojum forest again, the slender stalks sticking up from fields of boulders. Near here forty-niner Smith noted, "One mule made a dead set—would go no further. We shot her to save her a lingering death." This was the driest of the deserts on the desert peninsula. Only recently, a tourist from Los Angeles, stranded on a dirt road by the coast, had tried to walk for help; his mummified body was found weeks later, curled beneath a cactus.

As for Father Arnés, alone at the sizzlingly hot and nearly water-less Calamajué, he was desperate to relocate his mission. His neo-phytes told him about a stream to the north called Cabujakaamung. The stream had little water, but it was sweet. This would be the site of the Jesuits' last mission, Santa María Cabujakaamung. In May 1767, Arnés arrived and began to evangelize some three hundred Indians. He and his soldiers and neophytes built an adobe church and a house, "wretched cabins," according to the Jesuit historian Clavigero, "covered with palm leaves." Then, on the barest patch of arable land, they planted a crop of wheat and another of cotton.

I'd seen photographs of Santa María Cabujakaamung. It was noth-ing more than a few humps of melted adobe on a sandy rise, pink stone-strewn mountains in the background, a line of palm trees, and that huge, ever blue sky. From Rancho Santa Inés just outside of Cataviña, it was a hard drive over a very bad road. Like Missions Santa Getrudis, San Francisco de Borja, and Calamajué, the highway bypassed Mission Santa María Cabujakaamung by many miles. No one lives there. No one has lived there for nearly two hundred years.

Santa María Cabujakaamung: that beautiful name, its sound like bells in the wind. Its remoteness intrigued me; also, that it was the last Jesuit mission. I knew that Arthur North camped there with his mules and his Mexican *mozos,* and for six delicious days he hunted bighorn sheep, sipped wild honey, read Balzac, and scribbled in his diary. Erle Stanley Gardner helicoptered in. I had arranged for a guide with a truck through the Hotel La Pinta in Cataviña.

We were almost there. One last stop, though: the "golden spike" at San Ignacito where the Transpeninsular Highway crews working from the north met those from the south. It was not a spike, but a stained and peeling cement block embedded with a brass plaque.

Beneath the plaque—dated 1973—was a bullet hole.

Cataviña: Maybe

THE HOTEL LA PINTA in Cataviña did not have a telephone. Like the Californios up in the sierras, the people here relied on radios. Therefore, I had called the La Pinta in Ensenada, and they relayed my reservation for both a room and a guide who would drive us to Mission Santa María Cabujakaamung. The La Pintas were a chain, originally called the Presidentes, built in the 1970s as part of President Echeverría's grand gesture for the peninsula's development.

Our room was ready. The receptionist flashed a smile as she pushed our key across the counter.

And our guide?

"Oh, yes," she said vaguely. "We got the message. But the person who was going to go can't go. He was going to send someone, I think—" she looked at the ceiling as if she were trying to remember. "But maybe that person has to work tomorrow."

And might it be possible to find someone else?

"Yes," she said. "Maybe. I'll send a message to your room. Maybe by nine."

I was optimistic. All the "maybes" were a bad sign, but in my experience, those willing to pay well could invariably find a guide, even on short notice. My experience in that regard was limited to city hotels, however; Cataviña was basically the hotel, a gas station, and a trailer park. Blink and you'd miss it.

On the other hand, the La Pinta was not what one might expect. It was clean, modern, and airy, a sort of Holiday Inn à la *mexicana*. There was a large courtyard with a sparkling pool and clay pots of well-tended bougainvillea. There was a game room with a pool table and Ping-Pong. In our room—spacious, freshly painted—we even had satellite TV.

We ate dinner in the restaurant. Then, at nine, not having received a message, I went back to the front desk, where I found a different receptionist, a man in a navy blazer and a tie. He had slicked-back hair the color of shoe polish, and he smelled strongly of lime-scented shaving lotion.

No, there was no message for us.

And the woman who'd been here earlier?

"Ah," he said. She'd left for the day. And how did I learn to speak such good Spanish? How long had I lived in Mexico City? He was from Oaxaca.

I explained that my sister and I wanted a guide for the next day.

"Hmmm," he said. Maybe there was someone who might know someone. "I think that maybe he's at a birthday party at the trailer park."

One of the waiters from the restaurant had come up to the counter for change. The receptionist began to count out a pile of coins for him, peso by peso, *plink, plonk.*

I was concerned, I said. It was already nine, and we wanted to leave for the mission early in the morning. I explained that I'd called ahead, that we really wanted to go.

The waiter admired my Spanish, too. His name was Fidencio, he said with a blinding smile. He was from the Estado de México, from a village near Mexico City. His coins were stacked on the counter now, neat as a little tower.

"*Ay,* Fidencio," the receptionist said. "Why don't *you* take them to the mission?"

"Sure! I've always wanted to go there."

That was not what I had in mind, I said. I wanted a guide who knew the territory.

"*Bueno,*" Okay. Fidencio shrugged. He stuffed the change in his pocket and sauntered back to the restaurant.

"Well," the receptionist said. His voice had a hollow ring. He played with his tie, flipped it up and down.

In an hour—maybe—he would let me know.

Alice and I waited in our room, watching *Sopa de Videos,* Video Soup, an unabashed rip-off of *America's Favorite Home Videos.* From Chihuahua someone had sent a video of a man doing pushups as his pet cockatoo nodded in unison. From Puebla, a clip from a wedding video, a couple about to cut their three-tiered cake when a guest ran up from behind and shoved their faces into it. The groom turned around and started punching, while the bride simply stood there, stunned, her face bearded with white goo. The one we liked was of a dalmatian swinging a cherry-red hula hoop with its neck. And this was the winner, squealed the buxom blonde announcer, seven thousand pesos in national savings bonds, to Gabriela Ramírez of Mexico City!

At ten sharp, to our immense surprise, came a knock on the door. It was the waiter Fidencio. "No problem!" He had a friend in the trailer park who had a jeep, and we could all go for 150 U.S. dollars. But: only if we left after nine o'clock and returned before six, because he, Fidencio, had to be back at work at the restaurant.

Two Ruins

I HAD A better idea about how Alice and I might get to Mission Santa María Cabujakaamung. I realized now it was what we should have done in the first place. At dawn, we checked out of the La Pinta and drove down the highway to Rancho Santa Inés.

We'd want mules, the ranch hand said. That's how bad the road was. They'd find some for us. We could stay in the bunkhouse and leave with our guide at sunup the next morning.

So we had the day for other ruins.

Only a ways north on the Transpeninsular, then a short drive west down a dirt road, we came to the ruins of Mission San Fernando Velicatá. This was the watered site that would have been the next Jesuit mission after Santa María Cabujakaamung had the Jesuits not been expelled. Mission San Fernando Velicatá was Franciscan, founded by Father Junípero Serra on his way north to establish the missions of Alta (Upper) California. Having seen the peninsula's poverty, Serra was glad to be rid of it; in 1772, Baja California was given to the unwitting Dominicans.

The morning was yet cool when we arrived, the air still. We could smell the water, coldly burbling over stone and grassy weeds. The ruin of Mission San Fernando Velicatá was funny looking, two skinny hunks of adobe wall sticking up from a mound like a pair of Brobdingnagian teeth. There was a ranch here—a corral and a shed. The ground was littered with beer bottles, rusted soup cans, bald truck tires. Someone had fastened a basketball hoop to the top of a weathered cardón skeleton. There were no animals. We called out. No one answered.

Closer to Cataviña we found the onyx quarry at El Mármol. Once known as Brown's Camp, after the resident Southwest Onyx and Marble Company manager, El Mármol was compared by one transpeninsular traveler to Khartoum on the journey between Cairo and Cape Town. No self-respecting American would pass by without shaking Mr. Brown's hand. He appears in one of Erle Stanley Gardner's books, a middle-aged man in wire-frame glasses, his clean-shaven face as hard-boiled as a New England parson's. In its art-deco heyday, El Mármol's onyx was shipped to San Diego by the ton, where it was fashioned into bathroom fixtures, desk sets, tabletops and doorknobs, floor tiles and wall panels. Movie actress Theda Bara ordered a bathtub carved from a solid block of it, outfitted with gold faucets. But after World War II, with the flood of cheap plastic sub-stitutes, it became less profitable to work such a remote quarry. Brown's Camp was abandoned in 1958.

Only one building was still standing: a schoolhouse made of rough-cut, dull beige onyx blocks. It was a stout little thing with massive buttresses, alone on a field of dirt and rubble. One wall had been bashed down; it had no roof. The sun was directly overhead now. The only sounds were our footsteps on the gravel, our own breathing.

"Look at this," Alice said as she splashed a handful of water from her canteen onto the schoolhouse wall. It glistened as if it had been polished, striped with pearl, amber, bubblegum pink, and blushy lip-stick red.

Up on a hill we found some cement foundations filled in with pickleweed. Perhaps this had been the site of Mr. Brown's house. Perhaps not. We paced it, imagining where the living room would have been, the bedrooms. Then we hiked up another hill, which was covered with quarried onyx, slabs the size of armchairs and sofas.

Steel cables rusted with age lay coiled like snakes on the dirt. As we hiked, stepping over chunks of rusted machinery, insects hummed and clicked. A lizard darted into a clump of pickleweed.

From the crest was a view like a dreamscape: the plain of the Central Desert, parched and red as Mars. Rimming the horizon, far in the distance, were the lavender-blue peaks of San Pedro, San Pablo, and San Miguel.

The wind had begun to blow, hot and full of grit.

Just and Inescapable Reasons

"MY LABOR has borne little fruit," lamented the Jesuit Father Baegert of his seventeen years on the peninsula. In 1767, seventy years after Salvatierra landed at Loreto, Baegert's fellow missionaries—now fifteen in all—might have said the same. Always, there was the rock-embedded soil and the lack of water—if not the sudden raging torrents of it. In the previous four years, locusts had ravaged most of the missions' scanty crops. For lack of forage, as well as poaching by Indians, their herds of cattle and goats had shrunk by half. The ex-soldier-cum-miner Manuel de Ocio and his ilk were a constant irritation, setting bad examples for the neophytes, exploiting the mission lands, challenging the authority of the fathers. And the Indians, as ever, were dying. In the South there were but two hundred now, almost all of them sick with syphilis. Epidemics had begun spreading north; in that final year, Father Linck's Mission San Francisco de Borja was under siege with smallpox and typhus.

As for those Indians who remained—the object of this great enterprise to "save souls"—they were, wrote Father Baegert in his *Observations*, "stupid, awkward, rude, unclean, insolent, ungrateful, mendacious, thievish, abominably lazy . . ." To get any work done, "nothing is accomplished unless one drives the natives on every turn. During such periods there are sick Indians every day until the week is passed and it is Sunday, the day of miracles, I called it because all those who had been sick the whole week were unfailingly well on that day."

Pilfering and poaching were an ongoing problem. As Baegert wrote to his brother,

> they stole the unripened figs from some trees which I have here; they forced me to tear out all melon plants with still unripened fruit; they took one hundred fifty pounds of sugar; dug out newly planted sugar cane; reduced four hundred goats and sheep to such a small number that I had to give the remaining ones into the care of my neighbor. Partly my own Indians, partly those of the neighboring mission, killed over four hundred horses and cattle.

It was a problem, in his view, without solution:

> How should such thievery be punished? For example, as usual with rope and stick? But what happens when the Indian is free after six or eight months, six or eight weeks? He does it as before. And when they shot nine such thieves and robbers in one day at the neighboring mission eight years ago, this punishment made so little impression that they killed that night the mule of the missionary who was called to a sick man to hear his confession and he had to go back to his mission on foot. Aren't they quite a people?

The Indians were equally exasperating when it came to mass, confession, and prayer: "they have to be forced," Baegert told his brother, "with threats or even with thrashing." As another missionary conceded, the faith moved forward "with very slow steps on feet of lead."

Communication remained challenging. For all their experiments with reviving drowned flies, the priests never did learn the word for *resurrection,* at least not in the Guaycura language. That was because, according to Father Baegert, it did not exist. Neither did the Guaycura have words to express whatever is not material and not perceptible by the senses. . . . They possess only four words for denoting all the different colors. . . . They have no names for the separate parts of the human body, no terms like "father," "mother," "son," "brother." . . . They lack the comparatives and superlatives, the words "more" and "less," and nearly all adverbs. . . . They have no conjunctive, imperative, and almost no optative mood. . . . They know nothing of metaphors. . . . [And none of] the following words: holy, church, God, Ghost, communion, grace, will, cross, virgin, name, hell, kingdom, bread, guilt, temptation, creator, indulgence, or forgiveness . . .

Christ on the cross is a disturbing image, its meaning, like that of the Virgin Birth or the Holy Ghost, complex. When the Indians were first shown a crucifix, they asked one another, Why do they show this to us? Was this an enemy they killed?

Most of the literature blithely assumes that the priests made Christians of the Indians. But how much of the Gospels could the Jesuits have conveyed in the languages of hunter-gatherers? Translation, as every translator knows, is not always possible.

Yet the Jesuits' efforts were prodigious. Several of them compiled grammars of the various California languages and dialects, tomes that had taken them years of painstaking study—all of which were confiscated and lost in the expulsion. During his exile in Bologna, Miguel del Barco, the missionary at San Javier de Biaundó, recorded what he could remember in a manuscript that lay forgotten for more than two centuries. A decade after the expulsion, Franz Benno Ducrue, a Bavarian who had spent fifteen years in the missions, jotted down what he could recall of the Cochimí language: the numbers one through five, and twenty-six phrases, all of them short and crude. Here are the first few:

Diosjua ibiñi, God does not die
Tamma amayben metañ aguinañi, Man does not live many years
Uamibutel guiwuctujua nangassang, This man loves his wife

Wakoebutel wakameta, This woman was pregnant
Whanu wamijua wangata, [She] gave birth to an infant son
Uybetel luhu, [He or she] is still sick
Wahanu awiangga, The baby is crying

The Indians must have had their theories about the missionaries. At first, like the Aztecs and the Mayans, they may have believed the white men were gods, or, like the Indians Cabeza de Vaca encountered in his wanderings through the North, that they came from the sky. Like all precontact peoples, the California Indians had no concept of a human world beyond their own. Nazareth, Jerusalem, and Rome must have been places as unfathomable to the Californians as Madrid, where their Catholic king, the Bourbon Carlos III, reigned from the splendor of his Palacio Real.

"But that is enough now about these Indians," wrote Baegert to his brother. "Let us pray for them so that all are beatified."

Pray they did.

A few letters survive from the missionaries to their families. "My beloved father and dear relatives," wrote Lambert Hostell, "you will be so good as to remember me in your prayers in order that I be a capable instrument in promoting the glory of God and effect the salvation of the Christian and pagan California Indians. This is and this will ever be until I die, my one desire." Wrote Franz Inama, "[M]y dearest sister, implore the grace of God that I also live the life of this apostle and walk in his footsteps."

When I read these words I hear them in my mind like whispers.

In answer to the charges that they ran secret silver mines and so on, the Jesuits called the bluff. In a letter to the viceroy, they offered to renounce their two remaining missions in the South, Santiago and Todos Santos. Further, the Father Provincial offered to renounce all of the Jesuits' Mexican missions, including those in peninsular California. These offers were under consideration even as Father Arnés was erecting his "wretched cabins" and sowing the first crops in the rocky soil at Santa María Cabujakaamung. But they were soon made irrelevant, because King Carlos III's Order of Expulsion had arrived in Mexico City. The sealed envelopes that read "not to be opened before April 2, 1767 on pain of death" had been opened. The order, which covered Spain and all of its colonies, was for troops to surround the Jesuit colleges and residences in the night, arrest the priests, and jail them until they could be shipped out. All Jesuit assets—monies, churches, seminaries, libraries, haciendas, furnishings, even the personal effects of the priests—were to be seized. The king's order was explicit: "If a single Jesuit, even though sick or dying, is still found in the area under your command after the embarkation, prepare yourself to face summary execution."

In Mexico the arrests were made on the night of June 25. At four in the morning, the Jesuits were assembled in their dining rooms or chapels, and read the Order of Expulsion. There was no explanation, other than a vague allusion to "just and inescapable reasons," which the king would keep "locked in the depths of my royal soul." Without a chance to return to their rooms, the priests were shackled and herded into jails with shoves and insults. The fifty missionaries of the northwest missions in Sonora, Sinaloa, and Pimería fared the worst, forced to march to port through swamps and jungle in a pouring rain. Within a few days, twenty of them died. In the Bajío north of Mexico City and in Michoacán, Indians and mestizos rioted. The king's visitor general José de Gálvez arrived with six hundred Spanish soldiers, who hanged eighty-five men, flogged seventy, and jailed more than six hundred. Many of the dissidents were marched away, their skin hanging in bloody strips from the floggings, to work as slave labor. "Vassals of the throne of Spain," ranted Visitor General Gálvez, "were born to be silent and obey—not to debate or discuss the affairs of Government."

But in far-off California, no one knew any of this. The pearl fishers did not arrive that summer of 1767. Months would pass.

Rancho Santa Inés: Fast!

AT RANCHO SANTA INÉS there were no mules for our trip to Mission Santa María Cabujakaamung. The ranch hands had looked, but the mules had wandered through the desert too far in search of forage. Literally, they could not find them.

Nearing sundown, Alice and I sat at a picnic table under a thatched awning while the cook made scrambled eggs with *machaca* (shredded dried beef) for our supper. A pot of beans bubbled on the stove. The smell of the cooking wafted out from the open kitchen. The wall by the counter was plastered with bumper stickers: I'D RATHER BE IN BAJA read one; KILL A BIKER . . . GO TO JAIL. Several were from the Baja 1000 off-road race, which used the ranch as a pit stop. Alice and I were the only guests tonight.

A small, white poodlelike mutt nuzzled our legs. Palomito was his name, the cook said. A calico cat slunk up as well, meowing loudly. And her name? *"Gato,"* she said. Cat. She broke out laughing at me, that I would ask.

A capable-looking woman with short hair graying at the roots, her name was Matilda Valdez. She sat with us at the picnic table while we ate. She'd lived here for twenty-four years, she said. No, she'd never been out to the mission. Her husband didn't like her to leave the ranch house. "He says, you're a housewife, so this is where you belong."

As we spoke, the light faded. The ranch did not have electricity; Matilda switched on a small gas lamp.

When we were finished eating, she sighed and rested her chin in her hands. "I would like to go to the United States," she said. "I like the style of life there. But I'm too old now. I wouldn't know how to live there. What would I do?"

In the morning, for breakfast, we ate eggs and *machaca* again; it was all they had. Matilda shooed away the cat, then went back into the kitchen where she lingered like a shadow, washing dishes. At eight o'clock, it was already broiling hot. And strangely quiet—there were no chickens here, no goats. I watched Palomito sniff around our jeep, lifting his leg on each tire, and I thought of all the dogs that had marked them over the past several days.

"Doggie bush mail," I said.

Alice sipped her coffee. "More like message in a bottle."

Matilda's husband was named Oscar Valdez. Trim and tough-looking, he had a pencil-thin mustache and eyes that peered out hard and slitlike from beneath a crisply molded white cowboy hat. On his belt he wore a turquoise-encrusted silver buckle.

I still had my hopes of getting to Mission Santa María Cabujakaamung. Was the road really impassable?

"Es malo," It's bad, Oscar said, *"muy malo."* It used to be better; he'd built it himself, together with his father and cousins in the sixties. But it hadn't been kept up; *chubascos* had washed out large sections. We could hike to the mission and camp overnight, he suggested.

We'd lost that time, I explained. Alice had to catch her flight from Loreto, to be back at work.

He swung a leg over the bench of the picnic table. Palomito leaped up and laid his chin on Oscar's lap. The mission was just ruins, he said, not much to see. But he had a picture in a book from the 1920s that showed the adobe walls still standing. Gently, he patted the little dog behind its ears.

A German film crew had recently come to make a movie about the mission. "They filmed what happened two hundred years ago when they sent the priests home. Then some others came and they took the Indians to Alta California. They put them all in chains. The actors wore soldiers' uniforms from then, very different from today!" He raised his eyebrows and smiled, and shook his head. "They had a book, and they were reading the history from that book, two hundred years ago! Oh, how can they know about this place and I live here!"

Oscar, I realized, was much more interesting than some old lumps of adobe.

"¡Todo rápido!" Everything goes fast now, Oscar said, fast! He wanted to tell me how things were before the Transpeninsular

Highway was built. Before, he said, a car might pass by once a week, maybe once every ten days. "You could lie down and go to sleep in the middle of the road and nothing would happen to you!" He threw back his head and laughed.

Oscar may have looked slick—the big white cowboy hat, the flashy belt buckle—but he hadn't owned a pair of shoes, he said, until he was fourteen years old. One day, a mounted salesman arrived with his burro train from the sierras, selling shoes. Oscar had a bitch he liked, so they made a trade. "She was a good dog," he said as he stroked Palomito's curly white scruff. "But I really wanted those shoes. My first shoes."

When they needed to go to Ensenada they went on burro. "It took us two or three weeks. And sometimes I would go south to Santa Rosalía. I would eat at the ranches on the way for free."

There was no doctor. "You would ask yourself, am I sick? And you'd have to say, no, I'm not sick. Because if you are, well,"—he pointed to the yard—"there's the cemetery!"

He leaned over to the sugar bowl and raised a spoonful. "My father didn't know sugar until he was sixteen," he said, letting the sugar cascade back into the bowl. "'How can this be sweet?' my father said. 'It looks like salt!' He only knew honey."

"And bullets . . ." he said. "We only had a very few," *poquitas, poquitas*. "They were very expensive, my father would keep them wrapped very carefully in a handkerchief. We had to save our bullets for deer, because that was food. If you were going to shoot a deer, you'd better aim well, kill it on the first try. You couldn't shoot coyotes or mountain lions, nothing like that." He laughed scornfully. "Not like today. Today bullets are cheap, they just go around shooting at whatever."

I mentioned the bullet hole I'd seen on the "golden spike" monument down the road at San Ignacito.

"I was on the road crew," he said proudly. He'd worked as a tractor driver for the local section. He'd been there at San Ignacito when the road crews met. "There was a big party. They gave us lots of barbecue, and trailers and trailers full of beer." The governor arrived with newspaper reporters to cover the ceremony. "There were a thousand people!" Oscar said, eyes wide. "I had never seen so many people in one place at the same time." That was in 1973.

The highway opened vistas for Oscar. Working on the road crew, he met people from other parts of Mexico. And instead of herding goats, he was able now to make a living from tourism. Every week Rancho Santa Inés had a handful of guests, not just Americans and Mexicans, but also Italians, Frenchmen, Germans, Canadians, even Japanese.

Now there were a lot of people passing through on the highway, Oscar said, all kinds of people. There had been a number of holdups, several bad accidents. Like most Baja Californians, Oscar was wary of mainland Mexicans. Some of them were good people, he allowed, but they had different customs. Many were drunks. Some of them would fight with guns and knives. "Here in Baja California," he said sternly, "we fight with our hands."

Bad roads, good people, goes the saying, good roads, bad people.

Now, strung along the highway, there was the hotel, the gas station, the trailer park. And added to all that, as of three years ago, they had TV, Televisa from Mexico City.

"Everything goes so fast!" Oscar said again. His eyes nearly disappeared in the creases of his grin. *"Fast!"*

Fast, indeed. In less than two days' drive we were back in Loreto.

Loreto: Terminus ad Quem

THE SAD STORY of the Jesuits ends this way. As Visitor General Gálvez and his soldiers were putting down the rebellions on the mainland, the appointed governor of California, Don Gaspar de Portolá, was trying to sail to Loreto. He tried in June 1767 and a second time in August. Not until mid-October was he able to cross the Sea of Cortés in a storm-tossed voyage of forty-two days. Portolá had planned to land in Loreto, surround the presidio and the mission, and arrest the Jesuits as the king had ordered, but he was blown far off course, all the way to San José del Cabo.

That sandy, cactus-studded shore. Governor Portolá and his soldiers were nervous. They'd heard that the Jesuits had armed their Indians with ten thousand rifles and kegs of gunpowder. Here was immense treasure, they were certain: for California, as Father Baegert so acidly put it, was "a land paved with silver," where "pearls could be swept up with a broom."

Portolá and his men were met by Father Ignác Tirsch. Tirsch was a Bohemian who liked to make watercolor drawings in his spare time. His painting of San José del Cabo survives: a cluster of thatched shacks, and an adobe chapel the size and shape of a shed. Tirsch offered no resistance; to their surprise, he received Portolá and his men politely and brought them to his mission at Santiago. From there Portolá reconnoitered the ex-soldier Ocio's fabled silver mines in the sierra, where he saw the crude works and the abject poverty of the mining camps.

They then proceeded to Loreto by land, a journey that gave Portolá, wrote Father Baegert, "the best opportunity (more than he liked) of observing with his own eyes on his arrival at this promised land how this beautiful and noble kingdom of California is level, shady, green, rich in water, and populous."

After ten days marching through the rocks and cacti of the nearly waterless Sierra de la Giganta, Portolá and his soldiers arrived at Loreto. And as for Loreto, wrote Baegert, "He who has seen the Muscovite realm, Poland, or Lapland will know whether there is any small village in these countries or whether there is a milking shed in Switzerland more dilapidated than Loreto and its huts."

They were—there is no other word—flabbergasted.

The father visitor of the California missions was Franz Benno Ducrue. He was not at Loreto, but Mission Guadalupe de Hausinapí in the sierra west of Mulegé. It wasn't until five days before Christmas that Ducrue received the news of the expulsion and Portolá's summons to Loreto.

His neophytes were confused and frightened. Why would their missionary leave them? How would they find clothing and food? Father Ducrue had lived among them for thirteen years. The mission system, good or bad, was all that most of them had ever known. Who would come now? They would not know them; they would not speak their language. As the Indians crowded around him, kissing his hands, Father Ducrue began to cry. When he mounted his horse some of the Indians started sobbing. Many of them followed him for miles; some followed him all the ninety miles to Loreto.

At the other missions it was the same. A curtain had been brought down: the missionary and the Indians would never see one another again. Wrote even the flinty Baegert, "I, too, was moved to tears and could not restrain myself from weeping all the way to Loreto. Even now, while I am writing this, tears enter my eyes."

From all over the peninsula the missionaries began to arrive at Loreto: from the South, Ignác Tirsch and Johann Bischoff; from Dolores, Lambert Hostell; from San Luis Gonazaga, Johann Jakob Baegert; José Juan Díez from La Purísima, Franz Inama von Sternegg from San José de Comondú, Miguel del Barco from San Javier. Francisco Escalante came from Santa Rosalía de Mulegé, José Rothea from San Ignacio, and Victoriano Arnés from Santa María Cabujakaamung, leaving still green his first crops of wheat and cotton. At Mission Santa Gertrudis, Georg Retz had broken his leg and could neither walk nor ride; his neophytes carried him on a litter the nearly two hundred miles through the canyons of the Sierra de San Francisco, the Vizcaíno Desert, and the Sierra de Guadalupe. Wenceslaus Linck arrived last, because he was delayed tending to the dying in an epidemic at his Mission San Francisco de Borja. When the missionaries reached Loreto, Governor Portolá embraced each of them, and, as was the Spanish custom, he kissed their hands.

Portolá had read the Order of Expulsion and taken possession of the Jesuits' treasury and storehouse: a meager supply of gold and silver coins, a few bolts of cloth, tools for the soldiers and other *gente de razón,* and some dried meat and grain. No one was arrested.

The Jesuits were to sail on February 3, 1768. Their ship, the poor two-masted *Concepción,* waited at anchor in the harbor. They would cross the Sea of Cortés, then travel overland to Veracruz; from there, they would be sent to exile with their fellow Jesuits in the Papal States and Germany.

Against the king's explicit orders, Governor Portolá permitted the missionaries a final High Mass. Father Retz celebrated before the Virgin of Loreto, which was draped for the occasion with a black shroud. Father Ducrue gave the sermon. After supper, the missionaries returned to the church, to pray for California and ask God's mercy and assistance. And then, as they walked toward the shore, wrote Father Ducrue,

> behold we were surrounded on all sides by the people, the Spanish soldiers among them. Some knelt on the sand to kiss our hands and feet, others knelt with arms outstretched in the form of a cross and publicly pleading for pardon. Others tenderly embraced the missionaries, bidding them farewell and wishing them a happy voyage through loud weeping and sobbing.

The Indians carried the priests on their shoulders through the surf to the launch. There the priests recited the Litanies of the Virgin of Loreto, their voices carrying over the darkness of the water.

"We were sixteen Jesuits in all," wrote Father Baegert. "Exactly the same number, that is, sixteen Jesuits, one brother and fifteen priests, we left behind, buried in California."

The Jesuits had been on the peninsula for nearly seventy-one years.

At midnight they boarded the *Concepción*.

Flight

ON OUR LAST NIGHT in Loreto, I dreamt again about the room in my house that I hadn't known was there. This time, it was a large white room empty of furniture. I floated easily around it, as if the air were some light, gelatinous substance.

≈

IN THE LORETO airport we found a crowd of suntanned Americans returning to Los Angeles. Most sat reading paperback novels. The man next to us wore wraparound sunglasses like the ones given to cataract-surgery patients. He munched loudly from a bag of potato chips. Two women with backpacks sat cross-legged on the floor and took turns braiding each others' hair.

And then it was time to board. Slowly, the crowd shuffled forward, forming itself into a line. Alice and I hugged good-bye. I watched her walk out onto the tarmac and climb the steps of the plane. It was a clean-swept day, bright and blue.

An hour later, I boarded my flight.

III

the sea of cortés

many secret and marvelous things

"I would marvel at nothing," replied Don Quixote.

—MIGUEL DE CERVANTES, *Don Quixote*

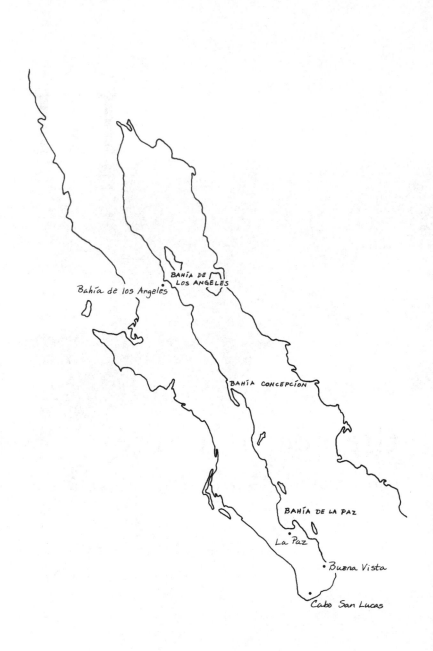

BAHÍA DE
LOS ANGELES

Bahía de los Angeles

BAHÍA CONCEPCIÓN

BAHÍA DE LA PAZ

La Paz

Buena Vista

Cabo San Lucas

The Sea Is Cortés

Cabo San Lucas to La Paz

Blue

AS I FLEW down the coast from Loreto toward La Paz, the land was
an unrelieved dun-drab brown, but the Sea of Cortés was impossibly
bright, brighter than the chemical blue of a Hollywood swimming
pool. Islands lay on its surface like blobs of dough flicked from a
spoon: Santa Catalina, then Santa Cruz inched by my window, then
the long, beige bony-backed mass of Isla San José. I could feel the
chugging of the engine through my seat back; I pressed my forehead
to the Plexiglas, and it made my teeth chatter. The plane was flying
low enough that I could make out individual cardón cacti, wee as the
props in a flea circus. Clustered on the shores of certain coves like
flecks of confetti were the shacks and sheds of fish camps. But what
fascinated me was the blue. It was a breathtaking, even painful blue.
From the air this blue looked hard, like polished stone. To fall from
this height, of course, it would be.

The plane began to descend over the vast, sparkling Bahía de la
Paz. We were over Isla Espíritu Santo now, banking for landing at the
La Paz Airport. Espíritu Santo, Holy Ghost: different from the other

islands, jagged, with many fingerlike peninsulas. In its narrow little inlets the water shimmered the honeyed-green of a jewel, so shot with sun it looked as if it were floodlit from within.

Paulino Pérez, an artist I would later meet in La Paz, painted a picture of a woman floating in that jewellike green water. Her face, which emerges like a mask, is fine-featured, even beautiful but for the grayish blooms (of decomposition?) at her nostril and her lip. From a distance, she seems to be sleeping, dreaming as she floats. When I first saw the painting at the Galería de Todos Santos, I turned it sideways, then upside down. I wasn't sure which way it was supposed to hang.

Neither was Paulino Pérez. "I like to turn my paintings around," he told me. He laid his ear on his shoulder. Then he laid his other ear on his other shoulder.

"Is the woman rising or is she drowning?"

I landed at La Paz, then caught a connecting flight home to Mexico City. I cannot say I missed the chaos of the smog-choked capital, its noise, its snarls of traffic, the crime. Over the next year I escaped whenever I could, making my way up the Sea of Cortés, not in any single fluid voyage but rather fly-in, fly-out, connect-the-dots: Cabo San Lucas, the East Cape, La Paz, Bahía de los Angeles. Sometimes the Sea of Cortés was choppy, flecked with white; sometimes it was gunmetal gray, terns and gulls looping listlessly overhead. But mostly, whatever the season, it was that brilliant, brilliant blue, so smooth, like polished stone, as endless as a vision in a dream.

Things leaped out: a dolphin, a flying fish like a little burp of silver.

The water is alive, Paulino Pérez will tell me. Put your hand in the water and look at the light. Look how many colors you see.

Cabo San Lucas: Blue Marlin

BLUE MARLIN leap out from the sparkling carpet of sea, black marlin, striped marlin, huge and sleek, their bills as long and sharp as swords. They might weigh anywhere from 200 to 500 pounds; often they top 600 or 700. The largest certified marlin to date was a female that weighed in at 1,070 pounds. Minerva Smith, an International Game Fish Association representative, weighed it on the scales in her tackle shop in downtown Cabo San Lucas, here in the marlin capital of the world.

I met Minerva Smith at her shop across from Baskin Robbins 39 Flavors; then we drove out a few blocks beyond Planet Hollywood to a restaurant called Cannery Row. A TV was going over the bar, weather news in English.

"I don't know anyone who doesn't feel good about themselves after catching a marlin," Minerva said as she dug into a plate of corned beef and cabbage. "They've got blisters, they're bruised from the rods and the reels, their thumbs are burned, but they're so happy! They feel so *good*."

Minerva was a large woman with a pretty, boxy smile. Her thick black-coffee hair tumbled over her shoulders like a mantilla; she wore white shorts and sandals and a diamond ring the size of a dime. When she touched her hair—a pretty gesture—the ring flashed. Everyone in Cannery Row seemed to know her; Hey, Minnie, they would say, stopping by our booth, how's it goin'?

She'd grown up in southern California, and so she spoke English with the same lilting, flat-toned accent I had. I wouldn't have guessed if she hadn't told me: she was a Mexican citizen born in Sonora. The name Smith was her husband Bob's, and it was because of him that she'd come back to Mexico. "He wanted to marry me, but only if I agreed to live in Cabo San Lucas. Cabo San Lucas? I didn't even know where that was! I got a map and looked. I thought, it must be beautiful because it has water all around it."

It *was* beautiful. Bob and Minerva married in 1976 and set up house here in a trailer in what has since become a bustling neighborhood of condos and shops barricaded from the sea by a wall of hotels and the Plaza Bonita mall. But back then, there was nothing. "There was no one, *no one,* on the beaches. From my trailer, every night I could hear the waves, and the sea lions barking. The water was so clear! Bob took a picture of me standing in the water up to my chest. When the photo was developed, I could see all the little red flowers on my bathing suit."

They brought down a thirty-four-foot boat they named the *No Problema*. Their first client was a Spaniard. "He wore this huge medallion covered with rubies, emeralds, and diamonds. Each gem represented a billfish he had caught somewhere in the world. His goal was to catch a striped marlin, and he caught it on the first day. Then—" she touched her hair and smiled—"he fished for twelve more days."

Back then a boat might have hooked as many as twenty marlin in a day. Some were released, some died during the fight, but most were killed. In fact, so many marlin were dumped on the beach near the ruins of the fish cannery that marlin became a staple of the local diet. "You have to understand, there was no refrigerator in town. There was one ice machine, that was it. Not even the grocery store or the butcher had a refrigerator. The townspeople would cut the marlin into steaks, butterfly them, salt them down, and then hang the meat over a clothesline to dry. It would keep for months that way. Later, they would soak it in water and cook it up to eat in burritos."

When Cabo began to boom in the 1980s, Bob and Minerva Smith's sportfishing business prospered along with it. In 1989 Minerva opened Cabo's first tackle shop. "I opened in the fall, when people were getting ready for the tournaments. I still had things in boxes, and all these people came in. They'd say, Do you have a three-way swivel? I'd say, Go hunt in the box! Here I was, boxes not even open! There was such a need."

Minerva's tackle shop (air-conditioned, jam-packed with merchandise) continued to do brisk business, and people would shell out several hundred dollars plus tips to go out on one of her and her husband's boats for the day. She had competition now—I'd noted half a dozen other fleets and tackle shops in a stroll down Cabo's main boulevard and around the marina; nevertheless, I knew for a fact (a friend had tried to get one) that Minerva's sportfishing boats were booked solid for the next two weeks. I couldn't help staring at her ring.

In Cabo, it seemed, people had money to burn.

"One time we had a couple from Texas get on the boat. The husband offered a five hundred–dollar tip to the crew for his wife to get a blue marlin. She was a tiny little thing. Well, she hit a blue marlin and it almost took her overboard. She was yelling, 'Cut the line! Cut the line! *Please!* My husband will give you the five hundred dollars anyway!'" Minerva giggled.

But wasn't all this fishing affecting the marlin population?

Catches had declined, Minerva conceded. "There's no data, it's just my feeling. Back in the 1970s a boat could hook sixteen, twenty marlin, but now a boat might get four in a whole day." But the problem, she stressed, was not the sportfishing, but commercial fishing— Japanese long-liners and seiners, especially. A single long-liner might take in a day what all the sportfishermen together took in an entire year. As for the local population's taste for marlin tacos, that was dampened back in the mid-1980s when the sportfishing fleet owners began to encourage local people to eat other kinds of fish—easier to do now that refrigeration and American-style supermarkets had arrived—and urged their customers to practice catch-and-release. Posters and bumper stickers appeared all over town: *"Suelteme, Suelteme,"* (Let me go, Let me go), said one with a cartoon of a marlin; "Fish 'Em and Release 'Em," said another; "Let Him Go to Fight Again."

"'The idea is, take what you can eat, take what might be a record, but otherwise, let it go." A "catch," she explained, constitutes bringing the fish alongside the boat. For release, the deck hand leans down over the gunwales, and either cuts the line or pulls out the hook. Whether the fish is killed or released, the boat chugs into harbor flying its flag: red for shark, yellow for dorado, orange for wahoo, green for roosterfish, dark navy blue—the most coveted of all—for marlin.

So far, three American women had come over to our table to say hi to Minerva, one of them with a Boston terrier that planted itself by our booth and gazed longingly as I ate my french fries. And now here was Roger, Minerva's boat-propeller repairman, an American retiree with a tousle of sun-bleached hair. Briefly, before he went back to the bar, they discussed a storm that was moving out to sea. It had been Minerva's idea to do the interview here at Cannery Row. I guessed now that Minerva had wanted to show me this part of herself, her place in this community, her many friends. Yet—and this intrigued me—Minerva was a Mexican come back to Mexico. Her life had made a loop, from Mexico to a Mexicanized area of the United States, to this Americanized tourist town in Mexico. She seemed thoroughly Americanized herself—her accent, her sportfishing business, these friends. What had it meant to come back to Mexico? Minerva smiled. She said her grandmother, who still lived in Sonora, was thrilled because her son, born here, was the only grandchild who could speak Spanish to her.

In Cabo, both Mexicans and Americans had embraced Minerva. For example, she said, her son was born during a *chubasco*. The water and electricity were cut off for five days. Yet several of the local people drove through the flooded arroyos to see her at the hospital. Minerva sat up tall at the memory. "The doctor slept on his desk, for me." She talked for a while about the clambakes she and Bob used to go to, "Someone with an ice chest full of clams, you bring the bread, I'll bring salad . . ."

And there was still a sense of community—a bicultural community, if I understood her correctly—although it was cloudier now. Like so many of the people I'd talked to in Cabo, Minerva had watched as the little fishing village filled with Mexicans from the mainland, and Canadians and Americans. "They come and go," she said of the latter. "It's not for everyone."

She could have said that about marlin fishing, too. It sounded dangerous, I said.

"Catherine," Minerva said, "people have been killed."

She waved to a weathered-looking blonde in a purple T-shirt.

"It's hard, it's not easy," Minerva said. She meant fighting a marlin. She smiled her big, boxy smile. "That's why it feels *so good.*"

❧

WROTE ANOTHER sportfisherman, Jeff Klassen, "[N]othing compares to the release of a tired marlin after a grueling battle." But release could be dicey: the marlin, if it was still alive, might be in shock. As Minerva had told me, sometimes the marlin might need to be revived with a massage, by patting the gill plates, maybe swinging its bill back and forth. And sometimes, as Klassen pointed out in an article for *Baja Life,* the marlin might not be as tired as it looked.

Klassen found this out when he took two friends out marlin fishing. The friends may have been greenhorns, but Jeff was the owner of the Los Cabos Fishing Center and holder of seven different International Game Fish Association world records, no less. Within two hours, they'd hooked a 250-pound marlin. After a fight that lasted an hour and a half, Jeff pulled the exhausted marlin alongside the boat. As he'd done more than a hundred times before, he gripped the marlin's bill with his gloved left hand, and with the pliers in his right he clamped onto the steel hook stuck in the marlin's bill, and pulled. The hook looked something like an anchor, with another arm, a second little hook; one was in the marlin's bill, the other dangled free. The two friends leaned over the gunnel to watch, and water started pouring into the boat. Jeff turned to tell them to move back, and suddenly, the marlin tossed its head and the trailing hook caught Jeff's right hand between his first two fingers, through the muscle, around the bone, and out the other side of his hand. The marlin was still hooked, and tossing, ready to sound. Jeff grabbed the marlin's bill with his left hand: if he were to let go, the marlin would dive and he would drown. "Boosted by sheer adrenaline," he wrote, "I hoisted the thrashing marlin into the boat. Its bill slapped against my head as my friends put it down with a club."

Two years later, he still could not straighten the injured fingers. "I did not give it the respect I should have," he told me when I met with him in his tackle shop in downtown Cabo San Lucas. And he was a person with a lot of respect for fish, Jeff said. Some of them, marlins especially, could be dangerous. But also—he said this reverently—fish provided him with entertainment and a livelihood.

His tackle shop was crowded with customers. We had an appointment for an interview, but Jeff was so busy at the cash register that I'd had nearly half an hour to peruse his many trophies (one—a bass?— with a cigar stuck into its mouth), the framed certificates and awards, the Peg-Boards crammed with hooks and knives and fish thumpers and lures. The lures were curious little things, acrylic squid-shaped heads with eyes (some painted on, others with a moveable pupil like a teddy bear's) attached to rubbery, fringelike skirts of sparkle-flecked purple, shocking pink, lemon-yellow, or cherry-red. The shop smelled strongly of plastic and coconut-butter suntan lotion. "HAFTA FISH," announced the T-shirt of one beefy-looking customer on his way out.

"I don't like killing anything," Jeff averred when I finally got him into the restaurant next door. He was a big Canadian with a mustache and strong-looking arms. "Not even spiders," he said.

And all those trophies on the walls of his tackle shop?

Fiberglass. "I've always practiced catch-and-release. If I'm not going to eat it, it goes back." But it was an effort to educate people. Tourists often wanted to kill a marlin just to have their picture taken with it. "And for some reason, people think it's the big one you need to release. It's the other way around!" The smaller ones were usually juveniles; let go, they could reproduce and fight again another day. The big ones might be records, and anyway, they tended to die in the course of the fight. "They have a heart attack, or they get 'tail-wrapped,' brought in backwards and drowned."

Fighting: so that, more than a trophy, was what Jeff Klassen, Minerva Smith, et al., were selling. What I understood from Minerva was that the fight felt good in the way an aerobics class might: you're all sweaty, brain pumped up with endorphins. Fighting per se didn't seem to be Minerva's style; but Jeff, when I asked him how he came to Cabo San Lucas and started his business, described a life that sounded like a lonely battle. "A lot of people think, *Oh, tropical Cabo San Lucas!* But you can't just come down here and open your restaurant, your little coffee shop or boutique. You have to pay your dues."

Klassen had paid his dues, and paid again. He began working at a downtown tackle shop, then struck out on his own with an American partner. They faced the usual complications of setting up a business in Mexico. "And I got some resistance. People here are nice, but they're worried about their jobs." At first, most of his business came from Americans. To bring in the Mexican customers, he needed to be able to speak Spanish. "I learned quick. I picked up fishing words first. It was a question of not being afraid to talk. If I knew ten words, I'd use those ten words. I'm not shy." Things seemed to be going well. Then, a year and a half into the enterprise, his partner snuck in at midnight, unloaded the contents of the store into his truck, and disappeared. "Down to the posters, the furniture, the Peg-Board hooks!" Four years later, Jeff was still in a rage. "I got zero support. It was a fully legitimate business! I'd paid my taxes." He tried to sue, but he couldn't get the case into the local courts. He lost everything. He considered going home. Instead, he borrowed money to reopen the store. For the first two years, he barely kept the doors open. "I worked fifteen hours a day. I put everything into that store. I'm thirty-five years old. I can't pick up and move whenever I feel like it." His business had not only recovered; it had taken off. But in the midst of all those long hours, his wife left him. Now he was sharing a bachelor pad with rock-and-roller Sammy Hagar's brother (I didn't catch his name), owner of the Cabo Wabo discotheque.

Which played into the celebrity angle, Jeff said. "Sammy comes down three times a year and gives shows. So we fish with Sammy." Recently he'd taken out the rock star Alice Cooper—"such a nice guy"—Oscar de la Hoya, the boxer; and Joe Montana. He'd seen many actors around town: Kiefer Sutherland, Sylvester Stallone . . . Singer Chris Isaak would be showing up in a few days. And in a sort of boomerang effect, Jeff was becoming a bit of a celebrity himself. Already well known in fishing circles for his seven world records, he'd been featured in numerous travel-magazine articles, and his store had been in the TV show *Land's End*.

Cabo was booming, but yes, there was a downside to that, he agreed. All the construction, the topless bars, the sports-betting bar, the cheesy franchise restaurants. "The Hard Rock Café," he sneered. "They'll never get their money out of there. Then they have to put in a Planet Hollywood, the *last* thing we need."

I wanted to ask him where he thought his roommate's Cabo Wabo discotheque fit into this scheme, but there, before I could open my mouth with my rude question, was the very man, come up to our table to invite Jeff for a beer.

"Sammy Hagar's brother," Jeff said—again, I didn't catch his name.

The brother wore several large rings. These brought to mind brass knuckles.

Did I want to join them?

※

IS SHE rising or is she drowning?

I think again of the floating woman's mottled face framed by the ripples of yellow-green water. I admire Paulino Pérez's painting, though I wouldn't want to hang it in my living room. I said to him: "She looks dead to me."

Paulino rested his chin on his hands. He has the mustache and chiseled profile of a Hollywood *bandido*. Yet Paulino is a kind person, open and relaxed.

"Todo depende," he said. "It all depends on what you want to see."

The East Cape: Hell, I Knew It Was Paradise

RAY CANNON wanted to see a dying dorado. It is an uncanny sight: once hooked, its silvery blue back turns an iridescent green, its flanks saffron with bright-blue polka dots, while its fins blush peacock blue. But the dorado—also called mahimahi—is not an easy thing to kill. After a typically acrobatic fight, when the some thirty pounds of twisting, leaping rainbow of a fish is finally subdued, the fisherman must club it, and then once the fish is brought on deck, he must club it again. ("Incidentally," advise the authors of *The Baja Catch,* "when we say you need a 'club,' we're not talking about 10 inches of broomstick. For big dorado, you want something on the order of a kid's metal baseball bat, or better.") When, at the Rancho Buena Vista Lodge, Ray Cannon made his request known, it was Bob Van Wormer who was enlisted to assist.

That was how the two first met, here on the East Cape in 1957. Cabo San Lucas was just a ramshackle village with a fish cannery then, its one hotel—the Palmilla, out on the dirt road to San José del Cabo—but two years old; Rancho Buena Vista, fifty miles up the Sea of Cortés near Los Barriles, was its sole competitor. Ray Cannon didn't get to see a dying dorado—as it turned out, all they could hook that day were sailfish. But a friendship was formed, which deepened as Cannon continued to fish, photograph, and write about the "biggest angling news scoop of half a century." Rancho Buena Vista Lodge—one of a number of Baja California hotels and airlines that, over the years, would host Cannon for his PR services—began to fill up with fly-in sportfishermen. By the time his book, *The Sea of Cortez,* appeared in 1966, Rancho Buena Vista's reputation as one of the premier sportfishing resorts in the world was shining bright. Ray remembered his young friend "Bobby" in his book. And Van Wormer, now a snow-haired paterfamilias, owner with his Mexican wife, Chacha, of three East Cape resort hotels and the peninsula's largest sportfishing fleet, remembered Ray.

"Ray Cannon . . . ," he said, and a look came over his wrinkled face like a little boy's on Christmas morning. We were sitting on the patio of his Hotel Palmas de Cortez, just up the road from the fabled Rancho Buena Vista. A band was playing *ranchera* music as his guests—American men mostly—snaked by the buffet of enchiladas and chicken mole. The air felt like a lazy embrace, warm and salty; moonlight fell on the water below in a sweep of silver.

On nights like this, Ray would sit on the porch and tell jokes and stories. I'd seen his picture on the jacket of his book *The Sea of Cortez:* an old man in shapeless, water-stained khakis and a captain's hat, cigarette clenched in his mouth, hoisting a giant black snook by the gills. Ray had been a bit player in Hollywood; later, a director and producer; and then he left it all to fish and write about fishing. A flicker of interest had been awakened north of the border by Steinbeck's *Log from the* Sea of Cortez; but Ray's magazine articles and glossy coffee-table book chock-full of fish stories were what brought down the first wave of big-spending tourists. As an industry, Baja California's sportfishing began with him.

Bob chuckled. His was a round Dutch face with hooded pale-blue eyes. He was in his seventies now, looking back on a lifetime. The surf lapped the shore below with a soft *shush;* forks clinked against plates, men's voices hummed in conversation over the drums and guitars of the *ranchera* band, yet I could hear clearly every word that he said.

"Herb Tansey owned Rancho Buena Vista then, he was the one who put up Ray Cannon. They were great friends. Tansey was an ex-captain for Trans-World Airlines. He was the sole survivor of a crash in Shannon, Ireland. He lost his leg, spent a year in the hospital. But with the compensation from TWA, he bought Rancho Buena Vista. My brother used to come down, and he would tell me how great the fishing was."

Bob didn't get down to Rancho Buena Vista until New Year's of 1957. At the time, he was working as an aircraft mechanic in San Diego. A farm boy from St. Joseph, Missouri, Bob had seen some of the world during World War II, when he was stationed in North Africa and India. But Baja, that was something else.

"God!" He laid both his hands flat on the table. "Jeeeeee-zus! Miles of beaches!"

Bob came right back and stayed to work for Herb. It was an idyllic time. Bob was young, unmarried, a man who liked to fish in a place where the fishing was fantastic. His welding and handyman skills, not to mention his English, made him a valued, in fact the most valued, employee in a resort that, thanks to Ray Cannon's publicity, had become the biggest business on the East Cape.

But Herb Tansey, the one-legged pilot, liked to drink. Late one afternoon in 1959, after hitting the bars in La Paz, he got in his plane with his friend Arty Young to fly back to Buena Vista. He got lost; soon it was dark. He flew around in circles until he ran out of gas and crashed on a mountaintop near the little mining town of El Triunfo. Bob was the one who went to retrieve the bodies.

"It was a miserable sight, just pathetic. He and Arty had all these liquor bottles in the back that broke when they crashed, so they were covered with liquor. But it was amazing, the people didn't take anything. Wallets, rings, I found everything on their bodies. I took Herb's wallet out of his pocket. And they had the payroll for Buena Vista, it was all there in a paper bag. I had to take it out and count it in front of the mayor. I hired a flatbed truck to cart the bodies out, and since we had to drive over washboard roads, I had to get six Mexicans to sit on the back of the truck to keep the bodies from rolling off. I buried Herb in front of his house at Buena Vista. He'd said to me, 'I love this place and these people more than anything in my life.' I could write a book about the parties he used to give. He'd have an open bar. The Mexicans *loved* that guy! I'd never seen so many people cry at a funeral. The cab driver who helped, going back and forth with all the business about the funeral, he would not take one penny."

Slowly, Bob shook his old white head. "That's why I fell in love with this place: the people. Hell! I knew it was Paradise."

After Tansey's death, Rancho Buena Vista was sold to a retired United States Army colonel named Eugene Walters. The first season went well, but when it ended Colonel Walters wanted to cut Bob's pay in half. "So I left. But then when things started rolling again, the colonel wanted me back, offering me the moon and green cheese. I said I'd go back if he offered me a 5 percent cut. It was a gentlemen's agreement. I worked there for several years, and he never paid me my commission. So finally, I left. Then what do you know, I get a letter from Ray Cannon. He said, 'Bobby, you are really part of Rancho Buena Vista.' In other words, You go back home, boy. I got the same letter from the colonel's son. Two letters arrived on the same day— go figure! That night the colonel came by. I told him, 'I don't see any future for me here.' I'd been working my you-know-what off, and they just used me all those years."

But it was then, free of Rancho Buena Vista, at the age of forty, that Bob began to build his fortune. In 1965, he married Chacha Ruiz, the daughter of a local cattle rancher. A few miles down the coast they built a resort at Punta Colorada—"the roosterfish capital of the world"—catering to fly-in sportfishermen, then, on land where Chacha's family had grown corn, the Hotel Palmas de Cortez. Soon the Van Wormers were the moguls of the East Cape, with a third hotel, a Pemex gas station, a trailer park, a fleet of sportfishing boats, and a family of three strapping sons.

"I laugh about it now," Bob said, "but I was bitter when I left Rancho Buena Vista. Goddammit! I'd worked in good faith. I went right ahead, though. I became successful, and maybe six or seven years later, I thought, that was an education! An education in the School of Hard Knocks. It cost me, but it was cheaper than what I would have had to pay to go to Harvard Business School. And Harvard Business School, none of those places could have taught me what I needed to know about running a hotel in a place like this."

Ray Cannon came out to Punta Colorada soon after the hotel opened, and he and Bob took some underwater photos of the swarms of roosterfish—big, exotic jacks with a spikey, comblike dorsal fin, rare everywhere in the world but the southern Sea of Cortés. "Once in a while Ray would make a courtesy mention of Punta Colorada. But Rancho Buena Vista was *the* place, and the colonel was keeping Ray happy." Ray came back and forth for quite a few years, staying at Rancho Buena Vista mostly. Then in June 1977, he died suddenly in California, of a brain tumor.

Bob was getting ready to go to the funeral when he stopped in to see Colonel Walters. "I'd been away from Rancho Buena Vista for some years by then, and I'd gotten over it. The colonel didn't want to get on an airplane because he'd fallen and hurt his hip badly. But he felt guilty about not going to Ray's funeral. He just talked and talked about the old days. I said to him, 'You know, I'd rather remember Ray the way he was. I get so sick of funerals. They're the biggest bunch of crap I ever saw in my life. Wouldn't you rather remember Ray with his big belly sticking out, his captain's hat?' And the colonel said, 'By God, I'm glad I talked to you.' I said, 'Don't go. Tell your son to represent you. You remember Ray the way he was, not in a box.'"

Bob looked off into the distance. A stand of palm trees inked out the stars. "That was the last day I saw the colonel alive. He died three or four months later."

Louder now, insects chirped and sawed. The dishes had been cleared, and the waitresses were gathering the tablecloths, ghostly pale in the moonlight.

We would meet again in the morning.

Bob, the Blue

THE *clomp clomp*ing woke me at six. Men's voices, laughing, "hubba hubba," *clomp clomp a-clomp*. I slid open the door and stepped out onto the balcony. The sun had not yet pushed above the horizon; the sea was molten silver and the sky ribboned with red and flame yellow, like a sky for the Apocalypse. The men made a line like a rabble of an army, marching with their fishing gear along the sand, then out onto the wooden pier, *clomp* and *clomp.* "Up and at 'em." They slapped each other on the shoulders, *heh heh.* And they kept coming in groups of four, two, six, three, *clomp*ing out and then into their skiffs that would take them to their boats—the yachts that were anchored a ways out, white and waiting like belles on a dance floor. The skiffs roared as they went slapping across the water.

Back inside, I pulled the pillow over my head and tried to sleep, but "hubba hubba," *clomp clomp,* the engines bagpiping away, they were still coming: the grand parade of the American billfighters.

When they were gone, the sun was up and the sea was blue, that impossible, painful blue.

"It feels so good," Minerva Smith had told me. Well, I thought, maybe for her. I wasn't interested in plowing out into the hot sun, wrestling with a fish I wouldn't kill. My father didn't fish either, but he'd been out off Cabo San Lucas with friends. Several times they'd hooked a marlin that already had one, even two fish hooks dangling from its bill. All this fishing: that's what I wanted to know more about. I met Bob Van Wormer in his restaurant for eggs and toast and coffee.

Catch-and-release, I ventured, sounded like the sportfisherman's new mantra.

There was nothing new about it, Bob said. Back in 1957, he'd hooked his first marlin, fought it, and let it go. He said, "I don't think I've ever killed a marlin."

And roosterfish?

"This year at Punta Colorada," he said proudly, "was the thirtieth annual International Roosterfish Tournament. Unless you think you have a record, everything is released. Thirty fishermen are out there for three days, and they don't kill more than five roosterfish." The guests liked the catch-and-release policy, he said, because then the fish could fight again.

True, he admitted, there was the occasional sportfisherman who needed a little education. Not long ago, someone hauled in twelve roosterfish. "I said, 'Goddammit, what'd you do that for? Why so many? You bastard! You do that again I'm going to report you!' It was some gung-ho diver with a speargun. He says, 'Well, there were so many it was like shooting fish in a barrel.' Shooting fish in a barrel! God! Damn it!"

Fish in a barrel: this was "the world's greatest fish trap," as Ray Cannon wrote in *The Sea of Cortez,* with "acres of roosterfish," "mile long schools of migrating totuaba," "teeming swarms of Cortez grunion," and all classes of marlin, sailfish, jack and snook and bass and grouper and sardine and tuna, "massive aggregations," "hordes," and "throngs." Most spectacular of all were the "fish pileups," when the sea would suddenly erupt into a boiling curtain of silver, up to a mile long and two to three feet into the air, as the sardines were literally driven out of the water by schools of migrating game fish.

"Back then you could spear grouper," Bob said, "cabrilla, pargos, there was such an abundance of good eating fish." But in the early 1960s, the Japanese came in with their long-lines, some of them thirty to even sixty miles long, strung with thousands and thousands of baited hooks. "So many marlin and sailfish were taken that by 1969 and 1970, their average weight was down to only thirty-five pounds. That's how little they were. The Japanese were selling all that sashimi. And the Mexican government was helping them!" Bob's face was livid. "We raised hell! The hotel association here and in Cabo San Lucas. Finally, the authorities in Mexico City realized what was up, and so the billfish started recovering. We got that turned around. Last year was the biggest marlin fishing season ever."

And the other fish?

Well now, that was another story because of gill netting, shrimp trawling, and spearfishing. Industrial netting and trawling had been going on in the Sea of Cortés for more than fifty years. I'd read a bit about that in Steinbeck's *The Log from the* Sea of Cortez. In 1940 he and his friend the marine biologist Ed Ricketts had gone aboard a Japanese dredger to cadge specimens from the tons of "trash fish" the fishermen would discard after having picked out the shrimp. Horrified, Steinbeck and Ricketts watched as the fishermen tossed mountains of dead and dying animals overboard—manta rays, sharks, tuna, anemones, pompano, small tuna—into a cloud of clamoring gulls swarming like flies off the stern. That the Japanese were doing this, and that the Mexican government would permit it, was, Steinbeck railed, "a true crime against nature and against the immediate welfare of Mexico and the eventual welfare of the human species."

Bob agreed. And now, having overheard us, one of the guests, a bearded man in a baseball cap, approached our table and introduced himself: he was a doctor from Anchorage, Alaska. The same thing was happening there, he said, Japanese and Korean fleets out with nets, sterilizing miles of ocean. "We've got this area called the Donut Hole between Russia and Alaska. It's illegal to fish there, but it went on anyway for years, until they went out with helicopters and filmed them."

Bob nodded vigorously. And if all this wasn't bad enough, there were the Mexicans living in fish camps on isolated stretches of coast and on the islands who worked with scuba gear and spearguns. "All your yummies—cabrilla, pargo, snapper, grouper—they're one-tenth of what they used to be. *One-tenth!* There's no one to monitor these fishermen, to check what size fish they're taking. They'll take these tiny little fish for these tiny little fillets, so the fish can't grow and reproduce." The Mexican fish and game authority, PESCA, did not have the resources to police the entirety of the Sea of Cortés. Bob had offered to help: "I told them I would gladly have one of my sons patrol the area, for free, not one penny." But PESCA wasn't interested.

"Ninety percent of it is gone already! Gone!" Bob wiped his mouth and laid his napkin by his plate. "What's it going to be like in ten years?"

His question hung there in the air like a ball thrown up with no one to catch it. The doctor from Alaska had left. The other guests were all gone . . . fighting the fish.

I may not have been a fan of sportfishing, but I really liked Bob—Don Roberto, as his employees called him—his good-old-boy air-force talk ("Goddammit"), his generous and genuine affection for the people, both Mexican and American, of the East Cape. Bob was someone who had integrated—married a Mexican, had a family, built several businesses here. Most Americans (and Canadians) I knew in Mexico were temporary residents barricaded into the local expat community. In Mexico City, for example, there was the Union Church, the Newcomer's Club, the American School, and so on; they would eat at McDonald's, shop at Wal-Mart, and watch CNN and the Disney Channel on cable TV. North Americans here in Baja California had their cliques and clubs too, like Jeff Klassen hobnobbing with American sports stars and rock royalty, the retirees in their trailer parks, artists hanging out at the Caffé Todos Santos sipping their smoothies. They might have a few Mexican friends, they might even speak passable Spanish, but to integrate, to have the Mexicans accept you as one of their own: that was another order of existence.

In fact, Bob had started out speaking Spanish to me. When I'd first called him on the phone, Roberto, as he called himself, went on talking with me for a good ten minutes before we both realized we could switch to English. And it was the damnedest thing: he sounded exactly—not a trace of an American accent—like an East Cape fisherman.

So did his boys. I'd spoken with Bob Junior, bartending at the Hotel Palmas de Cortez—his English was fluent, though thick with a Mexican accent. While Bob and I were having breakfast, another son, Chuck, stopped by with his baby daughter, Julia, a little bundle of pink with tiny gold earrings. Chuck spoke Spanish with his father, and Bob cooed at the baby, *"¡Qué preciosita!"*

The Van Wormer family name had taken its place alongside names like Fisher, Ritchie, and Wilkes, true-blue *bajacalifornios* all. And yes, of course, Bob had heard of Thomas "Captain" Ritchie, that legend of nineteenth-century Cabo. He'd read all about him in the book by J. Ross Browne.

"Ritchie," he said, drawing himself up, "was a very prominent person."

Like Captain Ritchie with his big wooden house–cum-hotel on the beach at Cabo San Lucas, in his neck of the woods Bob Van Wormer had built a house that was without question the largest and most luxuriously appointed. It stood off to one side of the parking lot of the Hotel Palmas de Cortez, grand and columned, like a cross between a suburban bank and a Greek temple. Bob gave me a tour: great expanses of white shag carpet and pearlescent onyx, black lacquer furniture, mirrors, and Italianate bric-a-brac, the rooms arrayed around a central nave fitted with a pool of darting bullet fish.

For years, he and Chacha had lived in a room in the hotel and saved their money, Bob said. All the while Chacha would clip pictures from magazines, dreaming of how it could be. And there she was, deep in her gleaming, creamy-white kitchen, a handsome woman with tawny skin and brushlike orange-blonde hair, sitting at the counter eating a bowl of *menudo*.

"Aqui tiene usted su casa," she said kindly. This is your house.

And the tour continued around to the front door, above which was a tabletop-size stained-glass medallion window. It depicted the state of Missouri and the cape of Baja California Sur spanned by the Gateway Arch of St. Louis, from his hometown of St. Joseph to hers, Los Barriles. Below were a stalk of corn and a cardón cactus; leaping over the Gateway Arch was a bright-blue marlin.

"Our family crest," Bob said. He'd designed it himself.

But if their house was Chacha's dream house, the Hotel Punta Colorada, "roosterfish capital of the world," was Bob's. This was the hotel they had built after Bob left Colonel Walter's Rancho Buena Vista. It was a half-hour drive down the coast on a washboard dirt road: a good, solid sportfisherman's lodge, quiet in the early afternoon. Inside it was cool and dark. We ate lentil soup and stewed chicken. Bob told me more stories, about a pet lion they'd had to give to the zoo in Santiago, and about a beggar he'd seen during World War II in Calcutta, a blind man entirely covered with coins. We talked some more about Captain Ritchie.

Afterward, I asked if I could take his picture. We went outside onto the patio overlooking the sea. Bob scooped up a gray kitten and held it close to his face, that round, smiling Dutch face. The sea behind him was dazzling.

My photo didn't come out; alas, the negatives on that roll were all blank. But I can see that photo in my mind, as clear as if I held it now in my hand: Bob, the blue.

La Paz: Such Glory

THE LAND may be poor, but the Sea of Cortés is rich. Not nearly as rich as it once was, but still it is rich. *Rich,* the waves caress the pebbly shore, *rich.* It is late September, and I am walking along the waterfront of La Paz, a whiff of the afternoon wind they call the *corumel* shivering the fronds of the palms and skidding the terns in the sky. This is the capital of the state of Baja California Sur, a sleepy little city of 150,000 on the southern rim of the vast Bahía de la Paz. Out on the water lies the long lick of mangrove-covered sand known as El Mogote; to my left are shops, taco stands and seafood restaurants, houses (their air conditioners dripping like runny noses), a hotel. A boy cycles by, a bunch of bananas trailing on a cart. A dog lies panting in the shade of a sign that says—in English—LOBSTER TACOS.

Nearing the root of El Mogote, the waterfront jogs into the bay, running alongside a new development of shops and restaurants and coral-pink high-rise condominiums. At the gated entrance to the condominiums stands a bronze statue of a little boy, fat-tummied, his swim trunks stuffed with periwinkle shells. He holds out a starfish as if offering it to a grown-up. . . . *Compartiré contigo mi oasis / la tierra perfumada del sur,* begins the poem by Fernando Jordán on its plaque, . . . *I will share with you my oasis / the perfumed land of the South.*

I walk back slowly. The heat is like wearing a hot, wet towel.

The abundance of the sea: *rich.* Once the Sea of Cortés was rich with pearls; now the pearls are gone. Still, the sea is rich with fish— despite the long-lines, the gill nets, the trawlers, and the spearfishing. *Rich.* I stoop to dip my hand in the water, warm and silky. The water is as clear as gin, flecked with tiny fish. Among the pebbles are a Coke bottle cap and bits of black plastic.

"Sea of *Cortés?*"

It is evening; it is still hot. I am in Paulino Pérez's studio, a white space covered with his artwork, a floor fan humming in the corner. We are sweating; we slap at bugs. "Why Cortés?" Like most Mexicans, he disdains Hernán Cortés, Spanish conqueror, gold-greedy destroyer of the Indians. "Why don't you call it Gulf of California? Or better yet, Vermillion Sea?"

The Vermillion Sea. I can never quite picture that, a sea as red as a movie star's fingernail. It does sound pretty, I agree. To say it is like mouthing a little candy slippery with sugar: Vermillion. The name was given by the explorer Francisco de Ulloa in 1539 when, nearing the mouth of the Colorado River, he first saw its bloodred tides.

Sometimes, at night, because of another type of dinoflagellate, the sea lights up with pinpricks of phosphorescent green.

But to me, the sea is blue and the sea is Cortés.

Amazing but true: Cortés dreamt of it years before he set sail across its azure waters to California, the island of the Amazons. His soldiers also knew of it: around the campfires, those who could read would have read aloud to the others about knights and fair maidens, enchanted isles and fountains of youth, wicked Turks and man-eating griffons, "idols of solid gold," as in the *Exploits of Esplandián,* "all inlaid with enormous precious stones and a huge mother-of pearl." And then one brilliant morning of their long march inland from Veracruz, Cortés and his men came to a broad causeway at the southern edge of what is now Mexico City. Wrote the old soldier Bernal Díaz in his memoir, *The True History of the Conquest of New Spain:*

> And when we saw all those cities and villages built in the water, and other great towns on dry land, and that straight and level causeway leading to Mexico, we were astounded. These great towns and *cues* and buildings rising from the water, all made of stone, seemed like an enchanted vision from the tale of Amadis. Indeed, some of our soldiers asked if it was not a dream. It is not surprising therefore that I should write in this vein. It was all so wonderful that I do not know how to describe this first glimpse of things never heard of, seen or dreamed before.

They entered the Aztec capital in 1521, Cortés and his five hundred men and their sixteen horses. And in time, with Indian allies and reinforcements from Cuba, they smashed the temples and the blood-splattered idols of Tezcatlipoca, Tláloc, and Huitzilopochtli; they took the gold, the glittering mounds of masks and necklaces, nose rings and bracelets, armbands and helmets. They left nothing but the stench of thousands of rotting bodies in smoking ruins.

May 3, 1535, fourteen years later: Hernán Cortés, conqueror of Mexico, Marqués Del Valle de Oaxaca and captain general of New Spain and the South Seas for his majesty, the Catholic king of Spain, is here, on this far shore of what he called Santa Cruz and we call the Bahía de la Paz, the Bay of Peace. He has arrived with men and horses, and now, in a brief ceremony, he takes possession of this land, what he believes is the island of California. "[H]e walked back and forth across the said land," wrote his majesty's scribe, "and with his sword struck certain trees which were there."

Whuck. He probably chipped a cardón cactus.

Audacious, cautious, Machiavellian, devout, avaricious: "Like all mortals," writes José Luis Martínez in his monumental biography, "Hernán Cortés was a complex weave of good and bad, of just and unjust acts, of grandeur and misery, valor and cruelty, generosity and crimes. He was, moreover, a surprising personality." "Above all," wrote his secretary, Francisco López de Gómara, Cortés "had a great heart and spirit." He liked women, cards and dice, drinking, good eating. His appearance was unremarkable: he was somewhat bow-legged with a pale and serious face that, according to the soldier Bernal Díaz, would have looked better had it been bigger. But, as Bernal Díaz remembered, "he gave signs of being a great lord," and although his dress was plain, it was rich, with "a slender and very valuable golden chain bearing an image of Our Lady." He often swore, "On my conscience!" or "Confound you!" and he would scold his soldiers, "It's a worthless sheep that can't carry its own wool."

Son of a minor nobleman, Cortés was born on the cusp of the Spanish Renaissance. He was a child of seven in that fateful year of 1492, when Moslem Granada finally fell to the armies of Aragón and Castile, and Christopher Columbus sailed across the ocean to the New World. As a teenager, he studied Greek, Latin, and logic at the University of Salamanca. He may have been a dreamer, a reader of Amadises, but his four surviving letters to the king, the *cartas-relaciones* about the conquest of Mexico and an ill-fated expedition to the jungles of Honduras, reveal a cool and forceful mind. Cortés may have been a conquistador, but he was not a bloodthirsty lout, a Nuño de Guzmán, a Francisco Pizarro. And if he destroyed the Aztec capital of Tenochtitlán, he rebuilt a Mexico City, strange phoenix, of palaces and hospitals and churches.

"Cortés!" Paulino Pérez spits out the name like a putrid bit of cheese.

In Mexico, "the nation of statues," as historian Enrique Krauze calls it, not one is of Hernán Cortés. There are paintings, however: in a mural in Mexico City's Palacio Nacional, Diego Rivera portrayed the conquistador as a hunchbacked syphilitic cupping his hands for coins. José Clemente Orozco painted Cortés as a robot, screws bolted into his metallic knees, driving a sword into the belly of a corpse. These, for the twentieth century, were the politically correct images of the conquistador of Mexico—this surprising personality with whom modern Mexico begins.

He died in Spain at the age of sixty-two, a broken man. "I am old, poor and in debt," he complained in his last petition to the king. Scribbled on the back, in the hand of a royal secretary: *"Nay que responder,"* No need to reply. Like a hot potato nobody wants, his bones have been moved eight times, no less. Currently they rest in Mexico City in the little-visited chapel of the Hospital de Jesús, mortared into the wall behind a plaque that says no more than this:

HERNAN CORTES

1485–1547

But such glory was expected from California. The first wonder: it existed! Many more rich islands could be found in the South Seas, on this Cortés had staked his fortune and his reputation. Already Ferdinand Magellan had sailed around the cape of South America and across the ocean to discover the Philippine Islands. Cortés had laid waste to the Aztec capital, that city that was "like an enchanted vision from the tale of Amadís," and so conquered an empire. Now what worlds might he conquer? The king had given him command

of the South Seas. Yonder lay the Spice Islands and the riches of
Cathay. There too might be found Quivira, or the Seven Cities of
Cíbola, the roofs of their many houses domed with gold.

First stop: California, Island of the Amazons.

There is no diary of Cortés's last great adventure, his attempt in
1535 to found a colony at La Paz. A fragment of a letter survives, a
brief and vague few pages in the biography written by his secretary,
and another few pages, also vague, in Bernal Díaz's *True History*. It is
an awful story, one Cortés would have wanted forgotten. He, the
conqueror of Mexico, had washed up on this remote desert land that
more than two centuries hence the Jesuit missionary Johann Jakob
Baegert would dismiss as "nothing . . . but a pile of stones full of
thorns." We can imagine the men's thirst, the heat, the Indians. "Of
the soldiers that were with Cortés," wrote Bernal Díaz, "twenty-
three died from hunger and illness and many others were ill, and they
cursed Cortés, his island, his bay, and his discovery."

"Cortés?" Paulino says. He is sorely disappointed in me.

"If we examine things," wrote Bernal Díaz, "Cortés did not have
fortune in anything after we won New Spain."

Things Appear, Disappear

THERE WERE no Amazons, no Seven Cities of Cíbola, no hoards of
gold—only pearls, which the Pericú wore in necklaces strung with
red berries and bits of shells. The pearls were ugly, blackened little
nubs because the Indians had no knives; to open the oyster shells they
threw them into a fire. The Spaniards slipped in their sharp and slender knife points: many of these yielded good Oriental pearls, white
and gleaming.

Beginning in the sixteenth century, pearl fishers from the mainland crossed the Sea of Cortés to work the rich beds around the
Bahía de la Paz, Isla Espíritu Santo, and points north—Loreto and
Bahía Concepción as far as Mulegé. The divers worked most
efficiently during the warm months, from May to September.
Usually enough pearls were found to make the crossing profitable,
but never enough to support a settlement. None of the colonies at

La Paz had survived: Cortés's failed in 1535; another headed by Sebastián Vizcaíno in 1596 also failed; Admiral Atondo's failed in 1683; even the Jesuits' Mission La Paz failed, its poor thatched adobe huts smashed and burned in the Rebellion of 1734. By the time the rebellion was quashed, too few Indians survived to justify a full-time missionary. And already the pearls, heavily fished for more than a century, had apparently become scarce.

But then in 1740, perhaps because of a *chubasco,* an immense quantity of pearl oyster shells was thrown up on the beach north of Mulegé. The Indians there, hoping to please the soldiers, brought some of the shells to the mission at San Ignacio. Manuel de Ocio was one of those soldiers. Abandoning the mission, he left for the pearl beds at once. Bane of the Jesuits, within a few years Ocio had sold hundreds of pounds of pearls and parlayed his fortune into properties in Guadalajara, silver mines in the mountains south of La Paz, and, grazing over the mission territories of the cape region, that voracious herd of sixteen thousand head of cattle.

Pearl fishing continued over the next century, primarily in the beds around the Bahía de la Paz and Isla Espíritu Santo. When the U.S. forces invaded in 1847, as many as a hundred boats were pearl fishing in the area. As Lieutenant E. Gould Buffum recalled in his memoir, in those heady days before the battles with the *Guerrilla Guadalupana,* he sailed out to the pearl fisheries off Isla Espíritu Santo one "clear and beautiful moonlit night" with "a delicious land breeze which blew our little boat so rapidly over the water." In the daytime he watched the Yaqui Indian divers at work, naked but for their loincloths and a sharp stick that they used to dig out the oysters and fend off sharks.

It was a primitive method of production for so precious a commodity. From the crude little canoes bobbing in the Bahía de la Paz, the pearls found their way into coronets and scepters, velvet robes and satin gowns. ("We attended a gala event at the theater with the most beautiful ladies of Mexico," boasted the Empress Carlota in one of her letters, "who arrived covered in pearls from the Gulf of Cortez [*sic*] and dressed in the latest fashions from Paris.") "The most esteemed ones," according to the Jesuit historian Clavigero, "are those which, besides being large, white, and lustrous, are spherical or oval; and especially valuable are those which are pear-shaped." As was the four hundred–grain Pearl of La Paz, made a present to the queen of Spain.

By the early twentieth century, when journalist Arthur North came through, La Paz had become the chief producer in the world's pearl-fishing industry. In his 1908 book, *The Mother of California,* North noted that the peninsula's "annual output is valued at a quarter of a million dollars, gold, and is promptly marketed in London, Paris and other great European marts." Using modern diving apparatus, the divers could dive deeper now, and dig out more shells from more beds. With the ensuing glut of pearls, pearl prices fell, and so the divers dove yet deeper and brought up more pearls. Each diver harbored the hope of a treasure—an egg-size find, perfectly round, or perfectly oval, brilliantly lustered, a pearl that would be, as Steinbeck called it in his novella *The Pearl,* "the Pearl of the World." But most oysters, cracked open, were empty, nothing but quivering gray tongue. As time went by, the pearls, when the divers found them, were increasingly unremarkable specimens, tiny things to be strung on a simple necklace or glued to the end of a hat pin. By 1940, when Steinbeck and Ricketts came through on their collecting expedition, almost all that was left were stories. An unknown disease had decimated the sparse remaining beds, and though the large companies based in La Paz attempted to limit pearl fishing, individuals—often women in nothing but a loincloth and a helmet with an air tube—continued to work isolated stretches of the coast.

By the end of World War II, Baja California's pearl oysters had all but disappeared, and La Paz's pearl industry, the economic engine of the peninsula for nearly four centuries, was dead. Like the Pericú themselves with their burnt little pearls strung together with berries and shells, a world is gone.

❧

IS SHE RISING or is she drowning?

Her face emerges, perfect oval, like a mask from the rippling yellow-green water.

Strange, the way the blue is swallowed into those narrow little inlets of Isla Espíritu Santo. From the air, the island looks empty, a claw-shaped lump of sand and rock and cactus. Yet there are ruins on its southern tip—the cement basins of a Frenchman's failed pearl-oyster farm. Pericú Indians once lived on this island, surviving on clams and fishes, pitahaya fruits, mice, and black cinnamon-eared jackrabbits. When the island's Pericú died, their bodies were laid in the caves that gouge its coast. Over the centuries, most of these bones were washed out to sea; others were bagged by souvenir hunters. Some years ago, the National Institute for History and Anthropology collected what was left for display in the museum in La Paz. I'd seen them there, ochre-red skulls, blackened femurs, and spidery rib cages chipped and flaking onto the white Formica floor of their display case.

Once, as he hiked along the island's shore of pebbles and shells, Paulino Pérez picked out a thumb-size bone. He took it to the museum in La Paz. They told him it was the tailbone of a child.

Paulino likes to draw the bones of Isla Espíritu Santo. He likes their colors and textures. He goes to the museum in La Paz, so cool and light, and he sits there for hours, sketching.

SO AS THE pearl oysters were dying, the pearl fishers switched to sharks. When the Nazis occupied Norway in 1940, cutting off the world's largest supply of cod-liver oil, a prime source of vitamin A, Baja California's fishermen took up the slack, trolling for the sea's rich population of blacktips, blues, bonitos, hammerheads, common thresher sharks, and more. Shark liver yields a clear, butter-colored oil richer in vitamin A, it turned out, than even cod-liver oil. The boom was on. Whole communities up and down both coasts turned to shark fishing. Men working from canoes would hook the sharks, haul them in, beat them to death with clubs, then cut out the livers and pack them into five-gallon gasoline cans. Throughout World War II, the peninsula's coasts were littered with rotting shark carcasses as truckload after truckload of livers moved across the border into the United States.

In the late 1940s, however, when vitamin A began to be synthesized in laboratories, the demand for shark livers plummeted. It was a poor business, but Baja California's shark fishermen kept on fishing, this time for the meat, the cartilage (used for drugs), and fins. The fins—sliced off the living animal, which is then tossed back in the water to sink and slowly drown—are a delicacy in Asia, used for soup. A pound of dried shark fins might sell for three hundred dollars in Hong Kong. And now, with shark populations crashing throughout the Sea of Cortés—and the world—they are still fishing. And not only are sharks being overfished for their fins, but millions—estimates range from twelve million to more than one hundred million worldwide—are killed each year by gill nets, long-liners, and trawlers meant for tuna and shrimp. The tuna boats and shrimpers have limited storage space and ice; for them, most sharks are "trash fish," tossed overboard for the gulls.

"The sharks will all be gone in twenty, maybe thirty years. There are much fewer sharks than there were five years ago. Ask anybody in La Paz, they'll tell you the same." Paulino Pérez sighs and looks up at the ceiling. A green lizard is resting there upside down, its tiny toes splayed in a grip. Over the hum of the floor fan, the night outside his studio crackles with croaks and chirps.

He is a painter, but Paulino knows a lot about sharks: he spent three years researching their eating habits for his thesis in marine biology at the Universidad de Baja California Sur. That was why he'd come to La Paz, to study marine biology; he grew up on the mainland, near Guadalajara. He obtained the shark specimens for his thesis research from local fishermen. When he'd finished, he took his data to PESCA, the Mexican fish and game authority.

"They needed it," he says, "because what they had was a big mess." PESCA registers catches of *tiburón*, or shark, and *cazón*, which means, roughly, small shark. "But *cazón*," Paulino explains, "can be shark species as different from one another as elephants and chickens. And not only that, PESCA counts a kilogram of dried shark meat the same as fresh. Age, size, species, none of these are differentiated."

Paulino put together some conferences, but the PESCA officials were not interested in his data. That was disheartening, as were his prospects as a researcher-professor. The pay was, as they say, *una miseria*. Even worse, as far as the sharks were concerned, more research wouldn't be of much use anyway. "Everyone will tell you the sharks are disappearing, although there's no really good data on the trend. To get really good data I'd have to do a ten-year study, but in ten years the subject of my research might not exist! What's happening is happening, whether I study the sharks or not."

What the PESCA officials were interested in were his photos and illustrations. Rather than despair, Paulino took that as a signal. "I can make art, I can transmit a feeling. And that, I think, is a contribution."

The walls of his studio are covered with his paintings, all of them of things submerged in water: a shark, a fish, a hand, two swimmers, the light playing on their bodies like tangles of ropes. Paulino is fascinated by the water; he always has been. When he was small, he would put his head in the washtub and look back up at the surface, shimmering like a layer of mercury. As a teenager, he took up skin diving. It always attracted him, the way light moves through water.

"It's very fast. Things appear, disappear. You don't see anything, and then all of a sudden: a whale! You see bubbles, a whole cloud of bubbles, then nothing. And colors—" he is on the edge of his chair now, waving his hands, his face pinkly glistening in the heat, the harsh bright light of the lamps—"in the sea there are *thousands* of colors."

The Bones of Cortés

PLAY GOD, scissor the Sea of Cortés out of the map, and move it around the globe. Seven hundred miles long, and an average of eighty miles wide, "the world's biggest fish trap," as Ray Cannon dubbed it, would spill over the Adriatic and drown the whole of Calabria. It would span the Portuguese, Spanish, and French borders, from Lisbon to Marseille. Or to try something vertical, say, from the prairies, over the Appalachians, and down into Dixie: you could lay the mouth of the Colorado River over Chicago, and Cabo San Lucas would touch Mobile, Alabama.

It takes nearly two hours to fly its length in a jet plane. I flew that length on my way home from the holidays in California, arrowing straight down the peninsula, the Pacific out the right-hand window, the Sea of Cortés out the left. I recognized the juts and scoops of the coastline now, each island. Nearing Loreto, Isla del Carmen came into view, beige like cookie dough, fish-shaped, wider than I'd imagined it. Then Santa Catalina, Santa Cruz, San José, Espíritu Santo. And then, after a brief stop to go through customs at the Los Cabos airport, home again to Mexico City, the valley of asphalt and concrete.

It's always a shock, the view on landing. *"Ay, el monstruo,"* mumbled the woman next to me. Ay, the monster. She crossed herself and kissed her thumb as we descended into the haze.

꩜

MEXICO CITY, like modern Mexico, begins with Hernán Cortés. And yet—that fantastic fact—in this city studded with statues there is none to honor this greatest of the conquistadors. We have only the paintings: Rivera's syphilitic, Orozco's evil robot.

"Cortés?" I could sense Paulino Pérez's revulsion like a shiver.

The Aztecs believed he was the plumed serpent Quetzalcóatl, god of wind and learning, returned from the East. And so, when his five hundred white-faced men and their sixteen horses and their translator, Doña Malinche, descended into the valley of Mexico, into that vision from the Amadises, they were received as beings from the sky. "Who could now count," recalled the old soldier Bernal Díaz, "the multitude of men, women, and boys in the streets, on the roof-tops and in canoes on the waterways, who had come out to see us?" As Cortés and his soldiers marched through Coyoacán, the chiefs touched the ground before them and kissed it. Approaching the island city of Tenochtitlán, they encountered the Aztec emperor Moctezuma on his palanquin, his lords shielding him with a canopy of green feathers decorated with gold and silver and pearls. Moctezuma, whom none of the other Indians dared look in the face, wore sandals of beaten gold; when he alighted from his palanquin, his lords swept the ground and laid down their cloaks for him to walk on.

Cortés presented him with a necklace of glass beads. Moctezuma reciprocated with a necklace of exquisitely worked golden crabs.

"Our lord," said Moctezuma, "I am not asleep or dreaming; with my eyes I see your face and your person." The terrible prophecy had come true. This was the will of the gods.

Then it happened, went an Aztec poem, *That the sky was crushed.*

Wrote Octavio Paz in *The Labyrinth of Solitude,* "[W]e shout *'¡Viva México, hijos de la chingada!'*" Literally, "sons of the raped woman," that is, sons of Hernán Cortés and Doña Malinche, Ur-*chingada.* The modern Mexican, goes this line of thinking, is a mestizo, both con quered and conquerer, member, in the words of José Vasconcelos, Revolutionary philosopher-politician, of *"La Raza Cósmica,"* the Cosmic Race.

Most Mexicans are indeed mestizo. But what of the many millions who are Huichol, Nahua, Mayan, Mixtec, Mayo, Tarahumara, Purapecha, Yaqui, or Zapotec? Some Mexicans are part African—for there were Negro slaves brought here, too. And Baja California with its Van Wormers, Wilkeses, Fishers, Ritchies, Davises, and Drews is not unique in its tradition of immigration. Two hundred thousand descendents of Lebanese immigrants live in Mexico City alone. There are Jews, Sephardic and Ashkenazi; there are Japanese, Chinese, French, Italian, and Irish Mexicans. One Mexican friend has a Russian great-grandfather who was emigrating to New York but got on the wrong boat. Many Mexican citizens are exiles: from the Spanish civil war, from Castro's Cuba, from the terrors of Argentina and Chile of the 1970s, Guatemala and El Salvador of the 1980s.

I have lived in Mexico City too long: I no longer see a forest, only trees.

In Mexico nothing is as it seems. The Hospital de Jesús, for example. One could drive right by what looks like a shoestring Bauhaus imitation, circa 1950, unremarkably ugly, like so many other buildings in Mexico City. But within, intact, is the charitable hospital founded by Hernán Cortés, on the very spot of his first meeting with Moctezuma, still in operation after nearly five hundred years. In its courtyard—beautifully proportioned, framed by graceful stone columns—one might be in Madrid or Seville. It is cool so deep inside this shell, the light strangely blue. Sounds from the city outside, of traffic rushing by, a street vendor's radio, are muffled.

Around to the back is the stone chapel where Cortés's bones are mortared into the wall. When I went there one weekday winter morning, there was no one. My footsteps sounded as I walked down the nave, past a glass-encased life-size Christ shouldering his cross, his forehead gouged and bloodied beneath his crown of thorns. I viewed the mural that swept over the choir ceiling, a riot of flame and soot— *Apocalipsis,* by Orozco. Finally, I found, on the wall by the altar, that humble bronze plaque. There were no flowers on the altar. It was very quiet.

Bay of Angels

Bahía de los Angeles

> ...and the voice of the turtle is heard.
>
> (Song of Sol. 2:12)

In the Air

IN LATE SEPTEMBER I was back on the Sea of Cortés with my sister, Alice. Six hours down from the border, in the thick of the boojum forest, we'd cut east toward the Bahía de los Angeles, the Bay of Angels. More boojums, sandy flats, bald sun-sizzled sierra that Alice said reminded her of the Alaskan tundra. At kilometer fifty-three we first saw the sea. Alice said, "Oh, my God."

We stopped the car to take a photograph.

Did it look anything like Alaska?

"No."

The Bahía de los Angeles was swimming with islands: tiny guano-bright hillocks, a massive volcanic cone, and one—Angel de la Guarda (Guardian Angel)—so vast it looked like a swath of mainland, strangely near. The town of Bahía de los Angeles, however, was a pitiful thing, far off in the distance, a clutch of cinder blocks like a splotch on the southern cup of the bay.

The road descended. A trio of vultures circled as we passed through the garbage dump. And then, hard against the barren shore, we came to the string of ramshackle houses and ramshackle RV parks.

Guillermos RV Park had a room behind the office. It was fairly clean, only three cockroaches (thumb-size, belly-up) on the bathroom floor. But there was no water or light until six in the evening. The deal was, water and light from six to four in the morning, and from six to eleven in the morning. Twenty-five U.S. dollars, cash in advance.

Outside, by the water, lingered a smell, faint but rank, something not unlike raw sewage with limburger cheese. A pack of dogs lazed in the sand. Some tables were set up beneath a palapa. A group of Americans was getting trashed on margaritas.

So this was it, the famous, beloved by Baja buffs, "Bay of L.A." Even back in 1940, Steinbeck found it too modern, with its airstrip and its one little airplane. When detective novelist Erle Stanley Gardner flew in with his entourage in the early 1960s, the Casa Díaz—which he touted as "this most interesting medium-priced resort"—had already been in operation for a number of years, catering to fly-in sportfishermen. Judging by the photographs in Gardner's books, Bahía de los Angeles had grown very little in the last thirty-odd years—these few RV parks, mom-and-pop groceries, a liquor store, a scattering of houses (shacks most of them) thrown up on the hill. It had changed in less obvious ways, however. The fishing wasn't what it used to be. And now, with the Mexican government trying to fight the cocaine barons, closing airstrips up and down the peninsula, fewer Americans were flying in. The airstrip was still open here, but there was no aviation fuel—or gasoline, for that matter. The last functioning Pemex station was in Cataviña, three hours north, and even there the supply was uncertain. (Alice and I were lucky: we'd had to wait only half an hour for the attendant to finish his breakfast.)

It had been a long drive down from the U.S. border, nearly twelve hours. We'd come to a town that was poor and dusty and ugly, but: on the Bahía de los Angeles, one of the most stunningly beautiful bays in the world.

If only it weren't for that ghastly stink.

The Right Idea

ALICE HAD the right idea: kick back, read, sip a margarita. But I had an agenda. There was a museum here—here of all places—and a sea-turtle research station. I wanted to interview the woman who'd founded the museum—she was an American named Carolina Shepard—and I also wanted to meet the marine biologist who ran the turtle research station. There were no telephones (as far as I knew), no way to know whether they would see me or not, no way to know if they were even in town. I had two days, that was all; then Alice had to get back to work. I'd come so far. I felt rushed, which was all wrong for a place like this—like wearing a tuxedo to a picnic, or trying to rollerblade through a supermarket. I speed walked out of the parking lot, *ni modo,* no matter.

The Museo de Naturaleza y Cultura was across the street from Guillermos RV Park, up the hill behind a stark, shadeless plaza and the municipal offices. It was a modest, square cinder-block building with reproductions of the cave paintings decorating its walls. A gray-whale skeleton was mounted on a platform out front; mining equipment from the abandoned mines in the nearby sierra, rusted buckets and shovels, were displayed in back. A cactus garden ringed the little building, each plant neatly labeled. The one by the door said: "Lophocereus schotti, Old Man, Garambullo, edible fruit, tea for ulcers, fish poison."

The museum was closed.

As I walked back down the dirt road to the municipal offices, the view of the bay was breathtaking. But again, the ugliness of the little town: parked in the dirt in front of the offices were two dust-encrusted police cars, both with their windshields smashed and tires punched flat. A policeman and another man stood by the door, huddled in a triangle of shade, watching me.

"*Buenas tardes,*" I said, that magic incantation. Did they know where I might find Carolina Shepard?

The policeman introduced himself and shook my hand. Happy to help! He presented me to the other man, a fisherman with a deeply creased face, dark as pickled walnut wood. Carolina? Oh, yes! He knew where Carolina lived; he would take me there. It was right up the hill, behind the museum. He began to walk, with strides so large I nearly had to jog to keep up. He wore big rubber wading boots that slapped loudly against his calves. As we passed the little museum, he flipped his hand as if to shoo a fly, and grinned sheepishly. *"Yo no sé nada de esas cosas,"* I don't know anything about those things.

He left me at the gate to Carolina's garden—a garden of cacti. It was a simple stuccoed house with a verandah. Through the screen window I could see a living room: chairs, a bookshelf with a row of encyclopedias. No one answered the bell. I left my card with a message. Then I walked back down the hill again, the bay a cobalt panorama before me.

Next, the sea-turtle research station. I took the car, plowing up the long, bumpy dirt road to the north shore. Already the light had begun fading to sepia, shadows stretching long. I followed the signs— a little turtle—through an abandoned trailer park. The asphalt was cracked and rubbly, but the cacti and elephant trees that had been planted (how long ago?) were still thriving. At the end sat the turtle research station, a thatched-roof enclosure. Sea-turtle carapaces were strung up all along its sides, huge leathery things rimed with salt and pocked with age.

The motor of a boat made a thin sound, far out on the water. A strong fishy smell wafted over me; the bay, I supposed, but then I realized it was coming from inside. As was the most curious noise: snuffly breaths like babies with bad colds. I walked right in to find three cement tanks, their rims as high as my chest. Two were empty, but one, painted blue, was filled with turtles. There were about ten of them, some as small as a handbag, several as big as coffee-table tops. Each turtle had a green silver dollar–size tag affixed to a flipper. They were swimming, around and around, bumping their noses against the sides of the tank. I watched them swimming, ceaselessly circling and bumping. They exhaled through their nostrils, a little *phsch! ssth.* The intervals between each breath were longer than a human's. They would put their heads back under after a breath and circle, bump, bump. Even in the dim, the water in their tank made crazy patterns of light, like shattered glass. I thought of Paulino Pérez's paintings, the light, like this, alive.

Then the turtles saw me. They crowded close, piling one on the other, slapping their flippers against each other, and raised their scaly heads, snuffled, blinked, frowned—like dogs hoping for a treat.

"*Cuidado las tortugas muerden,*" said the sign. "Caution the turtles bite."

Evening was falling when I found Alice sitting on the sand in front of Guillermos RV Park, fiddling with her shortwave radio. A light breeze had carried away that sewagey smell; the air held only a whiff of saltwater, fresh and cool. It was really very wonderful, to lie back on my elbows, the sand soft between my toes. We listened to the gentle crackle of the BBC, and the *shush* of the sea. The lighthouse on Isla Angel de la Guarda had begun to blink. It was an inky night with many stars.

At dinnertime there was a message for me, the waiter said when we sat down under the palapa outside Guillermos. Carolina Shepard had stopped by. That put me in a good mood; and so did dinner—fried scallops in homemade flour tortillas, and flan for dessert, eggy rich and laced with vanilla, the best flan, we both agreed, ever.

But then we came down to earth. There was no light in our room. Alice, however, had come prepared: Chemsticks from her survival kit. She took one out of its wrapper, snapped its top, and *voilà:* phosphorescent green light.

"Lasts for hours," she said.

There was no water, either.

Kind of Special and Wonderful

AT 7:45 A.M. the sun was a ball of fire, yellow-hot light streaming in through the window of the restaurant at Guillermos. I'd left Alice still sleeping (the Chemstick weakly glowing). I was gulping my coffee, shuffling through my collection of newspaper clippings, making notes—I was still in my tuxedo, as it were, ready to rollerblade. But I didn't have to go anywhere, because suddenly, there before my table like an apparition, stood a slight, red-haired woman in a gauzy purple cotton sundress. She gave me a huge sunbeam of a smile. Carolina Shepard—she held out a slender, freckled hand—director of the Museo de Naturaleza y Cultura.

A museum: the audacity of it. In this tiny little town of 520 people? Wherever did she get the idea?

She laughed, pulled out a chair. "You know that old saying, 'One man's trash is another man's treasure'? The first American couple to build a house here decided to go back to the U.S. after twenty years. The people who bought the house didn't want the junk they'd collected, so they hauled it all to the dump. I saw that they'd thrown out things they'd picked up from the mines. So I got to thinking, lots of things must be here. We tend to be souvenir happy. I began asking around."

The response was immediate and generous: local people brought in mining equipment, snakes and scorpions, family photographs. Indian artifacts turned up, and leather goods from the ranches. An American couple donated a professional collection of shells. "There are six hundred species of shells in the Sea of Cortés, of which we have five hundred. It's a beautiful collection."

But if the museum was her idea, it was built, Carolina stressed, by the efforts of many different individuals and groups. Financing came largely from jewelry and T-shirt sales. The city donated the land. The town's soccer team dug the foundation; a group of marine biology students from Glendale College in California helped with the construction; students from the university in Ensenada assembled a juvenile gray-whale skeleton that hangs from the ceiling. A tourist from Mexicali named Fabio and a woman visiting from Oregon did the cave-painting murals. "People just volunteer out of nowhere. It's kind of special and wonderful."

But Carolina was no naive do-gooder. When the museum opened in 1988, she'd already been living in Bahía de los Angeles for nearly twenty years, married to a local Mexican. Plus, she'd studied marine biology at the University of California at Berkeley. The idea of a museum may have been audacious, but she knew what was needed and what was possible.

Still, there were challenges. The local people didn't know what a museum was; they'd never seen one before. "They thought it was something for tourists. It was a hurdle to make them feel the museum was a part of their community, their history, their Sea of Cortés. Little by little they're warming up."

I mentioned the fisherman who'd taken me to her house the day before. Clearly he was fond of her, yet the museum—*"Yo no sé nada de esas cosas"*—intimidated him. I was reminded of Todos Santos, I said, another town with an American community and a population of locals somewhat stunned, like deer frozen in the headlights, by change. The big change here, it seemed to me, was the increasing fragility of the Sea of Cortés. A museum's raison d'être was education. Didn't that bring her into some conflict with the fishermen?

"We're generally very diplomatic. When you live in a small town you have to be. You know, you criticize and then when you need your car repaired, the parts just don't come—or you run out of gas while you're out in your boat, who's going to help you? The local people have a very poor economy. It's problematic for institutions to tell people, 'You can't fish yellowtail, you can't fish turtles,' when they need shoes. That's what they do for a living. There are not many alternatives here, there's not much know-how.

"The key is to educate the children. The schoolteachers bring them to visit the museum. And, we're now in our sixth year of offering kids' classes in the summer. We do arts and crafts, which is kind of new for them because they don't get that at school. A U.S. dive shop donated snorkel equipment for thirty kids, and another donated wetsuits and fins. So we take the kids out. We try to get them interested in their surroundings. We go out in a boat, we look at birds, we pick up trash, we hike in the desert. We're trying to get kids to think: What things affect other things? But again, it's touchy. You can't tell them their fathers or brothers are wrong to catch, say, turtles. But we can make them more aware, teach them about the food chain. It's very basic, but it's new for here."

New, after all that had happened? I had a thick sheaf of clippings about the factory ships that used to come into the bay, and the bait boats that wiped out the anchovies and sardines back in the 1980s—

the entire food chain, from birds to porpoises, even whales, had been affected. Overfishing had decimated all classes of sharks and game fish, as well as clams, mussels, squid, octopus, and, of course, turtles. So few were left that in 1990, the Mexican government outlawed turtle fishing and trade in turtle products.

"Until now, the local people haven't realized what it is to deplete a species. It's like the U.S. was fifty years ago, this eternal optimism." Slowly, an awareness was "coming into their consciousness," as she put it, most notably last year when the sea-cucumber population collapsed.

Four years ago, an Asian buyer had shown up. "They were bringing in a ton per boat per day, filled to gunnels with biomass. This went on for about three years, a big economic shot in the arm. Local people worked as divers, then people had to gut and cook the sea cucumbers, then people had to cook for the people who were working. People buy things from the stores—lots of 'trickle down.' The sea cucumbers were shipped to Los Angeles; there they filled cargo containers to go to Japan. Now there's no product left. They wiped it out. We don't know about the life cycles of the sea cucumber, its maturity. We don't know how it would reproduce in captivity. And now it's gone."

Gone: like the "mile long schools of migrating totuaba," the "massive aggregations," "hordes," "throngs," and "pileups," the waters, as Ray Cannon wrote only three decades ago, "so full of life." Fishing, I ventured, was not the future.

"Seventy percent of the income in this town comes from tourism, which is mostly based on natural history. Less and less is sportfishing. We don't get the Cabo crowd; there are no Jet-Skis to rent, no nightlife. You either really like this place or you don't. It's rough. You have to come to see the birds or the whales or the desert. Hopefully we'll see more ecotourism. And hopefully, the museum can help get young people to stop and think. Take care of your economic source, otherwise it will slowly fade."

❧

AGAIN: THAT FUNKY, god-awful smell. The dogs lying in the sand. A boat roaring over the water. At midmorning the air felt as hot as a furnace. The light was a white glare. Alice and I plodded up the dirt road to the museum. Entering the little cinder block felt like a cool drink of water. We had to stand still for a moment, waiting for our eyes to adjust.

Hanging from the ceiling, like a fantastic mobile, was the thirty-foot-long skeleton of a juvenile gray whale—the one assembled by the students from Ensenada. We moved forward, past the shell collection. We reviewed a fossil collection, and dried crabs and pufferfish and seahorses. Then: a cabinet displaying Mexican money, bills and old coins. There was a satellite photograph of the bay, Indian arrowheads, a skull, and a pelican-feather shawl, soft-looking, like beaver fur. Partitions zigzagged through the center of the one big room, festooned with posters and photographs, wedged up against cabinets and shelving. Here were photographs of the cave paintings; there, a display of leatherwork from the ranchos. A shelf was stocked with chunks of onyx from El Mármol; from Las Flores and San Juan, rusted shovels and picks. And too—not at all subtle—photographs from the 1960s of the turtle fishermen "harvesting their abundant crop."

But what fascinated me were the photographs of local people. Here was Dick Daggett Jr. (1893–1969), a grizzled old man in a plaid shirt. I knew who he was— "a rough and ready mechanical genius," as Erle Stanley Gardner called him. Son of a sailor and a *bajacaliforniana*, Dick Daggett Jr. was the town mechanic, in fact the only mechanic for miles. In the days before the Transpeninsular, he was the savior of many a stranded traveler. The story of how his father, Dick Daggett Sr., arrived in the 1880s has been told in nearly every book written about Baja California. An English sailor on a German ship bringing machinery to the mines, he'd had a fight with the captain, and when the ship anchored in Bahía, Daggett escaped and hid in a cave. After three days of searching for him the captain gave up and set sail; Dick Sr., soon to become the "Grand Padre of the Waist of the Peninsula," as Arthur North called him, remained to work the gold mines. And there, in a little Plexiglas case, were Dick Sr.'s binoculars, one of the few possessions he had with him when he jumped ship. *Donado por Ricardo Daggett.*

Casa Díaz, "this most interesting medium-priced resort" as Erle Stanley Gardner dubbed it, was represented with a framed blowup of an article about its owner, Antero Díaz. There were photographs of his wife, Doña Cruz Díaz, and of the airplane of "Capitán Muñoz"—Gardner's gap-toothed bush pilot—parked on the tarmac out front. And there were the three Smith boys, Memo, Nene, and Nelo, barefoot, their shirts hanging out. I recognized Nene from one of Gardner's books, a jug-eared kid in a tattered straw hat, "an alert, intelligent lad who . . . did a man's work."

I was very moved by what Carolina had done. She'd trawled through what looked like junk and netted treasures. And if so many people had helped her, it was because the museum mattered.

Even to Alice. She was calling me to come look, "Look!" She had pointed at a photograph of Doña Cruz Díaz with an American man, mild-faced and middle-aged, in khaki pants and a shirt. Entirely ordinary looking.

"That is Charles Lindbergh."

A Complex Situation

THINGS HAD A way of working out today. I'd gotten my interview with Carolina Shepard; now I was back at the sea-turtle research station with its director, Antonio "Toño" Resendiz. Someone else had gotten to him first, however, a shaggy-haired American with a video-camera. He was a dive master from Sacramento, eight years in Cozumel, the American said, shaking my hand. He was discussing plans to bring down a busload of schoolkids from California: "You make it through high school drug free, you get to come here and experience Baja."

"Sounds good," I said.

"Yeah." He aimed the videocamera at the turtles. "See the turtles, see the whales, dolphins, sea lions, pelicans. Help with the research." He pushed the stop button. "And, it's real cheap!"

Toño and the dive master went off; they had logistics to discuss. I waited, my elbows on the rim of the tank, watching the turtles. There was something mesmerizing about the turtles, their incessant circling, bumping, circling. I liked the way light played around in the tank, quivering threads and tangles. And the turtles' breathing, *phsch! ssth.* In spite of the fishy smell, and the sign—*Cuidado las tortugas muerden*—it was tempting to lean down, dip a wrist into that cool blue water.

Phsch! ssth.

"Three million dollars!" Toño Resendiz came walking back with the American, spitting with indignation. He was talking about the turtle research station in Oaxaca, on the mainland's Pacific coast. "It's all political," Toño was saying, "Salinas' show for NAFTA." Toño had a visceral, authoritative energy, a thick brooding brow, hair frosted silver at the temples. "Then came the devaluation, and the peso went from three to more than seven to the dollar. Imagine!"

He looked at the both of us, fiercely. "Before, it was three. Imagine!"

Unfortunately, I didn't have to.

For the interview we went to his house, upshore at the end of a sandy road, and we sat on the porch, which was strewn with his daughter's toys and a tricycle.

He was forty-two years old, Toño said, born in Mexico City. He'd studied marine biology at the university in Ensenada. When he was only twenty-four, he'd been given a two thousand–dollar government grant to study the turtles in the Sea of Cortés for PESCA. "The idea was, it's OK to fish turtles, but why not some order? A calendar? A turtle might live for a hundred years. But what is their life cycle? Their sexual maturity?"

Soon the government built the trailer park and gave him more money, enough for two assistants and a pickup truck. "My generation is the hippies, Clinton, Enrique Krauze.[1] We had a lot of opportunities. This was the time of petrodollars, the boom."

I was familiar with Mexico's economic history. True, in 1976, President Echeverría— *"arriba y adelante México"*—had left the country in a mire of debt and inflation. But by the late 1970s, with the bonanza of newly discovered oil reserves, Mexico had become a major exporter. In 1976, oil exports generated 3.6 billion dollars; by 1981, they'd soared to nearly 20 billion. Dollars washed into Mexico like a Niagara, and President López Portillo spent them with an abandon that made Echeverría, by comparison, look pusillanimous. López Portillo's attempts to *"administrar la abundancia"* amounted to hosing money over the economy in a random spray: expressways, theaters, pipelines, hotels, hospitals, loans to Cuba, workers' vacation centers, junkets, gifts to the Sandinistas, skyscrapers, advertising, grants for research, for graduate study abroad, concert halls, TV shows, newspapers, airports, airplanes, archaeological excavations, tortilla subsidies, movie production, museums, metro lines. Toño Resendiz's turtle research grants were just spare change, tossed off like a handful of pennies. It was a time of crass excess: politicians sported Rolexes, labor bosses hopped into private jets to roll the dice in Vegas. The wife of one prominent politician traveled with her baby grand piano (which on one occasion involved having to break the roof of the hotel open and lower it down into her penthouse via helicopter). The son of Mexico City's mayor bought a million-dollar mansion in New Canaan, Connecticut; López Portillo himself had the audacity to construct for his personal use a five-mansion complex in plain view of Mexico City's main commuter expressway. Debt piled on top of debt, until by 1982, with oil prices falling and U.S. interest rates rising, the spigot began dribbling dry. In February, the peso plunged from twenty-two to seventy to the dollar.[2] On Friday, August 13, with the peso hovering around one hundred, the minister of finance flew to Washington, hat in hand. Mexico was bankrupt.

For Toño, everything collapsed. Over the next two years he survived as a sportfishing guide. During this dark period, he met Dr. Grant Bartlett, a biochemist from San Diego. Until his death in 1990, Bartlett sponsored the turtle station's research, donating a pickup truck and the equipment and shed for the laboratory.

By the early 1990s, Mexico's debt had been renegotiated. With a sweeping series of reforms—liberalization, deregulation, privatization, and, finally, NAFTA—President Salinas had engineered what appeared to be a solid recovery. Dollars had begun flooding into Mexico, and once again, Toño had his government research grants. He still worked with PESCA; older and wiser now, he'd joined the local *ejido,* and was supplementing his income by renting out palapas to campers. He'd also learned, as he put it, "to present an image" for the turtle research station, garnering donations from as far afield as Germany and Japan. The U.S. Fish and Wildlife Service granted use of their satellite. And so, to a degree, Toño was better able to cope with the crisis that exploded in December 1994.

As Yogi Berra would say, it was déjà vu all over again: devaluation, economic depression, and the evidences of corruption crawling out of the woodwork like worms from a burning log.

"Salinas! All those guys with doctorates in economics! And Clinton, he invites them to Washington and he eats with them! White-collar criminals, they're the most corrupt. They're the ones who traffic in drugs, in children. The jails are filled with poor people! Rich people go free, even in the United States—look at O. J. Simpson."

Toño gazed out toward the water, his eyes hard and, at the same time, far away. You could hear the water from here, *shush, shush* ... A pair of pelicans skimmed by.

"I'm forty-two years old. If I died now it would be all right. I've done what I wanted in life."

It hadn't been easy. With reason, Paulino Pérez had given up on the sharks and turned to painting. But here was Toño Resendiz, after more than two decades, still studying the turtles. He'd weathered what he called the *"surrealismo nacional."* And not only that: Bahía de los Angeles was a world away from Mexico City's conveniences and culture. There was no gas, little water; the electricity flickered in from generators. The town's first and only telephone had just been installed—in a closet-size grocery store—last year. "My friends in Mexico City and Ensenada, they think I'm crazy."

But there was opportunity here, and Toño's efforts had yielded a resounding success. The Sea of Cortés is an area where juvenile turtles feed and grow. His mandate was to gather biological, ecological, and life-history information; to study behavior, sexual maturity, migration, and captive caring techniques; and to contribute to an international DNA database. Turtles were captured, studied, tagged, and released. So little was known. For example, where did the loggerhead turtles come from? Once grown, where did they go? The theory was, somewhere near Japan. It was one of Toño's turtles, a 213-pound loggerhead named Rosita, that provided the first hard evidence. Rosita was released off the peninsula's Pacific coast in July 1994. Fourteen months later, she turned up off the shore of Kyushu, drowned in a Japanese fisherman's net. Noting her plastic tag, the fisherman alerted a local biologist who, in turn, e-mailed a colleague, Wallace Nichols at the University of Arizona. Because Bahía de los Angeles didn't yet have a telephone, Nichols drove all the way down to break the news to Resendiz.

"He was bouncing off the walls," Nichols told the *San Diego Union-Tribune.* "This is the culmination of ten years of work for him." Toño, beaming, had handed me a copy of the newspaper article. The theory was that Rosita had swum all the way to Japan on the equatorial current that swings south of Hawaii. As a juvenile, she would have made her way to Baja California on the current that arcs north of Hawaii and down the west coast of the peninsula. A map showed the route: two arcs like a double jump rope spanning the 6,500 miles of open ocean.

No wonder the turtles were bumping their noses against the sides of the tank.

We walked over to the laboratory, the shed donated by Dr. Bartlett. Inside, the walls were decorated with posters of whales and turtles. A generator powered a laptop and printer. The station also measured seismic activity, Toño said, and tides and weather. He had an assistant, a schoolteacher named Félix who lived in a trailer by the water.

One thing had struck me, I said. He'd not mentioned anything about the precarious situation of the various sea-turtle populations. Despite the ban, they were still being fished. Worldwide, thousands drowned in the nets meant for tuna and shrimp. Their nests were raided, too: a single turtle egg—prized as an aphrodisiac—might sell for as much as two dollars in Mexico City. It was common knowledge that there weren't enough PESCA inspectors to police even a fraction of Mexico's waters, and it was also common knowledge that most were willing to look the other way for the equivalent of twenty dollars, or less. I understood his elation about Rosita. But it seemed so sad, I said, that she'd swum those thousands of miles only to die in a net.

Toño had zero patience with this kind of sentimentality. "Look," he said. "Illegal fishing is a problem of corruption, but it's also a problem of poverty. How are people going to live?" Turtles were meat, especially for poor fishermen.

A different issue was industrial shrimp and tuna fishing on the high seas, the fleets with factory ships, spotter helicopters, miles-long nets.

"You know what? A bluefin tuna might sell for eighteen thousand dollars. *Really!* I told that to some reporters, and they didn't believe me. There are cases when a single tuna has sold for sixty-two thousand dollars. All sorts of things die as bycatch—turtles, dolphins, birds. But look at what somebody is getting: thousands of dollars! What do they care if ten turtles get caught in the net? It's a complex situation."

He shrugged.

I could come back, he said, and watch him feed the turtles.

Shrimp Tacos Twice

FOR LUNCH Alice and I had shrimp tacos, and big, wide-mouthed icy glasses of limeade. The straws kept popping out, skittering off the table onto the sand.

"Wow!" It was the man at the next table, one of a group of Americans. Their four-wheel-drive Ford truck with a gleaming stainless-steel camper shell the size of a small house was parked out front. "Will ya look at that!" One raised his margarita, the same big, wide-mouthed glass, at Alice. "Serious drinking there!"

"It's just limeade," Alice said.

"Oh, right, *ha ha!*"

I was afraid we might not get rid of them, but their attention had already careened over to their waiter. "What's yer name! Igor? Eeegor! *Ha ha!*" And the rest of our lunch was punctuated with their calls to "Igor! Need some napkins here! Eeeegor! Salt!" We were on our coffee when one of them started singing, *Oh, she thinks she's got some class! But babeee! Yore jus' a horse's ass!*

The wind shifted and that smell, ranker than overripe limburger, wafted through the palapa.

"Whew!" one of the Americans elbowed the other. "What crawled up into you and died?"

The smell was worse, even a few yards down the beach. The air, away from the little square of shade under Guillermos's palapa, was grillingly hot. We'd walked over the dirt boat ramp to Casa Díaz next door because we were curious about Charles Lindbergh's visit. Alice, quite the Lindbergh expert, hadn't known about it.

Casa Díaz was a compound like a small town in itself. The rooms, in long shoebox-shaped buildings, framed a large, open yard with a stone chapel, a mechanic shop, a Pemex station (out of business), and, tucked along a verandah, a grocery store and the offices of the ministry of tourism. Behind loomed the sierra, baking in the afternoon sun.

Char-les *¿qué?* No one knew anything about him in the grocery store. No one had seen the photo in the museum, either. One of the cashiers, a gangly-legged boy, led us outside to an old man in a baseball cap who was resting, hands on his stomach, in the shade under the verandah.

Charles Lindbergh? The famous pilot? He would have visited here, Alice guessed, sometime in the late 1960s.

"Oh, yes," the old man said, brightening. "I think we have a picture."

We followed him around the side of the grocery and into an enormous light-filled room, a rec room of sorts, with a shelf of paperback novels gathering dust in a corner. Everything was dusty, the floor, the broken-down piano with its chipped keys, the stacks of misshapen cardboard boxes. On the walls hung faded family photos (I recognized the long-gone founders of the hotel, Antero and Doña Cruz

Díaz, from the museum), and, oddly, a large, framed oil painting of astronauts walking on the moon.

"There it is," the man said.

It was a blown-up black-and-white photograph, about the same size as the astronaut painting, of a heavyset, jowly man posing in front of a small plane.

"That's not him," Alice said. It wasn't Erle Stanley Gardner or Capitán Muñoz, either.

Antero Díaz Jr. might know, the man said. And at that very moment—we could see through the window—Antero Jr. was hauling his launch up the boat ramp. We made our way, painfully, back across the griddle of the open yard.

Antero Jr.'s boat, gleaming white as a new refrigerator, was named the *Chubasco;* the same name was embroidered on his shiny white cap. He was cigarette-slim and very tan, and he wore a gold chain with a gold pendant in the shape of the peninsula, which flashed brightly.

He remembered Lindbergh's visit, he said. Lindbergh didn't like to have his picture taken. That photo in the museum with his mother, Doña Cruz, was probably the only one. But no, he himself had not actually met Lindbergh; he'd been away at school in Ensenada at the time.

❧

THE HEAT was so strong that simply trekking back and forth over the parking lot for this Lindbergh business had exhausted us. Back in our room at Guillermos, Alice collapsed on the bed. But we had only one more day before we had to leave; I hoped to go out on a skiff the next morning and see the islands. To arrange this, once more I trudged out into the glare.

Then, late in the afternoon, I drove up the hill, past all the little houses that clung to its steep slope as though by their fingernails. The sun had slipped behind the sierra, and shadow, grayly soothing, bathed the little town and the shore far below. Angel de la Guarda still blushed a warm rosy-pink, even as the water lightened to a pale, silvered sapphire.

It was twilight when I shook Alice awake. We went for a walk along the beach. A black dog followed us partway, now and then stopping to sniff at something, then trotting along again.

On our way back we took a stroll through Guillermos RV Park. It wasn't at all like the trailer park in Todos Santos, the uniformly tall, shaggy palapas, the neat, shaded patios. This was a patchwork jumble of construction, rickety plywood and thatch, cinder block, a double-wide mobile home, a fussy little cactus garden rimmed with stones. One house looked like a barn. Along the shore the spaces were spanned with constructions, shoulder to shoulder. Farther back from the water, the rows became sparser. Decks had been constructed on top of some trailers to provide a view. There was a Winnebago hooked up, and a pickup truck and a pup tent strung, oddly, with Christmas lights. Most of the spaces for transients were empty; late September was the off-season. It was dark now, but in the dim flicker of a streetlamp, we could make out the sign nailed to one structure: FOR SALE. Just beneath the sign, under a palapa, a man lolled on a cot in the flickering blue-gray light of a TV.

For dinner we had shrimp tacos again. I'd made Alice sad, telling her about the turtles, how they drowned in the shrimp nets. But not that sad.

"But you have to admit," she said, glopping on the guacamole, "they *are* a heap better than Gardenburgers."

We almost didn't notice that stink.

A Vast, Strange Place

WE WOKE while it was still dark, our room aglow with the eery green light of a Chemstick. Within minutes, we were dressed and outside, stumbling our way down to the beach. Dawn appeared in an instant, a peach-colored haze rising from behind the islands, stone-dark, hulking shapes. We found our guide, Igor Galván, pushing our skiff down the boat ramp. It scraped over the sand and settled with a *sploosh* through the limpid surf. We waded into the chill, jelly-yellow water. The skiff rocked with our weight. And we were off, the noise of the motor buzzing through the stillness, obscene, like a saw.

Igor was the son of the owner of Guillermos RV Park. Tall and hefty as a college football player, Igor was a poker-faced, almond-eyed twenty-something year old with a mustache and a goatee. He wore plaid shorts and a gimme cap that said "J&B." He'd grimaced when I'd said we didn't want to fish. "Ecotour," although Carolina had used it, was a tad highfalutin a term for this place. We just wanted to "see things," was how I'd put it, "islands, birds, whales, you know."

The stink, limburger-sewage, was making us gag. Finally, we found out what it was: *"Ballena muerta,"* Igor announced. Dead whale. The bloated rot-brown carcass lay onshore just above the waterline, covered with an army of birds, pecking. I grabbed my shirt and wadded it over my mouth and nose. Alice buried her face in her sleeve. I leaned over the gunwales, and I thought I would but I didn't heave.

Igor swiveled the rudder and made a wide U-turn on the water, arcing out toward the northeast. *"Vamos ahora a La Ventana,"* he announced. We were off to Isla La Ventana, Window Island.

The sky had turned a fragile blue, and the clouds—at first pearl gray, then corraline and orange—looked bleached and luminous. The islands beyond were raw with sun, pale now as if they were made of nothing but sand. Was that a mist rising off the water near the horizon, or sun glare? "The very air here is miraculous," wrote John Steinbeck, "and outlines of reality change with the moment." It was like traveling into a dream, a vast, strange place where anything might be possible. A gull swooped over the prow, yellow legs flat against its snow-white belly. Alice's hair snapped back in the breeze.

Far in the distance was a milling cloud of birds.

"Feeding frenzy," Igor said. As we approached the cloud of birds, the water appeared to be erupting in little bursts. Soon the cawing and squawking was a cacophony louder than the boat motor. *Splash, splash, splash,* it was a rain of birds falling from the cloud, terns and gulls and geese and pelicans, folding their wings and diving, straight like bombs. Dolphins porpoised through the melee, squealing lustily. The whole party, fish, birds, dolphins, roiled through the water at a fast clip. We watched them move on, toward Isla Angel de la Guarda.

After about twenty minutes, we motored alongside La Ventana, a rocky island striped white with guano. A curious rock formation, a triangle with a hole in its center, gave the island its name. Starboard hulked the great mass of Isla Angel de la Guarda. In between that and these smaller islands stretched the Canal de Ballenas, Whale Channel.

There were more whales here in the winter, Igor said, including two or three killer-whale pods. Dolphins stayed in the bay year-round, as did a seal colony on La Calavera, the Skull, a puff-shaped rock frosted like a cupcake with guano.

Within minutes, we were rounding La Calavera, close in along black wet rocks draped with seaweed. The seals, some twenty-five or thirty with many little pups, lay basking in the sun, massed like vacationers on a beach. The seals were a harem belonging to a huge bear-brown male, shiny-sleek and fat. He pushed himself up on his flippers and shook himself like a dog. Their barks sounded like a cross between a dog's and a duck's honk, and their little snouts were sharp and whiskered.

"The killer whales take the seals down and drown them," Igor said. "They like to play football with them."

Suddenly, Igor stood up in the boat and started barking. The whole colony rushed, squealing with terror, slapping their fat bodies over the rocks, *plosh, plosh,* into the water. They stayed there, watching us, all the little heads bobbing up and down.

"You can swim with them if you want," Igor said. "No problem."

Igor had wanted to fish. To go out and just look at things, this wasn't his style.

And then we were nearing Isla Coronado, a long squiggly-shaped island crowned with a massive volcanic cone, when another skiff puttered by. I recognized the fisherman who'd led me to Carolina Shepard's house.

Catch anything? he asked by raising his chin.

Nah, Igor made a thumbs down.

The fisherman looked at me and Alice and laughed.

"Ha caído mucho," It's fallen a lot, Igor confessed when I asked about the fishing. The grouper were almost gone. "They took out tons." But now the commercial boats were relegated to the sea beyond the bay. "We don't let them in; we'll run them out. They can come in to get water and food, but that's it."

Now a skiff—what the locals called a *panga*—might take fifteen to twenty dolphinfish on a good day of sportfishing. And there were still lots of bass, sierra, and tuna. Divers could harvest lobster, octopus, clams, and scallops—although not so many sea cucumbers as before.

The economics were tough, Igor explained. "A *panga* costs two thousand dollars. The motor will cost you six thousand. It costs thirty-five dollars to fill the gas tank. To cover your costs you have to work, both sportfishing and for your own account, for one full year, all day, every day." The going daily rate charged to sportfishermen and other tourists was eighty dollars. "And with sportfishing," Igor said, "sometimes you get to keep the fish as a tip."

And the tourists who wanted to see the animals?

"Every two or three weeks, we get some people, yeah."

Now we were going to see a very pretty beach, Igor said, steering the *panga* to the north. We hugged the shore of Isla Coronado. At the far end of the island rose the cone of its volcano, nude and rubble gray. Pelicans perched on the rocks along the water's edge in twos and threes. They watched us with their beadlike yellow eyes, their bills tucked to their breasts like suspicious old ladies. We'd rounded the volcano and were heading south down the west side of the island. The shoreline was ruffled now with pickleweed. Above, on the crags, a stand of cardón cactus. The sun was warm and honey-yellow. We passed a kayaker.

"We get lots of kayakers." But this was the slow season, Igor said. High season was Christmas and Easter week.

And summer?

"Too hot."

I hadn't gotten the impression, as in Los Cabos, that Bahía de los Angeles was booming. True, the tiny town relied heavily on tourism

—the RV parks were evidence of that. But none of them looked new. The one by the turtle research station had been abandoned. How did Igor see the future?

He'd thought a lot about that, he said. He'd written his undergraduate thesis at the Technological Institute in Ensenada on developing the area for tourism. Above all, Bahía lacked infrastructure. "To develop tourism, you need light twenty-four hours a day, water twenty-four hours a day, otherwise there's no refrigeration, no gardens." Two years earlier a water pipeline had broken, and for an entire year the town's water supply had had to be brought in by truck. Sewage was handled by septic tank; none was going into the bay— not yet. The dump—right on the road into town—was an eyesore. There hadn't been any gasoline for more than a month and a half. The airport didn't have security.

"I was offered a job in the ministry of tourism when I graduated. But I couldn't do it." He shook his head vigorously. "Office jobs, they're for people with clean, soft little hands, right? Four walls, no way!" He was standing up now, angling our boat into a cove. The water was shallow here, pea green and placid. *This* was where he belonged, Igor said: water, sun, sky.

"I went to Mexico City once. I got lost in the airport. I couldn't find my way out. Then I got on the wrong bus." He rolled his eyes. "I wouldn't go back there if you tied me up and dragged me!"

Small, freckled manta rays flitted over the sandy bottom. A school of fish, striped yellow and blue, burst past, bright as a spray of flowers. The water was brindled with anchovies. Our boat nosed onto the beach, a thin neck of sand: on this side, the pea-green cove and a view of Bahía de los Angeles; on the other, the sparkling turquoise Canal de Ballenas and Isla Angel de la Guarda, massive with mountains. A songbird chirped; a white butterfly fluttered in the pickleweed.

Igor took a luxuriously deep breath.

"The minute this town gets a stoplight, I'm outta here."

We had been on the water for hours, and yet it had seemed only a short time. The throbbing of the motor lulled me into a sort of trance, half asleep yet awake to my surroundings, the sun playing on the water, the weave and ripple of its surface, the flocks of terns and gulls, pelicans gliding, as serene as kites. Returning, we passed the big bear-brown sea lion again. Out in the open water, he was fishing—a whiskered snout, then his tail, raggedy like a shrimp's, arcing above the surface.

The islands, even the massive Angel de la Guarda, were empty of buildings, of any sign of human life. And this, perhaps, was what gave this vast place its feeling of timelessness. The volcano might have erupted only yesterday. Perhaps we were the sole survivors. Indians might raft by, or perhaps, a white-sailed wooden ship. The explorer Francisco de Ulloa passed through these waters in 1539. Over the next two centuries, only three parties of explorers sailed through this bay—beings from the sky, the Indians must have thought. In 1765, but two years before the expulsion, the Jesuit missionary Wenceslaus Linck arrived. Some of his neophytes had reported fires on Isla Angel de la Guarda—campsites of unconverted natives no doubt, in need of eternal salvation. So Father Linck sailed there with a retinue of soldiers and neophytes. They found nothing, not even a footprint, no water, no animals but rattlesnakes.

Already it was past noon; Igor arrowed the boat back toward town. The light was harsh, and it made the buildings on shore look haggard. "WELCOME AMIGOS" was spray painted on a rock. A Volkswagen bus was parked beneath a tilting palapa, the ground around it scorched. We passed Toño's turtle research station, then trailers, first a scattering, then denser, strewn beneath the majesty of the sierra in an ugly clutter. In front of Guillermos RV Park, Igor cut the motor. The silence was sudden, like a death.

What's Real and What Isn't

GUILLERMOS RV PARK may have been depressing, but the food was fantastic: fish tacos, fluffy and breaded, spiked with fresh lime and green-chile sauce. Everywhere, it seemed, were these little surprises, twists and contradictions: a museum, a turtle that swam all the way to Japan, Mexican fishermen named Daggett and Smith. Igor Galván had been a surprise too, a waiter and a sportfishing guide who'd written a thesis, who argued for more infrastructure for touristic development, but did not want what more tourists would engender: cars and, perhaps inevitably, traffic lights.

"It's a complex situation," Toño Resendiz had said about the turtles, but he might have been talking about the sea cucumbers, or touristic development, or, for that matter, the role of the museum. "It's touchy," Carolina Shepard had said. Different groups wanted different things.

And one of the most different were the Americans living in the RV park. I thought of the man we'd seen lolling on his cot, watching TV. His house—constructed on a concrete pad over the packed dirt of Guillermos—was for sale. What was he asking? What was he offering?

(What on earth was he doing here?)

"Sixteen thousand dollars," he said. His name was Bob Luigi. He was a big, grizzled bull of a man with a tattoo above his left elbow. "But I've put twenty-six thousand dollars into it."

"Sounds expensive," I said.

"Depends on what you want. You want the air conditioner? The microwaves—I've got three microwave ovens—the satellite dish? I mean, we can negotiate."

I explained that I wasn't serious about buying. I was writing about Bahía de los Angeles. Would he show me his place anyway? He nodded and swung open the front door.

"I've got a generator, a fireplace, hot and cold water, and a septic tank, real deep, real good." We were in the kitchen, a narrow, hallwaylike space. "Two refrigerators, sink, stove." And yes, there were the three microwave ovens. Insulation drooped from the rafters; the cramped space flickered under the pale light of fluorescent rods that dangled from the ceiling. The main area, dim and stale smelling, was crammed with three lumpy old sofas and two large beds.

"And here's your bathroom." He yanked the string to a bare lightbulb. "*Really* hot water." He flipped a switch on the wall for hydraulic water pressure and turned on the sink. "Feel that."

I had to agree—my hand turned bright red—it was impressive.

The dining room was outside, a hand-hewn wooden table and chairs shaded by the palapa, packed in with the boat and the folding cot and the TV. He'd built the palapa so he could watch baseball games at night. He also watched TV in the morning. "I get the satellite feeds," he said, "so I watch *Northern Exposure* at 8:00 A.M. Mostly though, I watch CNN."

He was selling because he and his brother, Tom, were building a house nearby. They lived in Las Vegas, Nevada, for half the year, the other half here in Bahía. Tom appeared: grizzled but slightly shorter and without a tattoo. He wore blue swimming trunks and black running shoes without socks.

What was it they liked about Bahía?

"Good air here," Tom said. "It's quiet and peaceful."

"We're all coming here for the same reason," Bob said. "To get away from the crazy people."

What did they do all day?

"I rest in the daytime," Bob said. "Then I sleep at night."

And besides that?

"Bake," Bob said. "I like to bake cookies and cakes."

"We have barbecues," Tom said.

Bob said, "I like to make pizza parties. We all watch football, twenty, thirty people. We make a potluck, you know, somebody brings the buns, somebody else brings the toppings and the ketchup, we all chip in for the meat. Good people living here."

"Some people play chess," Tom said.

Bob said, "They get together, go fishing, play canasta, go over to each other's houses. All are couples but us. I had a wife, but I got rid of her. Traded her in. Gave her some money, she went away."

"And people go camping," Tom said.

"Here you have time," Bob said. "In the U.S. you buy stuff. Here, you make stuff. You don't have to do anything but live and die."

Didn't they get bored sometimes?

"No," Bob said. "It's a totally different way of doing things."

Tom said, "Your values change. Your attitudes change."

Bob said, "Before, you have to work. You never have enough

money. Monday you're broke. I was in the bar and restaurant business before I retired. I had a lot of kids, maybe a dozen of them, delivering pizzas. That was ten years ago, and they were making 150 dollars a day. And every Monday they were broke. Kids are making the same money today, and still, every Monday they're broke. In the U.S. you're born a consumer. You work and spend, work and spend, that's all they teach you. But here, you relax. You're not competing anymore."

Tom said, "You have peace of mind. You have a comfortable, healthy life."

"There are two doctors here," Bob said. "One is here year-round, plus a clinic. They won't give you a transplant, but they're OK. There's a good hospital in Ensenada. Mexican insurance is good and cheap, and here the medicines are cheaper, although they don't always have the variety you need. I had a kidney transplant five years ago, and I've got diabetes. I spend about 3,000 dollars a month on medicines."

"You know what?" Tom said. "Car insurance is 135 dollars. No way could you get that in the U.S! There they'd want 5,600 dollars."

Bob said, "The baby boomers, 80 percent of them will have to retire abroad. They can't afford to live in the U.S. They have no idea! They don't even know it yet."

So it was cheap to live here, I said.

They both shook their heads no. "Nothing's cheap here," Bob said. "Everything comes from Guerrero Negro or Ensenada. Materials are double here. People think Mexico is cheap, but only once you're set up. It depends on how you want to be. I've got a couch, TV, you name it, I got it."

"He's even got a workout bike!" Tom interrupted.

Bob went on, "But you don't need all this. The key is to *already* own your trailer and your boat and your car. Then you just pay your rent, insurance, food, and gas. You can live like a king on five hundred to six hundred dollars a month."

As for food, they kept their expenses down by doing their own cooking. Bob said, "We bring a lot of our groceries down with us from the border. And then every Thursday at about nine-thirty the produce truck arrives. All the Americans, everyone is there. You get what you need for the week. He has a very good selection of what's in season. Last week he had lettuce, cabbage, carrots, limes, garlic, string beans, corn, eggs, grapes, oranges, good peaches, bell peppers, you name it! Full of variety, all good. For meat, there's a couple of places here that sell good meat from the U.S., top sirloins, New Yorks."

"You can also buy good meat in Guerrero Negro," Tom said.

"I only use olive oil," Bob said. "I eat really well. I use no fats or sugars."

It sounded like a nice life. But after all, they were in Mexico. How did they get along with the locals?

"I get along well with the Mexicans," Bob said. "Some of them are drunks, but they're outcasts, and no one gets along with them anyway." The big problem in his view was the *ejido*, the cooperative comprised of about two hundred people—nearly half the population. "They're not educated; they're not smart. There's a very poor education system in this town. The government hasn't provided. My theory is that they want to keep people ignorant and poor so they can control them. The government wants to keep wages low. Do you know what the minimum wage for a day's work is? Thirty pesos! And you know how many hours a day's work that is? Ten, twelve hours! It's ridiculous. So anybody who owns a business makes a lot of money. Everybody else is exploited. Too many kids are born here, and there aren't enough jobs. You can't blame them for going across the border. But then they get exploited in the U.S.—it's not like people think."

"Maybe I'm wrong," Tom said, "but every town here has a military camp. Why? To suppress people. To protect who? We get stopped and checked five or six times coming down from the border. They're looking for guns."

"Mexico's scared of revolution," Bob said. "Like in Chiapas, all they want is food and schooling. That's all they want! Clean water, just basic survival."

"So many Pemex stations are closed," Tom said. "Why? To keep people from moving around."

"It's all about learning," Bob said. "You are what you eat. Why does the government subsidize so much junk? The government sells lard and sugar and flour, all cheap. And the corn oil they sell, maybe it's not even corn oil. I've tasted it—it's terrible! I think it's a conspiracy. There are too many young people, so the old people have to eat junk and die."

Tom said, "The superwealthy people own and run everything. They must educate the people."

But television had arrived in Bahía about six years ago, and with that, the *tele-escuela,* educational programs beamed into the schools via satellite by the ministry of education in Mexico City. Hadn't they noticed a change?

"The kids are getting smarter," Bob conceded. "There's a big difference, especially with the TV at school. On the other hand, the more TV they have, the more trouble they're going to have. They watch those commercials, and they see all those nice cars and clothes. They don't know what's real and what isn't. People in this town think all Americans are rich. They don't understand that people have saved to retire. They think we've had all this—the truck, the boat, the trailer—all along."

"There's good and bad," Tom said.

Bad drivers, that was another problem in Mexico. "They do nutty stuff," Bob said, "like pass on curves. The truck drivers are half asleep. And you gotta watch out for the buses! They're nuts! They think they're pilots. I know one lady, she said, 'If I see a young guy is a driver, I step down. I do *not* get on the bus.' That's why I drive at night— it's safer, there's no other drivers. I have really strong headlights, and I can see real good."

He'd be driving back up to the United States soon, Bob said, because he had to have a heart-bypass operation. It was going to be dangerous because of his diabetes. He would also have to have a vein in his leg replaced. "I'll be back here in January, I hope."

We were standing out on the dirt walkway between the trailer spaces. We'd shaken hands, but Bob didn't seem to want to let me go.

He pointed to the trailer across the way, which was boarded up. "His girlfriend got cancer two years ago. He hasn't been back here since." The house next door had a dust-covered truck parked under an awning. "That guy owned a trash-collection business. He came down here every other weekend in his own plane. He was a real alcoholic. He crashed his plane and died about a year ago."

There were a lot of people who weren't coming back. Another was a photographer who'd been arrested for stalking an American woman who had a penchant for sunbathing in the nude. The Mexican marines marched him to jail, all his cameras hanging around his neck. "The whole town knew. He sold his trailer, he was so humiliated."

And how long had Bob's house been on the market?

"About three years." He crossed his arms over his chest. "I haven't tried very hard, though."

Dark

ON THIS last evening, I decided to take Toño Resendiz up on his invitation to watch him feed the turtles. Near sunset, I drove out to the turtle station with Alice. This was going to be fun, I'd convinced her. I told her how they'd piled up close to me, slapping one another with their flippers, heads high and hoping for a treat. A bagful of meat thrown into the tank? I envisioned a frenzied free-for-all. And indeed, it appeared we were in for something special, because when we arrived, several people were standing around the turtle tank. There was Toño's wife, Betty, and their little daughter, her legs dangling over the edge. Félix, the hefty, mustachioed laboratory assistant and schoolteacher, stood next to them. The principal of the school was there too, and his wife, and two women teachers, one from Mexicali, the other from Todos Santos.

Toño emptied a bag of fish offal into the water. The stuff floated. *Psch! ssth*. The turtles continued circling, bumping, circling. The fishy smell was strong, relieved only slightly by the faint breeze coming in from the bay.

The teachers, who seemed to have all the time in the world, wanted to know what we were doing in Bahía. In turn, I asked about their school. There were 210 children in Bahía, of whom 127 were in primary school and 37 in secondary. They were poor, the principal said. A work party of volunteers had just laid the floor for the new kindergarten, his wife said.

Did they bring the children to see the turtle research station?

"We try to get the kids involved," the teacher from Todos Santos said. She had long, raven-black hair and a girlish, oval face.

Toño and his family had left; Alice and I were alone now with the teachers. The turtles pecked listlessly, tiny bites. The light was fading fast, and the water in the tank looked gray and flat. I wondered why the teachers were here; the turtle feeding was spectacularly uninteresting. It turned out they all lived near the turtle station, in trailers.

"Aquí tienes la comunidad intelectual de Bahía," said the principal. Here you have the intellectual community of Bahía.

"Menos Carolina," said his wife. Not counting Carolina.

The key is to educate the children, Carolina had said, and here, strung out around the turtle tank, were the educators themselves. I was curious about the *tele-escuela,* which was meant to supplement the scarce number of teachers in rural areas. Even Bob Luigi had acknowledged an improvement. What did the teachers think?

"It's great!" the teacher from Todos Santos said. They all loved it. First, because the lesson plan was fixed in Mexico City.

"We guide the students," the principal said, gesturing with his hands.

"It opens the world to them," Félix said. "They hear about and see things they'd never know of otherwise. Before, I'd tell them and they wouldn't believe me! Now they see it on TV, and they say, *'Ah ha!'* It's especially good for technical subjects. Their world is much bigger now."

Carolina had said, We can make them more aware. What things affect other things?

I asked, "How about turtles?"

"Pues," said one teacher. Well. "For many of them, turtles are still food and money."

It was almost dark. We could still see the turtles swimming below, their flippers fat and slick. The teacher from Todos Santos gazed down at them longingly.

I wondered, had any of them tried turtle meat?

No one answered. I had embarrassed them. "But it wasn't illegal until 1990," I offered. I'd heard—from many of my friends who'd tried it years ago—that turtle was really very good.

"*Blanda*," Soft, said the teacher from Todos Santos. And spongy, very greasy.

"I had turtle once in a sausage in a Chinese restaurant in Mexicali," Félix said.

"*Sopa de aleta*," Turtle fin soup, said the teacher from Todos Santos.

But the light was fading fast. Within seconds, we were shrouded in murk. The turtles were only dim shapes, more smell and sound, the snuffly breathing, a lazy sloshing.

Psch! ssth.

"Next week I think I'll bring my kindergartners here to see the turtles."

It was a pretty voice, but in the dark, I couldn't tell whose it was. It floated out, disembodied, like the voice of an angel.

Postscript

A few weeks after my return to Mexico City, I received a letter from Alice. Lindbergh had flown down to Bahía de los Angeles on a trip organized by Kenneth Bechtel, the San Francisco philanthropist and preservationist. This was in 1973, when Lindbergh was seventy-five years old and a roving ambassador for the World Wildlife Fund. He was still world famous, although he was no longer caught in the klieg lights of celebrity. To his relief, in most public places, his white hair and middle-aged paunch let him pass unrecognized.

Alice had enclosed a copy of one of his articles, "The Wisdom of Wildness," which appeared in Life *magazine in 1967. It was a very personal essay. He talked about his childhood in Minnesota and the stories his father had told him about the frontier. "Woods were full of deer, he said; the sky was often black with duck; every lake and river held its fish. Chippewa Indians built their tepees near his home." But by the time Lindbergh was born, the deer were hunted out, the forests had been felled for lumber and cropland; the ducks and fish had become scarce. The Chippewa had been shunted onto reservations. He reflected on his career in aviation, and how he'd chosen it because it combined science and wilderness. He wrote about the things he'd seen from the air, the "great bends of the Mississippi Valley; sweeps of Western plains; Appalachian, Rocky and Sierra ridges, dividing a continent." He'd seen such beauty: caribou galloping over the tundra, herds of elephants in Africa, tropical jungles, Himalayan mountaintops, and "Pacific islands set gemlike in their reefs."*

His own lifetime, he noted, had spanned the Wright brothers' flight at Kitty Hawk and manned-satellite orbiting. (A year and a half later, Apollo 11 would rocket to the moon.) He had devoted the best years of his life to aviation—science, technology, progress. And yet, what had "progress" wrought? He could see it from the air: "Stumplands appeared where forests had been. . . . Ditches graded marshlands; dust hazed prairies; highways and power lines kept scarring ground from horizons to horizons. I watched crossroads become villages; villages, towns; towns turn into cities; suburbs spill over hills." There were fewer and fewer wild animals, and these were too often shot and gaffed with impunity.

If he had his life to live over, he would have chosen a different career, one closer to nature than science. He wrote of walking in an Indonesian rain forest, a mystical experience in which "ages turn to seconds," and his sense of individuality meshed into the infinitely complex web of life all around him.

Science, he argued, needs to be combined with the wisdom of the wild. "In wildness," wrote Lindbergh, ". . . [t]he smell of the earth, the touch of leaves, sounds of animals calling, myriad qualities interweave to make one not only aware but aware of one's awareness. With stars above, a planet below, and no barrier between or after, intuition reaches out past limits of the mind." As an African tribesman had told him, "God is in everything. . . . He is in the rivers, the grasses, the bark of trees, the clouds and mountains. We sing songs to the mountains because God is in them."

꧁

When I put the article down, I had a sudden vision of Lindbergh flying over the bay. The noise of the engine was loud. The plane soared over a great, bright emptiness.

IV

the pacific coast

leviathan

But where shall wisdom be found?

and where is the place of understanding?

(Job 28:12)

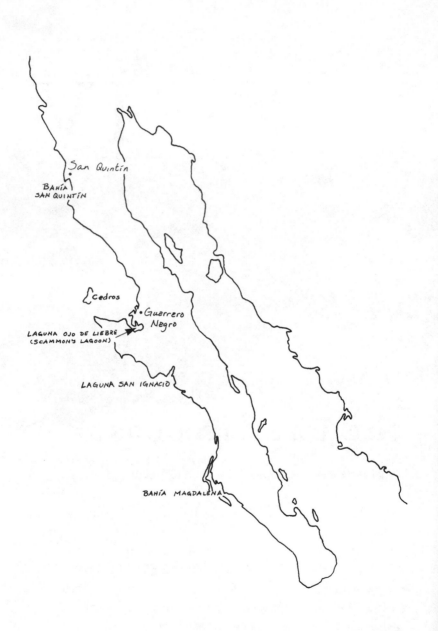

San Quintín

BAHÍA
SAN QUINTÍN

Cedros

Guerrero
Negro

LAGUNA OJO DE LIEBRE
(SCAMMON'S LAGOON)

LAGUNA SAN IGNACIO

BAHÍA MAGDALENA

Lay Thine Hand upon Him

Laguna San Ignacio

> Lay thine hand upon him.
> (Job 41:8)

Call Me Ecotourist

"HOPEFULLY WE'LL SEE more ecotourism," the museum director
Carolina Shepard had said about Bahía de los Angeles. As for putter-
ing around on the bay with Igor and Alice, I wasn't sure that quite
qualified. What, really, was this newfangled class of tour like? Who
were the people who went on these ecotours and did their attitudes
change as a result? And what about those for whom ecotourism was
a job? If ecotourism was to play a role in the salvation of Baja
California's endangered ecosystem, it seemed to me that these were
questions worth exploring.

In any event, I had long wanted to visit Laguna San Ignacio, one
of the most remote bays on the peninsula's Pacific coast, and the
número uno place to watch gray whales. Getting there, however,
would not be easy: the road was often washed out, there were no
facilities, and because it is a protected area, it is illegal to go out on
the water without a licensed tour guide. Signing up for a tour was
not something I had contemplated—until it occurred to me that on
a tour, not only could I get out to Laguna San Ignacio to watch
whales, but I could also watch the watchers.

Thus, courtesy of Baja Expeditions out of San Diego, California, the slickly glossy brochure arrived in my mailbox. "San Ignacio is a whale watcher's paradise," purred the copy for the five-day tour. "Our 'safari styled' camp is awaiting your arrival." In the photo, a skiff-load of tourists reached out their hands to pet the muzzle—humongous, glistening gray cone—of a whale.

Here, as a Mexican friend wryly put it, was *el turismo industrial en su máxima expresión.* In other words, the Cadillac of ecotours.

Day 1: Here, Kitty Kitty

A DEEP HOLE burned in my bank account, I found myself having landed on a dirt airstrip midway down the peninsula's Pacific coast and, along with some twenty fellow ecotourists, hanging onto my seat as we jounced down a washboard road toward Laguna San Ignacio. This was the western edge of the Vizcaíno Desert, a vast flatness of sandy ground encrusted with shells. There were no cacti here, only low scrubby bushes and skeletal ocotillo not yet in bloom. The afternoon sky was light and scraped with thin licks of salt-white clouds. In the distance a coyote bounded away, kicking up scuffs of sand.

Chris Peterson, one of our two naturalists, had to shout to make himself heard over the roar and rattle of the bus. Fortyish with a round, clean-shaven face, Chris wore a Day-Glo pink and orange anorak with purple sleeves, and a baseball cap that said "WILD AMERICA."

"Everybody has their own technique for finding whales," Chris shouted. "Some people tap their foot against the bottom of the boat. Some people sing, *'Here, kitty kitty!'*" With that the bus kiltered into a pothole, and I had to grab the seat in front of me to keep from bouncing into the aisle. Slowly, gears screeching like a wounded animal, the bus hauled itself forward and Chris resumed.

"One lady finds whales by standing at the front of the boat and singing 'Amazing Grace.'" Laying his hand on his chest, our guide dropped his jaw to sing, "*Ama-a-a-a-a-a-zing gr-a-a-a-a-a—*Ah!" He pointed out the window to an imaginary whale. *"Ah, ah!"*

We were driving across a muddy depression now, nude of any vegetation. The road had become an uncertain trace of tire tracks, filled in here and there with puddles of saltwater sparkling in the sunshine. A flock of sanderlings flew low to the ground beside us, flashing their white bellies as they flittered back and forth.

"By the time you leave," Chris boomed with a splendid authority, "all of you will have your own technique."

I hadn't known about these whale-finding techniques, but I had done a bit of reading about the whales themselves. The adult gray whale *(Eschrichtius robustus),* a medium-size baleen cetacean with a mottled, shoe-leather gray appearance, ranges from thirty-nine and a half to forty-six feet from nose to fluke tips, that is, the length of a four-story building laid on its side, and may weigh anywhere from fifteen to thirty tons. Summers they spend feeding in the plankton-rich Bering, Chukchi, and Beaufort Seas; in early January, after a migration of some five thousand miles—the longest of any mammal on earth—they begin arriving in Baja California, where in the warm, shallow waters of the peninsula's inner Pacific bays, cows give birth to their ten-foot-long half-ton calves. Their three main calving grounds are Bahía Magdalena, Laguna San Ignacio, and Laguna Ojo de Liebre (Scammon's Lagoon); of the three, Laguna San Ignacio is the true mecca for the modern whale watcher, because there the gray whales will swim right up to the skiffs, and allow the whale watchers to touch them.

In the past, however, whales were considered extremely dangerous. When one Yankee whaler first attempted to hunt the grays in Baja California, they destroyed two of his catcher boats and staved the others fifteen times. Of the eighteen men he'd sent out, six were gravely injured, one with both legs broken. Nearly a century later, the few Americans who ventured down in airplanes and jeeps found the recovered population of "devilfish" as devilish as ever. When a researcher tried to attach a wire to a basking gray to record its heartbeat, with a single slap of its flukes, the whale smashed the rudder, knocked off the propeller, and bent the drive shaft at a forty-five-degree angle. Then, having swum away a short distance, it charged again and smashed in the hull.

When Erle Stanley Gardner visited in the early 1960s, he thus had good reason to caption one of his grainy photos of a gray whale "In Dangerous Proximity." But his was a mild, even amusing encounter: a lost calf nosed up underneath one of the skiffs, letting it slip off his back. Not long after, Jon Lindbergh, swimming in a wetsuit, found himself being butted by a playful calf. Something was changing: was it the whales, or the people? By the early 1980s encounters with "friendlies" had become an almost daily occurrence during the calving season in Laguna San Ignacio. And U.S. tour companies like Baja Expeditions were Johnnys-on-the-spot, marketing trips that featured the chance to pet the friendlies from a skiff.

The sun hung low over the Pacific when our bus, casting a long shadow, finally ground to a halt up on a slight rise over the southern shore of the lagoon. We clambered down onto the sandy ground. Scattered over about an acre stood a dozen gray dome-shaped tents and two nearly house-size regulation-green army tents: our "safari styled" camp.

The sky had paled and was nearly white at the horizon, but Laguna San Ignacio was so blue it looked like one great brush stroke of Joan Miró cerulean. A ragged file of pelicans headed inland, silhouetted against the peaks of the Sierra de Santa Clara that rose beyond the far shore.

And the whales?

"Where *are* you whales?" Lisa, a middle-aged blonde who wore wooden earrings with orcas painted on them squinted into the distance. "Oh," she said, one arm akimbo and her earrings bobbling in the breeze, "I'm just *dyin'* to touch a whale!"

"Here, kitty kitty," someone joked.

All we saw was water. A flock of cormorants.

"Look!" Lisa giggled at the pair of heart-shaped sprays that burst from the middle of the lagoon, perhaps a mile out.

Like a good shepherd, Chris was with us. "You can actually hear them breathing when it's calm."

We stood for a while, all twenty of us, watching the enormous landscape.

It was extraordinary, the thought that such creatures would let us touch them. But it was even more extraordinary, I thought, that we would want to.

We were herded into the mess tent, fed a snack, introduced to the smiling staff, given a tour of the camp, and shown to our tents. This was all done with such smooth efficiency that I couldn't help feeling we were being shunted along on a conveyor belt, as at Disneyland, ever closer . . .

To touch a whale: Writes Roger Payne in *Among Whales*, "It's the kind of experience that can change one's life." Marvels Michelle Gilders in *Reflections of a Whale Watcher*, "Ask me to describe the emotions of the experience and I cannot. Ask me to say how I felt during the encounter, and I can only smile and laugh at remembering the episode. How does it feel to be in love? Sheer elation."

Sheer elation! An experience that might change my life?

When we regrouped in front of the mess tent, the stars had begun to come out, impossibly close. In what seemed like a matter of minutes the Milky Way ribboned above us in a sparkling canopy. There appeared only a sliver of a moon, but it was bright enough to cast our shadows on the sand.

Chris was holding a plastic model of a gray whale, showing us how it "spyhops," resting its flukes on the lagoon's muddy bottom as it raises its head straight up out of the water. A little girl named Holly trained her flashlight on it so we could see.

"We are too anthropomorphic," Chris was saying. "We say the whales 'spyhop,' but why should we think they want to look at us? If you watch closely you'll see that most of the time when whales do this, their eyes don't even come out of the water."

I couldn't help thinking, as Chris arced the plastic whale over his other hand, that he would have made a wonderful school teacher. He went on, "This is what dolphins do, 'bowing,' or 'porpoising,' as if they're going through a hoop. But whales 'breach.' They thrust up—" he showed us with the toy—"they twist around and crash back on their sides into the water. Whales also show their tails when they dive, but not so much here because the lagoon is shallow. If they tried to dive like that here—" he smashed its nose into his palm—"they'd hit their heads."

"Ow," Holly winced.

In the mess tent we were served a supper of tuna casserole, then given more instruction. Glenn Neumann, the deeply tanned and ponytailed Baja Expeditions base-camp director, led this session. For nights, he handed out lanterns; for whale watching, wading boots and, as featured in the brochure, candy-colored life jackets. Mine was cherry-red. As we tried them on, someone joked that it was like wearing the cushions of his sofa.

Holly wanted to know: how do you touch a whale?

"That's a good question," Glenn said in his beautiful voice, deep and mellow as melted caramel. "I'm glad you asked that." Not around the eyes, he explained, the blow hole, or the flippers. "Their flippers are *really* powerful, and they could slap you up the side of your head. Some whales like to have their baleen stroked. When you pat them, you can rub really hard. These guys are *huge!* And we are really small. So rub away!"

Holly gripped the edge of her plastic chair and bit her lip. Suddenly the only sound was a faint *whap whup* of the wind against the canvas of the tent. The lantern swayed, slightly, from its pole.

"I know," Glenn said with a fatherly chuckle. "Everybody's *dying* to touch the whales! But I have to stress that I hope you won't be disappointed if you don't actually touch one."

"Got to cover themselves," muttered one man to his wife. Lisa nodded, bobbling her little wooden orca earrings.

Day 2: Ah! Eeee! Oh, Oh, Oh!

ALL THROUGH the night the frame of my little dome of a tent creaked in the wind and gusts of numbingly cold air whistled through the cracks between the panels. I slept fitfully, with the sleeping bag pulled over my head. Near dawn I woke to the sound of the tent's entrance flap slapping loose against the ground. I found my sleeping bag sodden with dew. I reached my bare toes into the chill for my sneakers: they too were sodden. I shuffled, miserably, out into the fog.

In the army-green womb of the mess tent I poured myself a mug of steaming-hot coffee. I sat at the table, cupping its warmth in my hands. Breakfast was hearty, a thick eggy cake with Mexican pastries and fruit salad. Lisa sat with me. In a moment, another middle-aged woman named Brenda joined us. Brenda had a grandmotherly, apple-cheeked face. A lace-edged, pink-flowered flannel nightgown peeked out from beneath her raincoat. When she sat down, the nightgown's hem dragged on the sandy ground. Her friend, who wore a helmet of permed yellow hair and designer glasses, was named Rennie. Divorcées from Los Angeles, Brenda and Rennie traveled together.

"Our kids are all grown up now," Brenda said.

"Last year we went to China," Rennie said.

"It's better to travel," Lisa said. "Why leave your money to your kids?"

"Yeah," said Brenda.

"That's what I tell my dad," Lisa said. "I don't want your money, Dad. Take a trip. Enjoy life."

Rennie said, "He's got some problems with walking, but I think I'm going to book my dad on a Princess cruise to Scandinavia. It goes to Norway, Sweden, and . . . what's that other one there?"

"Finland?" I suggested.

"Yeah. Then it goes on up to Russia and you get a tour of St. Petersburg."

Lisa wrinkled her nose. "Oh, but St. Petersburg, the crime—"

Brenda said, "The food in Russia is *terrible*. It's just rotten onions and cabbage, and God-knows-what they put in the sausage."

Holly's dad, Hal, joined us. Hal was an orthopedic surgeon with a strong-jawed and fleshy face not unlike the young Teddy Roosevelt's. A better trip, Hal informed us, would be to go to the Galapagos. "You do two islands a day. You get to stay in these little cabins, and they all have hot water."

"Hot water?" Lisa said. "Lord, I don't know *how* I'm going to manage without hot water."

"Me neither," said Brenda, and she drew the lapels of her raincoat tight at the throat and shivered.

By ten o'clock the sun had burned through the fog. In all my whale-watching gear, I felt like a clown: over my clothes, I had on a lemon-yellow rain poncho, the cherry-red life jacket, a bandanna, a baseball cap, and sunglasses; over my sneakers, enormous rubber wading boots; and swinging around my neck, a camera, binoculars, and a canteen.

"Laguna San Ignacio!" Chris yelled, and he hugged himself tight. "It's so GOOD to be back!"

And we were off, the spray flying in our faces. At last, we were heading out toward the mouth of the lagoon, to the Designated Whale Watching Area. There were eight of us in this *panga,* plus the Mexican driver. Everyone was smiling wide, clutching their cameras and video cameras beneath their rain ponchos as we sped over water dancing with sun. Behind, we could see the tallest cone of the volcanic Tres Virgenes, clear on the other side of the peninsula. Ahead of us, a flock of cormorants flew in a wedge, onyx-black against the jewel-blue of the sky. At the horizon, a whale was breaching, hurling out waves of silver as it crashed down again and again. Lisa splayed her hand out into the wind, as if for practice.

We passed several pairs of cows with their calves. The calves were smooth and dark, unlike their mothers, who were blotched with barnacles and whale lice. The cows swam close to their calves. When they surfaced, they spurted tandem heart-shaped blows of mist, one big and one—just a *piff*—very small.

"We've got to get farther out," Chris shouted. "We want to find more single adults because the calves are newborns and the cows are going to be too protective." This was only the last week in January, the first of the tour season.

We'd gone two or three miles from camp when the driver slowed the engine to a burble. All of a sudden, not ten feet from the prow, a massive snout rose up out of the water as straight as an obelisk, perhaps twenty feet high. Covered with barnacles and clumps of lice that looked a gelatinous pink in the sunlight, thick rivulets of water rushed down; the skin glistened. The line of the whale's mouth curved slightly, as if in a rueful smile, and the baseball-size eye, only inches above the water, swiveled in its socket. Then the whale turned, slowly, and opened its jaws, revealing a comb of flax-yellow baleen. It stayed like this for perhaps thirty seconds. Then, noiselessly, it slipped back down into the lagoon.

So this was "spyhopping." I'd been too stunned to take a photograph.

How had the driver known to stop here?

"You look for the fluke prints," Chris said, "a circle of what looks like grease floating on the water. The fluke prints don't tell you where the whale is, but they tell you where the whale was. Then you can guess where it might come up."

We waited for a while to see if another whale would surface. About a quarter mile to our left, two other Baja Expeditions *pangas* had found what looked like a friendly. The hump of its back filled the space between the boats, and the people were leaning out, tipping the gunwales dangerously close to the water as they tried to touch it. Lisa raised her binoculars for a better look.

"I am so jealous," Rennie sighed.

"Two *pangas* to a whale, that's the rule," Chris said.

"We can't go over there?" Brenda said.

"No." Chris chuckled. "And you'll see, you'll get very possessive about your whales."

After another ten minutes, a cow and her calf approached our *panga*. Chris plashed the water with his hand. *"Here, kitty kitty."* Rennie and Lisa leaned out and plashed the water too. "Try this," Chris said, tapping his foot *dup-dup-dup* against the floor of the boat. But rather than come closer, the cow settled just beneath the hull. She was as big and dark as a submarine, and we could see her splotchy white barnacles through the jade-green water.

"She's *so* close," Lisa said, clenching her fists.

The calf poked its nose out of the water, tantalizingly near. "Oh!" Rennie reached out, her hand like a fat white star. "Oh, oh, oh!"

The cow surfaced and blew. The wind carried the mist away from us, and the sunlight shining through it prismed into a rainbow.

Back in camp, we compared notes. None of us had had the luck to touch a whale, although in three hours of whale-watching, we'd all had at least a dozen close encounters. The big news at lunch was that the *panga* with the Carpenter family—Jim, Joanne, and their two boys—had filmed a live birth.

"The cow was lifting her tail and slamming it down and lifting it up," Joanne said. "We couldn't figure it out, it looked so strange."

Jim said, "And then suddenly, there was all this blood on the water, and out it came, a little calf!"

Spirits were high when we hiked back down to the *pangas* for our afternoon whale-watching session. Along with Chris, I switched *pangas* to go with the Carpenters. I told Jim, "My technique for finding whales is to go with you guys." He patted his video camera, a Sony as big as a shoe box, and grinned.

But, again, the whales proved shy. We would see a blow or a flipper, motor up close, and then the whale would dive away. We seemed to be going in circles around the Designated Whale Watching Area. After a while, Jim left his video camera on his lap with the lens cap on.

It was torture sitting in the afternoon sun in all this rubber gear, the boots, the rain ponchos. The life jacket felt bulky and as hot as being sandwiched between two boards. We'd seen what there was to see, the birds, the sandy shore, the mountains bleached pale in the distance.

Sometime around four o'clock, another Baja Expeditions *panga* motored by. Holly was lying prostrate across the bow in an agony of boredom.

All of us were languishing. But a few minutes later, after we'd motored up to yet another whale that swam away from us, Chris seemed to come out of suspended animation.

"Look at that!" Hadn't we noticed its flukes, crisscrossed with deep white scars? "Those are orca bites. Orcas hunt in pods, and they'll hunt grays. One takes a flipper, one takes a fluke, and *then*—" He had our full attention. "One goes in and bites out the tongue!"

"Oooooh," Johnny Carpenter said. A skinny boy who must have been about thirteen years old, he wore a sports watch that bristled with dials.

Chris said, "There was a gray whale that came here for several years that had no flukes on his tail. They were all bitten off by orcas."

"Oooooh," Johnny said again. This seemed to please him immensely.

"There are two things in the ocean," Chris said. "Orcas and orca food."

Now that we were on the subject of food, was it true that the Japanese ate whale meat?

"Oh, yes," Chris said brightly. He'd been a Mormon missionary in Japan. "I ate whale meat when I was there. You can buy it in the supermarket."

What was it like?

"Purply red, like beef except that it's got these huge blood vessels—" he made a circle with his hands. "When you cook it, it falls apart like fish."

"I ate whale meat once," Joanne Carpenter volunteered. She was sitting in front of us, and she swiveled around to join the conversation. A handsome woman with cropped champagne-blonde hair, she wore silver butterfly earrings and a touch of pink lipstick. "I didn't really want to eat it, though. We were in Japan. Jim was there on business, and I didn't want to offend our hosts. They kept saying please, *please,* try some. It was three chunks of sushi arranged on a plate with three different sauces."

"Remember the zebra steak we ate in Africa?" Jim grinned at his wife.

"Oh, yes, that was really good."

"That was great! Barbecued."

Back in camp again, it was a sad score: no one had touched a whale in the afternoon either. At dinner, as we lined up in the mess tent to serve ourselves from an iron pot of fish stew, we were sullen, like passengers on an overseas flight wedged into tourist class, with hours yet to go.

I sat off by myself at the far corner of the table.

"Do you like it?" This was Alejandro, one of the cooks. He meant the fish stew.

It was wonderful, I said, and I meant it. Chunks of tender flounder were tossed with chopped fresh tomatoes, onion, sprigs of oregano, and a delicate lacing of garlic. I'd made a taco with a floury grilled tortilla.

He had a beard, but it seemed to me that Alejandro was very young. He was wearing a T-shirt with whales on it. So he liked whales?

"I *love* the whales! I *can't wait* to go out!" Alejandro seemed to rocket around in his chair with enthusiasm. "I get to have a turn when there's room on the boat. I made a video of the whales—" he was breathless with happiness—"and I sent it to be edited, and I sold it for twenty-five dollars."

We stopped talking because Chris had started his slide show. It was an expert slide slow, zippy and informative. In a little less than an hour, he'd covered the feeding and mating habits of the whales, what we know and what we don't know. Finally, why was it that some of the grays allowed people to touch them? Apparently because grays like to rub, perhaps to remove barnacles and lice.

"The whales probably don't even know that we're human," Chris said. "They see our boat and they probably think, what a funny hard white animal that is floating up there. When you swim up close all these little tentacles come waving out at you—" he wriggled his fingers—"and it goes '*Ah! Eeee! Oh, oh, oh!*'"

Day 3: "Real Close"

I PEEKED OUT the flap of my tent to see the rim of the sky bleeding like a wound. A white bird swooped low over the water, as if an invisible hand had pushed it down from the sky. When I stepped outside, I was nearly flung over by the wind. It rushed at my ears and made my eyes water.

Too much wind, Glenn said when we'd all arrived in the mess tent. It would be a long wait this morning before we could go out whale watching—if we could go out at all.

After breakfast Sergio Flores, our other naturalist, joined me in killing time in the mess tent. Younger than Chris, he was in his midtwenties perhaps, and his English was spiced with a Mexican accent. He specialized, he said, in cetaceans. He had just finished his masters in oceanography at the University of Baja California in Ensenada; in the fall, he would be going to do his doctorate in biotechnology at Dalhousie University in Halifax, Nova Scotia. He told me all this with a crisp self-assurance, leaning forward with a smile to punctuate this point or that.

Why had he chosen to study whales?

Sergio flashed another smile. "I could write a poem about whales. Whales are super! But I could live without them in my academic career. I could write about, say, abalones. How do they respond to their environment? Their predators? How are they distributed, why are they there, how have they adapted? For me that's the challenge. If we understand ecology we can make better decisions, manage our resources better. That's what I want to do: research and help formulate and carry out policy."

He'd chosen a bramble path of a career. I thought of Paulino Pérez, the shark expert turned artist. Toño Resendiz had managed to do some important research at his turtle station in Bahía de los Angeles, but only after many years of lonely struggle. I wondered, when Sergio finished with his doctorate in Canada, would he come back to Mexico?

Sergio drew himself up tall. "Of course! I cannot be disloyal. I owe it to my country."

By ten-thirty the wind had died down enough for whale watching. Chris poked his head into the mess tent and shouted, "You snooze you lose!"

Out on the water, we motored to the Designated Whale Watching Area. A whale was breaching, but so far in the distance that it looked like a potato bug. We passed a cow and her calf; they dove away from us.

I was sitting in between two women from Los Angeles, the willowy Amy and Kelly, who had blunt-cut hair and a dimpled Peter Pan face. Amy and Kelly had met in Panama seven years ago; ever since then, they vacationed together.

"Twice a year," Kelly said.

Our driver steered us into the middle of a fluke print and cut the motor. We waited. The boat rocked gently.

"Look!" Kelly nearly jumped out of her seat as three fins slid by. "Dolphins!"

Amy said, "Last year we went snorkeling with the dolphins in St. Croix."

"Yeah," Kelly said. "Remember those funny signs there underwater?"

"Yeah, like, Here's some coral, in case ya didn't know."

"Actually," Kelly said, "my favorite marine mammal is the penguin. I love dolphins, but I *really* love penguins. We went to the Galapagos Islands to see the penguins. Did you know that the penguins that live on the Galapagos are the northernmost penguins in the world?"

I confessed I hadn't known that.

"You should see them swim." Kelly made a gliding motion with her hand. "They are *so* beautiful."

And what was their next trip?

"Australia," Kelly said.

"The Great Barrier Reef," Amy said.

"But first she's gotta learn to dive." Kelly elbowed Amy in the ribs. "She can't even swim."

"I get around with my flippers on," Amy said.

So whose idea was this whale-watching trip?

"Mine," Kelly said. "If it were up to her, we'd be in a Holiday Inn somewhere in the Caribbean doing nothing."

"Oh, yeah," Amy said dreamily. "My next vacation is gonna be in a hotel with *hot water.*"

"Well," Kelly said, "it would be great to swim with the dolphins in the Bahamas." She picked up her camera. After a while, she said to no one in particular, "I *really* love dolphins."

The morning, like the two whale-watching sessions the day before, was, friendly-wise, a disappointment. On our way back, we saw a coyote trotting along the shore, its tail between its legs.

Exhausted, I skipped the afternoon whale-watching session. And now, as it apparently did every night, the wind was picking up, and the temperature began dropping rapidly. The sides of the canvas mess tent shook, and the tent poles rattled as we lined up for dinner.

There was only one more day of whale watching, Kelly said as she took a plate. "And gosh darned if I'm not gonna touch one!"

"They're shy right now," Lisa said. She was standing behind me in line. "Chris says they're more friendly by about mid-February."

"*Now* they tell me." Amy laughed.

"So you didn't touch one either," I said, spooning chopped steak onto my plate.

"We saw a whale trying to mate with a dolphin," Kelly said.

"Poor dolphin!" Lisa said.

"That kind of thing happens," Amy said darkly.

A woman named Cheryl said, "You know those Earthwatch trips where you get to help with the orangutan research in Borneo? They tell the women not to walk in the jungle alone."

"Eew," Lisa said. She held the spoon in midair.

"Oh, yeah," Cheryl said. "Orangutans."

Amy said, "Sounds like some men I know."

I found a place at the table next to Holly's dad, Hal. "What you want to do," Hal was saying in a loud voice, "is go on one that has a barge." Those were your first choice for a biking tour in Holland, because then if you got tired of biking, you could just ride along on the barge.

"And the food!" his wife said. Her name was Rhonda. She was a petite woman with a riot of frizzy red hair.

"Great French food," Hal interrupted. "Really great, and they give you wine with every meal."

"It's so rich you couldn't possibly bike it off," Rhonda said.

"We tried!" Hal patted his stomach.

"Well, I dunno." This was Sam, a retired dentist from Salt Lake City. He and his wife were celebrating their forty-fifth anniversary with this whale-watching trip. "I'd do the biking thing in Holland, but Dotty's got a mind to go see the polar bears."

"You mean one of those tours out of Churchill, on Hudson Bay?" Rhonda asked.

"Yeah," Sam said. "They have these vehicles, kind of like armored trucks? You can get real close."

It seemed the talk about other tours never stopped. I was fascinated to listen. I had not imagined I would find people who would regularly travel to such a variety of far-flung places, spending thousands of dollars, but always—or almost always—as members of a tour.

As I walked back to my tent I winced in the chill. The night was like the others: the stars so bright and close, the stiff damp wind blowing in from the ocean. A cloud blew across the face of the moon, thin like a scarf. I remembered then something that Chris had said in his slide show, that as recently as ten thousand years ago, Laguna San Ignacio did not exist. A million years ago the sea flooded the Vizcaíno Desert, turning the peaks of the Sierra de Santa Clara into islands. That was why everywhere around the bay—even on the floor of our tents—there were shells and bits of shells embedded in the sandy soil. Three million years before that—yesterday by the scale of evolution—the Sea of Cortés did not exist either. I thought of another thing Chris had said, that the whales first emerged twenty-six million years ago.

An uncanny sight: with the lanterns on inside, our tents looked like a string of glowing orbs half-buried in the sand. The tents creaked and flapped in the wind, a sad sound, like little animals crying.

I ducked into my tent, yanked off my shoes, and with all my clothes on zipped myself into my sleeping bag and curled up tight into a ball.

Day 4: "I Hope Today!"

DAWN WAS a dim gray glow that didn't seem to be coming from any one direction. I made my way through the swirling murk to the kitchen tent. Inside, a gas-powered lamp cast weak blue light over a jumble of crates and coolers stacked on the sandy ground. Alejandro, the cook who had told me about his whale video, was cracking eggs into a skillet. He wore an apron, but otherwise he was dressed for a ski resort in a heavy flannel shirt and deerskin snow boots. Next to the stove were a basket of brown eggs and a tub piled high with tiny limes. A boiling kettle of coffee clattered on the back burner.

Alejandro poured me a mug and brought me a chair. The menu this morning was omelettes, and he was making two at a time. I'd been impressed by his enthusiasm for the whales, I said, his whale T-shirt, the fact that he'd made a video. What was it that was so special about the whales?

He frowned as he sprinkled a handful of cheese over the eggs. "For me, whales are something that have to do with work."

He was from La Paz, and he'd worked on a variety of Baja Expeditions trips—cruises, bike tours, diving, and kayaking. "I like kayaking best because there's snorkeling, hiking, volleyball, lots of activities. But diving—" he shrugged. "Diving is just diving."

And whale watching?

"I started with the whale trips seven years ago."

And what did he think about the whale trips?

"You feel desperate because you start at a low level. If you're married it's difficult. You've got to be single. We work for eight months. We do various things. I like what I do. If you like what you do, that's best." He pulled down the oven door, eased an omelette onto a cookie sheet, slid the sheet back in, and pushed the door shut, all in a single graceful motion.

"There are salary differentials," he went on. "You go from C to B to A to double-A and then triple-A. Head guides are almost always Americans, like Glenn and Chris. They have a university education and a lot of experience. You've got to speak English."

But his English was very good, I said.

"Oh, but perfectly, you have got to speak English *perfectly*. Or you've got to go to university, like Sergio. To move up with experience alone is really difficult. But I learn a lot here. I've always had this idea that I want to be a chef in a hotel in La Paz. So I have to learn to cook with more elegance. That's why I'm trying new things, like using oregano."

And the whales? He'd seemed so thrilled when I'd asked him about them the other night.

"The whales . . ." Alejandro cracked another egg into the skillet. He stirred thoughtfully. "Well, they are very special because they come here. They need this shallow lukewarm water."

I tried another tack. "When you were growing up in La Paz, did you know about the gray whales?"

"No. I didn't know that the whales came here or why they would come here—and I was living one block away from the sea! When I came here with Baja Expeditions, I was surprised that tourists would pay to come see this—that there was work in this, that's what really surprised me."

He folded another omelette and slid it into the oven. "I used to be a *panga* driver. But now I have to wait a turn to go out. Maybe I'll get to go out today." And at the thought of this, Alejandro was transformed, suddenly as happy as a little kid, waving his spatula like a wand. "I hope today! I hope I can go out today and find a whale!"

How did it feel to touch one?

"Smooth, smooth." His voice trailed off to a whisper as he lidded his eyes. "Oh, very *smooth.*"

Luckily, today the sun had burned off the fog by the time we were ready to go out whale watching. Like everyone else, I was keen to touch a whale; but I just could not bear it, the thought of sitting out there for another several hours in the hot sun, motoring around in circles. We still had one more whale-watching session in the afternoon; I decided to skip the morning session and read.

I settled into a chair by my tent on the bluff overlooking the lagoon. It was hard to concentrate; the breeze ruffled the pages, and the water sparkled like a carpet of jewels. After a while, I left the book in my lap and closed my eyes. A fishing boat roared by, heading out toward the Pacific. I could hear pots and pans clattering in the kitchen tent, and scrubbing. Someone (Alejandro?) was singing, but with the shifting breeze, I could make out only a few words, *mi corazon . . . cuando fui al otro lado . . . te quiero.* A bird cried out: *caw-ki-ki;* someone in the kitchen tent whistled sharply. Soon the breeze began to calm and the air warmed. I dozed.

CHU! I woke to a noise, very loud, like someone blowing full-force into a bottle.

CHU! A whale was spouting, out in the middle of the lagoon.

Another: louder. Where? Another! This time I spotted the puff of vapor toward the mouth of the lagoon, perhaps two miles away. A moment later, a blow shot up so far east, toward the head of the lagoon, that it looked as though it were coming from the base of the Tres Virgenes—yet I could hear it full and clear. CHU!

The blows came singly and in pairs, a few seconds to more than a minute apart. Chris had said that there might be as many as four hundred whales in the lagoon at any one time. I'd found that hard to believe until now.

For a long while, I scanned the hard blue shimmer: listening.

"You snooze you lose!" Chris shouted when it was time for the afternoon whale-watching session, our final one. Holly had touched a whale in the morning, a calf, right on the tip of its nose. And not only that, Holly bragged, but her dad had filmed it too.

Sheer elation? An experience that might change my life? It still seemed possible that I might actually touch a whale.

The *panga* driver motored us out to the Designated Whale Watching Area. It was hot. We saw a whale; it swam away. We saw a cow and calf; we motored up; they swam away. We saw the hump of a gray's ridged back; we saw it blow. It sank down and disappeared.

The bench felt as hard as cement. In our rubber boots and rain ponchos and thick, bulky life jackets, we began to sweat. Jimmy and Johnny Carpenter sat at the front of the *panga,* their elbows on their knees, moping. An hour passed.

And another hour passed.

The engine burbled, the water sloshed gently against the hull. The sun was sinking; flocks of pelicans began to fly inland, one after the other. Another whale surfaced, blew, and sank down.

Lisa, who I had imagined to be a comrade-in-suffering, her jaw grimly set, eyes glinting narrowly over the waters of our folly, blurted: "This is so great!" Beneath the halo of her floppy white golf hat, she smiled beatifically. "It's like when I was on the tour in Canada off Vancouver Island to see the orcas? We went out on little Zodiacs, and we were right up close, surrounded by whales, just like this."

With her video camera she began to film a whale, yet another ridged hump, perhaps fifty feet away. "The funny thing is, there was a big cruise ship nearby? They sent out a guy in a Zodiac with a camera so he could feed back a live video of the orcas to everybody on board." She turned to me. "Isn't that just awful?"

There was a little red square on her forehead where she'd pressed it against the viewfinder.

"Tell me," she said. "Why would anyone *pay* to go all the way to Vancouver Island and then watch the whales on *video?*"

Now she had her Nikkon camera out. She adjusted the zoom lens and started clicking: a whale was swimming toward our *panga*. It dipped beneath us, came up on the other side, and blew, CHU! The mist rained on the water. The whale came back again, sinking down to glide below. In a moment, its head bobbed up again just—barely—beyond arm's reach.

"A friendly!" Johnny cried, and he stood up, wobbling the boat.

His mother, Joanne, leaned out and lightly plashed her hand in the water. Jim began filming, swinging his big box of a video camera first right, then left as the whale swam back and forth, each time passing just a shade closer to our *panga*.

"Ah!" Lisa said as it bobbed its head up, inches—tantalizing inches—beyond her fingertips. "Oh! Oh!" The *panga* tipped starboard as Lisa, Joanne, Johnny, and Jimmy all leaned out, trying to touch it. It sank down; it surfaced on the other side. CHU! We all reached out to it with a chorus of, "Oh, oh, oh!"

My God, I thought as I reached my hand out, I might actually touch a whale! This wild, living thing the length of a four-story building! The boat listed with our weight, its rim inches from the water's surface. My fingers stretched long until my shoulder ached. And my fingertips were not three inches from the table of slick, glistening skin when—out of nowhere—another *panga* came roaring up. With a foot on the prow like Washington crossing the Delaware, a burly man in a camouflage jacket and a cowboy hat aimed his video camera like a weapon at our whale. Three hefty blondes were crowded in the boat with him, all in black biker's shorts and big baggy T-shirts that hung down from underneath their life jackets.

Painted on the hull of their boat was the name KUYIMA—the cheaper Mexican tour operator. Within spitting distance from our *panga,* the trio of blondes leaned over the sides, butts in the air, and started shoveling the water with their hands.

"HERE!" They shouted at our whale. "HERE! Get over HERE!"

One of the blondes pounded her fist against the hull of the boat. "Come ON!"

Stunned, we sat on our benches and watched as our whale bobbed around the interlopers. One of the blondes started snapping pictures—with a disposable camera.

Lisa hissed: "Trailer people."

"That's it," Joanne huffed. "Now I don't want to whale watch anymore."

We all laughed. Meanwhile, with all three blondes at the same end, their *panga* was severely listing.

"I hope they fall in!" Johnny said.

"Vultures!" Jim chuckled as he started videotaping them.

Perhaps we hadn't tried hard enough, I thought, as I watched the blondes so vigorously thrashing their arms in the water, shouting and banging. Like almost everyone else on the Baja Expeditions tour, I had been content to simply sit, as if I were on some genteel amusement ride, and wait.

Chris was right: by the end of the week I did have my own technique for finding whales. Not that it worked.

It was small consolation, but before any of the blondes could touch it, our whale lost interest and swam away.

"Served them right," Joanne harumphed. We watched the *panga* roar off, our own *panga* rocking in its wake.

The sunlight had faded to a rich gold. It was nearly six; time to head back to camp for dinner. Flock after flock of seabirds was heading inland after the day's fishing: a line of pelicans, a crowd of forktailed terns, a wedge of cormorants, white-tailed brant geese, more pelicans. Here and there, a straggler flapped by low over the water.

"It's just not fair!" Lisa said. We'd come all this way, sat hour after hour in a *panga;* we'd slept in tents, we'd baked, we'd frozen, we'd put

up with having to use a latrine, we'd had *no hot water.* "Why, even—"
she laughed at herself—"the driver feels sorry for us!"

Without a word he cut the engine. He'd spotted a whale lolling on
its side, one flipper in the air, maybe twenty feet away. It was a long
shot, but worth one last try. We bobbed on the chop of the lagoon
for a minute or so, waiting. *Dup-dup-dup,* we tapped our feet against
the bottom of the boat. I plashed the water with my hand, halfheart-
edly. And then, with a great lazy slap of its flukes, the whale sank
down and disappeared. The wind was blowing now, and the water
moved by swiftly, carrying its fluke print away.

The driver had just revved the motor when Joanne spotted a tern
that was standing on something in the water. As we approached, the
bird fluttered up and hovered, its bright-yellow legs dangling like
twigs.

"It's a turtle!" Johnny shouted. "The bird was standing on the back
of a turtle!"

Lisa pursed her lips. "That's just a buoy."

The driver let the *panga* drift in closer. A grayish-green oval was
floating there—an oval with flippers and a head. It *was* a turtle. The
tern alighted again on its perch. We all started filming and photographing.

"Cool," Johnny said.

But the turtle wasn't moving. I said, "I think it's dead."

"*Sí,*" the driver said. "*Está muerta.*"

"Dead!" Joanne was terribly disappointed. The bird flew off. We sat
for a moment bobbing on the water in peevish silence.

"Well I don't care," Joanne finally said. "If I can't touch a whale—"
she turned around and gestured at the driver. "Come on, pull right
up."

He swiveled the rudder and let the boat drift closer. Jim shoul-
dered his video camera and began taping as his wife leaned out and
rapped the carapace with her knuckles.

Thook.

"I did it," she said, and she sat back down.

"And I filmed you doing it," Jim said nicely.

She turned to her boys. "Don't tell anyone it was dead."

They rolled their eyes.

Day 5: Finally

THE NEXT MORNING we were back on the bus heading for the airstrip.

"So," said Sam the retired dentist from Salt Lake City. "Did you touch a whale?"

"No," I confessed. "And you?"

"Nope. But we had a good time anyhow."

His wife, Dotty, patted his hand. "Yes, we did. It was a great trip."

It was hard to talk. We were bouncing over the washboard road, the bus scranching loudly in low gear. I looked out the window: pickleweed, ocotillo, the great bowl of weepy sky. An osprey sliced low through the air, heading toward the water.

Holly was the one member of this tour who, as far I knew, had actually touched a whale. She was an experienced traveler, she'd told me on the first day. She'd already been to many places in Mexico: Cabo San Lucas, Costa Rica, and Ecuador, for instance. She seemed a happy, talkative child, but now that the trip was finished—we were at the airstrip now, waiting for our luggage to be unloaded from the bus—she stood away from everyone else, scowling and kicking at the sandy ground with her sneaker.

"How about you?" I asked Kelly. "Did you touch a whale?" She hadn't.

"But I did," her friend Amy said. "Finally."

What was it like?

"Slick like a stingray." Amy shrugged.

"I *loved* the dolphins," Kelly said as Glenn, the camp director, joined us. "You know what?" she said to Glenn. "This was even better than seeing elephants in Africa."

"Oh, yeah," Amy said. "In Africa you see so many, it's like, elephants, elephants, elephants, all the time. You totally get sick of elephants."

"But this was great," Kelly said. "This was even better than the Galapagos."

"Oh, yeah," Amy said.

"Well," said Glenn in his deep and mellow voice, a broad smile crinkling his sun-weathered face. "I'm glad you liked it."

Black Warrior, White Salt

Scammon's Lagoon (Laguna Ojo de Liebre) and Guerrero Negro

> ...remember the battle, do no more.
> (Job 41·8)

Oceans of Tears

HOME IN MEXICO CITY, as the weeks went by, the memory that stayed in my mind was of the morning I'd sat alone on the bluff over Laguna San Ignacio, listening. I could still see the color of the sky, the mountains a pale Maxfield Parrish pink in the distance. I could feel the tingly heat of the sun, the way I had to squint from the water's sparkle. The whales' blows were etched in my mind like a song. I'd taken a tour—an often silly conveyor belt of a tour—and yet come away with this. It seemed as strange as having found a plum in a lemon tree. I held it in my mind. I turned it over, and over.

In truth, I'd never given much thought to whales. Whales were something to do with a homework assignment, cobwebbed skeletons in a natural history museum. I'd gone to Laguna San Ignacio more curious about Baja California's ecotourists than the whales they'd come to watch. I did not touch a whale, but seeing them up close did, after all, change the way I thought about them. It took a while for me to admit to myself, but seeing them like that, and hearing them, so many, in that huge, nearly empty place, was one of the most fantastic experiences of my life.

Ecotourism was not without its drawbacks, however. The tourists brought dollars, but also garbage and sewage. There were small Mexican tour operators on Laguna San Ignacio, but the serious money went largely to U.S. tour companies, like Baja Expeditions, that had the infrastructure and know-how to sell packages to people who just as easily might decide on the Galapagos, biking in Holland, or, for that matter, a few days baking on a beach outside the Holiday Inn somewhere in the Caribbean.

"Ecotourism doesn't leave much for the locals except low-level jobs," the Mexican activist and poet Homero Aridjis told *Newsweek*. It's an old argument. As V. S. Naipaul pronounced back in 1962, "Every poor country accepts tourism as an unavoidable degradation." I could see it for myself: it was the Mexicans who drove the *pangas* and dug the latrines and washed the dishes.

On the other hand, ecotourism did provide some good jobs, including for Sergio Flores, the well-spoken cetologist, and Alejandro Flores, the cook who hoped to work one day as a chef in a hotel. It also provided an incentive to care for the environment at a time when too many people were fishing too few fish. In short, like so many others, it seemed to me a complex situation.

And one I was very privileged to have been able to explore. Not many Mexicans can shell out for an ecotour, nor would many be interested even if they could. "Environmentalism is a luxury that developing countries can't afford," I've heard a top-ranking government economist say on more than one occasion (echoing none other than President Echeverría). But there is this: they may never go on an ecotour, but millions of Mexican children care about whales because they care about one whale that they saw and they heard— Keiko, the orca that performed at the Reino Aventura amusement park in Mexico City, the star (along with an "animatronic" rubber orca) of the phenomenally popular movie *Free Willy*.

On the single day of January 6, 1996, nearly thirty thousand parents and children filed past Keiko's tank at Reino Aventura. Later that night, as many as one hundred thousand people lined the expressway and crowded onto its pedestrian overpasses to wave good-bye as Keiko was driven, packed in ice water in a UPS crate with a sticker reading "THIS SIDE UP," to the Mexico City airport. So many of his fans attempted to accompany the "Keiko Express" flatbed rig in their cars—some of the police in the motorcade even brought their children—that the fifteen-mile trip to the airport, which began a little after midnight, took until three-thirty in the morning. Mexican TV and newspapers gave the event full coverage, interviewing Keiko's pretty young trainers, and showing Keiko's handlers coaxing him into his sling to be transported, the huddled families wrapped in ponchos and blankets, and the children crying and waving.

"Que se quede, que se quede," Let him stay, they chanted, let him stay. "Keiko! Keiko!" One man held up a placard that said, *"¡SUERTE KEIKO! Familia Sánchez."* Good Luck Keiko! The Sánchez Family.

Keiko was being flown in a C-130 cargo plane to his new $7 million tank at the Oregon Coast Aquarium, paid for by the Free Willy Foundation with donations from all over the world. The Reino Aventura amusement park, which had bought Keiko for $350,000, was letting the Oregon Coast Aquarium have him for free. Keiko was being rescued, just like Willy in the movie.

Keiko/Willy was instantly recognizable because of his fallen dorsal fin, which was the result of a vitamin deficiency. Rather than standing up straight like a big triangle, it curled over like a broken finger. For ten years he had been kept in a tank that was barely large enough for him to turn around in. His water was chlorinated and artificially salted, far too warm, and inadequately filtered, so that he was often swimming in his own wastes. He suffered from warty eruptions on his skin; his teeth were worn down from nervous chewing on the edge of the tank; and he was, at 7,700 pounds, more than 1,000 pounds underweight. Keiko's job was to perform, dancing to disco music, leaping for a mackerel, letting his trainers plunge their heads into his mouth, and giving kisses to his "girlfriends"—young women selected from the audience.

Then, in 1993, *Free Willy* hit the movie theaters. When it became known that its star was living in similar circumstances as the fictional Willy before his rescue, there was an international outcry. Reino Aventura did not have the resources to build Keiko a larger and better tank. They attempted to find him a new home, but his skin disease made this impossible, since the parks and aquariums that considered taking him would have had to put him in a tank shared with other whales or dolphins. *Free Willy*'s producers tried to send Keiko to Cape Cod; Michael Jackson offered to build him a home at his Neverland Ranch in California. Finally, Dave Phillips, director of the Earth Island Institute, established the Free Willy Foundation and marshaled the millions of dollars—and the support of both Reino Aventura and the Alliance of Marine Mammal Parks and Aquariums—to build Keiko his new home in Oregon.

It was terrible that this orca had been made to live in a cramped and dirty tank. But was it a tragedy that Keiko came to Mexico? Millions of Mexican children saw him perform at Reino Aventura, as well as on TV and in films. They watched *Free Willy, Free Willy II,* and *Keiko en Peligro* ("Keiko in Danger," a side-splittingly bad—I actually watched it—Star Trek rip-off about visitors from outer space returning to Earth for their orca). They bought stuffed Keiko toys, rubber Keiko toys, Keiko T-shirts, Keiko baseball caps and backpacks and lunch boxes. To a degree, this was cheap mass merchandizing no different from the onslaught of Barney and the Power Rangers and the Teenage Mutant Ninja Turtles. But Keiko was not a cartoon, he was a living animal, a prisoner of human hubris. Still, even as he wriggled to disco music and leaped up like a dog for a snack, for many of these children he was an ambassador to Mexico—not only for whales, but for all the animals in the seas, and for the seas themselves.

I think the greatest tragedy was that Keiko had to leave Mexico. Every Mexican, whether he watched Keiko leaving from the side of the Mexico City expressway or saw it on TV or read about it in the newspapers, was reminded of how poor his country is in comparison to its neighbor, where $7 million can be marshaled to build a tank for a single animal. Keiko's new home, the Mexicans were told, was four times bigger than his old one in Mexico City. It was filled with cool seawater that was exchanged and purified every twenty-four hours. It had water jets for Keiko to play with; reversible currents for him to swim against; submerged rocks for navigation practice; and reeflike designs on the bottom to rub on. Every day Keiko would be fed three hundred pounds of restaurant-quality fish, and he would no longer be made to perform.

When Keiko's team of wetsuit-clad handlers tried to herd him into a holding pen in his tank at Reino Aventura, he porpoised over the webbing of the net and escaped. The crowd broke out in an ecstatic cheer: *"¡No se quiere ir!"* He doesn't want to go!

Keiko jumped over a second time, and the crowd went wild, cheering and clapping and hooting at the TV cameras. But then, when the handlers dragged him into the pen and eased him into a sling, there was an eerie hush. As the crane hoisted him high up into the air and aligned him above his UPS crate, Keiko cried out, *zzzeee!*

"Keiko se nos va," Keiko leaves us, said Mexico City's *Reforma* the next morning in a full-color spread on the front page of its "People" section. *"Lloran a 'mares,'"* They cry oceans of tears.

"Poor Mexico!" lamented the dictator Porfirio Díaz. "So far from God and so close to the United States." It is a saying repeated in Mexico again and again. His predecessor, Benito Juárez, had a formula for dealing with the Yankees: "Say yes, but never say when." On too many occasions, however, what Mexico had to say wasn't of much concern to the United States. Octavio Paz characterized the United States as a giant that "neither sees nor hears us, but keeps striding on, and as it does, enters our land and crushes us." Every Mexican schoolchild learns the litany of invasions, bombardments of ports, interventions, intimidations, vast chunks of territory lost: Texas, Arizona, New Mexico, Nevada, Utah, California.

Not far from my house in Mexico City, schoolchildren are led through the Museo de las Intervenciones (the Museum of Foreign Interventions), where room after room of maps and flags, rifles and cannon, portraits, placards, and sundry mementos tell the stories of Mexico's victimizations by Spain, France, and, above all, the United States. "QUE EL ENEMIGO NOS VENZA Y NOS ROBE, SI TAL ES NUESTRO DESTINO..." are the words of Benito Juárez at the entrance: "May the enemy conquer and rob us, if that be our destiny; but we should not legitimize such attempts, voluntarily delivering what is demanded by force." "SEREMOS LIBRES SI ESTAMOS UNIDOS," says another sign. We will be free if we are united.

The museum is in the Convento de San Diego in Churubusco. Like neighboring Coyoacán, where I live, Churubusco was once a small village, now thick within the sprawl of Mexico City. A major battle of the U.S.-Mexican war was fought here. On that "Bloody Friday," Santa Anna lost as many as four thousand men, killed or wounded, and three thousand captured, among them eight of his generals. Less than a month later, General Winfield Scott, "Old Fuss and Feathers," would ride through the center of Mexico City to the hurrahs of his troops.

"Leviathan comes floundering down upon us from the head-waters of the Eternities. . . ." The Mexicans might well have quoted Melville. The Treaty of Guadalupe Hidalgo was signed in 1848. The Manifest Destiny of the United States had been realized: it was the will of God, said some, that the Republic should span "from sea to shining sea." Go west, young man! With the discovery of gold in California, thousands did. Once they reached the Pacific, some of them blithely slipped south into Lower California, Mexican territory.

A good many of these men were whalers, their unlikely hero a native of Pittston, Maine, named Charles Melville Scammon.

Scammon's Lagoon

A DAGUERREOTYPE of Charles Melville Scammon taken not long after he arrived in San Francisco in the early 1850s shows a mild-eyed man with a Mona Lisa–like expression. His hair neatly combed behind his ears, he sits on a fragile-looking parlor chair with his hands—a scholar's hands, fine-boned and smooth—resting loosely in his lap. Only in his midtwenties, he is already the captain of a whaling bark that prowls the North and South Pacific. It would be difficult to guess from his appearance, but soon, for his ventures hunting grays in Baja California, he would become world famous as one of the greatest and bloodiest whalers of all time.

Nonetheless, his first attempts to hunt the gray whales were disastrous: two boats destroyed, the others staved fifteen times, and eleven men injured when the "devilfish" attacked. Scammon had no intention of returning to Baja California. But two years later, he reconsidered, when, having spent the spring and summer of 1857 cruising the South Seas in command of the *Boston,* his takes of whales and seals were so meager that his men would have had to return to San Francisco penniless.

Scammon had heard rumors of a lagoon within the Bahía de Vizcaíno where grays were said to congregate in vast numbers. No whaler had dared approach the lee shore of the bay, which smaller boats had reported to be mined with shoals. But Scammon was desperate for a bonanza. He sent his tender schooner ahead to scout. It was dangerous, came the report two days later, but there was a navigable passage into the inner lagoon. And yes: it was filled with whales, in countless numbers.

Straightaway, Scammon headed south. The venture that was to make his reputation began, however, with one mishap after another. The wind failed just as the *Boston* approached, forcing them to anchor near the shoals as night came on and a sickening swell began to heave against their hulls. On the third day, four of the catcher boats were swept out to sea and the carpenter drowned. On the fourth, a norther whipped down, blew the ships adrift and buffeted the lagoon for three more days. Finally, when the wind calmed, the crew ventured into the lagoon and killed two cows. But their luck was brief: early the next morning an enraged cow staved one of the catcher boats, splintering it to bits and badly injuring four men. The boat that went to its rescue was also staved, and yet another boat had to be sent to pick the men out of the water. Aboard the *Boston* the wounded were laid out on mattresses, their broken bones set, their cuts and bruises dressed. Almost half the men had been injured.

Nearly a week passed before crews could be mustered for two catcher boats. Bravely, the volunteers rowed out among the whales. But when they came close enough to launch the harpoon, all hands jumped overboard, including, as Scammon wryly noted, "a bulky deserter from the U.S. Army, who had boasted of his daring exploits in the Florida War."

It was, in Scammon's words, a situation "both singular and trying." The whalers were surrounded by hundreds of whales, the water was calm, the weather mild—and the men paralyzed with panic.

This was when Scammon came up with a remarkably simple innovation. Instead of harpooning the whales—which gave them a chance to fight—and then finishing them off with a bomb gun, he tried having his marksmen shoot them with the bomb gun first, from the vantage point of water too shallow for the whales to approach. From that day on, the tryworks were kept going until the last cask was filled with whale oil—and the bread casks, and the mincing tubs, and the coolers, and the deck pots, and finally, even the try-pots themselves were cooled and topped with oil. Scammon and his men sailed into San Francisco Bay that spring with 740 barrels of whale oil, the *Boston* so heavily laden that her scuppers were awash.

Laguna Ojo de Liebre: Whales and Salt

FLATLY SHIMMERING water: it was difficult to tell where Scammon's Lagoon—or as the Mexicans called it, Laguna Ojo de Liebre (Jackrabbit's Eye)—began. Sixty thousand acres of evaporation ponds spread for miles around the bay, separated from one another by the thin lines of dikes of piled dirt and stones. Owned by Exportadora de Sal, a partnership of the Mexican government and Mitsubishi, these works were one of the wonders of Baja California, and I had been fortunate enough to obtain, through friends, a private tour. I was riding in a van with the company's biologist, Julio César Peralta. Water lay on either side of the narrow dirt causeway, broad reddish-blue expanses crowded with birds. Julio pointed out an osprey flying overhead, a glisten of fish wriggling in its talons. A flock of ducks dipped low over the road, darted out toward the horizon. There were 150 bird species here, Julio told me, including peregrine falcons.

This was stark desert country with endless, empty sky. When Arthur North passed by with his mule train, he found nothing but a foul little watering hole crawling with insects. He shivered when he recalled the *Tower Castle,* a whaler shipwrecked in 1838, whose crew swam ashore only to perish of thirst. ("I have observed the symptoms of my companions," scribbled the last survivor in the ship's log, found with their sun-bleached bones. "It is but reasonable to expect that my time will soon come, for I now experience these same symptoms.") North would nearly die of thirst himself some days later, staggering through the thickets of cactus on the pitiless Vizcaíno, his tongue swollen like a knot. Now the town of Guerrero Negro was only a short drive away, although from this wilderness, it could just as well have been on the other side of the earth.

Nearing the saltworks, the evaporation ponds became shallower. Globs of salt foam blew across the road. Along the causeway, salt had accumulated like a ring of slushy snow. A flock of white pelicans floated on the water, as serene as swans. A heron stood at the edge of the road, then took flight at our approach, wings wide.

Salt does not evaporate, Julio said: that was the trick. Lagoon water was pumped into the ponds where it evaporated in the sun; pond by pond it flowed, ever saltier, until it was finally scooped up from the crystallization fields—which was where we had arrived. The van rumbled off the dirt road onto a plain of salt, blazing white to the blue horizon like a prairie farm in winter. The biggest truck I'd ever seen—each wheel was taller than a man—was out in the middle of it, grinding slowly forward as its chute rained salt into a gargantuan hopper. Each harvesting truck weighed 360 tons, Julio said.

It felt strange to be walking on solid salt. It did not crunch.

And then we drove on to the plant. Next, the salt had to be cleaned. Julio showed me where the trucks dumped their cargo over a grate. Below, the salt was caught in tubs, then funneled onto conveyer belts. He walked me through an impressive-looking control room, with instrument panels and blinking colored lights. "PELI-GRO," Danger, said several signs.

Outside, by the loading dock on the lagoon, was a bizarre sight: a mountain of salt high enough to ski down. A small tractor roared back and forth over the top of it.

From here the salt was ferried to Isla Cedros, where it was loaded onto oceangoing ships, some 120 annually carrying a total of 7 million metric tons. Most of it was bound for Japan.

Later, in the Exportadora de Sal's executive boardroom in Guerrero Negro, Julio told me that there were fourteen thousand uses for salt, from making aluminum and glass and fertilizer, to paper and plastics. About 85 percent of the salt went to the chemical industry, 7 percent for water softeners, a mere 4 percent was used for deicing roads and airports, and 4 percent for table salt and food processing.

It was easy to take notes now; I sat in a comfy leather swivel chair, my elbows on the gleaming expanse of table; Julio stood at the chalkboard. A portrait of Ernesto Zedillo in his presidential sash smiled down upon us.

The salt company was founded by an American named Daniel K. Ludwig, Julio said. He saw that the climate here was perfect for producing salt: lots of sun, very little rain. Already there were massive natural salt deposits around the lagoon. In 1954 the American company constructed a pier and a road and dike. In 1957 it shipped out the first load of salt, 8,807 metric tons. Little by little, the company built the town of Guerrero Negro for its workers. Mitsubishi bought the company from the Americans in 1973; three years later, the Mexican government purchased a majority share, a total of 51 percent. Unlike most state-owned companies, Exportadora de Sal was hugely profitable, one of Mexico's top foreign-exchange earners, public or private.

And now they were planning to expand into Laguna San Ignacio. I'd heard the environmentalists' point of view—outrage. What was Exportadora's de Sal's?

"We are in love with this project! Salt evaporation, it's very clean, it's 'green' industry, just what Mexico needs."

Carefully, Julio sketched a map of Laguna San Ignacio on the chalkboard.

"We're talking about 51,150 hectares, 2 percent of the total Vizcaíno biosphere. We want to inundate 28,000 hectares around the lagoon. We'll put a pier out near Punta Abreojos, two and a half kilometers from the mouth of the lagoon, but that won't bother the whales, because their route is four kilometers from the coast."

What about affecting the salinity of the lagoon?

"Six hundred million cubic meters of seawater come into the

lagoon every twenty-four hours. We're talking about pumping out only 2 million cubic meters per day."

But the project involved building housing for fourteen hundred workers and their families. What about sewage treatment?

The salt company would do what it had already done here in Guerrero Negro: install a treatment plant.

And all the ships, wouldn't the noise bother the whales?

Julio laughed. "If that were a problem, the whales wouldn't be coming into Lagunas Guerrero Negro and Ojo de Liebre."[1] I could see for myself, he said. Tomorrow we would go out on Laguna Ojo de Liebre—Scammon's Lagoon.

Big Business

SCAMMON'S LAGOON: within months news of this marvel had raced over the Pacific, from San Francisco to the Sandwich Islands and Oceania, from the Kamchatka Peninsula to the Galapagos to Bahía Magdalena. When Scammon returned the following winter of 1859 with his 205-ton bark *Ocean Bird,* he was at the head of a parade. Six of the vessels managed to find their way through the shoals into the lagoon, and a total of nine lowered thirty catcher boats, at least twenty-five of which by Scammon's estimate were daily engaged in whaling.

"The scene of the slaughter," recalled Scammon, "was exceedingly picturesque and unusually exciting." Some whalers adopted the method of harpooning the calf, quickly towing it ashore, then blasting the cow with a bomb gun as she swam up after it. Different boats often chased the same whale, the men shouting and cursing at each other. On one morning, he recalled,

we distinctly heard a burly fellow, who stood at least six feet in his stockings, bareheaded, with his long locks streaming behind, shouting to his opponent: "That won't do! that won't do! cut your line! I struck my whale first! Cut that line or you'll be into us! Cut that line or I'll put a bomb through you!" But the officer on the opposing boat very coolly replied: "Shoot, and be d—d, you old lime juicer! I won't let go this line 'till we git 'tother side of Jordan!" Then, turning to his crew, he said: "Haul line, boys! haul ahead! and I'll give old Rip-sack a dose he can't git to the 'pothecary's! Haul ahead, and I'll tap his claret-bottle!"

Scammon may have been a bloody-minded man, but while his men were out in the catcher boats he stayed aboard ship, and in the long hours, he made sketches and watercolors astonishing in their detail and beauty. I like to imagine the captain with his mild Mona Lisa smile, daubing his brush into a watery Egyptian blue, or burnt sienna for the barks and schooners and catcher boats. They fill his lagoons from end to end, the ships with their towering masts, the dozen catcher boats—no bigger than whale watchers' *pangas*—with their oars protruding like the legs of strange swimming insects. The dark slivers that dot the water are the backs of whales. In the foreground, a harpooner stands at the prow of a catcher boat aiming his weapon, a few black strokes as spare and deft as Japanese calligraphy.

There is another daguerreotype of Scammon, made some ten years later. He has the same mild face, but a beard now, stippled with white, and an old soldier's wistfulness about the eyes. He wears the full-dress uniform with epaulets, a coat with tails and two rows of coin-size buttons down the front (two unfastened for his hand, à la Napoleon), and a sword sheathed in a scabbard with the seal of the United States. No longer a whaler, Scammon was now a captain of the United States Revenue Marine, playing a new role in his nation's Manifest Destiny, one that would spur him on to a far greater achievement than any of his whaling exploits. Twice he ferried a group of scientists from the Smithsonian Institution and the Chicago Academy of Sciences to Alaska to explore that territory and conduct surveys for a trans-Bering cable. The cable project was suspended when a cable was successfully laid across the Atlantic in 1866; nonetheless, their surveys were put to good use when, the following year, the United States purchased Alaska from the Russians. Inspired by the scientists he had worked with in Alaska, Scammon came back to San Francisco and began writing a book. Published in 1874, *The*

Marine Mammals of the North-western Coast of North America is an extraordinary tome, large and fine, with a lengthy discussion of the history and methods of the American whale fishery, and more than forty illustrations by Scammon himself, ranging from an elegantly simple display of tools (blubber fork, stirring pole, skimmer, bailer, fire poke), to fully realized scenes such as *California Grays among the Ice*. A number of leading naturalists gave *Marine Mammals* their endorsement, among them the great Luis Agassiz. But Scammon was not to enjoy his fame. Ill, he retired to his apple farm. His publisher could not sell more than a few of what was then—at ten dollars—a very expensive book. Unbound copies remained in stock until 1906 when they were destroyed in San Francisco's earthquake and fire. Scammon died in 1911 at the age of eighty-six, believing no doubt that his writings were a forgotten footnote. But as his friend the naturalist William Healy Dall wrote in Scammon's obituary, *Marine Mammals* "forms the most important contribution to the life history of these animals ever published, and will remain a worthy monument to their memory."

The whalers of Baja California may have been long gone, but whales were still big business. During the whale-watching season, Guerrero Negro's dozen motels and two RV parks were filled. A five-minute drive from the Transpeninsular Highway, the town clung to the Boulevard Zapata, an artless automobile-influenced layout. Many of the side roads were still unpaved; taco stands and liquor stores stood cheek-by-jowl with used-clothing vendors, a video-rental shop, a hardware store, the bus depot, a pharmacy, a grocery, a beauty parlor. Guerrero Negro, I couldn't help noticing, had a surprising variety of commerce for a town of ten thousand.

In the van again, we turned off Boulevard Zapata into the neighborhood of Exportadora de Sal's company housing. It was like another world. The roads were all paved, the houses looked like they'd been transported from some churchgoing Republican subdivision in Orange County, California: modest but solid, freshly painted, with well-tended gardens and satellite dishes on the roofs. New cars were parked out front, Fords and Chryslers, Volkswagens and Nissans. An Irish setter lay snoozing on a sidewalk. We drove past the school and the church—a soaring A-frame construction not unlike the one I'd attended as a child. We rounded the neighborhood's park, refreshingly lush with palms and bougainvillea.

"The saltworks *is* Guerrero Negro," Julio said. "Take it away and the town would disappear."

And the whale watching?

He blinked, I thought: as if I'd surprised him.

"That didn't become important until the early 1990s."

We ate lunch at the Malarrimo Restaurant, one of several on the Boulevard Zapata, but according to Julio, the best in Baja. My platter of fish, shrimp, and lime-spritzed melt-in-the-mouth clams convinced me he was right. We were joined by an economist from the Banco de México, and Leonardo Villavicencio, a manager with the salt company. The Malarrimo was a bustling restaurant, perhaps twenty tables, all of them full. Among them was a group of Japanese women, dressed in suits with stockings and high heels—executives' wives from the salt company. They were celebrating someone's birthday with a chocolate cake.

Leonardo was born in San Ignacio, his surname, Villavicencio, from a soldier in the Jesuit presidio. Leonardo had bushy eyebrows and a thick office-bound waist. In his younger days he'd moved to Guerrero Negro to work for the American salt company. "It was very hard at first," he said. There was no town; the workers were living in tents. The wind blew in cold and clammy from the ocean. "We hired welders and carpenters from the mainland, and we paid them very well. But then they'd come here and see the dirt roads and the tents, and they'd say, 'OK, where's Guerrero Negro?'" He burst out laughing at the memory.

Even the name Guerrero Negro was American, in a way. Guerrero Negro means Black Warrior, which was the name of a Yankee whaling ship that sank at the entrance of the lagoon in 1858, overloaded with whale oil. Julio told the story: the salt company needed a name for its town. In 1954, Ludwig's right-hand man drew up a list of possibilities: Salinitas, Vizcaíno, and Guerrero Negro. He got the workers together and they took a vote.

Julio's parents were from the mainland, but he had been born here in the new town. He went back to the mainland to study biology. For a while, in Michoacán, he got into exporting avocados. He also sold frog legs to Mexico City restaurants. But then he realized, "salt was better." It was here in his windblown little hometown in the Baja California desert that he had the opportunity, golden in Mexico, to work as a biologist. Guerrero Negro had taken shape during his lifetime; even now it was growing.

The Transpeninsular Highway had been bringing in travelers since the early 1970s who tanked up on gas, stayed in the hotels, bought groceries, and ate in the restaurants. Then in the early 1990s the whale-watching business took off. And now, with the army base around the monument at the twenty-eighth parallel, there were soldiers and their families, too.

"It used to be that if someone died, all the weddings and dances were canceled," Julio said. "But not anymore."

Just the other day, one of the salt company workers had had his car stolen. He'd left it in front of one of the taco stands on the Boulevard Zapata with the keys in the ignition. His friend said, You shouldn't leave your keys like that. But the worker said, Oh, don't worry. When they'd finished eating, the car was gone.

"It can't have been someone from here," Leonardo said.

"*Alguién de fuera,*" Julio said. Someone from outside.

"This is very strange here."

Julio agreed: "Very strange."

🦂

I WAS LODGED in Exportadora de Sal's guest house. The living room was cool and comfortable, high-ceilinged, with a late-model TV and a stereo and a well-stocked bar. The house would not have been out of place in a Los Angeles suburb, except that to walk out the front door was to step onto a broad, sand-swept road, surrounded by sand.

In the morning Leonardo asked me if I had signed the guest book. "*Gente muy importante,*" Very important people, he said, his bushy eyebrows dancing up and down his forehead.

The guest book lay on the coffee table. Of course, I'd looked at it:

apart from the rows of Japanese characters and a few stilted attempts at Spanish *(Gracis!)*, it was a Who's Who of Mexican politics.

The one missing was Luis Donaldo Colosio, I said.

Colosio had visited, Leonardo said. He just hadn't stayed in the guest house. This was in 1992, when he was minister of social development and ecology, before he was named candidate for the presidency. Hadn't I seen the little brass plaque on the wall at the Malarrimo, where we'd had lunch yesterday? Colosio had eaten there, at the table in the far corner.

Colosio: he was a reminder of everything that had gone wrong. The investigation of his murder was a travesty of flip-flopping theories, suspects arrested, tortured, released, rearrested. "Who killed him?" the old schoolteacher Néstor Agúndez had fumed back in Todos Santos. "I think it was Salinas. But why?" There were a dozen different theories, any one of which might have been the truth. It still remained a mystery.

Opening scene: Baja California. Leonardo said, "Colosio was in La Paz with Juan Ignacio Bremer, the head of Exportadora de Sal, and about twenty other people." I guessed that Leonardo had told this fragment of the story many times, worrying it like a rosary bead, telling and retelling as if enough telling would make it make sense. Bob Van Wormer had told me the same story when I was visiting his sportfishing resort on the East Cape: Colosio was in La Paz; he was about to fly to Mexico City when he got the phone call ordering him to go to Tijuana.

"Tijuana," Oscar Arce had told me down in the canyons of the Sierra de San Francisco, shaking his head sadly. "That is a lost city."

These thoughts so flustered me that I had to cross out what I'd written and write it again.

❧

ON THIS BRILLIANTLY blue morning, faint trails of white were feathered across the sky. The water was as smooth as butter. We motored past a buoy with a trio of sea lions sunning themselves on it, fat chocolate-brown lumps with whiskers. One raised a flipper at us and yawned. In the distance, a barge loaded with salt chugged slowly out toward Isla Cedros. Along the shore loomed tall ivory-white dunes carved round by the wind, a ravishing landscape, as unforgiving in its way as the ice fields of Antarctica.

I thought of the men from the shipwreck of the *Tower Castle,* their bones parching in the sun, and of Arthur North and his mules, his Mexican guides, his can-do wanderlust.

And, of course, I thought of Charles Melville Scammon. He would have known a morning like this, the sun dappling on the sea, the air sweet with salt. I had my camera at-the ready, lens cap stowed, my finger poised on the button. Within minutes we saw our first gray whales, a baby as dark as marble, and its mother. At the horizon—not far from two whale watchers' *pangas*—a whale was breaching, a huge, violent thing.

In the Land of the Clouds

San Quintín

> ...because they had all come from a place of
> sadness and worry and defeat ... they huddled
> together; they talked together ...
> —JOHN STEINBECK, *The Grapes of Wrath*
>
> There are those who leave their town and
> don't come back, God knows why.
> —FELIPE LUIS SANTIAGO, quoted in *Mixtecos en Baja California*

San Canteen

SAN QUINTÍN, as Arthur North advised, "is pronounced San Can-téen, a pronunciation which no visitor is apt to forget, for assuredly the canteen is patron saint of this flea-bitten pueblo."

Alice was reading from North's *Camp and Camino in Lower California*. Its brittle old spine had finally cracked, its edges frayed and yellowed pages loosened. Five hours south of the border, we were driving by tomato fields now, vast expanses swathed in strips of black plastic, like an artwork by Christo. In several fields, gangs of workers stooped along the rows, picking the ripe red fruits. By the roadside a boy was pushing a bicycle, his face covered with a handkerchief like a bandit. A refrigerated truck—EMPACADORA ABC—blasted by, and *poof,* the boy and his bike disappeared in a swirl of sandy dust.

"San Quintín," Alice read on,

> a small village of perhaps a hundred two-legged inhabitants, and
> a hundred million fleas ... situated on the edge of the Pacific, just

above the thirteenth parallel of north latitude, and hard by five strange hills. . . . Briefly, San Quintín has a harbor which needs dredging, wonderful salt beds from which, for some unknown reason, no salt is extracted, a flour mill which is enjoying a long vacation, and a lobster factory which does nothing to interfere with the numerous lobsters thriving along the coast.

San Quintín's heyday as an English colony was a decade past, its railroad and flour mill already in ruins, when North rode into the little "flea-bitten pueblo" in 1906. A quarter of the way down the peninsula's Pacific coast, it was almost unimaginably remote. The nearest mission was the Dominicans' Santo Domingo, twenty rock-and-cactus-strangled miles north, a few melted lumps of adobe abandoned in the early nineteenth century. A tribe of Paipais survived in the sierra near the border, but for the most part, the Indians of the peninsula were dead—"stone dead," as a traveling miner told North, "the whole blooming outfit."

But now the Indians were back. From Oaxaca, deep in the belly of the mainland, some twenty thousand had ventured across the Sea of Cortés to settle in the San Quintín Valley; thousands more crowded into the shacks and tents of the growers' camps during the May to October season. If the English had tried to farm here and failed, a century later Mexican growers, most of them from Sinaloa, succeeded. Deep wells for irrigation, strong demand for winter fruits and vegetables in the United States, dirt cheap migrant labor: they made a lucrative combination.

San Quintín was so tied to the U.S. economy that, though I was coming from Mexico City, it was considerably cheaper to get there by first flying to San Diego. Within five hours' drive here we were: a liquor store, a pharmacy, a roast chicken stand, fish tacos, clams, used clothing, the Mueblería La Cuatita, the Discoteca Flamingo. As in Ciudad Constitución and Guerrero Negro, the main street of San Quintín was the highway, lined with cinder-block shops set back behind dirt aprons. Another liquor store: TECATE CERVEZA FRIA COLD BEER. On the dirt a man in a tattered black T-shirt and huaraches sprawled conked out, a bottle at his feet.

"San Canteen." Alice made a gruesome little chuckle.

And then we whizzed through Lázaro Cárdenas, its sister pueblo just down the highway, equally flea-bitten, equally endowed with liquor stores—plus an army base.

But Arthur North hadn't said enough about those "five strange hills": volcanic cinder cones as nude and smooth as gelatins slipped from their molds. They surrounded the shore, calm sentinels over an even calmer bay. Nor did he say enough about the bay: such a beautiful bay, still—so it appeared from the distance of the highway—as a mill pond, polished silver in the afternoon light.

We bumped down the rutted dirt road to the water, dust billowing behind us. Farms lay on either side, a few pigs, a shack, a flock of chickens, cows munching at a trough of green and pale-orange tomatoes. After perhaps a quarter of an hour, we pulled up to water's edge. In the distance two cinder cones loomed over the bay. The sky gleamed as blue as crystal, not a cloud in sight. The tide was trickling out. A pelican sat calmly, letting the water slowly carry it backward.

The Old Mill and the Tomb of the Tomato King

THE ENGLISH COLONY was what first piqued my interest in San Quintín. Such an unlikely venture: a folly, to dry farm wheat in the desert. And like so many other enterprises in Baja California, a source of small, sad ruins. As with the sugar mills in Todos Santos, the windswept hovels of El Arco, the El Mármol onyx quarry, and the Franciscan Mission San Fernando Velicatá, I felt a curious satisfaction in seeking them out, tramping around the rubble, photographing whatever was left to photograph. To see the ruins was like viewing the Very Bones in a filigreed reliquary: She lived. He suffered. This actually happened. As with the bones, so with the rubble: It was the stories of the people associated with them that mattered—small, sad stories perhaps, but stories nonetheless, each one opening like a bud into a many-petaled flower: more stories. A thousand and one stories.

Here by the water a long, narrow bed of earth once covered with railway track jutted into the bay. Surrounded by a careful planting of pink geraniums and a park bench stood a gargantuan rusted iron wheel—what was left of the English flour mill.

Appropriately, "The Old Mill" was the name of the motel here, two rows of brick-walled rooms separated by a gravel parking lot and a cubbyhole of an office with a slapping screen door. A boardwalk led next door to Gaston's lobster and steak house. This was a place for sportfishermen ("the perch are large," enthuses *The Baja Catch,* "comparable to what was found off San Diego thirty years ago"). The parking lot was filled with high-clearance trucks and jeeps with California plates.

"Foreign influences," *El Diario Peninsular* had grumbled back in Cabo San Lucas. *"Nos están invadiendo,"* They are invading us, the toothy-smiled girl had told me at the roadside stand near Todos Santos. From La Paz to Loreto, Bahía Magdalena to Mulegé, in the trailer parks in Bahía de los Angeles, whale watching on Laguna San Ignacio and Ojo de Liebre, from the U.S.-Mexican war, whaling and mining, farming and fishing, ranching, even salt production: in the past as in the present, invited in or hacked back, the Yankee influence on the peninsula proved as hardy as kudzu. Across the bay, at the foot of the cinder cone known as Kenton Hill, was the seedling of an American colony, some dozen vacation houses. I could see them from here.

But the English were gone. They'd bought the concession to farm four hundred thousand acres around San Quintín from a group of bankrupt American investors. In the early 1890s they began to construct a railroad. They built a pier, a warehouse, and a mill for the great quantities of wheat they expected to grow and ship north. Their Mexican Land and Development Company was headed by Colonel Charles Edward Hamilton, Francis Baing Dupre, and, improvidentially, one J. A. Drought. It did not rain for many years. In 1909—three years after Arthur North's visit—what could be salvaged of the railroad track and the mill was shipped to a copper mine in Arizona.

So little was left: this fragment of causeway, odd finger in the bay; this iron mill wheel dignified by geraniums. And a graveyard, of course. More stories? Names, at the very least, and dates. The sky was paling, and the masses of the volcanos Kenton and Ceniza, moments ago a reddish brown, had dimmed to purple as we plowed down the dirt road toward the mouth of the bay. It was soft in places, powdery with sand. Dust blew over the road like snow. The fields on either side were empty of animals or crops, nothing but dust and pickle-weed. Near the graveyard, a break of pine trees wavered in the wind, ragged and yellow with dust.

The English graves dotted a small rise overlooking the water, over-grown with scrub. Their markers were made of wood, simple cross-es that had splintered and broken, their surfaces bleached over the years of sun and rain and sun. Nothing was legible, not a name, not a date. One grave was marked by a wooden bed frame. A woman who died in childbirth, Alice guessed. Behind the ruined bed frame a pita-haya cactus threw out its arms like crazy tentacles.

But there were other graves, the modern cement markers of Mexicans—among them a marble monument, a pillared temple ris-ing up, as ostentatious as something out of a Las Vegas casino. Beneath its shelter a life-size bronze statue of Christ blessed the small, bent figure of a campesino with a hoe. A plaque spelled the story of Luis Rodríguez Aviña, born in Michoacán in 1914, son of humble peas-ants, orphaned at an early age. He worked hard, and although he did not enjoy the advantage of schooling, he was honest. He loved rodeos and music and fiestas. He married at the age of eighteen and had twelve children. In the 1950s he arrived in Baja California, and his greatest dreams and happinesses were achieved in this valley. He was an admirable father and a loving grandfather. He died on September 12, 1992. May he rest in peace.

I later learned that Luis Rodríguez Aviña was the founder of one of San Quintín's largest tomato-growing concerns. The Tomb of the Tomato King, as I came to think of it: a story that opened into other stories and connected in the most unlikely ways. Here was one dead in childbirth, leaving bone-dry land on the outer edge of nowhere; the other dying old and rich and honored with many children and grandchildren and fields full of big, ripe tomatoes. There they lay by the silvery bay, not fifteen feet apart.

Sky Ranch

ON OUR FIRST night in San Quintín, Alice and I stayed at the Old Mill Motel. But our room was cramped and our neighbors—six sportfishermen guzzling their way through a cooler of beer—loud. The only (non-flea-bitten) alternative was Rancho Sereno, a bed-and-breakfast run, so my guidebook noted, by the "friendly Atkinson family." To my surprise, Rancho Sereno wasn't out across the bay in the American colony, but near the Old Mill, plunk in the middle of these dusty pickleweed-covered fields.

The little oasis of Rancho Sereno began with a water tank up on stilts, an arch made of two whale ribs, and a graded dirt driveway neatly lined with rocks. The house—a ranch house like any other in, say, suburban Los Angeles—was sheltered by a grove of yucca and leafy green acacia trees.

"Welcome!" Susie Atkinson's one hundred–watt smile greeted us at the door. "Welcome, welcome!" Slight, with a puff of carrot-colored hair, Susie was a bundle of grandmotherly energy embracing us right into the bosom of her home. There in the living room watching TV were her husband, Jim; daughter, Julie; and a black labrador named Moxie that gave us the once-over with bright eyes and began, lazily, to thump her tail.

Where were we from, where were we going, what did we think of Baja? Jim, a tall man with elfin features and a halo of white hair, jumped up from the living room sofa to make us margaritas. The blender roared. Conversation resumed once we were seated with our drinks. It was all so oddly, suddenly intimate. Julie sat smoking a cigarette, her bare feet up on the ottoman. Moxie lolled on her side and let out a little snore.

The Atkinsons had bought this house nearly ten years ago. Before that—back in the late 1960s—they ran Sky Ranch. I'd heard of Mike's Sky Ranch, a dirt-bike resort up in the Sierra San Pedro Mártir.

"Not *Mike's* Sky Ranch!" Susie rocked back, clenching her fists in mock fury. "I just *hate* it when people say, *Oh, you mean Mike's* Sky Ranch."

"Ours was before that one," Jim said.

"They copied the name," Susie said indignantly.

"We were really famous," Jim said.

But the "we" was more sentimental than proprietary. The Atkinsons had merely managed Sky Ranch, Jim explained, which belonged to a businessman named Walter Hussong and his partners. It consisted of two airstrips, a restaurant and bar, and a ten-room hotel down the bay, not far from the English graveyard. Now it was in ruins.

"People flew down here to hunt geese and deer, dig clams. There was lots of fishing," Jim said.

"Before, there were a lot of ducks," Susie said.

"Half a million brant geese," Jim said. "Now there's only maybe eighty or ninety thousand."

"People would fly in for the day from Los Angeles and San Diego just for our lobster tacos," Susie said.

"Big flour tortillas piled with fresh lobster meat," Jim said.

"Erle Stanley Gardner flew in," Susie said.

"And Claude Ryan."

"Claude Ryan?" Alice was impressed. He was the original owner of the San Diego company that built Lindbergh's *Spirit of St. Louis.*

"Yep," Jim said. "Flew down with his son just for lunch. I saw him climb out of his airplane. What d'ya know."

But then in 1968, Hussong got into a wrangle with his partners and Sky Ranch was closed. The Atkinsons took over a nearby chicken farm, but that was a short-lived venture. Not until nearly twenty years later, when they bought this house, did the Atkinsons return to live in San Quintín.

"I was so happy," Julie said. Sky Ranch and San Quintín had been her childhood; to move to the United States was a cruel uprooting. A petite woman with a cigarette-roughened voice and long, honey-blonde hair, Julie was my same age, born in 1961. For her, Mexico was home.

Jim took down the Sky Ranch photo album. Susie said, "Aw, they don't want to have to look at all that." But we did. Slowly Alice turned the yellowed pages of snapshots, their colors faded to pastels. Guests in blue jeans posing with their fishing poles, a woman with a bouffant hairdo and capri pants in front of her airplane, a truck bed piled high with giant clams—"huge clams," Jim said, "big as a man's face and there for the taking." There were the little cabins with their roof tiles of clam shells, more guests, laughing, eating.

And then a larger black-and-white photograph: maybe twenty Mexican children, their stern-faced teacher, and a tiny blonde girl looking away from the camera as if she was about to cry.

Julie chuckled. "Somebody must have been teasing me."

She hadn't known Spanish when she first went to school in San Quintín. "But I learned it in three months," she said proudly. "I learned to read and write in Spanish before I did in English."

It was hard not to stare at the photograph: that one small, sad blonde child.

Why

Sabrá Dios por qué, God knows why anyone would want to stay here, I couldn't help wondering. As for the Oaxacans, after the tomato harvest, most would go home to mountain villages, perhaps to a little wooden house set in a forest of pine trees and oaks, and a plot of corn and beans. They would participate in all the many baptisms and weddings, so pretty with their music and their decorations of colored tissue paper, and the funerals, and the saint days with their fiestas of firecrackers and parades.

Why leave? Money. Family. Religious freedom, political freedom. A chance to learn. *Pueblo chico, infierno grande,* Small town, big hell? Or—*à la americana*—"Anywhere but here"? Everyone who leaves, like everyone who chooses not to go back, has their reasons. I had mine for living in Mexico City. What were Julie's for staying here? She had, after all, spent seventeen years in the United States, a U.S. citizen. I would have liked to have asked her, but in the morning she was gone.

The Atkinsons' cook, a large, plain woman with her lank hair knotted into a ponytail, stood frying bacon at the stove. Coffee dripped and gurgled through the Mr. Coffee machine. Four places had been set on the red-and-white-checkered tablecloth: for Jim and Susie, Alice and me.

As we started on our coffee, Jim and Susie continued reminiscing. Back when they ran Sky Ranch, the San Quintín Valley was a rumble of a ride from the border; the Transpeninsular Highway hadn't been built yet. "There was so little traffic," Susie said. "It was perfect for potty stops because there was no one to see you!" Jim met the government officials who'd arrived on the presidential yacht on a fact-finding mission for incoming president Luis Echeverría. "They landed on an abandoned beach. They had to roll up their trousers and wade in." He laughed at the memory. "They asked me, what do you need more than anything else? I said: A road."

Lázaro Cárdenas, the sister town with the army base, was a dirt field then. Industrial tomato growing hadn't yet started. San Quintín amounted to three little stores that served a handful of hardscrabble ranches growing wheat and chiles—a tough business: "You could grow a thousand acres of chiles and not break even."

Why did they come back?

"The dust!" Susie laughed.

"The people," Jim said. "But you know, it's changing. We're getting an awful lot of people from Sinaloa, Nayarit, Jalisco, Oaxaca—"

"Vienen por el trabajo," the cook interrupted. They come for the work. She understood English; she knew that we understood Spanish. *"En Sinaloa, no hay segundas,"* There's nothing secondhand in Sinaloa. "But here I can buy my kids used clothes and shoes. In my hometown I had to buy everything new, so they had to do without. Here life is easier. You earn more money. People come and go for two or three years, they see that it's better here. There are lots of institutions—health centers, schools. The INI even sends social workers to the camps to teach people better hygiene and nutrition.[1] My whole family moved here. I have three kids. When we moved I was pregnant. In my hometown we never had enough food. I was always hungry—oh, that was awful the way we were always hungry! I don't

want my children to suffer the way I suffered." She shook her head no, no. *"Por eso me quedo,"* That's why I stay in San Quintín. That's why people come here.

And with that, she set our plates on the table: fluffy cheese omelettes, crisp Oscar Mayer bacon, fried potatoes with onions, buttered toast, and a big bottle of ketchup.

Elephant in the Living Room

IN THE COUPLE of days Alice and I spent around San Quintín we ventured into town only twice, both times to make phone calls from the pharmacy. The Old Mill Motel didn't have a telephone; neither did the Atkinsons. Pharmacies appeared to have a monopoly on the business: four pesos a minute long distance, eight pesos to the United States. The clerk would dial, then direct us to a booth. After five there were lines of workers waiting to make calls. Aged school buses—one said ST. LOUIS SCHOOL DISTRICT—groaned by on the highway outside, ferrying workers back to the camps. Other workers ambled in the dust along the road, gangs of men and women in long sleeves and baseball caps, their faces covered with filthy bandannas.

I'd come to San Quintín for the story of the English colony, which turned out to be thin gruel. Instead, I found the Atkinsons, their memories, and their faded photographs of Sky Ranch. I'd never been a fan of bed-and-breakfasts; they seemed to me unnaturally chummy, too precious. But I liked Rancho Sereno; I liked the Atkinsons. American expats in Mexico, they were of my tribe. Just to hear their voices was comforting, and the little things, like the flowered bedspreads and color-coordinated towels in the bathroom, the TV showing *The Price Is Right,* that big bottle of ketchup, they soothed. Outside, there was the dust and the pickleweed, the tomato fields and the Oaxacans: Mexico. It seemed a world away.

And too, I found the bay and its five hills, so grand and sober, changing with the light like Monet's haystacks. Alice and I drove out along the dirt roads around the bay and the bay behind it, Bahía Falsa, where we found an oyster farm with oyster cages floating like a necklace across the water. We saw cinder quarries, deep pits of reddish gravel, and black lava in the surf. Once, two ebony snakes striped with gold slithered across the road. We ate at Gaston's by the Old Mill Motel: lobster brochettes, lobster linguini, New York–style cheesecake. Alice brought her watercolors. I tramped around taking photographs. We had a wonderful time.

I was avoiding it, this story as utterly obvious as an elephant in the living room: the migrant field-workers, the Oaxacans—*los oaxacalifornios,* as one of the waiters at Gaston's called them. I remembered what people had told me down in Todos Santos: "We don't want them here." Like the Atkinsons' cook, the Oaxacans came to San Quintín for the money, a better life.

Better: it was hard to imagine something worse than the backbreaking work in the sun, the stink of the fertilizers, the dust. We'd driven by some of the camps: shacks surrounded by chain-link fence, children with swollen bellies playing in the dirt.

On our way out of town, we drove by another man passed out on the roadside, clutching his bottle of beer with grime-black hands.

They

I WAS BACK in San Quintín in April, the start of the growing season. The winter's rains had left the roadside green with wild grasses and tufty bushes of tumeric-yellow daisies. I'd driven down from the border in a rented fire engine–red Oldsmobile. Already it was coated with dust, grit even down around the gas cap, and a fine crud-yellow spray over the dashboard. I'd come back to the Old Mill, and here I was sitting in the dim of Gaston's lobster and steak house, interviewing my first contact, Félix Pérez (not his real name), the director of a government-sponsored microenterprise program for Oaxacans in San Quintín. My calling card was that, as a professor of economics at Mexico City's ITAM, I'd written a book about how low-income Mexicans make use of financial services. On the mainland, I'd researched several microenterprise programs, most of which were more "hype and heart" than anything sustainable, but a few of them—perhaps—did some good.

Tall and big-bellied, Félix Pérez was just the size to play a shopping-mall Santa. But he spoke with a bluntness that surprised me.

"Les gusta ser pobres," They like to be poor. This was the first thing I needed to understand about the Oaxacans.

They like to be poor? It was absurd! But I hadn't come to argue; I listened, I kept taking notes.

Mixtecs and Triquis were the two most important groups from Oaxaca in San Quintín, he went on. There were also a few Zapotecs, and from Guerrero and Michoacán, Náhuatls and Purapechas. Some 20,000 Oaxacans had settled on *terrenos invadidos,* invaded lands, that is, they were "parachutists," like Lupe in Cabo San Lucas. The rest of the Oaxacans—as many as 150,000—were migrants who began arriving in April and stayed in the camps through October. They earned about fifty pesos, or a little less than six dollars, for an eight- or even ten-hour day of planting, tending, or harvesting.

The Oaxacans were crammed into shacks, or surplus United States Army tents, families with children, newlyweds, grandparents, all mixed up, the families cordoned off from one another with cardboard or plywood into spaces the size of a closet. Inside in the summer heat it was sweltering and foul. Some camps had electricity, some didn't. Same with drinking water. In general, they lacked sewers. Growers provided latrines, although the Oaxacans rarely used them. "They go on the floor," Félix said, wrinkling his nose.

He seemed to have a curious mixture of contempt and heartfelt concern. I asked him how he'd gotten into this line of work. He said he'd been a professor of international economics at the Universidad Autónoma de Baja California in Tijuana, specializing in Soviet cooperatives and Marxist theory. *Not*—he wanted me to be sure to know—that he was an unabashed admirer of all that was Soviet. He'd visited Russia in 1984, the first days of Gorbachev's perestroika, and been shocked by what he saw, "a shameful kind of feudalism, very far from socialism." Later, he left the university and rolled up his sleeves to work in a Tijuana slum for Solidaridad, the nationwide community-development program launched by President Salinas.

I already knew a bit about Salinas's Solidaridad. By the early 1990s, with the economy going full-blast and the government's coffers spilling over from the recent reprivatizations of the banks, Solidaridad morphed into a massive shower of spending—the equivalent of 2.6 billion U.S. dollars in 1993 alone. But it wasn't a replay of *fin-de-sexenio* López Portillo: this time the spending was aimed at infrastructure in poor communities. From the tiny mountain pueblos of Chiapas to the shanty towns around Chihuahua, Solidaridad paved roads, brought in drinking water and electricity, built drainage systems and health centers and schools. There were those who called attention to the old-fashioned ward politics behind Solidaridad, the way the purse strings were so often controlled by local members of the ruling party, the PRI. Many—like the Mexican political scientist Denise Dresser, who famously dubbed it "a neopopulist solution to neoliberal problems"—criticized Solidaridad as weak salve for the hardship inflicted on the poor by the "structural adjustments" that came with Salinas's market-oriented reforms. But such voices were soft, mere annoyances. These were the glory days when Salinas was feted by everyone from U.S. investment-fund managers to the throngs of campesinos who met him on his weekly tours through the countryside. Solidaridad glittered brightest of the jewels in the jewel-encrusted crown of Salinas's economic "miracle," concrete evidence—here was the school, there was the drainage system—of, as Salinas's finance minister put it, "the higher mission of the government before its people."

The government official in charge of Solidaridad was the minister of social development and ecology, Luis Donaldo Colosio. "So," I said, "you worked for Colosio?"

"That's right." And, Félix continued, when Colosio was named the PRI's presidential candidate, he joined the campaign, helping to organize youth for the various rallies.

Including the one at Lomas Taurinas?

"Yes," Félix said. "I was there when he was killed. I saw his body carried by on the stretcher. I followed the ambulance to the hospital."

This story as painfully sudden as a knife slash, it was like the interview with Professor Agúndez in Todos Santos. And Colosio—who seemed so unreal, an idol's face blown up on a billboard—collapsed into a man I might have known "We lost a great hope!" Professor Agúndez had said. "And we don't know why. Who killed him?"

Some people said it was Salinas.

"Why would he do that?" Félix said, indignantly. "Salinas always supported Colosio. He made him head of the PRI, he made him minister of social development and ecology, and then he, Salinas, personally chose Colosio to be the presidential candidate."

Félix looked at me hard, my pen, my notebook. He wasn't going to say anything more about it.

We walked outside onto the gravel of the parking lot. Across the water, solid and enduring, loomed Kenton and Ceniza. The sky, a perfect unblemished blue, seemed to shimmer. Seabirds wheeled overhead, chittering and honking.

Why didn't more people come out here, where it was so beautiful?

"They don't see it like you do," Félix said.

They: the Oaxacans who came here to work but, according to Félix, liked to be poor. But if I found Félix's reasoning muddy, he was thoroughly confused by mine. What was I getting at? I'd told him I was interested in the Oaxacans, and that in learning about their business that his program sponsored, I might begin to gain some insight about their lives here.

And so: what was the point?

Again, I tried to explain. Judging from the expression on his face, however, I might as well have been speaking Chinese. *Ni modo,* No matter, he shrugged as he folded himself into the passenger seat of the Oldsmobile. We were going to proceed with the tour of three of his "clients," Oaxacans in a profit-sharing scheme to raise chickens.

I'd done this kind of interview many times before. They were always fascinating. Once, in a slum in Mexico City, I'd talked to a man who made a business of buying scraps from a blue-jeans factory, then sewing them into children's backpacks. With a loan, he'd bought a used sedan, which he drove all over the state selling his backpacks at street markets. I toured a clandestine factory that employed seven people making chile-coated lollipops. I met a woman who used her loan to build a ceramic oven in her living room. Once a month, she would pack up several boxes of the little baked-clay party souvenirs she'd made and take them to a store downtown. Her problem, she told me, wasn't so much getting credit as it was not having a telephone to take orders, or a less expensive way of getting to the store than a taxi. The bus wouldn't allow her on with the boxes; she couldn't afford a car. These were all things I wouldn't have thought of. Many people, even very poor people, told me they didn't need credit so much as they did a savings service that would yield interest. Again, that surprised me.

How about savings? I asked Félix. How did the Oaxacans save?

We were passing through the ramshackle trip that was downtown San Quintín. In the parking lot of a liquor store, a pack of dogs nosed a pile of rubbish.

The Oaxacans were too poor to save, he said. They didn't have any financial culture.

I'd found some interesting things in other parts of Mexico, I offered. Even very poor people might keep a silver coin or two tucked under the mattress. A trusted employer, a priest, or a teacher might act as *"guardadinero,"* safekeeping savings in a bank account or even a locked suitcase. Oftentimes poor people mixed their "savings" with "consumption" and "investment," for example, by raising goats or rabbits. How about chickens?

The chickens in his program were meant to be a business, he said.

How about *tandas,* then? Some form of the informal savings and credit groups could be found almost everywhere in Mexico—I'd heard of them even among some of the poorest indigenous people in the remote Sierra Madre, albeit with foodstuffs rather than cash. Did the Oaxacans here have *tandas?*

"¿Cómo?" How? Humph. Félix scowled and crossed his arms over his chest. *"Prestando entre jodidos,"* Lending among the screwed. Ridiculous.

Maybe *guelaguetza,* the Mixtec's ritual bartering system, would constitute some variant of *tanda.* What about that?

He didn't have a very clear idea of what *guelaguetza* was.

I had to admit, neither did I.

Félix switched on the car radio to 1290 A.M. *"La Voz del Valle,"* said the announcer. *"La voz que rompe el silencio,"* The Voice of the Valley. The voice that breaks the silence. This was the radio station run by the INI for Oaxacans in the San Quintín Valley. Sometimes *La Voz del Valle* broadcasted in Mixtec or Triqui; now the announcer was reading messages in Spanish. "Rocio Edith Morales, it is urgent that you call 298-91 and speak with Señora Morales in Oaxaca. Epifanio González, please write to your father in Justlahuaca, Oaxaca. He needs to know where you are and if you are all right."

The workers listened to the radio in the fields, Félix said. Under their baseball caps and bandannas they wore Walkmans. Some of the growers didn't like it because sometimes the announcer would read the federal labor laws in Mixtec and Triqui.

"Heladio Martínez," intoned the announcer in his mellifluous baritone, "please wait for a call from your brother in Oxnard, California, at the pharmacy in Lázaro Cárdenas on Sunday at 5:30 P.M."

Several miles north of town now, the highway arrowed through a patchwork of green, expanses of black plastic strips, and raw plowed fields. The midafternoon sun radiated with a cruel harshness, and though there were all these fields, and the wild grasses and daisies bunched in the dust along the roadside, the landscape felt parched and lifeless.

We turned off onto a dirt road, jolting over the gashes and mounds of dried mud. This was the Colonia Ampliación San Ramón, a *terreno invadido,* invaded land. Cinder-block and tar-paper shacks had been built here and there. Most of the lots were still empty, although marked off with wire. Electric wires drooped overhead. The settlement was less than two years old, Félix said. It didn't yet have running water; residents had to buy what they needed from a truck.

We pulled up in front of a tar paper–and–plywood shack. On the dirt was parked a dust-encrusted raisin-brown hatchback with Oregon plates, so battered it looked like it had been pelted with bricks. This was the house of Herminio Chávez, a Mixtec who had migrated back and forth from San Quintín to Oregon working the strawberry crops, until the year before, when he'd stayed behind to raise chickens with Félix's microenterprise program. Herminio's handshake was brief, his hand hard and rough. A tiny jut-jawed man with a muscular chest, Herminio wore a Nike baseball cap, a frayed blue T-shirt, and huaraches with soles cut from old tires. His daughter, as tiny as a china doll, in pink maryjanes and a filthy ruffled dress, stared up at me, strange white person. Her hair had not been combed, and her face was smeared with food. An enormous black dog trotted up, plunked itself down next to her, and commenced scratching furiously at its ear.

There was nowhere to sit and talk. Down the street a thin rectangle of shade fell from the corrugated metal awning of a soda shack. He would buy us all sodas, Félix said.

Let me, I said.

An old couple, the man with a row of greenish-yellow teeth, the woman still pretty with salt-and-pepper braids, were already leaning on their elbows on the counter that opened out onto the street, and were staring at me.

I bought the sodas, and an orange juice for the little girl.

I followed Félix's lead. Apparently the only thing to do was conduct the interview standing here by the counter with our open-mouthed audience.

He didn't have any chickens now, Herminio said. He would get more, but he was pissed off about what had happened. He'd gotten 7,000 pesos as risk capital from Félix's program, *"muy poco dinero,"* very little money. He'd always kept a few chickens, but these fryer chickens, they were another class of business: vaccinations, medicines. The program had hired a technician who was supposed to provide guidance, but that hadn't worked out. "He didn't show up and didn't show up, and then he shows up at ten o'clock at night!"

Yes, Félix acknowledged, the technician had been a disappointment. He had not done his job; he had not treated people with respect.

Meanwhile, the little girl had toddled off with her orange juice. She was halfway up the street now, being followed by the black dog and four others.

"The dogs might bite her!" the old woman cried.

"Eh," Herminio waved his hand as if to shoo a fly. He turned back to me. "I get 30 pesos for each one of a hundred chickens. That's 3,000 pesos. But out of a hundred chickens, ten, maybe fifteen are going to die. Then the hundred chickens eat twenty bags of feed, those fucking chickens, they eat a lot! Damn! Twenty bags of feed cost 115 pesos. That's 2,300 pesos. Three thousand less 2,300 leaves me what? Do the math." He dared me.

"Seven hundred pesos," I said.

"No es mucho pedo." Not a lot of fart.

"Now, now," Félix said, "don't swear so much."

"Tss," Herminio said.

We walked back to my car.

"Is that your car?" Herminio said. Even covered with dust, in the mercilessness of the sun the Oldsmobile gleamed a sleek and snazzy red.

It was rented, I said.

"But she's rich just the same," Félix said. "She's white." He sidled up to Apolinar and rolled up his sleeve. "You see? We are both dark. That is why we are poor."

I didn't know what to say to that. Oaxacans like to be poor, Félix had said to me back in the coziness of the sportfishermen's steak and lobster house; now, however, poverty boiled down to an equation of skin color. And why was he toadying up to Herminio?

Just then a man rode up on a bicycle. "Ah," Herminio said, and threw up his hands. "The Cadillac!"

This was Gerónimo, who lived across the street. He had a pudgy moon of a face and a Nike baseball cap that said, "JUST DO IT!" With risk capital from Félix's program, Gerónimo had bought some chickens. They were in a coop in his yard. He invited us in for a look.

They were chicks, as big as a man's fist, but still without feathers, a mass of them quietly huddled together. The coop was cobbled together with pieces of black plastic, wood, and chicken wire. They stank.

There was a plan to sell chicken mole to the workers in the fields, Félix said.

Oaxacan mole was very good, I said.

He hoped the program could expand, Félix said, as we headed back out to the street. Maybe some people could use the program's risk capital to buy ovens and sell roast chicken.

Herminio swore under his breath; I couldn't understand what he was saying. Gerónimo picked up his bike and pedaled off, no goodbye.

Félix had one more client we could visit this afternoon, a Triqui who lived in the neighboring Colonia San Ramón Sección Triqui. This was an older, squatter settlement; most of the plots had been built on. At the outer edge of the settlement, ringed by a fence grown over with bushes, herbs, and nopal cacti, Diego's house was a wood shack painted an eye-popping cobalt blue. The lemon-yellow flag of the PRD—the opposition Partido Revolucionario Democrático—fluttered on a pole next to the gate. Diego, a short man with a shaggy mustache and thick Jesus-length hair, appeared from behind, a broom in his hand. When he opened the gate for us, his flock of chickens swarmed out, strutting and clucking across the road and under the wire fence of a field of alfalfa. They were beautiful chickens, jet-black with bright combs, black-and-white speckled ones, and penny-red ones, all of them tall and yellow-legged and fluffy.

Félix introduced me as "a researcher." Might she ask a few questions about his chicken business?

"*Pues sí,*" Of course, Diego said. We filed into his house, a stale-smelling, windowless room with a dirt floor. A PRD poster—DEMO-CRACIA YA! CARDENAS PRESIDENTE '94—was taped on one wall. A U.S. flag on a stick hung upside down from a beam next to his bed. His bed, pushed against the far corner, was heaped with what looked like wads of clothing. After such stark sunshine, I couldn't see well in this murk. I had a sense of chaos, crates piled here, a stove there, a chair, a clutter of soda bottles. Félix and I sat on chairs that faced a wooden bench placed, oddly, diagonally across the center of the room. Diego perched on his bed, arms crossed tightly, as far away from us as possible.

"*¡Se me murieron!*" They died on me! Suddenly, with both hands, Diego grabbed his head.

"Why don't you come sit here with us?" Félix interrupted.

Obediently, Diego shuffled over and sat facing us on the bench, and then, like an actor resuming position for a second take, he grabbed his head again.

"They died on me! Oh! There was one that died, then two, then five. Oh!" Still holding his head, he rocked back and forth. "I had forty chickens and twenty-five of them died! Then, just when they were ready to eat, another four died! So the next time I bought just twenty. I thought I'd be safe with fewer chickens. OK. Then I buy fifteen. OK. But then: a plague. Oh!" He grabbed his head. "The chickens start to cry, they cry and cry and cry. I have to buy this medicine with my money, very expensive!" He jumped up and took out two bottles of medicine from a cabinet. "I paid for these with my own money. My *own* money!"

I tried to take it slow. I hadn't gotten his full name when we were introduced, I said. Diego—?

"Diego Gabriel Torres, and I am not lying. I do not like people who lie. I do not lie. You see?" From his pocket he whipped out a card and put it in my hand—his voter ID card. "We are all the same, are we not? We are children of God."

I nodded, sure. And he sold his chickens in the market?

No, he said, people came here to his house. "Chickens and a little bit of sodas—a tough business." Immediately he swung back to God in a rapid-fire babble, "God loves us and God blesses us, and I don't like it that people call God by another name but that's OK, lots of things I don't like, God is with us, God is everywhere, we are children of God." He went on, round and round about God, nodding like a puppet on a string, never looking at me, always the floor or the ceiling—until Félix cut in:

"Oiga," Listen, what is *guelaguetza?*

"Ah!" Diego gave an explanation, something about the dead, but so fast that I couldn't understand what he was saying. So: was she—he pointed to me with his chin—going to give him a loan?

"No," Félix said. "She's a researcher."

"I thought she was researching me for a loan."

"No," Félix said. "She's just researching."

Diego laughed nervously, but his whole body seemed to relax. Apparently, he'd taken me for some kind of cash-happy evangelist.

"Look at this." Félix said to me and chuckled. A plastic toy of a naked President Salinas as *chupacabras,* the goat-sucking vampire, hung on a nail on the beam next to him. Félix picked it off the wall and handed it to me. Then he turned to Diego. "You should have been at the meeting," he said sternly. "I came all the way from Ensenada with my boss, and you weren't there."

Diego, sitting pigeon-toed, looked at the ground sheepishly.

"You need to fill out these forms for your next loan." Félix moved over and sat next to Diego on the bench. He was much larger than Diego, and he leaned over him, like a father reading a bedtime story to his child.

"Can you read and write Spanish?"

Diego nodded.

"Here, you put your name. Here, you put your address. OK, how many chickens do you have?"

Meanwhile, having examined Diego's President Salinas-as-goat-sucking-vampire, I hung it back on its nail.

Afterward, we walked around to the side of the yard to see the chickens. No, not those beautiful yellow-legged fluffy ones that had returned from their meal in the grower's alfalfa field: those were *pollos de rancho,* Félix said disdainfully. His program gave risk capital for *pollos de granja,* fryer chickens. Fryer chickens grew faster and yielded more and better meat, though it was true they were more delicate. Net of the ones that had died, Diego still had some dozen of them in a small coop. He led me around to the side yard to see them. They were ugly chickens, with thick wedges of white feathers and stubby gum-gray legs.

In the car, Félix let me know he was annoyed with me. "Why did you let him go on like that about religion?"

The truth was, until I realized he'd mistaken me for an evangelist, I'd thought Diego was a chucklehead. What I said was, "Sometimes when you let people go on they tell you the most interesting things."

Well, Félix said, it didn't sound very interesting to him.

We were on the highway, heading back to San Quintín. He said he didn't like the way I drove.

"Too slow," he said. "Typical woman."

"That's why women have fewer accidents," I said.

"Yes, but you cause them."

I decided to laugh. It was a long drive back to town.

Félix had one more thing he wanted to show me, a migrant-worker camp, half of which had burned down. It was on Los Pinos—the farm founded by Luis Rodriguez Aviña, whose marble tomb I'd found in the English graveyard. The camp was hard against the highway: a gaily painted school, a store, and a line of shacks and latrines backed up to a field. A chain barred the entrance. The guard approached my car.

He was with the government, Félix said, showing the camps to *la compañera investigadora,* the comrade researcher. Could we pass?

"No." The guard did not blink.

We'd come a long way, Félix said.

"No."

Well, Félix said to me, this was where half the shacks burned down. The workers cried, not so much for their things, but for their savings. Some of them had lost ten thousand, even fifteen thousand, in peso bills—the equivalent of twelve to eighteen hundred dollars.

"Imagine," Félix demanded. "Imagine what that is to someone who earns three hundred pesos a week." He looked at me, then, gravely out the windshield, past the chain, at the shacks.

So: some of the Oaxacans did save and, in fact, managed to scrape together some substantial amounts. Why had Félix denied it? Never mind his program with those troublesome chickens; the people here might have been greatly helped to have had a reliable, nearby savings service. But I didn't have the heart to say anything.

A bus—another that said ST. LOUIS SCHOOL DISTRICT—swooshed past, heading north. The fields spread out on either side of the highway, an endless patchwork of black plastic, green, and raked powdery dust.

After I dropped Félix off, I bumped down the dirt road toward the

Old Mill and the water. On the radio, a woman was speaking Mixtec, soft and shushy sounds, hard sounds—*k* and *ch*—and tonal inflections, singsongy, like a mix of Portuguese, Japanese, and Chinese. It was a strange and beautiful language.

Behind me, my car hurled up billows of dust.

Ahead: the cinder cones, and the bay glazed blue like sky.

The Land of the Clouds

FIFTEEN MINUTES LATER, at the edge of the shimmering water, I was in another world. But the Oaxacans, in their shacks out on the yellow dust, had come from another world, beautiful too, in its way. *Ñuñuma,* the Mixtecs call their country: the Land of the Clouds. They call themselves *Ñusabi,* the People of the Clouds, just as the Zapotecs call themselves the same thing in their language: *Ben Zaa.* Oaxaca is a land of pine-forested mountains, rich valleys veined with small rivers, and jungle-covered lowlands spreading dense and steaming along the Pacific coast. In the highlands, the People of the Clouds built palaces and pyramids, ball courts and observatories. Zapotecs constructed a fabulous city on a mountaintop at Monte Albán; Mixtecs then turned it into a royal necropolis, mining it with tombs as splendid as those of ancient Egypt, filled with jade and gold, exquisite earrings, necklaces, even tweezers and tiny bells. Their polychromed pottery was vivid with gods, humans, animals, numerals, and hieroglyphs, as were their codices, "books" of pictures painted on deerskin.

In the fifteenth century they were conquered by the Aztecs, in the sixteenth by the Spaniards. Pedro de Alvarado and his men rampaged through the valleys, the richest of which was granted by the king to Hernán Cortés, made Marqués del Valle de Oaxaca. The Dominicans followed with the True Faith. European diseases killed as much as 75 percent of the population. But unlike Baja California's sparse tribes of hunter-gatherers, Oaxaca's indigenous populations were numerous enough to rebound—even as throughout the sixteenth, seventeenth, and eighteenth centuries they were shunted farther and farther up the rock-strewn slopes of the mountains. Those who remained in the rich valleys provided slave labor for plantations.

The conditions in Oaxaca were the most shocking of a *Barbarous Mexico,* as the muckraker John Kenneth Turner titled his book, the classic indictment of the dictatorship of Porfirio Díaz. If Santa Anna dominated Mexico in the first half of the nineteenth century, "Don Porfirio" dominated its latter decades and up to 1910. Son of a Oaxacan mule breaker, Don Porfirio ruled Mexico with an iron fist, selling chunks of Mexico to foreigners, enriching his cronies, jailing or killing his opponents, and winning election after unanimous reelection.

"No reelection!" and "The land belongs to those who work it" were the battle cries of the revolution that broke out in 1910. Díaz fled to a gilded exile in Paris, while a cast of liberals, radicals, conservatives, peasants, and opportunists crisscrossed the stage in a chaos of civil war that raged through the 1920s. Not until 1946 did the ruling party have the confidence to name a civilian president. That same year, the ruling party—which was to go on to win almost every election through the 1980s and hold the presidency throughout the 1990s—changed its name to the Partido Revolucionario Institucional, the Party of the Institutional Revolution. Marvelous oxymoron.

"Words, words, words," lamented the agrarian reformer Luis Cabrera in his memoir, *Twenty Years After.* "The Revolution has resolved none of the country's political problems." Too harsh an assessment—although perhaps not from the point of view of Oaxaca's Indians.

"Mexico is a nation of mestizos," I heard the writer Aurelio Asain say on the radio, not long after I returned to Mexico City. A commonplace. I had lunch with a Mexican friend that day, and I told her what I had seen in San Quintín, the Oaxacan workers, their poverty. I also told her about a riot that had broken out at Rancho Santa Anita, one of the tomato packing plants, in 1996. "Chiapas in San Quintín," the local press had reported (although, tellingly, not a word about it had appeared in Mexico City). Rancho Santa Anita had run out of cash. After three weeks of waiting, when the workers weren't paid, they rioted, burning buses and police cars. The army was called in; some sixty Oaxacans were arrested. Many were badly beaten.

My friend replied, very matter-of-factly, "Mexico is a nation *for* mestizos. And white people."

Then she told me about a friend of hers, a wealthy coffee planter from Chiapas. He had told her that it was true, when he walked down the street, if he met an Indian on the sidewalk, the Indian would step down into the gutter. Not so long ago, in Chiapas, if an Indian had not stepped down for a white man, he could have been shot or hanged for his impertinence.

Along with Chiapas, Oaxaca remains one of Mexico's poorest states. And its most Indian. The People of the Clouds are a conquered people, as Indians are everywhere on the continent.

"They like to be poor," was what Félix had told me.

But I think they just weren't too hepped about those fryer chickens.

🦋

I DIDN'T STAY in San Quintín for long. I tried to find the local head of the National Indigenous Institute (INI), but he'd gone to Ensenada. I interviewed another government worker who ran a program— another incarnation of Solidaridad—that helped Oaxacan workers build their own houses, and I interviewed the director of *La Voz del Valle,* the INI radio station. Like Félix Pérez, both were well-educated and well-meaning mestizos. The one who ran the house-building program kept a portrait of Emiliano Zapata on his credenza.

But trying to talk to the Oaxacans themselves—it had been naive to think that I might begin to understand their lives with a few questions about what turned out to be a ham-fisted government program. Herminio and Diego didn't entirely trust Félix. Why should they trust me?

The Atkinsons, on the other hand, had talked to me for hours. I missed them. Some months before, Jim had died—a heart attack, the clerk at the Old Mill Motel told me. Susie had rented the house to a youth group from California. Would she come back? I wondered.

And what about their daughter, Julie? San Quintín was changing, very fast.

It was late in the afternoon when I began the drive north to the border. The sky, which had been so clear, was quilted now with cottony gray clouds. Dust drifted across the highway, as fine as silt. I drove fast, passing the trucks and Winnebagos, slowing only through the towns, Colonia Vicente Guerrero, Camalú, Colonet, farm towns as dusty and flea-bitten as San Quintín. A bruised-looking twilight had fallen by the time I started winding down the mountainside into the Santo Tomás Valley, the lights of Santo Tomás twinkling in the distance. Each one was a story—so many stories, I could never hope to hear them all. I felt a sense of despair as I kept driving. North of Ensenada, the highway widened—I had to pay a toll—and then I kept driving. The highway ran between cliffs and the ocean. Fog was rolling in.

V

borders
the sound of one hand clapping

The atmosphere of the border—

it is like starting over again

—GRAHAM GREENE, *Another Mexico*

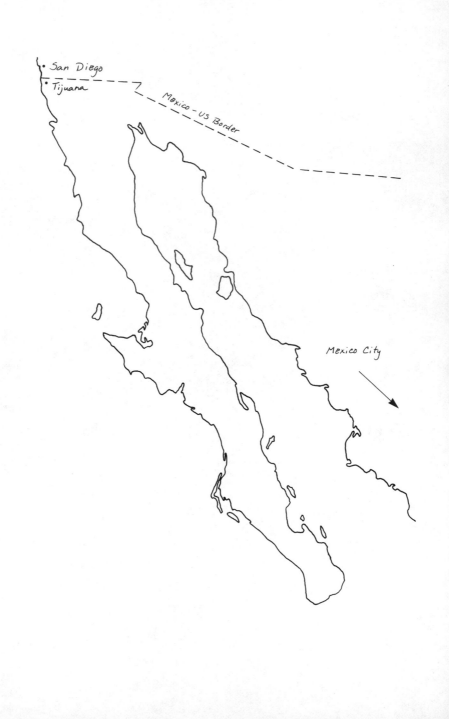

A Touch of Evil

Tijuana

> Why aren't you back in Mexico City?
> —U.S. detective to Miguel Vargas
> (played by Charlton Heston) in Orson Welles's *A Touch of Evil*

Tierra de Oportunidad

ON WEDNESDAY, March 23, 1994, Luis Donaldo Colosio was in La Paz, about to fly home to Mexico City when he got the phone call ordering him to go to Tijuana.

Tijuana, the Lost City. TJ, as the border people call it, Tia Juana, say the gringos. Sin city, poor city, city of dog races and discos, gray skies and trash, Tijuana crowds against a twelve foot-high iron wall that runs along the no-man's-land north of the border, up and down canyons, across fields and marshlands, more canyons, more fields, until finally, at the small park that faces Tijuana's Bullring-by-the-Sea, a public toilet, and the La Michoacana ice cream shack, it slopes down a hill of sand and into the water where it slices right through the waves.

People jump the wall, people burrow beneath the wall, they bash big holes in it. Every night, hundreds of people bolt through the no-man's-land, darting the searchlights of the helicopters, the headlights of the Border Patrol's Ford Broncos, the infrared nightscopes, and the shouting, billy club–wielding agents. Interstate 5 to San Diego posts warning signs showing not cattle, but running people, a little girl

329

with pigtails flying. Sometimes they make it, sometimes they don't. Sometimes they get robbed or raped. If they make it into the United States, they will wash dishes, pick lettuce, sew blue jeans, cut grass, lay bricks. Theirs is quite a story, well told in many books. Among the best of them are Ted Conover's *Coyotes* and William Langewiesche's *Cutting for Sign*. I'm going to tell you a different story.

I drove my big red Oldsmobile into downtown Tijuana and right up the ramp of the fruity-pink Camino Real Hotel. I tossed the keys to the doorman, I rode the escalator up, and I strode across the ice-rink white marble floor of the lobby.

"She's rich," Félix Pérez had said about me.

For the moment, consider this true.

In the bar I met a Tijuana-born, San Diego–educated multidisciplinary artist named Ana María Herrera, a young woman with glossy black hair and a movie star smile. We sat on a squashy black sofa. We ordered drinks. Flamenco strummed on the stereo, the notes weaving through our conversation like threads of silver. Overhead, the skylight poured down the golden light of a softly waning afternoon.

❧

THREE O'CLOCK on the afternoon of Wednesday, March 23, 1994: Luis Donaldo Colosio was flying up the Baja California peninsula. By this time, he would have been over the waist of the Central Desert. Brown; the sea on either side blue. He probably didn't bother to look. He'd been flying all over the country for the last four months, ever since his *destape,* or "uncovering"—President Salinas's announcement that he would be the PRI's presidential candidate. Colosio was a man with a lot of energy, however: he was young, only forty-four years old. Trim and photogenic, he'd earned a master's degree from the University of Pennsylvania; since then, he'd held his own with the technocrats of the Salinas administration, the Ph.D.'s from Stanford, Chicago, MIT, Yale, and Harvard. But unlike his Hermès-tied Mexico City colleagues, Colosio, a middle-class provincial, had the *afición* of a born politician. He thrilled to wade into the crowds, to clasp the hands that reached for him, touched his

back, his arms, his hair. At rallies, he would break free of his bodyguards and allow himself to be carried along, as in a river of love.

Below, along the scalloped coast of Baja California, the brown was
beginning to be relieved here and there with broad valleys patched
with green: San Quintín, Santo Tomás, Ensenada. And at last, Colosio's plane started its descent toward the Tijuana airport.

❧

ANA MARÍA HERRERA had brought slides of her work. I wiped my
hand on the cocktail napkin, then picked one up. I raised it over my
head to view it against the skylight: this one was *La Nena* (Little girl),
a banner that was currently hanging in the lobby of the Centro
Cultural Tijuana. On one side, a slender young girl stood wrapped in
white, the sky roiling above; on the other, a fat woman photographed
from below, all folds of worm-white globlike flesh.

Next slide: *El Ser* (The Being), an installation of twenty-three
tubes, each filled with a substance shed by the human body: hair,
skin, blood, urine, feces, mucus, sweat, saliva, semen, ear wax . . . "The
twenty-three tubes symbolize our twenty-three chromosomes," Ana
María explained. "At the end I put a fetus."

This wasn't anything like the art of Derek Buckner, canvases alive
with color and beauty, or like Paulino Pérez's paintings of figures in
water, or even the giant red-and-black figures of the cave paintings:
this was art stripped of any intention to charm.

"It's not about money," Ana María said. She was a member of a
group called Revolucion-arte, artists from both Tijuana and San
Diego committed to making art more universal—"not just Chicano
art or Mexican art. We want to make spaces for art, put art anyplace.
Why not a gas station?" One of her fellow Revolucion-arte members, Marco Ramírez, or "Erre," had just erected a giant metal statue
of a two-headed Trojan horse—one head looking south, the other
north—at the San Ysidro border crossing.

Ana María sipped her drink. "Tijuana needs the nurturing of art.
It's a young city, and its essential point is to make money, to eat. From
all over Mexico, that's why people come here. They work in the factories, they try to cross to the other side. They want a better life."

And then she passed me one more slide: *Tierra de Oportunidad* (Land of Opportunity). I held it to the light: it was of a large glass box hanging on a chain from a meat hook. Inside dangled a crumpled wad of real fifty- and one hundred–dollar bills. At the bottom of the box, Ana María explained, were two black polyester gloves. You could put your hands in the gloves and touch the dollars. But you couldn't take the dollars out.

SHORTLY AFTER four o'clock: Luis Donaldo Colosio shook hands and gave *abrazos* to the congressmen and PRI officials who had come to meet him at the Tijuana airport. Many more had turned out than he'd expected. Only three weeks earlier, his campaign had seemed adrift in the doldrums. Mexicans were still in shock from Archbishop Posada's assassination at the Guadalajara airport and the New Year's Day Zapatista uprising in Chiapas. Subcomandante Marcos with his ski mask and his pipe had mesmerized both the national and the international press corps. Reporters would hike for days into the Lacandon jungle for the chance of an audience with the guerrilla leader, this "Lone Ranger, Batman, and Darth Vader," as one wide-eyed journalist called Marcos, this green-eyed "Lawrence of Arabia" who dabbled in poetry and quoted Fuentes and Monsiváis.

Much as he loved the crowds, Colosio was beginning to look like just another apparatchik offering the same-old, same-old. Worse, Colosio's chief rival within the PRI, former Mexico City mayor Manuel Camacho, had been named the government's chief negotiator with the Zapatistas. What was President Salinas trying to do? The newspapers openly speculated on Camacho's chances of displacing Colosio.

On March 6, the sixty-fifth anniversary of the PRI, Colosio lashed back with a speech calling for justice in Chiapas, clean elections, and an end to authoritarianism. *"Declaro,"* boomed his voice over the thirty thousand party members assembled at Mexico City's Monument to the Revolution. *"El gran reclamo de México es la democracia,"*

The great outcry of Mexico is for democracy. "The country wants to exercise it fully. Mexico demands, we respond. As candidate for the presidency of the Republic, I am also ready."

Your typical campaign speech, grumped some pundits. Others argued that it constituted a declaration of independence from President Salinas and the PRI's old guard—the "Dinosaurs." Either way, Colosio's campaign began gathering steam. On Tuesday, March 22, Camacho stepped aside. And now, on Wednesday, March 23, 1994, at the Tijuana airport, the congressmen and PRI officials clapped loudly, and cheered. As he jumped up on the running board of the Chevy Blazer that would take him to the rally in Lomas Taurinas, Colosio smiled and waved good-bye. Good-bye.

La flor más bella

WHEN I WAS a professor of economics at ITAM, one of the courses I taught was a seminar on the Mexican economy. I should say I "directed" rather than taught, because I gave only a few introductory lectures; after that, the students made presentations. They were graduating seniors, most of them already working in treasury, Banco de México, investment banks, family businesses. They were bright kids, among the best prepared in the country. Every year several asked me for letters of recommendation for graduate school in the United States.

I let the students choose their topics, maybe something having to do with their jobs, I suggested, something they felt passionate about. They took it very seriously, with their slides chock-full of multicolor graphs and data bars and pie charts. I listened to so many presentations over the years, I couldn't possibly remember them all. The variety was astonishing, as was one single consistency: every semester I had a student who made a presentation on Tijuana and its *maquiladora* industry.

Usually it was a boy in a suit and tie. He'd gotten his data from the government. He'd give a little background, explain that *maquiladoras* were factories set up along the U.S.-Mexican border under a special

1970 program to take advantage of low-wage Mexican labor. Materials were imported tax-free, the *maquiladoras* added labor, and then final goods were shipped north again: televisions, stereos, cassette tapes, computer chips, clothes, toys. There were so many hundreds of plants, employing so many thousands of workers—mostly women. Part of the Free Trade Zone around the border, Tijuana was capitalizing on its "comparative advantage." With NAFTA, more so. The city was booming, high employment, housing starts, highways . . .

Not once in all the hoopla did any of my students mention what it might have been like to actually work in a *maquiladora*. Why should they have? This was a course in the Department of Economics, not Anthropology or Sociology. Still, I liked the idea of pushing my students to think beyond supply and demand, cost-benefit, trade theory. Have you read *La flor más bella de la maquiladora*? I would ask. It's kind of interesting, interviews with the workers themselves.

Stories were important, I'd said at the beginning of the course. As Donald McCloskey pointed out, "Economists have not lived without stories, not ever." I'd made McCloskey's book, *If You're So Smart: The Narrative of Economic Expertise,* required reading.

I would say to my student: You were just telling me a story right now. "Once upon a time, Mexico had a lot of low-skilled labor and very little capital, so it made this arrangement with the countries that had a relatively small supply of low-skilled labor and a lot of capital. And then, in some border cities like Tijuana, there was economic development . . ." Your story may well be nonfiction, I was always quick to say. But: is it the whole enchilada?

In one of the interviews in *La flor más bella de la maquiladora,* a woman named Elena tells about working in a factory that made Muppet dolls. Her job was to dress the Miss Piggys as they went by on the conveyor belt—grab it, dress it, grab it, dress it. She'd forgotten how many dolls she dressed in a day, but, Elena said, "I knew it was thousands, so many that at various times I dreamed that Miss Piggy was attacking and killing me."

Maybe some of my students went and read *La flor más bella de la maquiladora,* I don't know. I do know this: I found Elena's nightmare about Miss Piggy infinitely more interesting than any of my students' presentations.

I wasn't meant to teach economics.

Veo un México

FROM THE AIRPORT, Colosio's Chevy Blazer sped along the highway fronting the wall, through a landscape of dirt parks and warehouses—mile after numbing mile of *maquiladoras*. If these were evidence of economic development, they were, at the same time, symptomatic of his country's poverty. Beyond the graffitied metal wall—too tall to see over—lay the ordered, red-tiled suburbs of San Diego with their swimming pools and shopping malls. There lived the managers, owners, and consumers; here, in Tijuana, the workers.

"*Veo un México de trabajadores,*" I see a Mexico of workers, Colosio had said in his March 6 speech, "who do not find the jobs they deserve. I see a Mexico of workers who have greatly contributed to the productive effort and who should be offered work, with training and better salaries.

"*Veo un México de jóvenes,*" I see a Mexico of young people, "who daily face the difficult reality of the lack of jobs, who do not always have the opportunities of education and preparation. . . . I see a Mexico of women who do not yet enjoy the opportunities they deserve. . . . I see a Mexico of businessmen oftentimes dispirited by the bureaucracy, the oceans of paperwork, the arbitrary decisions of the authorities . . . a Mexico of teachers and professors and researchers who ask for professional recognition, who ask for better salaries and conditions. . . . I see a Mexico with hunger and thirst for justice. A Mexico of people aggrieved by the distortions imposed on the law by those who should serve it."

The usual demagoguery? Perhaps. Colosio had made his career in the PRI, the twentieth century's longest-ruling party, a corporatist behemoth riddled with mafias. Nevertheless, like many other members of the PRI, Colosio was deeply, personally committed to social justice and democracy. It was Colosio, when he was head of the party, who went on national TV to concede the 1989 loss of the Baja California governorship to the PAN (the right-leaning National Action Party)—the PRI 's first loss of a governorship since its founding. Local PRI strongmen—many of them based in Tijuana, skimming the fat off the drug trade, gambling, and prostitution—were enraged. Five years later, some of them still seethed.

Yet the PRI, in part thanks to Colosio's reforms, continued to work like a well-oiled machine. Nearing the outskirts of Tijuana, the Chevy Blazer passed beneath a billboard with his own name, big as a shout:

COLOSIO

La Bola

IN THE MORNING I walked from the Camino Real Hotel to the Centro Cultural Tijuana, "La Bola," as the Tijuanenses called it, the Sphere, after the Omnimax Planetarium at the entrance, which looked like an enormous egg half-emerged from its cracked shell. Behind La Bola spread a plaza crowded with children finger painting on sheets of brown paper. "¡Ven a pintar con nosotros!" called out a clown. Come and paint with us! He shuffled across a stage festooned with balloons, throwing out his arms to disco music. A little girl in a dress-size T-shirt spattered with blue paint had jumped up and was dancing with him. The plaza felt hot and busy and loud, but through the heavy glass doors of the cultural center itself, the air was hushed and cool. Huge banners hung down from the ceiling, high above. With the burst of air from the doors they swayed, slightly.

There was Ana María Herrera's *La Nena,* the vast, gross nude with its fleshy folds of fat; on the flip side, the pretty girl wrapped in white. The slide hadn't done justice to the shock of its scale, its masterfully harsh blacks and whites. I wandered among the other banners, some forty of them, by artists from all over Latin America, the United States, and Spain. One looked like lace; another, slick traffic-light yellow with a giant red question mark. Mexican Arturo Elizondo's was a portrait of Cortés transposed over images of the Virgin of Guadalupe; on the back were a native man and a native woman covered with tattoos. *In God We Trust,* by Venezuelan Milton Becerra, was fashioned of Bolivian bills tied together with string. The banner from Nicaragua by Raul Quintanilla portrayed a gargantuan grape-purple penis with a Barbie doll glued onto the tip of it. Its title: *Me Repugna Miss Lewinsky (Ugliest Dick in the World).* Sophomoric stuff. But I admired the spirit of it all, the unusual form and materials, art broken free of categories—photography, collage, silkscreen, weaving, oil paint, and canvas. Why not glue a Barbie doll onto the end of a giant penis? Why not make a glass box and stuff it full of dollars? Or make a mural for a gas station?

It was like breaking out of the straitjacket of economics: suddenly I could make use of, say, a dream about Miss Piggy. I could write not just about how Colosio's reforms might impact the *maquiladoras,* but also about what he was wearing when he was killed: brown pants, beige windbreaker, open-collared blue shirt. I could mention that Félix Pérez, the social worker I'd met in San Quintín, was there waiting in Lomas Taurinas, having organized a group of students for the rally. I could mention that it was late in the afternoon, nearing four-thirty. Shadows were growing long, the spring air beginning to cool. *Ranchera* music blared into the crowd of some three thousand as the Chevy Blazer bumped down the steep dirt hill into Lomas Taurinas.

Avenida Revolución

TIJUANA IS the most visited city in the world. Fact: there are seventy-two million legal crossings a year between San Diego and Tijuana. "Border people" make up much of the traffic—Mexicans, Mexican Americans, Anglo-Americans, and all other kinds of Americans with jobs, property, family, and friends on one side or the other of *"la línea."* Like Ana María Herrera, many are bilingual and cosmopolitan. Some are more limited: a Oaxacan *maquiladora* worker, say, whose son works in a restaurant in Los Angeles. They tend to speak "Spanglish," peppering their Spanish with words like *apartamento* instead of *departamento* (apartment), *trocke* instead of *camión* (truck), *waife* instead of *esposa* (wife). A whole paragraph of English may run by, then: *¿qué onda?*

The balance of those seventy-two million crossings is mainly tourists. They walk, they drive, they take buses and taxis into the downtown, the main artery of which is the Avenida Revolución, "a shopping district," trumpets *The Tijuana Handbook,* "famous around the globe."

Briefly, I had contemplated the notion that I too was a sort of border person, but here, in my shorts and sneakers, I was just another gringa. "Tourist!" shouted a tout. "Cheaper than K-Mart!" "Blankets from Oaxaca, Pottery, Stained Glass, Leather!" "*Amiga!* Cheap-o-rama!" Loud drums beat from a record store, muddied with rock-and-roll from the Hard Rock Café (the back end of a pink Cadillac hanging out of the wall). Tourists jostled down the Avenida Revolución, groups of two, three, five, hugging their purses tight, past the Jai Alai Palace, Chiki Hai, the tables of Tia Juana Tilly's. Get your Virgin of Guadalupe framed in shells, joss sticks, Jack-in-the-Box, KFC, Havana Room Fine Cigars, Aztec Massage. On almost every corner: a donkey painted to look like a zebra.

"Get your photo!" "Photo with the zebra!" "Step on up!"

Each donkey stood patiently, harnessed into a gaily painted cart with a backdrop of Aztecs or pyramids or some colorful scene of Tijuana. Alongside the backdrop, sombreros were pinned up that said: PANCHO VILLA; HONEYMOON; TIJUANA; I LOVE YOU. You put one on, they threw a serape over your shoulder, five bucks. It seemed the sporting thing to do.

The donkey's name?

"Bimbo."

And then, at the corner of Third and Revolución, I jumped in a cab. The seats were plush red velvet. A plastic Virgin of Guadalupe dangled from the rearview mirror.

Lomas Taurinas, I said.

Plaza de la Unidad y Esperanza

SMOOTH, THE RIDE was smooth, the little plastic Virgin barely bobbling as the cab sped through Tijuana, up hills, down and around through streets of apartment buildings, taco stands, shoe repairs, gas stations. The driver cut, he swerved, always smooth even as the streets grew narrower, the houses smaller and shabbier, flat-roofed cinder blocks, many of them unpainted, others dirty-white, cobalt, candy orange. And then down the sharp, steep hill of Lomas Taurinas, smooth over freshly laid asphalt.

"Colosio had to die before they'd pave this road," said the driver. He had a voice as loud as a buzz saw. His face was too large and pocked with scars. His name was Emilio. He laughed. He'd seen it all: he'd been living in Tijuana for fifteen years. He was from Nayarit.

We'd come to the bottom of the hill, to a bricked-over plaza.

"This used to be dirt," Emilio said. He swept his arm across the windshield. "All dirt."

We got out of the taxi. The plaza featured a small library, the Biblioteca Pública Luis Donaldo Colosio, and an even smaller room, the Centro Comunitario Diana Laura Riojas de Colosio, both freshly painted mint green. Behind the two tiny buildings was tucked a tiny, tree-shaded playground with a teeter-totter and a swing set. To the right, wedged into the far corner of the plaza, stood the monument to Luis Donaldo Colosio, a ten-foot-tall statue of the candidate in his open-collared shirt, one arm raised high. A wreath of white carnations lay propped at its feet. LA PLAZA DE LA UNIDAD Y ESPERANZA, read brass letters on the wall behind the statue: The Plaza of Unity and Hope.

"Dirt," Emilio said again. In part, the plaza had been built on top of a ravine, which had been filled in with cement. Before, Emilio said, the plaza was much smaller. When Colosio arrived for the rally, he'd had to walk across the ravine on a wooden footbridge. Below ran a river of sewage. "Oh, the flies! The stink!" Emilio laughed a hearty, deep-bellied laugh. "Colosio had to die before they'd fill in that ravine."

A group of teenaged boys was eyeing us from across the street. "Lots of tourists come here," Emilio said, sensing my concern. Not to worry. "I take two, three a month." Last month was the anniversary of Colosio's death. "*Oof!*" Emilio waved his hand. "Hundreds of people!" Politicians, newspaper reporters, TV cameras.

It had been more than four years. *"Piden que declare Zedillo sobre Colosio,"* Zedillo Asked to Testify about Colosio, headlined the March 23, 1998, Mexico City *Reforma*. President Zedillo had been Colosio's campaign manager. What had he seen? What did he know?

This much was known: on March 23, 1994, after having made his speech, at 5:10 P.M., as he waded through the throng, Colosio was shot once in the head and once in the abdomen. Mario Aburto, a twenty-five-year-old *maquiladora* worker who fancied himself the "Eagle Knight," confessed. There was the video filmed from a rooftop: the tight, bouncing crowd; confetti; *ranchera* music; then the flash of silver near Colosio's head and *pup!* a belch of smoke.

But was Aburto Aburto? The man tackled and pummeled at the scene did not resemble the thick-necked, clean-shaven prisoner. Official photographs showed him as having two different heights. Had "Aburto" acted alone? At the scene of the murder Aburto had pointed to Vicente Mayoral, one of Colosio's volunteer bodyguards, shouting that it was him— *"el viejo!"* the old man!

Certainly it was strange that on the night of the crime, Sonora governor Manlio Fabio Beltrones rushed to police headquarters in Tijuana to interview Aburto. Stranger still that President Salinas named as special prosecutor Miguel Montes, a career PRI politician with no experience whatsoever in criminal law, or criminal investigation.

Montes made a careful analysis of the video, which he presented on national TV, playing the video at normal speed, then slow-motion, little arrows pointing to each bodyguard, each jostle and push: the choreography of a conspiracy, he claimed. Four of Colosio's Tijuana bodyguards, including *"el viejo"* Vicente Mayoral, were arrested. The four turned out to be police, two of them former State Judicial Police who were well known to the National Center for Human Rights as extortionists and torturers.

On April 28, in Mexico City, Special Prosecutor Montes received an anonymous telephone call about a bomb in the Tijuana airport. Montes phoned Tijuana with the report; Tijuana police chief Federico Benitez left his office to investigate. Two hours later Benitez was ambushed on the Tijuana expressway and pumped full of rounds from an AK-47. Was it merely coincidence that on June 2, Montes ditched his elaborately detailed conspiracy theory and announced that Mario Aburto had, after all, acted alone?

Colosio's widow, Diana Laura Riojas de Colosio, responded with an open letter calling for further investigation into a possible conspiracy. Montes was replaced. But Colosio's widow could do little more than establish a foundation in her husband's name and settle her own affairs, because on November 18, 1994, at the age of thirty-four, Diana Laura—"our Princess Di," as some of the press eulogized her—died of pancreatic cancer, leaving her two small children orphaned.

Under President Zedillo, who took office in December 1994, the investigation played on like a farce noir In February 1995, a third special prosecutor, Pablo Chapa Benzanilla, announced that the bullet that had supposedly ripped through Colosio's abdomen was a plant, that, in fact, the real bullet was fired from a second gun. Othón Cortez, one of Colosio's guards at the rally, was arrested, beaten, and tortured so severely that when he was brought before the press to be photographed, he fainted three times. But in the video—that same video that had been played and replayed by Montes on national TV—Cortez was standing behind Colosio with both hands free. So Cortez was released. According to the next special prosecutor, Luis Raúl González, Chapa Benzanilla had paid witnesses to testify against Cortez. In any case, after having paid witnesses in the investigation of the murder of PRI secretary-general Ruiz-Massieu, among them a psychic named La Paca who'd planted her son's father-in-law's body on Raúl Salinas's ranch, Chapa Benzanilla fled the country.

The years went by, 1996, 1997, 1998: the investigation diddled on. Most recently, four agents of the Justice Department assigned to the Colosio case were detained for extortion and car theft. Another snippet of news on March 23, 1998: a video had come to light that "had to do with" Aburto's detention. The investigators who went to Guadalajara to retrieve it were chased by strange cars for three hours. *"Espero un milagro,"* I am hoping for a miracle, was what Colosio's father had to say.

Indeed. We will probably never know who told exactly what truth about which detail lost in the 47,403 pages of testimony. As journalist Alma Guillermoprieto put it, "In the frightening nightscape, anyone can be a murderer." Lone assassin Mario Aburto, say some; "intellectual author" President Salinas, insist others—or was it his brother Raúl Salinas, or the Dinosaurs, *narcopolíticos,* Gulf Cartel capo Juan García Abrego?

Maybe—just maybe—Colosio is not even dead, but living the high life off a secret bank account in Switzerland. That was the theory of a Mexico City taxi driver.

Emilio slammed shut the door of his cab. *"Nada de eso,"* Nothing of this would have been built—the ravine filled in, the library and social center, playground, pavement. "The road paved, *ha!"* He muttered to himself, shaking his head as the taxi glided up the hill, smooth. I leaned back into the plush red-velvet seat. The little plastic Virgin swung toward me, then, as the taxi pulled up level at the top of the hill, back. The sky had turned gray. I felt a sadness heavy like a winter coat.

La Línea

"TIJUANA," writes Luis Alberto Urrea in his haunting *By the Lake of the Sleeping Children, "is* the sound of one hand clapping." Maybe that's why I couldn't hear it. I wasn't getting a sense of place as I had everywhere else on the Baja California peninsula. This was no reflection on Tijuana: it may have been a poor, rough city, but it was also a city vibrant with commerce and culture. And the culture of the border should have fascinated me—after all, I was an American who had spent most of my adult life in Mexico. But it did not. I'd set out on my travels to make my "wheel" turn, and indeed it had, right back to where it was when I started: the squalor, the violence, the corruption.

"What's the nice part of Tijuana?" I'd asked a friend who'd grown up here. She'd looked at me and hooted. "San Diego."

I wasn't dying to get home to Mexico City, either. The smog there had gotten so bad that I often felt short of breath and headachy after just a walk around the block—if I dared walk around the block. Mexico City had degenerated into a "criminal free-for-all," as *Newsweek* called it. Many of my friends had been mugged in rogue taxis, punched in the face, glasses broken; one was hauled out right into traffic and stabbed. Many were led from cash machine to cash machine, until their accounts were cleaned out. Dozens of millionaires were kidnapped by gangs of police, their ears and fingers sliced off and sent to their relatives—but no one was safe: a friend's seven year old was pulled from the car at a stoplight and held for the few hours it took to come up with the equivalent of three hundred dollars. Everyone I knew, if not a victim themselves, had a close friend or relative who'd been attacked or kidnapped or killed. Crime was the topic of conversation at almost every dinner party, to the point where the pundit Carlos Monsiváis quipped, "Only three assaults per person per conversation."

As Octavio Paz railed after Colosio's assassination, "Every day they serve us the same dish of blood."

"Why do you want to live there?" my sister, Alice, had asked me. There were personal issues to consider. But I was asking myself the same question.

I checked out of the Camino Real Hotel. The porter placed my bag in the trunk of the Oldsmobile. And then I tooled down the ramp onto the avenue. North.

So: I had traveled the nearly one thousand–mile length of it, from Los Cabos to Tijuana. This dark denouement was not what I'd expected. But then neither was anything in my travels. It had been like living in a novel, one person leading to another, suspense, surprise—always the surprise. As John Steinbeck wrote, "We do not take a trip; a trip takes us."

Half a mile from the San Ysidro border crossing, the traffic bottlenecked. Street vendors worked the lanes between the idling cars: plaster Tweety Birds and Bugs Bunnys, woolen weavings, a sticklike cactus in a pot. The vendors walked quickly, faces grim, pausing only to hold up their merchandise at each window.

My car crept forward, past a billboard that advertised a U.S. pawnshop: *"Los Genios de las Casas de Empeño."* More vendors paraded past: a plaster Aztec sundial, a plaster Venus de Milo, Chiclets; window washers with their soapy squeeze bottles and rags; an Indian woman begging, her outstretched hand a welter of sores. I dropped a coin in her palm; I inched forward, braked. Vinyl seat pads, Winnie the Pooh dolls, a papier-mâché giraffe, sunglasses, roses. A boy walked by playing a wooden flute, two dollars? He stopped at my window and tooted out a few bars of "Happy Birthday." I shook my head no and, without a shrug, he moved on. From the side mirror on my car, I watched him walking, a spring in his step. But what a life, I thought, pounding the hot asphalt, breathing the exhaust of the cars.

A car: fabulous item. Yes, as Félix Pérez had so bluntly pointed out back in San Quintín, I was rich by the standards of the average Mexican—immensely privileged. Living in Mexico, this was something I was never allowed to forget. My privilege was always obvious, often awkward. The shock of it—a shock every tourist feels—had yet to wear off in all the years I'd been living here. But I'd had time to contemplate that shock, as well as the professional inclination to do so. Yes, I was privileged, but certainly not from the point of view of a Park Avenue matron, say, or the average investment bank vice president. To flip the coin: the average Mexican is rich compared to the average African—or for that matter, the average Peruvian, Afghan, or Filipino. I used to tell my students, Go look at the most miserable slum in Mexico City, count the TV antennas, and think of this: Louis the Sun King could not have bought one single television, even if he'd hocked the whole of France.

Herminio Chávez owned a hatchback.

What is "rich"? What is "poor"? A mountain of literature has been published on the subject without establishing a consensus. We can fiddle with definitions of "poverty"—and for public policy, these have their uses. But what disturbs us is difference, that the few should have so much, while the many have relatively little—that they *could* have a TV and do not, that they *could* have a car and do not. Make your wish list: healthful food, running water, medical care, employment, education . . .

With my education, I'd thought I'd learn the answers, something like a list of recipes: mix, shake, bake, and *voilà:* Economic Development. I did learn something at the University of Chicago. I remember Gary Becker chalking up his equations on human capital, lectures by D. Gale Johnson on import tariffs, a workshop where T. W. Schultz—a rail-thin figure in a gray suit—argued about the rate of return on primary education. But most of all, I remember Arnold Harberger—"Alito," as his Latin American students affectionately called him—talking about markets. "They are like the winds and the tides," he said, making big circles with his arms, "and he who tries to fight that operation is going to have himself one hell of a battle." Which was not to say that markets always worked, or that a market solution would always prove optimal. Diagnosing, he warned, was not so easy. "Reality—" I noted down his every word—"is supercomplex."

In my decade of working as an economist in Mexico, I learned much more. What I learned, boiled down to stock: there aren't any set recipes. The whole question of "economic development" is like a ball of mercury, you press your finger on it and it breaks into more little balls . . .

And because reality is supercomplex, as my old professor Arnold Harberger stressed, you need a structure to approach it with. A theory.

Which is, in a way, a story.

And as Flannery O'Connor put it, "When anybody asks what a story is about, the only proper thing is to tell him to read the story."

Still sitting in my car, I bought a package of peanuts from a woman in a wheelchair. The vendors kept streaming by: more plaster Tweety Birds, ersatz Tickle-Me-Elmo dolls, Jesus on a plastic cross, junk and more junk. The driver in the Winnebago ahead of me bought a sombrero (a tattooed arm held out a bill; the sombrero was handed up): the first purchase I'd seen in half an hour.

Closer to the crossing, traffic fanned into seven lanes, stop and start, stop. In the lane next to mine a beat-up yellow van had stalled.

Its two bumper stickers: DEMOCRACIA YA! and JESUS SAVE ME FROM YOUR FOLLOWERS.

On the right, just past a stand of palm trees, appeared Marco Ramírez's two-headed Trojan horse, its metal flanks gleaming in the harsh light. Nearing the booths, cement curbs with whitewashed steel posts divided the lanes. An Indian girl in a filthy red-checked blouse rested against a post. She wasn't begging or selling anything; merely sitting, her bare feet in the gutter, tears rolling down her cheeks.

I pulled up to the booth. I showed my passport.

"Welcome home," the officer said brightly.

Jewel Point

San Diego to Mexico City

Wings

THE FIRST AIRPLANE arrived at San José del Cabo in 1931. The people couldn't believe it, that this thing could stay up above the earth, swoop over them without falling. The pilot's name was Flores, but no one remembers his first name.

It was the *cronista de la ciudad,* the town historian, Don Fernando Cota, who had told me this story back at the beginning of my travels.

They stood watching, Don Fernando said, on the stoops of their houses, at the edge of their citrus orchards, in their fishing boats: a machine with wings, its body glinting in the sun, engine droning across the pale desert sky. It had come from the other side of the Sea of Cortés; this must be so.

The dogs began to bark, mules and burros neighed and whinnied and stamped their hooves. Someone rang the bells of the church, and someone else ran to ring the bells at Municipal Hall. Everyone gathered on the beach.

It was not possible! This Flores, he started to climb and climb— Don Fernando raised his hand—and then *paf!* he would stall and dive. He did the loopy loopies! The people stood there on the beach, and they clutched at their hearts because they thought he was going to die. Some of the old ladies fainted, right there on the sand.

The whole town—Don Fernando smiled—we were so grateful. We made Flores a party in Municipal Hall, a great ball, with dancing.

❧

HERE IN SAN DIEGO—palm trees and freeways, shopping malls and blue sea—I was clinging to this fragment of a story like a life raft. I'd shipwrecked, driven right across the border into the United States. Here, all was brightness, even the leaves on the trees in Balboa Park looked white with light. Cars gleamed, freshly washed. I wandered around a shopping mall, an everyday space of my childhood but, after the ruggedness of the peninsula and ragamuffin Tijuana, now wonderfully strange, a marble-floored palace rich and shining and fragrant with the smell of new. So many scarves, so many shoes; clothes; candy; blinking, beeping toys; kitchen utensils I never knew I needed. In the movie theater I had a choice of Bruce Willis or Brad Pitt, that golden boy with the face of an angel. I lounged in the flickering darkness, munching popcorn and sipping Coke.

Outside in the parking lot, lamplight fell in pearlescent pools on the asphalt. In the distance, the bridge to Coronado arced into the sky like a string of rhinestones. The air here smelled of the sea, cool and brisk and clean. Driving, I rolled down my window. For a little while, thinking of the pilot Flores, I imagined that I was flying.

Brief, Golden Glimpse

I'D FOUND more stories in Baja California than I'd ever imagined. But not all of them had endings. Who killed Colosio? And why? Who were the Painters, and what strange visions brought them into the labyrinths of those remote canyons? For that matter, who was Flores? Why did he show up that day at San José del Cabo? In the movies—as in the Amadises—the heroes are made known to us; they have their adventures, then face their fate, tragic or triumphant. Of course, sometimes, as the Mexican writer Juan Villoro put it, "Life can't come up with an ending." But I was trying.

In the morning, with a search through the San Diego Aerospace Museum's Mexican Archives, I found out who Flores was. It was a simple process of deduction. The only one of all the Mexican military pilots in the late 1920s and early 1930s named Flores was Feliciano Flores. A 1933 registry of Mexican pilots' licenses, both military and civil, listed only one Flores—again, Feliciano Flores, military, License no. 100.

Flores also appeared in several U.S. War Department Intelligence Reports. One noted that he had participated in the campaigns of 1926 and 1927, bombing raids against the Yaquis and the Cristeros.

Bombing raids: another clue. In the book *La breve historia de la aviación en México* (The brief history of aviation in Mexico) I found him again, Second Captain Feliciano Flores flying under the command of Colonel Roberto Fierro against the Escobardista rebels in 1929.

Roberto Fierro: clue. In his autobiography *Esta es mi vida,* Fierro mentions that Feliciano "El Piojo" Flores and five other military pilots flew with him to Kansas City for the air show of 1929. There they met the famous flying acrobat Fearless Freddy Lund whose "inverted looping" caused a sensation. Lund invited Fierro for a ride. ("I must confess," wrote Fierro, "that this was one of the most tremendous experiences of my life. I lost my breath and I was sure my heart would jump out of my chest when the airplane dove at enormous velocity only to then, abruptly, soar into the infinite blue.") And so, could it be that Flores— like his commander, Fierro— had been taught to do the loop-de-loops by none other than Fearless Freddy Lund?

In Fierro's autobiography, Feliciano "El Piojo" Flores appears once more, flying an airplane in Mexico City's 1930 air show. A brief mention, as fleeting as a ghost.

So many of these early aviators were killed in crashes. That was one of the reasons Lindbergh's 1927 flight from New York to Paris so captured the public imagination. Whether the "Flyin' Fool" or the "Lone Eagle," he was "Lucky Lindy," a man who it seemed might live forever.

To reciprocate Lindbergh's 1928 flight to Mexico, the Mexican military pilot Emilio Carranza flew to Washington, D.C., and New York. On his return, in a lightning storm over the New Jersey Pine Barrens, Carranza crashed and died. In 1930, Flores's commander, Pablo Sidar, and his copilot, Carlos Rovirosa, fell out of the sky over Costa Rica. Fearless Freddy Lund died only a few years later when, on a pylon turn, he skidded into the propeller of another plane.

Indeed, Flores's fellow pilots died like flies. In a folder I found a little sheaf of newspaper clippings, Mexican Air Force fatalities of 1936: January 26, Rafael Chazaro Pérez, director of military education; June 26, Lieutenant Emilio Sanmillán Alonso; July 5, Colonel Agustín Castrejón; October 5, José Fabriz Arce, army air mechanic. This last plane crashed when the engine failed near Mexico City. Arce burned to death, pinned beneath the wreckage. The pilot, Lieutenant Eduardo Iniestra Reyes, was found some distance away with both legs broken.

What happened to Feliciano "El Piojo" Flores? After Fierro's mention of his flying in the 1930 Mexico City air show, Flores disappears. In 1931—golden glimpse—he touches down in San José del Cabo. This was all I knew when I flew home to Mexico City.

You See

SPRING. I WAS sitting at my desk. The sky out my window was gray with smog. The leaves on the trees, flocked with dust, lay dead still. A heat wave had oppressed the city for days. Not even the birds were singing. All I could hear was the traffic, a grinding drone. I had lunch that day with a friend. His apartment had a stunning view— Chapultepec Park, the castle, the hills—but, of course, on this day, the view was soup.

We'd read the drafts of each other's books—his was on finance. Like mine, it lacked an ending.

We talked about Tijuana, the wall, the *maquiladoras,* La Bola, Bimbo the donkey painted to look like a zebra (which made him laugh). And then Lomas Taurinas. Just to think about it—the corruption, the sheer stupidity and incompetence—I was disgusted, I said.

"It's like JFK." He shrugged. "What did you expect?"

Still, I said. I gazed out the window.

"There's your metaphor," he said. "It's all a big, muddy cloud. But tomorrow, it might rain."

Like a miracle, when I came home from lunch, it rained. Just a patter at first, but soon thunder sizzled and crashed, and the rain began coming down in sheets.

The next morning the birds were singing. Everything looked glazed, fresh. For the first time in a week, I took a walk in Los Viveros, the park near my house in Coyoacán. It smelled of damp earth and eucalyptus. People were jogging. An old man tossed peanuts to the squirrels. In a grassy clearing, a woman in an ivory-white sweat suit was doing tai chi. I stopped and watched her for a moment, the way her arms moved, slowly, gracefully.

And in this moment, in Mexico City, I was happy.

"You see how this country is," Colosio said, shortly before his death. "Tomorrow who knows what will happen?"

For Instance

"*Bimbo Va al D.F.*," Bimbo Goes to Mexico City, as Ana María Herrera titled her performance-installation. It was one of several by Tijuana artists sponsored by, among others, the Centro Cultural Tijuana and Mexico City's Ex-Teresa Arte Alternativa, an "alternative" art gallery housed in the old Church of Santa Teresa, one of the historic center's most exquisite seventeenth-century baroque buildings.

I laughed out loud when I saw him, the little donkey painted to look like a zebra. He was standing patiently in the floodlights of the convent's flagstone courtyard, harnessed to his gaily painted cart. The backdrop of his cart depicted Aztecs and a pyramid; pinned around its edges, the brightly colored straw hats were painted with the words MEXICO, TIJUANA, HONEYMOON, I LOVE YOU.

Next to Bimbo, a whitewashed board displayed Ana María's framed black-and-white photographs of the zebra-donkey's visits: to Chapultepec Castle; to the wedding cake–like opera house Bellas

Artes; to Mexico City's first skyscraper, the Torre Latino; to the ancient floating gardens of Xochimilco; to the Monument to the Revolution; to the plaza of Coyoacán; and, of course, the ultimate of any pilgrimage to Mexico's capital—there was Bimbo and his cart at the Cathedral of the Virgin of Guadalupe.

"Well," someone said, crossing his arms over his chest. "The whole *Michelin Guide.*"

I was among the first to arrive; the artists and the public were still at a performance at the Plaza de Santo Domingo. I sat on the steps of the church. The air was filled with noise: the drums of the Aztec dancers, only a block away near the ruins of the Great Temple. Across the street, a fluorescent rod illuminated the narrow shiny-green foyer of a *vecindad*—a two-story rabbit warren of apartments. I watched as people filed into the foyer: a woman balancing a tray of pink meringues on her head; a man carrying a shoe-shine stand on his back—street vendors going home. From somewhere, a TV blared. There was the smell of tortillas toasting on a griddle.

Bimbo lifted a hoof. He twitched one ear.

The sky was luminous with electric light. I gazed up at the church's old stone bell tower, leaning like the Tower of Pisa, floodlit, gorgeous. Strange for a Mexico City evening: the air was as warm as a summer morning.

A little boy from the *vecindad* had come over to see Bimbo. He patted the donkey's flank, and up flew a little cloud of dust.

At the head of a parade, Ana María arrived with her movie star smile. She had her camera in hand.

Could she take my photo? she asked.

It seemed the sporting thing to do. I climbed up onto the cart. I chose the MEXICO hat.

I looked at the camera and *flash.*

Jewel Point

I STARTED OFF on this journey of a thousand miles in search of a place and people that might teach me to find once again the beauty in Mexico. I did find immense, if fragile, beauty, many wonders, and moments of joy. But what my travels in Baja California had taught me, I realized now, were simple truths, yet truths as hard and enduring as a diamond. That we are all connected, though we may often feel lonely and see one another as strangers. That our time here is precious, passing by as fast as a pistol shot. That we must make of it the best that we know how, though our goals and actions may be misguided, though all that we strive for may end in ruin, and will certainly end with our own deaths. We must have courage. We must do what we do with love.

"A journey of a thousand miles begins with but a single step," wrote Lao-tzu, and I had taken that step, and all the many, many others. Lao-tzu also said this: "The way to do is to be." In the end—and yes, my story does have one—I understood what he meant by that. It didn't matter whether my wheel turned, because I had found its center, the hub around which it turns, up then down, then around again. I'd come "home," I finally understood, not to any place on the map, but to a centeredness, this jewel point in my mind. I had learned to simply be aware, whether of a rainwashed morning in the park, or of a little zebra donkey lifting one hoof. Twitching one ear. The luminous sky filled with the orange of twenty million electric lights. Or a swarm of stars. As the mathematician John Allen Paulos said, "We are the stories we tell." We are the wheel, and rolling as we go, wrote Joseph Campbell, "difficulties melt and the highway opens."

·ℑ

AND SO, one last story: the fate of Feliciano "El Piojo" Flores.

In Mexico City I called the Pilots' Union, I tried the Military Aviation Academy. The number I was given by the operator for the ministry of defense was out of order. A photo archive had nothing; there was no aviation museum; a friend of a friend of a pilot suggested the Mexico City airport public relations department. The woman there suggested I call the Pilots' Union. It seemed I was going in circles.

Blindly, I called the Mexican Air Force. I told the story of the pilot Flores. I was put on hold. Someone else, a gruff voice, picked up the phone; I told the story again; I was put on hold. At last, one Captain Pedro Cruz Camarena took the call. He listened politely: the loop-de-loops, the people fainting on the beach, the great ball with dancing, Freddy Lund and Roberto Fierro, Kansas City, Mexico City's 1930 air show. When I was finished, Captain Cruz Camarena laughed. He said, "I have decided that I will help you." But how had I gotten his name and telephone? Ah—another laugh—I didn't know? This was the Office of Military Intelligence.

I still cannot believe my good fortune: Captain Cruz Camarena checked the archives and called me back.

Feliciano "El Piojo" Flores. "El Piojo" means "The Louse"—but in Spanish the connotation is not necessarily negative. A less literal but more accurate translation would be "Shorty." Indeed, Flores stood a mere five foot two. Born in Mazatlán on January 11, 1901, he entered the military in 1923. For his service in the campaigns of the 1920s, he was decorated for "extreme valor" and "irreproachable conduct." In 1929 he was commissioned to the ministry of trade to scout mail routes, among them one from the mainland to Santa Rosalía in Baja California. So that would explain his presence on the peninsula. Apparently, he went back and forth: not only was he in the Mexico City air show of 1930, but he was also jailed there for two weeks and a day as punishment for his high jinks of zooming over the city at an altitude of only fifty meters. Flores's career recovered quickly, however: by 1936 he was serving as an aide to the president. In 1940 he was promoted to lieutenant colonel; in 1945, colonel. In 1952 Flores was made brigadier general. He retired in 1967.

And then?

I had this fantasy that Flores might still be alive. A spry old man with flashing eyes. I saw him with a silver-knobbed cane, *swish swish*. His house would be nearby, old-fashioned and musty-smelling, green-velvet sofas with fringe. We would drink coffee, nibble crumbly little cookies.

San José del Cabo? I would ask, and he would throw back his wizened old head and roar.

And then he would tell me. He would tell me everything.

Epilogue

SINCE MY TRAVELS through Baja California in the late 1990s, Mexico has undergone a sea change. In 2000, after more than seventy years in power, the PRI lost the presidential election to an opposition-party candidate. This was the six-foot-four cowboy boot–clad Vicente Fox of the conservative PAN, or National Action Party, whose photo has been splashed on the front pages of newspapers from Mexico City to Manhattan. No longer yoked to the PRI's version of *presidencialismo*, the Mexican Congress has become dramatically more vocal and powerful. Meanwhile, the information revolution of the Internet has made censorship, should anyone attempt it, less effective, if not impossible.

Much has changed in Baja California as well. In March 2000, Exportadora de Sal's Laguna San Ignacio Project, long the focus of pointed attacks by environmentalists, was officially canceled. Environmentalists are already waging a new battle, however, this time against President Fox's Escalera Náutica, or Nautical Ladder, a 1.7 billion–dollar megaproject to build and improve a total of twenty-four marina-resorts on both coasts of Baja California and the eastern mainland shore of the Sea of Cortés. The Nautical Ladder also envisions an eighty-four-mile highway from the peninsula's Pacific coast to the Sea of Cortés for towing boats, among many other infrastructural improvements. By 2010, there will be an estimated twenty-three thousand new marina berths, seventeen thousand new lodging quarters, and thirty-four new golf courses. Read all about it at http://www.escaleranautica.com.

Whatever the fate of Baja California's Nautical Ladder, growing numbers of visitors and immigrants are streaming down the Transpeninsular Highway, arriving by ferry, or flying into the resorts. In Los Cabos, franchises and hotels have been springing up like mushrooms—though some businesses, such as that infamous neon sign–crowned Planet Hollywood, have closed. Dusty little Todos Santos has a handful of galleries now, new shops, new bed-and-breakfasts, and even an Internet café. At Mulegé, the Johnsons' Hotel Serenidad, the famous fly-in resort that had been taken over by *ejidatarios,* has been open for some time—and not only that, it even has an E-mail address for reservations: serenidad@bajaquest.com. Tiny and remote Bahía de los Angeles may not have an Internet café—yet. But it has a web presence: with a Yahoo search, I found more than twenty-four thousand matches.

As this book goes to press, San José del Cabo and Cabo San Lucas are gearing up for the September 2002 Asia-Pacific Economic Cooperation meetings. President Fox and the finance ministers and central-bank governors of the twenty-one member countries will arrive at the Los Cabos International Airport. I can see it in my mind: the tarmac a gleaming parking lot of airliners, Lear Jets, and Gulfstreams.

Mexico City, 2002

Acknowledgments

ENORMOUS THANKS to Agustín Carstens, Alice Jean Mansell, and Roger and Carolyn Mansell, who supported me every step of the way. Agustín and Alice, this book would not have been possible without you.

Nor would it have been possible without the people who appear in these pages. To all, my heartfelt appreciation.

Several people helped me with their time and advice, the gift of a book or articles, and/or put me in touch with sources, among them Homero Aridjis and Betty Ferber de Aridjis, Jacinto and Cecilia Avalos, David Haward Bain, the Baja Expeditions Laguna San Ignacio whale-watching camp staff, Carmen Boone de Aguilar, Helen "Chata" Carstens, Cristina Casanueva, Paula Colombo, Michael Cope, Ken Corben, Serge Dedina, everyone at Exportadora de Sal (and particularly Julio César Peralta and Leonardo Villavicencio), Santiago A. Flores, Jorge Flores-Kelly, Igor Galván, Adolfo García, Juvenal González, Patricia Krakov, Hans Lenz, Luisa Madrazo, Suzy Maieux, Juan Malagamba, Mike McGettigan, Rosa Elena Montes de Oca Luján, Gabriel Arturo Neri, Jorge Nicolín, Antonio and Betty Resendiz, Felipe Rodríguez, René Pinal, Fernando Salas, Carolina Shepard, Gregory K. Silber, Nancy Spitters, Celia Toro, Gabriel Vázquez Arroyo Carstens, Jan Wassen, and Robert Whiting.

A very, very special *gracias* to Captain Pedro Cruz Camarena, who answered my unlikely telephone call and took the trouble to go through the archives of the Mexican Air Force and call me back—for which I still cannot believe my good fortune.

My research was aided by the very helpful librarians at the University of California at Berkeley's Bancroft Library, the Library of the Museo Nacional del Virreinato (Tepozotlán, Estado de México), and the Library of the San Diego Aerospace Museum. I would especially like to acknowledge the splendid work of Santiago A. Flores, who assembled the latter's archive on Mexican aviation.

Yaddo and the Virginia Center for the Creative Arts each granted me two residencies, wonderful oases, and just when I needed them.

Thanks also to Esther Morales Pablo, Yolanda Ojeda, Benito Loaeza, and Juan Carlos Santos Loaeza for taking care of everything at home in Mexico City.

I have been fortunate to have had many readers at the various stages of writing this book. Harry W. Crosby not only provided a gracious and informative interview in his La Jolla, California, home, but also read through the entire manuscript and caught a few errors, for which I will remain eternally grateful. Others who offered helpful critiques of various drafts of the whole or parts include Julian Anderson, Kate Blackwell, Anne Borchardt, Agustín Carstens, Sofía Carstens, Cristina Casanueva, Martina Coppelman, Kathleen Currie, Susan George, William C. Gruben, Timothy Heyman, Alice Mansell, Ann McLaughlin, T. M. McNally, Elizabeth Mills, Mary Morris, Mary O'Keefe, Leslie Pietrzyk, Jennifer Redmond, Bertha Ruiz de la Concha, Nancy Spitters, Sara Mansfield Taber, Lex Williford, and Mary Kay Zuravlef.

For the design of the cover and text, thanks to Kristina Kachele. The maps were drawn by Joanne Poon. Annette Wenda copyedited the manuscript, Patricia Degges corrected the proof, and Rodger Reynolds shepherded it through to the printers.

For the painting of the angel flying the house of the Virgin to Loreto that graces this book's cover, thanks to Father Floriano Grimaldi, curator of the Museo-Pinacoteca della Santa Casa, in Loreto, Italy; Bruno Longarini; and Carlos Sassu, the surviving son of the artist, Aligi Sassu.

T. M. McNally and Sara Mansfield Taber, two sharp-eyed and elegant writers, thanks for cheering me on and calling it like you saw it. Trudy McMurrin, thanks for the tip. And finally, Dawn Marano, gracefully elliptical memoirist, you are the editor any writer would dream of finding.

Notes

Chapter 1: El Halloween and the Día de Muertos

1. Those who have read Cervantes's *Don Quixote* will recall that when the barber and the curate held their inquisition in Don Quixote's library, they spared *Amadís of Gaul* for its "unrivaled style," but tossed *Exploits of Esplandián* out the window to start the pile for the bonfire. "The goodness of the father," said the curate, "is not going to help the son."

Chapter 2: The Visitors

1. Adolfo López Mateos was the president of Mexico from 1958 to 1964.

2. Southern Arizona and New Mexico were acquired from Mexico in 1853 with the ten-million-dollar Gadsden Purchase, authorized by none other than Santa Anna. He embezzled the money.

Chapter 3: Like People You See in a Dream

1. Edward L. Schieffelin and Robert Crittenden, eds., *Like People You See in a Dream: First Contact in Six Papuan Societies*. Palo Alto: Stanford University Press, 1991.

2. *Piloncillo* is a cone-shaped molasses candy.

Chapter 7: Bay of Angels

1. Enrique Krauze is a Mexican editor and historian.

2. For accounting ease, three zeros were knocked off the peso in 1993. The devaluation of late 1994, from three to seven (new) pesos to the dollar, was thus the equivalent of three thousand to seven thousand (old) pesos.

Chapter 9: Black Warrior, White Salt

1. I later learned that the issue of noise pollution and whales is in fact problematic. In the murky depths of the seas, whales live in a world of sound, a "Jules Verne world," as cetologist Roger Payne put it, very different from the one we humans are adapted to. Sound propagates far better through water than through air, and low-frequency noises—such as the calls made by large whales—can actually be heard across entire oceans. Whales use "echolocation"—emitting noises that bounce back to give them a picture of their surroundings, very much like radar, to find each other, to "spot" the ocean floor, distant storms, schools of fish. They also squeak, roar, burble, boom, even sing long rhyming songs—communicating with one another in ways cetologists have only begun to understand. In the nineteenth century, hundreds of gray whales once entered San Diego Bay in (Upper) California. No more; they pass by now on their way south. It seems likely that the whales are frightened by the heavy boat and ship traffic of the port and naval base, although there may be some other explanation. I also learned that when the salt company began operations in Laguna Guerrero Negro, the gray whales, once plentiful in that lagoon during calving season, shied away. When operations moved to Ojo de Liebre (Scammon's Lagoon) in 1967, however, the whales returned to Laguna Guerrero Negro. At the same time, the whales have not abandoned Ojo de Liebre, despite the regular traffic of whale-watching boats and salt barges traveling to and from Isla Cedros. In short, whether and in exactly what way gray whales might be affected by noise pollution in the Baja California lagoons remain unclear.

Chapter 10: In the Land of the Clouds

1. The Instituto Nacional Indigenista, or National Indigenous Institute, is a federal government agency.

Bibliography

Adorno, Rolena. "The Negotiation of Fear in Cabeza de Vaca's *Naufragios.*" In *New World Encounters,* ed. Stephen Greenblatt. Berkeley and Los Angeles: University of California Press, 1993.

Aguilar Marco, José Luis, et al. *Misiones en la peninsula de Baja California.* Mexico City: Instituto Nacional de Antropología e Historia, 1991.

Alós, Gabriel. *Eclipse de sangre.* Mexico City: Grupo Editorial Planeta, 1994.

Andrews, Thomas F., ed. *English Privateers at Cabo San Lucas: The Descriptive Accounts of Puerto Seguro by Edward Cooke (1712) and Woodes Rogers (1712), with Added Comments by George Shelvocke (1726) and William Betagh (1728).* Los Angeles: Dawson's Book Shop, 1979.

Aridjis, Homero. "El silencio de las ballenas." *Reforma* (Mexico City) (Feb. 21, 1995).

——. "The Silence of the Whales." *Grupo de los 100* (Mexico City) (Feb. 15, 1995).

Aschmann, Homer. *The Central Desert of Baja California: Demography and Ecology.* Berkeley and Los Angeles: University of California Press, 1959.

——. "Historical Sources for a Contact Enthnography of Baja California." *California Historical Society Quarterly* (June 1965).

Baegert, Johann Jakob, S.J. *The Letters of Jacob Baegert, 1749–1761, Jesuit Missionary in Baja California.* Ed. Doyce B. Nunis Jr. Trans. Elsbeth Schulz-Bischof. Los Angeles: Dawson's Book Shop, 1982.

——. *Observations in Lower California.* Berkeley and Los Angeles: University of California Press, 1952.

Barco, Miguel del. *Historia Natural y Crónica de la Antigua California.* Ed. Miguel León Portilla. 2d ed. Mexico City: Universidad Nacional Autónoma de México, 1988.

Barthel, Manfred. *The Jesuits: History and Legend of the Society of Jesus.* New York: William Morrow, 1984.

Belt, Don. "Baja California: Mexico's Land Apart." *National Geographic* (Dec. 1989).

Berg, A. Scott. *Lindbergh.* New York: G. P. Putnam's Sons, 1998.

Bolton, Herbert Eugene. *Rim of Christendom: A Biography of Eusebio Francisco Kino, Pacific Coast Pioneer.* New York: Macmillan, 1936.

Bravo, Jaime, Juan de Ugarte, and Clemente Guillén. *Testimonios Sudcalifornianos: Nueva entrada y establecimiento en el Puerto de La Paz, 1720.* Ed. and trans. Miguel León Portilla. Mexico City: Universidad Nacional Autónoma de México, 1970.

Browne, J. Ross. "Explorations in Lower California." Parts 1 and 2. *Harper's New Monthly Magazine* 37/38 (1868).

Bruns, Rebecca. "Todos Santos." *Travel and Leisure* (May 1993).

Bryant, Mark, and Néstor Segovia. "La Masacre de la Caguama." *La Onda* (Tucson and Hermosillo) (Apr. 1996).

Buffum, E. Gould. *Six Months in the Gold Mines: From a Journal of Three Years' Residence in Upper and Lower California, 1847–8–9.* Ed. John W. Caughey. 1850. Reprint, Los Angeles: Ward Ritchie Press, 1959.

Campbell, Joseph. *The Hero with a Thousand Faces.* Princeton: Princeton University Press, 1949.

Cannon, Ray. *The Sea of Cortez.* Menlo Park, Calif.: Lane Magazine and Book Company, 1966.

Carmichael, Elizabeth, and Chloë Sayer. *The Skeleton at the Feast: The Day of the Dead in Mexico.* London: British Museum Press, 1991.

Carwardine, Mark. *Whales, Dolphins, and Porpoises.* London, New York, and Stuttgart: Dorling Kindersley, 1995.

Castañeda, Jorge G. *The Mexican Shock.* New York: W. W. Norton, 1995.

Cervantes Saavedra, Miguel de. *Don Quixote of La Mancha.* New York and Scarborough, Ontario: New American Library, 1979.

Chamberlin, Eugene Keith. "Nicholas Trist and Baja California." *Pacific Historical Review* (Feb. 1963).

Chaput, Donald, William M. Mason, and David Zárate Loperena. *Modest Fortunes: Mining in Northern Baja California.* Los Angeles: Natural History Museum of Los Angeles County, 1992.

Clavigero, Francisco Javier, S.J. *The History of (Lower) California*. Trans. Sara E. Lake. Stanford: Stanford University Press, 1937.

Coe, Sophie D., and Michael D. Coe. *The True History of Chocolate*. London and New York: Thames and Hudson, 1996.

Conover, Ted. *Coyotes: A Journey through the Secret World of America's Illegal Aliens*. New York: Vintage Books, 1987.

Consejo Consultivo del Programa Nacional de Solidaridad. *El Programa Nacional de Solidaridad*. Mexico City: Fondo de Cultura Económica, 1994.

Cook, Sherburne F. *The Extent and Significance of Disease among the Indians of Baja California, 1697–1773*. Ibero-Americana 12. Berkeley and Los Angeles: University of California Press, 1937.

Crosby, Harry W. *Antigua California: Mission and Colony on the Peninsular Frontier, 1697–1768*. Albuquerque: University of New Mexico Press, 1994.

———. *The Cave Paintings of Baja California*. San Diego: Sunbelt Publications, 1997.

———. *The King's Highway*. La Jolla, Calif.: Copley Books, 1974.

——— ———. *Last of the Californios*. La Jolla, Calif.: Copley Books, 1981.

Decorme, Gerardo, S.J. *La obra de los jesuitas mexicanos, 1572–1767. Tomo II, Las misiones*. N.p.: Antigua Librería de Porrua, 1941.

Dedina, Serge. *Saving the Gray Whale*. Tucson: University of Arizona Press, 2000.

Dedina, Serge, and Emily Young. "Conservation and Development in the Gray Whale Lagoons of Baja California Sur, Mexico." Final Report to the U.S. Marine Mammal Commission, Oct. 1995.

Delpar, Helen, *The Enormous Vogue of Things Mexican: Cultural Relations between the United States and Mexico, 1920–1935*. Tuscaloosa: University of Alabama Press, 1992.

Del Río, Ignacio. *Conquista y Aculturación en la California Jesuítica, 1697–1768*. Mexico City: Universidad Nacional Autónomo de México, 1984.

Díaz del Castillo, Bernal. *The Conquest of New Spain*. Trans. J. M. Cohen. New York: Penguin, 1963.

Dibble, Sandra. "Turtle's Trek across Pacific Awes Scientists." *San Diego Union-Tribune,* Mar. 7, 1996.

Diguet, Léon. "Note sur la pictographie de la Basse California." *L'Anthropologie* 6 (1895).

Dillon, Sam. "Mexican Cops Caught in Scandal." *New York Times,* Nov. 30, 1995.

Doyle, Mike, with Steve Sorenson. *Morning Glass: The Adventures of Legendary Waterman Mike Doyle.* Three Rivers, Calif.: Fusi Press, 1993.

Dresser, Denise. *Neopopulist Solutions to Neoliberal Problems: Mexico's National Solidarity Program.* Center for U.S.-Mexican Studies, University of California, San Diego, 1991.

Ducrue, Benno. *Ducrue's Account of the Expulsion of the Jesuits from Lower California (1767–1769).* Ed. and trans. Ernest J. Burrus, S.J. Rome: Jesuit Historical Institute; St. Louis: St. Louis University, 1967.

Eisenhower, John S. D. *So Far from God: The U.S. War with Mexico, 1846–1848.* New York: Random House, 1989.

Everitt, Sandra. "Keiko se nos va." *Epoca* (Mexico City) (Jan. 1996).

Fiedel, Stuart J. *Prehistory of the Americas.* 2d ed. Cambridge: Cambridge University Press, 1992.

Fierro Villalobos, Roberto. *Esta es mi vida.* Mexico City: n.p., 1964.

Fineman, Mark. "Bitter Standoff at Hotel Serenidad." *Los Angeles Times,* Jan. 30, 1997.

Fineman, Mark, and Craig Pyes. "In Baja, a Plane Is Buried and Drug Ties Are Unearthed." *Los Angeles Times,* Nov. 18, 1995.

Florescano, Enrique. *Memory, Myth, and Time in Mexico: From the Aztecs to Independence.* Austin: University of Texas Press, 1994.

Flores Kelly, Jorge. "Análisis bioeconómico de la pesquería sequencial de camarón en el Pacífico." Bachelor's thesis, Instituto Tecnológico Autónomo de México, 1995.

Francez, Padre James Donald. *The Lost Treasures of Baja California; Los tesoros perdidos de la Baja California.* Chula Vista, Calif.: Black Forrest Press, 1996.

Gante, Pablo C. de. *Tepotzotlán: Su historia y sus tesoros artísticos.* Mexico City: Editorial Porrua, 1958.

García Moll, Roberto, ed. *El Mundo Mixteco y Zapoteco.* N.p.: Editorial Jilguero, 1992.

Gardner, Erle Stanley. *The Hidden Heart of Baja.* New York: New York: William Morrow, 1962.

———. *Hovering over Baja.* New York: William Morrow, 1961.

———. *Hunting the Desert Whale.* New York: William Morrow, 1960.

———. *The Land of Shorter Shadows.* New York: William Morrow, 1948.

———. "A Legendary Treasure Left by a Long Lost Tribe." *Life* 53:3 (1962).

———. *Off the Beaten Track in Baja.* New York: William Morrow, 1967.

Garduño, Evardo, Efraín García, and Patricia Morán. *Mixtecos en Baja California: El caso de San Quintín.* Mexicali: Universidad Autónoma de Baja California, 1989.

Gerhard, Peter. "Gabriel González, Last Dominican in Baja California." *Pacific Historical Review* (May 1953).

Gilders, Michelle A. *Reflections of a Whale-watcher.* Bloomington: Indiana University Press, 1995.

Grant, Campbell. "Charles Melville Scammon: Sea Captain–Naturalist." In *The Marine Mammals of the North-western Coast of North America,* by Charles Melville Scammon. Facsimile ed. Riverside, Calif.: Manessier Publishing, 1969.

————. *Rock Art of Baja California.* Los Angeles: Dawson's Book Shop, 1974.

Guggenheim, Ken. "Four Years Later, Case Still Baffles." Associated Press, Mar. 23, 1998.

Guillén, Clemente. *Clemente Guillén, Explorer of the South: Diaries of the Overland Expeditions to Bahía Magdalena and la Paz, 1719, 1720–1721.* Trans. and ed. W. Michael Mathes. Los Angeles: Dawson's Book Shop, 1979.

Guillermoprieto, Alma. "Whodunnit?" *New Yorker* (Sept. 25, 1995).

Halleck, Captain Henry W. "Memorandum of Captain Henry W. Halleck Concerning His Expeditions in Lower California." In *The Mexican War in Baja California,* by Doyce B. Nunis Jr. Los Angeles: Dawson's Book Shop, 1977.

Hambleton, Enrique. *La pintura rupestre de Baja California.* Mexico City: Fomento Cultural Banamex, 1979.

Heitman, Phil. "The Lady Who Watches Over Pilots." In *Flight USA* (Dec. 1997).

Iglesias Prieto, Norma. *Beautiful Flowers of the Maquiladora: Life Histories of Women Workers in Tijuana.* Austin: University of Texas Press, 1997.

Iturriaga, José Mariano de. *La Californiada.* Trans. Alfonso Castro Pallares. Mexico City: Universidad Nacional Autónoma de México, 1979.

Janovy, John, Jr. *Vermilion Sea: A Naturalist's Journey in Baja California.* Boston: Houghton Mifflin, 1992.

Johnson, William Weber. *Baja California.* New York: Time-Life Books, 1972.

Jordán, Fernando. *El otro México.* La Paz, Baja California Sur: Gobierno del Estado de Baja California Sur, 1980.

————. *Mar Roxo de Cortés: Biografía de un Golfo.* Mexicali: Universidad Autónoma de Baja California, 1995.

Joselit, David. "Living on the Border." *Art in America* (Dec. 1989).

Juárez, Miguel Angel. "Revela Comisión Nuevo Video en Caso Colosio." *Reforma* (Mexico City) (Mar. 23, 1998).

Kandell, Jonathan. *La Capital: The Biography of Mexico City.* New York: Henry Holt, 1988.

Kelly, Neil, and Gene Kira. *The Baja Catch: A Fishing, Travel, and Remote Camping Manual for Baja California*. 2d ed. Valley Center, Calif.: Apples and Oranges, 1993.

Kira, Gene. *The Unforgettable Sea of Cortez, Baja California's Golden Age, 1947–1977: The Life and Writings of Ray Cannon*. Torrance, Calif.: Cortez Publications, 1999.

Kirchner, John A. *Baja California Railways*. Los Angeles: Dawson's Book Shop, 1988.

Klassen, Jeff. "Los Cabos Fishing." *Baja Life*, no. 5 (1996).

Knudson, Tom. "A Dying Sea." *Sacramento Bee*, Dec. 10–13, 1995.

Krauze, Enrique. "El Legado de Cortés." *Reforma* (Mexico City) (Dec. 7, 1997).

———. *Siglo de caudillos: Biografía política de México (1810–1910)*. Mexico City: TusQuets Editores, 1994.

Krutch, Joseph Wood. *The Forgotten Peninsula: A Naturalist in Baja California*. New York: William Sloane Associates, 1961.

Landauer, Lyndall Baker. *Scammon: Beyond the Lagoon: A Biography of Charles Melville Scammon*. South Lake Tahoe, Calif.: Flying Cloud Press, 1986.

Langewiesche, William. *Cutting for Sign: One Man's Journey along the U.S.-Mexican Border*. New York: Vintage Books, 1993.

Le Clézio, J. M. G. *The Mexican Dream; or, The Interrupted Thought of Amerindian Civilizations*. Chicago: University of Chicago Press, 1993.

Leonard, Irving A. *Books of the Brave: Being an Account of Books and of Men in the Spanish Conquest and Settlement of the Sixteenth-Century New World*. Cambridge: Harvard University Press, 1949.

Léon Portilla, Miguel. *Cartografía y Crónicas de la Antigua California*. Mexico City: Universidad Nacional Autónoma de México, Fundación de Investigaciones Sociales, 1989.

———, ed. *Loreto: Capital de las Californias; Las cartas fundacionales de Juan María Salvatierra*. Mexico City: FONATUR, Universidad Autónoma de Baja California, Consejo Nacional para la Cultura y las Artes, 1997.

———. *Testimonios sudcalifornianos: Nueva entrada y establecimiento en el Puerto de la Paz, 1720*. Mexico City: Universidad Nacional Autónomo de México, 1970.

Linck, Wenceslaus, S.J. *Wenceslaus Linck's Diary of His 1766 Expedition*. Trans. and ed. Ernest J. Burrus, S.J. Los Angeles: Dawson's Book Shop, 1966.

———. *Wenceslaus Linck's Reports and Letters, 1762–1778*. Trans. and ed. Ernest J. Burrus, S.J. Los Angeles: Dawson's Book Shop, 1967.

Lindbergh, Charles A. *The Spirit of St. Louis.* New York: Charles Scribner's Sons, 1953.

———. "The Wisdom of Wildness." *Life* (Dec. 22, 1967).

Lindbergh, Jon. "Lindbergh Lands . . ." *New York Times,* Dec. 15, 1927.

Lingenfelter, Richard E. *The Rush of '89: The Baja California Gold Fever.* Los Angeles: Dawson's Book Shop, 1967.

Lockhart, James, ed. and trans. *We People Here: Nahuatl Accounts of the Conquest of Mexico.* Vol. 1. Berkeley and Los Angeles: University of California Press, 1993.

Mackintosh, Graham. *Into a Desert Place: A 3000-Mile Walk around the Coast of Baja California.* New York: W. W. Norton, 1995.

Mahieux, Susana, ed. *Diagnóstico ambiental de Baja California Sur.* La Paz: Fundación Mexicana para la Educación Ambiental, Sociedad de Historia Natural Niparajá, Universidad Autónoma de Baja California, 1998.

"Man of Mystery." *Newsweek* (Jan. 18, 1960).

Mansell-Carstens, Catherine. *Las finanzas populares en México: El redesubrimiento de un sistema financiero olvidado.* Mexico City: Centro de Estudios Monetarios Latinoamericanos, Editorial Milenio, ITAM, 1995.

Martínez, José Luis. *Hernán Cortés.* Abbreviated ed. Mexico City: Fondo de Cultura Económica, 1992.

Martínez, Pablo L. *Guía familiar de Baja California, 1700–1900.* Mexico City: Editorial Baja California, 1965.

———. *A History of Lower California.* Trans. Ethel Duffy Turner. Mexico City: Editorial Baja California, 1960.

Mathes, W. Michael, trans. and ed. *The Conquistador in California, 1535: The Voyage of Fernando Cortés to Baja California in Chronicles and Documents.* Los Angeles: Dawson's Book Shop, 1973.

McCloskey, Donald N. *If You're So Smart: The Narrative of Economic Expertise.* Chicago: University of Chicago Press, 1990.

McDonald, Paula. "The Friendly Whales of Laguna San Ignacio." *Baja Life* 1:4 (1995).

McNally, Robert. *So Remorseless a Havoc: Of Dolphins, Whales, and Men.* New York: Little, Brown, 1981.

Melville, Herman. *Moby-Dick; or, The Whale.* Ed. with an introduction and commentary by Harold Beaver. New York: Penguin, 1972.

Messinacher, Miguel. *La búsqueda del signo de Dios: Ocupación jesuita de la Baja California.* Mexico City: Fondo de Cultura Económica, 1992.

Milton, Joyce. *Loss of Eden: A Biography of Charles and Anne Morrow Lindbergh.* New York: HarperCollins, 1993.

Moore, Lee. *The Todos Santos Book.* Brevard, N.C.: Todos Santos Press, 1996.

Morales, Cesáreo, and Samuel Palma. *Colosio: La construcción de un destino.* Mexico City: Rayuela Editores, 1995.

Morris, J. Bayard, trans. *Hernando Cortés: Five Letters, 1519–1526.* New York: W. W. Norton, 1928.

Moyano Pahissa, Angela. "La Compañía Inglesa." In *Panorama Histórico de Baja California,* ed. David Piñera Ramírez. Tijuana: Universidad Nacional Autónoma de México, Universidad Autónoma de Baja California, Centro de Investigaciones Históricas, 1983.

————. *La Resistencia de las Californias a la Invasión Norteamericana (1846–1848).* Mexico City: Consejo Nacional para la Cultura y las Artes, 1992.

Nápoli, Father Ignacio María, S.J. *The Cora Indians of Baja California: The Relation of Father Ignacio María Nápoli, S.J., September 20, 1721.* Trans. and ed. James Robert Moriarty III and Benjamin F. Smith. Los Angeles: Dawson's Book Shop, 1970.

Nordhoff, Charles. *Peninsular California.* New York: Harper and Brothers, 1888.

North, Arthur W. *Camp and Camino in Lower California.* New York: Baker and Taylor, 1910.

————. *The Mother of California.* San Francisco: Paul Elder, 1908.

Nunis, Doyce B., Jr. *The Mexican War in Baja California.* Los Angeles: Dawson's Book Shop, 1977.

O'Malley, John W. *The First Jesuits.* Cambridge: Harvard University Press, 1993.

Oppenheimer, Andres. *Bordering on Chaos: Guerillas, Stockbrokers, Politicians, and Mexico's Road to Prosperity.* New York: Little, Brown, 1995.

Padgett, Tim, and Sharon Begley. "Beware of the Humans." *Newsweek* (Feb. 5, 1996).

Pastor, Robert A., and Jorge G. Castañeda. *Limits to Friendship: The United States and Mexico.* New York: Random House, 1988.

Payne, Roger. *Among Whales.* New York: Scribner, 1995.

Paz, Octavio. *The Labyrinth of Solitude.* Trans. Lysander Kemp. New York: Grove Press, 1961.

Pepper, Choral. *Baja California: Vanished Missions, Lost Treasures, Strange Stories Tall and True.* Los Angeles: Ward Ritchie Press, 1973.

Pìccolo, Francesco María, S.J. *Informe on the New Province of California, 1702.* Ed. and trans. George P. Hammond. Los Angeles: Dawson's Book Shop, 1967.

Piñera Ramírez, David. "Tierras Deshabitadas y Concesionarios Extranjeros." In *Panorama Histórico de Baja California*, ed. David Piñera Ramírez. Tijuana: Universidad Nacional Autónoma de México, Universidad Autónoma de Baja California, Centro de Investigaciones Históricas, 1983.

Polk, Dora Beale. *The Island of California: A History of the Myth*. Lincoln: University of Nebraska Press, 1991.

Portillo, Alvaro del. *Descubrimientos y exploraciones en las costas de California, 1532–1650*. Madrid: Ediciones RIALP, S.A., 1982.

Proffitt, T. D., III. *Tijuana: The History of a Mexican Metropolis*. San Diego: San Diego State University Press, 1994.

Ravelo, Ricardo. "De 23 de marzo a 23 de marzo: 1,560 declaraciones . . . y nada." *Proceso* (Mexico City) (Mar. 22, 1998).

Reynolds, Christopher. "Baja Bohemia." *Los Angeles Times*, Apr. 21, 1996.

Río, Ignacio del. *Conquista y aculturación en la California jesuítica, 1697–1768*. Mexico City: Universidad Nacional Autónoma de México, 1984.

Río, Tayde del. "Lloran a 'mares.'" *Reforma* (Mexico City) (Jan. 8, 1996).

Roberts, Norman C. *Baja California Plant Field Guide*. La Jolla, Calif.: Natural History Publishing, 1989.

Ronstadt, Edward F., ed. *Borderman: Memoirs of Federico José María Ronstadt*. Albuquerque: University of New Mexico Press, 1993.

Rotella, Sebastian. *Twilight on the Line: Underworlds and Politics at the U.S.-Mexican Border*. New York: W. W. Norton, 1998.

Salvatierra, Juan María, S.J. *Selected Letters about Lower California*. Ed. Ernest J. Burrus, S.J. Los Angeles: Dawson's Book Shop, 1971.

Scammon, Charles Melville. *The Marine Mammals of the North-western Coast of North America and the American Whale Fishery*. San Francisco: John H. Carmany, 1874.

Schurz, William Lytle. *The Manila Galleon*. New York: E. P. Dutton, 1939.

SeaWatch. "Shark Fishery a Huge Disaster." *SeaWatch Alert* (Jan. 1995).

Shieffelin, Edward L., and Robert Crittenden, eds. *Like People You See in a Dream: First Contact in Six Papuan Societies*. Stanford: Stanford University Press, 1991.

Simpich, Frederick. "Baja California Wakes Up." *National Geographic Magazine* (Aug. 1942).

Smith, William C. S. "Baja California: The 1849 Journal of William C. S. Smith." Introduced and annotated by Harry W. Crosby in *Gold Rush Trails to San Diego and Los Angeles*, ed. George M. Ellis. San Diego: San Diego Corral of the Westerners, 1996.

Southworth, J. R. *Baja California ilustrada*. La Paz: Gobierno del Estado de Baja California Sur, 1989.

Steinbeck, John. *The Log from the* Sea of Cortez. New York:Viking, 1951. (The narrative portion of the book *Sea of Cortez: A Leisurely Journal of Travel and Research*, by John Steinbeck and E. F. Ricketts, 1941).

Sweet, David. "The Ibero-American Frontier Mission in Native American History." In *The New Latin American Mission History*, ed. Erick Langer and Robert H. Jackson. Lincoln: University of Nebraska Press, 1995.

Taraval, Sigismundo, S.J. *The Indian Uprising in Lower California, 1734–1737*. Ed. and trans. Marguerite Eyer Wilbur. Los Angeles: Quivira Society, 1931.

————. *La rebelión de los Californios*. Ed. Eligio Moíses Coronado. Madrid: Doce Calles, 1996.

Thomas, Hugh. *Conquest: Montezuma, Cortés, and the Fall of Old Mexico*. New York: Simon and Schuster, 1993.

"Todos Santos Water Crisis." *Baja Sun* (Sept.–Oct. 1996).

Toro, María Celia. *Mexico's "War" on Drugs: Causes and Consequences*. Boulder: Lynne Rienner, 1995.

Turner, John Kenneth. *Barbarous Mexico*. Austin: University of Texas Press, 1969.

Urrea, Luis Alberto. *Across the Wire: Life and Hard Times on the Mexican Border*. New York: Doubleday, Anchor Books, 1993.

————. *By the Lake of the Sleeping Children: The Secret Life of the Mexican Border*. New York: Doubleday, Anchor Books, 1996.

Van Atta, Dale. "Invasion of the Drug Lords." *Reader's Digest* (Sept. 1996).

Vargas, Enrique. "Cabo Klassics: The Hottest New Lure Design in Town." *Baja Life* 1:4 (1995).

Venegas, Miguel, S.J. *Noticia de la California y de su Conquista Temporal y Espiritual*. 3 vols. N.p.: Editorial Layac, 1944.

Villela Gómez, José. *La breve historia de la aviación en México*. Mexico City: n.p., 1971.

Warrick, Joby. "Sharks Vanishing from the World's Oceans." *Washington Post*, Nov. 10, 1997.

Zwinger, Anne. *A Desert Country Near the Sea: A Natural History of the Cape Region of Baja California*. New York: Harper and Row, 1983.

————, ed. *The Letters of John Xántus*. Los Angeles: Dawson's Book Shop, 1986.

Index

About the Author

C. M. MAYO is the author of *Sky Over El Nido,* which won the Flannery O'Connor Award for Short Fiction. Mayo's stories have been published in many literary journals, including *Chelsea,* the *Paris Review,* and *Witness,* and essays in *Fourth Genre, Tin House,* and the *Southwest Review,* as well as in newspapers, including the *Los Angeles Times* and the *Wall Street Journal.* She has received numerous awards, including fellowships from the MacDowell Colony, the Virginia Center for the Creative Arts, Yaddo, and the Bread Loaf, Sewanee, and Wesleyan Writers conferences. Mayo is the founding editor of the annual bilingual literary journal *Tameme: New Writing from North America/Nueva Literatura de Norteamérica.* A native of El Paso, Texas, raised in Palo Alto, California, and educated at the University of Chicago, Mayo is a longtime resident of Mexico City where for several years she was a professor of economics at the Instituto Tecnológico Autónomo de México. Her website is www.cmmayo.com.

DATE DUE

JA 26 '04			
DE 7 '04			

Please remember that this is a library book,
and that it belongs only temporarily to each
person who uses it. Be considerate. Do
not write in this, or any, library book.